Augusta Theodosia Drane

The Life of St. Dominic and a Sketch of the Dominican Order

Augusta Theodosia Drane

The Life of St. Dominic and a Sketch of the Dominican Order

ISBN/EAN: 9783337009687

Printed in Europe, USA, Canada, Australia, Japan

Cover: Foto ©ninafisch / pixelio.de

More available books at **www.hansebooks.com**

THE

LIFE OF ST. DOMINIC,

AND

A Sketch of the Dominican Order.

WITH AN INTRODUCTION,

BY

MOST REV. J. S. ALEMANY, D. D.

Pro Patre D[...],
T[...],
S[...] Jesus,
Pro bono certa [...].

PERMISSU SUPERIORUM.

NEW YORK:

P. O'SHEA, PUBLISHER,

7 BARCLAY STREET.

1 7.

INTRODUCTION TO THE AMERICAN EDITION.

St. Dominic's name is revered by many who never perused his life, and it is likewise execrated by others who gain their notions of him from false biographies, (if they may be so called.)

The fragrance of his sanctity fills the entire garden of the Church, and all within its holy precincts acknowledge his virtues, even without pausing to learn the peculiar causes of his distinction, while those without hear nothing but the foul reports of such as never saw him, never held any kind of communication with his associates, but who derived all their knowledge of St. Dominic from those who wrongly judged him.

England was not the last in joining in this hasty verdict, elicited from incompetent testimony ; nor is she the last in re-opening the case, setting aside all unqualified evidence,—nay, in arraigning before the majesty of reason and of truth the faithful contemporary eye-witnesses of the Saint, and in giving to the world, as the result of most careful and impartial scrutiny, the true life of St. Dominic, of which this is a mere republication.

This English portrait of St. Dominic is a gem, the precious offering to the sanctuary of Catholic truth, by a distinguished pen, admired for its rare powers while used out of the Church, now consecrated in its undiminished force and elegance by Divine faith. The English author in pencilling so exquisitely the portrait of the Saint, modestly forgot to state who depicted it ; but the merit of the life before us will be deeply appreciated by all its readers. The American non-Catholics earnestly searching after truth will see in St. Dominic the unflinching lover of truth,—the gentle yet powerful advocate of truth, and the undying martyr of charity to his fellow man.

And if American Protestants should read St. Dominic's life, Catholics should especially be familiar with it. It is well said that the reading of the lives of the saints makes saints. Our Saviour pronounced dreadful woes against those by whom scandal comes ; and if scandal be a great evil, because it occasions the ruin of souls redeemed by Christ's most precious blood, no Christian can doubt the incalculable blessings that naturally flow from reading the heroic examples set forth in the lives of the saints. But St. Dominic's should be peculiarly dear to all our Catholics, on account of his important relations with the Catholic world : for he gave to the world the most useful devotion of the Rosary, of which the Sovereign Pontiffs have proclaimed him the founder. He obtained from heaven the extraordinary power of living after death in thousands and tens of thousands of devoted preachers of the Catholic truth, through whom he has carried the gospel of Christ to the uttermost bounds of the earth.—He has adorned the Catholic libraries with the unsurpassed wisdom of St. Thomas, and a host of others ; he has given to St. Peter's chair distinguished and saintly occupants ; he has studded the altars of the Church with most precious gems of virtue and sanctity, and has given to America her first Saint—the fragrant Rose of Lima.

ADVERTISEMENT.

——※——

A few words of explanation may seem required as an apology for presenting the public with a new Biography of S. Dominic. The beautiful life of the saint by Père Lacordaire seemed to have furnished everything that could be desired, in clothing the legendary story of his great patriarch in modern dress. But although there can certainly be no temptation to pretend to anything like a rivalry with that eloquent writer, there are some reasons which appear to make a fresh biography desirable for those among ourselves who wish to form a more familiar acquaintance with S. Dominic than is furnished in the brief notices given in English collections of the lives of the saints. It is true Père Lacordaire's life has for some time been translated into our own language; but the very beauty of its style is so essentially French, that no translation can preserve its peculiar charm, or render it as popular as it deserves to be. But it is French in something more than idiom; it was written with the avowed object of advancing the order in France, and a prominence is therefore given to the Gallican associations of the Order of Preachers, which, by readers of another nation, is felt to be undue.

In the following pages, the course of the saint's life has been followed with no view save that of giving his character in its true historical light; and for this end, the simple narrative of facts, without comment or explanation, has been felt to be sufficient. We are much mistaken if the best defence that can be offered of S. Dominic's character, so long the subject of the strangest misrepresentation, be not to be found in the unvarnished story of his life, drawn from the testimony of those who saw him face to face, and whose writings form the principal material from which the following pages have been compiled.

There are some subjects which our readers may be disappointed in finding so briefly touched upon in a life of S. Dominic. But we have felt that several of the disputed points, commonly discussed by his biographers, have little real interest to the student of his character. We have not, therefore, entered at length into the history of the Albigensian war, or of the foundation of the Inquisition, preferring to leave the doubts arising out of these subjects to be resolved by others, whose object is the critical examination of historical questions. Our only task has been to lay before our readers the personal portrait of one whose influence in the Church of Christ must endure so long as the religious and apostolic life shall be found within her bosom.

The authorities from which we have drawn our sketch have been chiefly Mamachi's Annals, with the ancient chronicles and memoirs reprinted in that work, including the Acts of Bologna, the memoir of Sister Cecilia, and that of blessed Humbert; Polidori's life, which follows the facts, and in many places the text, of blessed Jordan; Ferdinand Castiglio's history of the order, and the life of S. Dominic by Touron; whilst in the account of the early fathers of the order, great use has been made of F. Michel Pio's work entitled "Progenie dell' Ordine in Italia" (which collects all the particulars given by Gerard de Frachet and the old writers), and of the biographical sketches of F. Marchese in his "Diario Domenicano."

The summary of the history of the Friars Preachers subsequent to the death of S. Dominic, has been chiefly taken from Touron's great work on "the Illustrious Men of the Order." In selecting a few out of the many names that called for notice, we have necessarily omitted a number that will readily suggest themselves to our readers; but our object has been to avoid wearying them with a mere enumeration of authors and learned works, and, without attempting such a complete sketch as our limited space rendered impossible, to suggest something of the general features of the order, as illustrated by the lives of its greatest men.

CONTENTS.

—⚒—

CHAPTER I.

The birth of Dominic. His youth and university life, 1.

CHAPTER II.

Dominic is appointed canon of Osma. His mission to the north in company with Diego of Azevedo, 6.

CHAPTER III.

Pilgrimage to Rome. First labours among the Albigenses, 9.

CHAPTER IV.

Dominic in Languedoc. The miracles of Fanjeaux and Montreal. The foundation of the Convent of Prouille, 14

CHAPTER V.

Diego returns to Spain. His death. Dominic remains in Languedoc. The murder of Peter de Castelnau, and the commencement of the Albigensian war, 20.

CHAPTER VI.

Proclamation of the Crusade. Simon de Montfort. Dominic among the heretics. His apostolic labours, 27.

CHAPTER VII.

The institution of the Rosary. The Council of Lavaur. The battle of Muret, 41.

CHAPTER VIII.

CHAPTER IX.

CHAPTER X.

CHAPTER XI.

CHAPTER XII.

CHAPTER XIII.

CHAPTER XIV.

CHAPTER XXII.

CHAPTER XXIII.

CHAPTER XXIV.

CHAPTER XXV.

CHAPTER XXVI.

CHAPTER XXVII.

PART II.

THE DOMINICAN ORDER.

CHAPTER I.

CHAPTER II.

CHAPTER III.

CHAPTER IV.

CHAPTER V.

CHAPTER VI.

CHAPTER VII.

THE LIFE OF S. DOMINIC.

--- ⚜ ---

CHAPTER I.

The birth of Dominic. His youth and university life

It was in the year 1170, during the pontificate of Alexander III., that Dominic Gusman, the founder of the order of Friars Preachers, was born at his father's castle of Calargo, in Old Castile. The history of a genealogy, however illustrious, seems scarcely to find its place in the biography of a saint; though indeed few families can boast of one more honourable than that of the Castilian Gusmans. But if their long line of chivalrous ancestors, and the royal privileges granted to them by the kings of Spain, have no claim to be noticed here, the immediate ancestors of S. Dominic possessed at least one distinction which had a more powerful influence on his life. They were a family of saints. The household of his father, Don Felix Gusman, was so remarkable for the religious character of its inmates, that it was said to resemble rather a monastery than a knightly castle. His mother, Joanna of Aza, after being constantly held in popular veneration, has, almost within our own time, received the solemn beatification of the Church. The same testimony has been borne to the hetric sanctity of Manez, her second son; and though Antonio, the eldest of the three brothers, has not indeed received similar honours, yet was he no unworthy member of his illustrious family. We read of him that he became a secular priest, in which position he might have aspired to the highest ecclesiastical distinctions; but, enamoured of holy poverty, he distributed his patrimony to the poor, and retired to an hospital where he spent the remainder of his days in humble ministering to the sick.

The future greatness of her younger son was announced to Johanna even before his birth. The mysterious vision of a dog, bearing in his mouth a lighted torch which set fire to the world, appeared to indicate the power of that doctrine which should kindle and illuminate men's hearts through the ministry of his words. The noble lady who held him at the font saw, as the water was poured on his head, a brilliant star shining on the infant's forehead : and this circumstance, which is mentioned in the earliest life which we have of the saint (that of Blessed Jordan), bears a singular connection with the beautiful description of his appearance in after-life, left by his spiritual daughter, the Blessed Cecilia ; in which she says, among other things, that "from his forehead, and between his brows, there shone forth a kind of radiant light, which filled men with respect and love." Nor were the expectations which were excited by these prodigies in any way diminished by the promises of his childhood. His early years were passed in a holy household, and his first impressions were received from the all-powerful influence of a saintly mother. Amid the associations of a Christian family, his mind was moulded into a religious shape even from his cradle ; and the effect of this training is to be traced in the character of his maturer sanctity. From first to last we admire the same profound and unruffled tranquillity of soul. So far as his interior life is revealed to us, he seems to have known nothing of those storms and agitations through which the human mind so often works its way to God ; nothing seems to have interrupted the upward growth of his soul ; and even the tales of his combats with the powers of evil give us more the idea of triumphs achieved, than of temptations suffered and overcome.

When seven years old, he was committed to the charge of his uncle, the arch-priest of Gumiel di Izan, a town not far from Calaroga. Here he grew up in the service of the altar, finding his pleasure in frequenting the churches, and learning to recite the divine office, in singing hymns, and serving at mass, and other public cere-

monies; and in all those numberless little devout offices
which make the life of so many Catholic boys much like
that of the child Samuel in the Temple. To Dominic
they were all labours of love; and his biographers dwell
on the devotion kindled in the hearts of those who saw
the grave and reverent manner with which he bore himself in the presence of the Most Holy Sacrament, or
busied himself in the cleaning and adorning of the altar.
At fourteen he was sent to the university of Palencia,
then one of the most celebrated in Spain. He was but
young to be suddenly removed from so retired and
sheltered a home into intercourse with a world, of which
as yet he knew nothing. With how many would such a
change have brought only the rapid loss of all which had
hitherto rendered his life so innocent and happy. But
to Dominic it did but give room for larger growth in
holiness. During the ten years of his residence at
Palencia, he was equally distinguished for his application
to study, and for the angelic purity of his life. Worldly
pleasures afforded no seductions to one who from his very
birth had received an attraction to the things of God.
Even human science failed to satisfy his desires, and he
hastened to apply himself to the study of theology, as to
the only fountain whose limpid waters were capable of
quenching the thirst of his soul after the highest truth.
He spent four years in the most profound application to
philosophy and sacred letters; often spending his nights
as well as his days over his books; and, convinced that
Divine Science can only be acquired by a mind that has
learnt to subjugate the flesh, he practised a rigid austerity,
and for ten years never broke the rule he imposed on himself at the commencement of his studies, to abstain entirely
from wine.

The influence of a holy life is never unfelt by those
who would be the last to imitate its example. Dominic's
companions bore witness, by their respect, to the sublimity of a virtue far above the standard of their own lives.
Boy as he was, none ever spoke with him without going
away the better for his words, and feeling the charm
of that Divine grace which shone even in his exterior

gestures. " It was a thing most marvellous and lovely to
behold," says Theodoric of Apoldia; " this man, a boy in
years, but a sage in wisdom; superior to the pleasures of
his age, he thirsted only after justice; and not to lose
time, he preferred the bosom of his mother the Church,
to the aimless and objectless life of the foolish world
around him. The sacred repose of her tabernacle was
his resting-place; all his time was equally divided between prayer and study; and God rewarded the fervent
love with which he kept His commandments, by bestowing
on him such a spirit of wisdom and understanding, as made
it easy for him to resolve the most deep and difficult questions."

Before we quit his University life, two circumstances
must be recorded, which happened during its course, and
illustrate the peculiar gentleness and tenderness of his
character. Such terms may seem strange to a Protestant reader, for there is, as it were, a traditional
portrait of S. Dominic, handed down from one age to
another by means of epithets, which writers are content
to repeat, and readers to receive, without a thought of
inquiry as to their justice. We can scarcely open a book
which professes to give the history of the thirteenth
century and its religious features, without finding something about " the cruel and blood-thirsty Dominic," or the
" gloomy founder of the Inquisition;" and under this
popular idea the imagination depicts him as a dark-
browed, mysterious zealot, without a touch of human
tenderness, remorselessly handing over to the flames the
victims of his morose fanaticism. The author of the well-
known " Handbook," from which so many English travellers gather their little stock of knowledge on Italian
matters, finds something of an almost providential signi-
ficancy in the fact that the tree planted by the father of
the Friars Preachers in his convent-garden at Bologna,
should be the " dark and melancholy cypress." And all
the while the true tradition of his character is one pre-
eminently of joy and gentleness. With his fair auburn
hair and beaming smile, he does not present in his exterior
a more perfect contrast to the received notion of the

Spanish Inquisitor, than may be found in the tales of tender-hearted compassion, which are almost all we know of him during the first twenty years of his life. We find him, in the midst of the famine which then desolated Spain, so sensibly touched with the sufferings of the people, that not only did he give all he had, in alms, selling his very clothes to feed the poor,—but he set a yet nobler example of charity to his fellow-students by a sacrifice which may well be believed to have been a hard one. His dear and precious books were all that remained to give; and even those he parted with, that their price might be distributed to the starving multitudes. To estimate the cost of such an act, we must remember the rarity and costliness of manuscripts in those days, many having probably been laboriously copied out by his own hands. Yet when one of his companions expressed astonishment that he should deprive himself of the means of pursuing his studies, he replied, in words preserved by Theodoric of Apoldia, and treasured by after-writers as the first which have come down to posterity, "Would you have me study off those dead parchments, when there were men dying of hunger?" This example roused the charity of the professors and students of the university, and an effort was soon made which relieved the sufferers from their most urgent wants. On another occasion, finding a poor woman in great distress on account of the captivity of her only son, who had been taken by the Moors, Dominic, having no money to offer for his ransom, desired her to take him and sell him, and release her son with his price: and though this was not permitted to be done, yet the fact exhibits him to us under a character which is strangely opposed to the vulgar tradition of his severity and gloom.

It is said by some authors, that his early desires led him to form plans for the foundation of an order for the Redemption of Captives, similar to that afterwards established by S. John of Matha; but of this we find no authoritative mention in the writers of his own order; and it is probable that the idea arose from the fact to which allusion has just been made.

CHAPTER II.

Dominic is appointed canon of Osma. His mission to the north in
company with Diego of Azevedo .

It was not until his 25th year that Dominic was called
to the ecclesiastical state. Until that time the designs of
God regarding him had not been clearly manifested; but
some important changes which took place in the diocese
of Osma were the means of bringing him into a position
where the latent powers of his soul were displayed before
the eyes of the world. Martin de Bazan at that time
ruled the Church of Osma; a man of eminent holiness,
and most zealous for the restoration of Church discipline.
Following the plan then generally adopted in most of the
countries of Europe, he had engaged in the difficult but
important task of converting the canons of his cathedral
into canons regular, an arrangement by which they
became subject to stricter ecclesiastical discipline and
community-life. In this labour he had been greatly
assisted by a man whose name will ever have a peculiar
interest to all the children of S. Dominic,—Don Diego
de Azevedo, the first prior of the new community, and
afterwards successor to Martin in the episcopal see. The
name of Dominic, and the reputation of his singular
holiness no less than of his learning, had already reached
the ears of both; and they determined, if possible, to
secure him as a member of the chapter, not doubting
but the influence of his example and doctrine would
greatly assist their designs of reform. In his 25th year,
therefore, he received the habit of the Canons Regular, and
the influence of his character was so soon felt and appreciated by his brethren, that he was shortly afterwards
chosen sub-prior, in spite of his being the youngest of the
whole body of canons.

Nine years were thus spent at Osma, during which time God was doubtless gradually training and preparing his soul for the great work of his future life. Jordan of Saxony has left us a beautiful sketch of his manner of life at this period. "Now it was," he says, "that he began to appear among his brethren like a bright burning torch, the first in holiness, the last in humility, spreading about him an odour of life which gave life, and a perfume like the sweetness of summer days. Day and night he was in the church, praying as it were without ceasing. God gave him the grace to weep for sinners and for the afflicted; he bore their sorrows in an inner sanctuary of holy compassion, and so this loving compassion which pressed on his heart flowed out and escaped in tears. It was his custom to spend the night in prayer, and to speak to God with his door shut. But often there might be heard the voice of his groans and sighs, which burst from him against his will. His one constant petition to God was for the gift of a true charity; for he was persuaded that he could not be truly a member of Christ unless he consecrated himself wholly to the work of gaining souls, following the example of Him who sacrificed himself without reserve for our redemption."

It is interesting, among the very scanty details left us of Dominic's early years, to find two books mentioned, the study of which seems to have had an extraordinary influence in forming and directing his mind. The one was, the "Dialogues of Cassian;" and the other, the "Epistles of St. Paul." In after-years he always carried a copy of the Epistles about his person, and he seems to have shaped his whole idea of an apostolic life after the model of this great master. In 1201, Don Diego de Azevedo succeeded to the bishopric of Osma, and two years afterwards was appointed by Alfonso VIII., the king of Castile, to negotiate a marriage between his eldest son and a princess of Denmark. He accordingly set out for the north, taking Dominic as his companion; and it was on the occasion of this journey that, as they passed through the south of France, the frightful character and extent of the Albigensian heresy, which then

infected the whole of the southern provinces, first came
under their notice. Though they were not then able to
commence the apostolic labours for which they saw there
was so urgent a demand, yet an impression was left on
the hearts of both which was never effaced; and Dominic
felt that his life, which had hitherto seemed without any
determinate call or destiny, had been, as it were, reserved
for a work which he now saw clear before him. Probably
this feeling was strengthened by a circumstance which
occurred at Toulouse, where they stopped for a night on
their journey. The house where they lodged was kept by
a man who belonged to the sect of the Albigenses, and
when Dominic became aware of the fact, he resolved to
attempt at least to gain this one soul back to the faith.
The time was short, but the dispute was prolonged
during the whole night ; and in the morning the
eloquence and fervour of his unknown guest had conquered the obduracy of the heretic; before they left the
house he made his submission, and was received back
into the bosom of the Church. The effect of this first
conquest on Dominic's mind was a feeling of unspeakable
gratitude, and a determination, so soon as he should be
free to act, to found an order for the express purpose
of preaching the faith. Castiglio, in his history of the
order, tells us that the embassy on which Diego and
Dominic were employed was not to Denmark, but to
the court of France, and that it was on this occasion
that, finding Queen Blanche in much affliction on account
of her being without children, Dominic recommended to
her the use of the Rosary. The Queen, he adds, not
only adopted the devotion herself, but propagated it
among her people, and distributed Rosaries amongst
them, engaging them to join their prayers to hers,
that her desire might be granted; and the son whom
God gave in answer to those prayers was no other than
the great S. Louis. This is the first direct mention of
the devotion of the Rosary which we find in S. Dominic's
life; it is probable, from the date of S. Louis' birth,
which is generally given in 1215, that the circumstances
referred to, if they ever really took place, occurred at

some later visit to the French court. But though there is evidently some confusion in the time, we do not like altogether to abandon the story as without foundation; for there is always a peculiar charm in the little links which unite the lives of two great saints together, and those who claim any interest in the order of S. Dominic may feel a pleasure in thinking of S. Louis as a child of the Rosary.

— ✧ —

CHAPTER III.

Pilgrimage to Rome.   First labours among the Albigenses

The death of the princess, whose marriage they were negotiating, whilst engaged in a second embassy at her father's court, having relieved Diego and Dominic from their charge in this affair, they determined to take the occasion of their absence from the diocese, to visit Rome on pilgrimage before returning to Spain. Many motives concurred in inducing them to undertake this journey; but with Diego the most powerful one was the desire to obtain permission from Pope Innocent III. to resign his bishopric, and undertake the labours of an apostolic missionary life among the Cuman Tartars, who were then ravaging the fold of Christ in Hungary and the surrounding countries. It would seem as if the impressions made on the minds of these two great men by what they had witnessed of the sufferings of the Church in their journey through Europe, had been of that kind which is never effaced, and which, whenever it touches the soul, is to it the commencement of a new life. In them it had kindled the desire to devote themselves to a far wider field of labour than the limits of one diocese; they had both received the heroic call of the apostolate. The state of the Church at that time was one which might well make such an appeal to hearts ready to receive it. "Without were fightings, within

were fears." Whilst hordes of savage and heathen enemies were pressing hard on the outworks of Christendom,
and watering the ground with the blood of unnumbered
martyrs, heresy, as we have seen, was at work within
the fold; and during this memorable year, Diego and
Dominic had in some degree been eye-witnesses of both
these evils. We know in what manner they had been
thrown among the Albigenses of France, and it is at
least probable, that in the course of their Danish journey
they had become in some way more vividly aware of the
dangers to which the northern nations were exposed.
Pope Innocent, however, knew the value of Diego too
well to grant him the permission he sought, and exhorted
him not to abandon that charge which God had given
him in his Church, but to reassume the care of his
diocese; and after a short residence in Rome, the two
friends accordingly prepared to return to Spain, it being
then the March of the year 1205.

They had come to Rome as pilgrims, and it was in the
same spirit that, on their journey home, they turned from
the direct road in order to visit the celebrated abbey of
Citeaux, which the fame of S. Bernard had made illustrious throughout Europe. The charm of its religious
character and associations captivated the heart of Diego;
doubtless the failure of his deeply-cherished plan had
been no little pain to him, and his return to Osma was
a hard obedience. He was suffering under that strange
thirst to strip himself of the world, which sometimes
attacks the soul at the very time when it bows to the
law that forces it back to the world's duty. Very willingly would he have remained at Citeaux, and commenced
his noviciate in that school of holy living; but as this
could not be, he contented himself with taking the habit
of the order, and soliciting that he might carry some of
the religious back with him to Spain, to learn from them
their rule and manner of life. It is interesting to us to
know that he was probably moved to this by the example
of our own S. Thomas of Canterbury, who, several years
before, had received the religious habit at the same monastery, whilst in exile from his diocese, and whose popu-

larity as a saint was just at that time at its greatest
height. After this he no longer delayed his homeward
journey; but, accompanied by Dominic and some of the
Cistercian brethren, he set out for Spain, and soon arrived
in the neighbourhood of Montpellier.

And here, if we may so speak, the will of God awaited
them. Those inward stirrings which both had felt, yet
had not fully comprehended, had truly been the whisper-
ings of the Divine voice; and dimly feeling in the dark,
in obedience to the hand that was beckoning them on,
the dream of a martyr's crown among the Cumans, or a
monk's cowl at Citeaux, had, as it were, been two false
guesses as to what that whisper meant. This feature in
what we may call the vocation of S. Dominic is worthy of
notice, because whilst we are often inclined to regret that
more details of his personal life have not been preserved,
there is a peculiarity in this early portion of it, not without its interest. His call was not sudden, or miraculous,
or even extraordinary; it was that which is the likeliest
to come to men like ourselves; particular impressions of
mind were given just at the time when circumstances
combined together gradually to develop the way in which
those impressions could be carried out. He was always
being led forward, not knowing whither he went. As
sub-prior of Osma he probably saw nothing before him
but the ordinary community-life of the cathedral chapter.
Then came the journey to Denmark, on a mission whose
ostensible subject was a failure, but whose real end in the
designs of God was accomplished when it brought him
into the presence of the heresy which it was his destiny
to destroy. Yet though we have reason to believe that,
from the time of his first collision with the Albigenses, a
very clear and distinct idea was formed in his mind of
some future apostolate of preaching, it is evident that
he had no equally clear and determinate view in what
direction he was to work; and it hung on circumstances
alone, and on the will of another, to decide whether or no
he were to end his days as a nameless missioner among
the Tartars. He was on the road back to his old home,
preparing to take up again the old duties and the old life,

which had been interrupted by two years, rich with new
thoughts and hopes now, as it seemed, to be for ever
abandoned; and then, when he had made what was probably a painful sacrifice of great desires, those mysterious
orderings of Providence, which we call chance and coincidence, had prepared for him, under the walls of Montpellier, a combination of events which was to make all
clear.

The alarming progress and character of the Albigensian heresy had at length determined the Roman Pontiff
on active measures for its suppression. A commission
had been appointed for that purpose, the most distinguished members of which were Arnold, abbot of Citeaux,
and Rodolph and Peter de Castelnau, the Papal legates.
These were, all three, Cistercian monks, and with them
were associated several other abbots of the same order.
They found their task a difficult one, for the country was
entirely in the power of Count Raymond of Toulouse,
the avowed protector of the Albigenses; and unhappily
the bishops and clergy, by their coldness and indifference,
too often even by yet more culpable irregularities, were
themselves the chief causes of the spread of the evil.
Innocent III., in a letter to his legates, speaks in bitter
and yet in touching terms of this degeneracy of those
who should have been foremost in the ranks. "The
pastor," he says, "has become a hireling; he no longer
feeds the flock, but himself; wolves enter the fold, and he
is not there to oppose himself as a wall against the enemies of God's house." This scandal was of course the
great weapon used by the heretics, in all their conferences
with the legates. It was a short and triumphant argument to quote the words of the Gospel, "By their fruits
shall ye know them;" and then to point at the careless
and worldly character of the priesthood. Baffled and
confounded in all their efforts, the Catholic leaders had
met to consult together in the neighbourhood of Montpellier; and it was whilst discussing the gloomy prospects
of their commission that they heard of the arrival of the
two travellers. Their reputation, and the interest they
had shown in the state of the distracted province on the

occasion of their former visit, were well known, and the legates sent them an invitation to assist at the conference. It was accepted, and the disappointments and perplexities of the whole case were laid before them.

The chief difficulty in their way was the impossibility of convincing the heretics that the truth of the Christian faith depended, not on the good or bad example of individuals, but on the sure and infallible word of God made known to them through the Church. Diego inquired very particularly concerning the mode of life adopted by the legates and their opponents, and gave it as his opinion that the great obstacle which had hindered the work of souls, had been the neglect of Evangelical poverty among the Catholic missioners. For "he remarked," says Blessed Jordan, "that the heretics attracted men by persuasive means, by preaching, and a great outward show of sanctity, whilst the legates were surrounded by a numerous suite of followers, with horses and rich apparel. Then he said, 'It is not thus, my brothers, that you must act. They seduce simple souls with the appearances of poverty and austerity : by presenting to them the contrary spectacle, you will scarcely edify them ; you may destroy them, but you will never touch their hearts.'" The words of Diego, if they convinced his hearers, were yet a little unwelcome. None had the courage to be the first to follow the hard counsel, and they felt the want of one possessed of the chief authority among them to set the example of an austere reform, and enforce its adoption by the others. "Excellent father," they said to Diego, "what would you have us do?" Then the spirit of God came upon him, and he said "Do as I am about to do;" and, calling his attendants, he gave orders that they should return to Osma with all the equipages and followers who accompanied him. A little company of ecclesiastics alone remained, of whom Dominic was one; but they retained nothing of external pomp, and affected only the bearing and manners of the humblest missioners. The example was instantly followed by the other legates, and each one sent away all his followers and baggage, retaining only the books necessary for the re-

cital of the Divine Office, and for the confutation of the
heretics. More than this, feeling the power of Diego's
character and influence, they unanimously elected him as
head and chief of the Catholic body, and Innocent III.,
to whom the whole of the circumstances were made
known, hesitated not to grant him the permission which
he had before refused in the case of the Cumans; he was
authorized to remain in the French provinces for the
service of the faith.

—※—

CHAPTER IV.

Dominic in Languedoc.   The miracles of Fanjeaux and Montreal.
The foundation of the Convent of Prouille

A NEW impulse had been given to the enterprise on
which the Catholics of Languedoc had embarked; with
the apostolic life came a daily increase of the apostolic
spirit.   It was a very different thing to set about evan-
gelizing a country encumbered with the pomp of a feudal
retinue, and to traverse the same country on foot with
" neither purse nor scrip," as Diego was wont to send out
his companions daily into the neighbouring towns and
villages to preach the faith.   For after the conference at
Montpellier they all set out together towards Toulouse,
stopping at different places on the road to preach and
hold disputations with the heretics, as they were moved
by the Spirit of God.   We are assured that they made
this journey barefooted, and trusting to God's providence
alone for their daily wants; and the effect of this new way
of proceeding was soon evident in the success which attended their labours.   At Carmain, a town near Toulouse,
the residence of two of the principal Albigensian leaders,
Baldwin and Thierry, the people received the missionaries
so warmly that they were only prevented from expelling
the Albigenses from their territory by the authority of
the lord of the place, and accompanied the legates out of
the town on their departure with every sign of respect.
They proceeded in this way to Beziers, Carcassona, and

other places in the surrounding country, confirming the faith of the Catholics, and in many instances reconciling great numbers of the heretics to the Church.

Hitherto Dominic's part in these transactions has seemed to be a secondary one; he has appeared before us rather as the follower and companion of the bishop of Osma, than as the man whose name was to be for ever remembered in future histories as the chief leader in this struggle of the faith. Few probably of those who witnessed these first openings of the campaign against the Albigenses, would have believed that the award of a deathless fame was to fall, not to the bishop, whose prompt and commanding spirit had been so readily recognized by those who had unanimously chosen him to be their chief, but to one who followed in his train, known only as Brother Dominic; for he had laid aside even the title of sub-prior, and took on him nothing but the inferior part of the subject and attendant of another. As soon, however, as the disputes with the heretics began to be held of which we have spoken, his power and value were felt. Perhaps they were best evidenced by the bitter hatred which the heretics conceived against him. The same sentiments had been so unequivocally evinced towards the legate Peter de Castelnau, that the others had persuaded him to withdraw for a while from the enterprise, in order not to exasperate those whom it was their object to conciliate. The masterly arguments and captivating eloquence of Dominic, which time after time silenced his adversaries, and conquered the obstinacy of vast numbers who returned to the obedience of the Church after many of these conferences, excited a no less vindictive feeling against him in the minds of those who might be confounded, but would never yield. They spoke of him as their most dangerous enemy, and did not even conceal their resolve to take his life, whenever chance should give them the opportunity. He behaved on this occasion with a surprising indifference; the service of God was the only thing that he saw before him; and as his days were spent in public disputations, his nights were consumed in interviews with those who secretly sought his counsel, or more frequently in those prayers, and tears, and strong intercessions with God for the souls of his people, which were more powerful arms in fighting the battle of the faith than were the wisdom and eloquence of his words.

Among the conferences held at this time, that of Fanjeaux was the most important, both from the preparations made by both sides, and the extraordinary nature of its termination. It would seem that the heretics had appealed to some final arbitration of their differences, and that the Catholic leaders had not only responded to the challenge, but even accepted as judges in the controversy three persons whose sentiments were commonly known as favourable to the Albigenses themselves. Each side had put together in writing the strongest defence of their cause; that of the Catholics was the work of Dominic. The three arbitrators having heard both parties, and read the written apologies, absolutely refused to pronounce any decision on the case; and in this perplexity the heretics loudly demanded a different mode of trial, and proposed that both books should be committed to the flames, that God might declare by his own interposition which cause He favoured. " Accordingly a great fire was lighted" (says Blessed Jordan), " and the two volumes were cast therein; that of the heretics was immediately consumed to ashes; the other, which had been written by the blessed man of God, Dominic, not only remained unhurt, but was borne far away by the flames in presence of the whole assembly. Again a second and a third time they threw it into the fire, and each time the same result clearly manifested which was the true faith, and the holiness of him who had written the book. This miracle is given by every contemporaneous writer. It is mentioned in the lessons for the Divine office, composed by Constantine Medici, bishop of Orvieto, in 1254; and in the following century Charles le Bel, King of France, purchased the house where the event took place, and erected it into a chapel under the invocation of the saint. A large beam of wood on which the paper fell when tossed away by the flames, was still preserved when Castiglio wrote his history; and there does not even seem to have been any attempt on the part of the heretics themselves to deny the fact. Yet in spite of this, there is a melancholy significance in the expression of the historian. "*A few* of the heretics were converted to the truth of our holy faith, but as to the rest, it produced no effect; this being the just reward of their great sins."* It would seem as if every age and every heresy were to act over again the scenes of Christ's ministry in Judea: signs and miracles were thrown away on those who had Moses and the prophets, and would not believe.

This was not the only occasion when a miracle of this kind was wrought. A similar prodigy took place at Montréal, in the diocese of Carcassona, under different circumstances. Dominic had, in the course of one of his public disputations, written down on a sheet of paper various quotations from the Holy Scriptures, which he had cited in the course of his argument, and these he gave to one of the heretics, praying him to consider them well, and not to resist the conclusion to which they might bring him. The same evening, as this man sat over the fire with some of his companions, discussing the subjects of dispute, he drew out the paper, and proposed submitting it to the flames, as a test of the truth of its contents. They consented, and thrusting it into the fire, kept it there for some time, and then drew it out unscorched. Again and again they repeated the experiment, and always with the same result. And a second time what do we find to be the effect on the witnesses of this new miracle? "Then the heretics were filled with great wonder, and, instead of keeping the promise they had made of believing the truths preached by the Catholics, agreed to keep the prodigy a close secret, lest it should reach the ears of the Catholics, who would be certain to claim it as a sign of victory."† One, however, more noble-minded than the rest, was converted by what he saw, and published it to the world, and from his testimony it was inserted by Peter de Vaulx Cernay, in his history of the Albigenses.

It is to be regretted that more particulars have not

* Castiglio, part i. cap. viii.　　　† Polidori, cap. vi.

C

been preserved of those memorable conferences, but we are only told in general that great success everywhere followed the footsteps of the missionaries, and that the numbers of the Catholics daily increased, which reduced the heretics to the necessity of using frauds and the most incredible ingenuity to preserve their ground against the power of their adversaries

It will be observed that we have made no attempt in these pages to give any account of the nature of that celebrated heresy, the name of which will be for ever inseparably united with that of S. Dominic; neither is it our intention to do so. An ample account of its doctrines may be gathered from so many works within the reach of the Catholic reader, that we feel it is wholly unnecessary to devote any space here to the task of unveiling its true character. Indeed, whilst alluding to its connection with this period of S. Dominic's life, we cannot but feel that this connection has been greatly overrated by many, who have made his biography little more than a history of political and ecclesiastical affairs, with which he had personally but little to do. In this way his own personal life and character have often been lost sight of, and confused with the troubles of the times, and the portrait of the Saint has been hidden by the shadow which rests, in some degree, on the Count de Montfort's crusade. With all this we have nothing to do; nor shall we allude to the political history of the time, except in so far as is necessary to explain and illustrate the details preserved to us of the life of Dominic. There is little doubt that the Albigensian heresy, besides its corruptions of the faith and its frightful immorality, had a directly political character, and was mixed up with a spirit of revolution and sedition, which goes far to explain the bitterness of those civil wars of which it was the immediate cause; and, like all revolutionary movements, it had a disorganizing effect on all social ties, so that the south of France was plunged by it into a state of civil anarchy, which was doubtless the chief reason which moved the civil arm against its followers with such peculiar severity. One of the consequences of these political commotions was the impoverishing of many noble families engaged in them, and this often led to their concealing their faith through the pressure of necessity, and suffering their children to be educated by the heretics, who eagerly made use of the worldly temptations which were in their power to offer, in order to get the children of Catholics into their hands.   This evil was very soon perceived by the quick eye of Dominic, and so deplorably did he feel the cruelty which exposed these souls to the certain ruin of their religious principles, that he determined on a very strenuous effort to oppose it, and to provide some means for the education of the daughters of Catholics in the true faith.

For this purpose he resolved to found a monastery, where, within the protection of strict enclosure, and under the charge of a few holy women whom he gathered together out of the suffering provinces, these children might be nurtured under the Church's shadow.   The spot chosen for the purpose was Prouille, a name illustrious in the Dominican annals, for there, unconsciously probably to its founder, rose the mother-house of an institute which was to cover the world.   It was a small village near Montréal, at the foot of the Pyrenees; and a church dedicated to our Lady, under the familiar title of Notre Dame de Prouille, was the object of considerable veneration among the people.   There, with the warm sanction and co-operation of Fulk, bishop of Toulouse, Dominic founded his monastery.   The church we have spoken of was granted to the new foundation, and it seemed as if the plan had no sooner been proposed than every one saw its fitness for the necessities of the times, and vied one with another in forwarding and contributing to it.   Peter of Castelnau, stretched on a bed of sickness, gave thanks to God with clasped hands for what he deemed so signal a mercy. Berenger, archbishop of Narbonne, immediately granted it considerable lands and revenues; and all the Catholic nobles, with the Count de Montfort at their head, gave their prompt and liberal aid to a scheme from which they themselves were sure to derive such lasting advantage.

The little community consisted at first of nine members, all of them converted from the Albigensian heresy by the preaching and miracles of Dominic. They were joined by two noble ladies of Catholic families, one of whom, Guillemette de Fanjeaux, though the last to receive the habit, was chosen by Dominic as their Superior. She continued in that office until the year 1225; but he himself governed the monastry, and thenceforth received the title of Prior of Prouille, residing in a house outside the enclosure, when his apostolic labours did not call him elsewhere. The community took possession of their new retreat on the 27th of December, 1206. Their habit was white with a tawny mantle; of the rule given them by their founder we know nothing, save that it bound them, besides attending to the education of children, to devote certain hours to manual labour, such as spinning. Prouille, afterwards associated to the Order of Preachers, became in time a flourishing monastry, never numbering less than a hundred religious; it was the mother-house of no less than twelve other foundations, and reckoned among its prioresses several of the royal house of Bourbon.

—◦◦◦—

CHAPTER V.

Diego returns to Spain. His death. Dominic remains in Languedoc. The murder of Peter de Castelnau, and the commencement of the Albigensian war.

DIEGO of Azevedo saw the foundation of Prouille before returning to his diocese of Osma. He had now been two years in the French provinces, and he felt it was time to revisit his own church and people. He left the country in which he had laboured so truly and nobly, with the promise soon to return with fresh labourers in the cause; but this promise was destined never to be fulfilled. His companions attended him to the confines of the province of Toulouse, all journeying on foot and preaching as they went. These last missionary labours of Diego were crowned with new successes. At Montréal 500 heretics

abjured their errors. A meeting of the legates and chief
Catholics also took place at the same town, and another
at Pamiers, when the increased courage and strength of
the Catholic party were plainly visible, and some of the
principal of the Albigenses made their submission with
the most unequivocal marks of sincerity. After this last
conference Diego turned his steps towards Spain, and,
still travelling on foot, reached Osma, having been absent
from his diocese exactly three years. He died before he
could carry his intention of returning to France into
execution; and thus he and Dominic never met again.
He was the first of a long line of great men with whom
the founder of the Friars Preachers was united in bonds
of no common friendship, nor was he the least worthy of
the number. So holy and stainless was the life he led,
that even the heretics were wont to say of him in the
words of blessed Jordan, that "it was impossible not to
believe such a man predestined to eternal life, and that
doubtless he was sent among them to be taught the true
doctrine." It was his influence that had consolidated the
weak and scattered elements of the Catholic party into a
firm and united body, and his loss was felt by all to be
that of a father and chief. Nay, it seemed as if his death
dissolved in a moment the tie which had bound them
together. They were again scattered, each in different
directions, and a few weeks after the news of his friend's
death reached the ears of Dominic, he found himself alone.

We cannot guess, or rather we can but guess, what
kind of solitude that was when the work remained to do,
but the fellow-labourers, and he among them whose company had been a brotherhood of fourteen years, were gone.
Yet Dominic was equal to the shock of that great lone-
liness : he saw one after another of the missioners depart,
the Spanish ecclesiastics to Spain, the Cistercians back to
their abbey, but he remained firm and tranquil at the
post where God had placed him. The sweetness of human
consolation had left it, but the will of God was clear as
ever, and that was the law of his life; and if hitherto he
had been displayed to the world as following rather in
another's track, than as himself the originator of the

enterprise in which he was engaged, it was for the test of
a crisis like this to show him to the world in his true
light. We have mentioned Fulk, bishop of Toulouse, as
co-operating in the foundation of the convent of Prouille.
His presence and influence in some degree supplied the
loss which the Catholics had sustained by the death of
Diego. Until his elevation to the episcopate, one of the
greatest drawbacks to the Catholic cause had been the
coldness and indifference of their own bishops; but the
vigorous example of the new prelate roused many of his
colleagues from their negligence, and infused new life into
the ecclesiastical administration of the diocese. He was
indeed in every way a remarkable man, one in whom the
energy of human passion had been, not laid aside, but
transformed and sanctified by the influence of grace.
Not many years before, he had been known to the world
only as a brilliant courtier, a successful cultivator of the
"gaie science," the very embodiment of the Provençal
character. The world spoiled him for a time, and then
deserted him; or we might rather say that God had determined to draw to Himself a soul too noble for the
world's spoiling. Deaths came one after another to strip
his life of everthing that made it desirable; then there
followed that period of bitter conflict and agony which
precedes the putting off of the old nature; and when it
was over, Provence had lost her gayest troubadour, and
Fulk was a monk in the abbey of Citeaux. In 1206 he
was raised to the bishopric of Toulouse, and in that capacity his energy and enthusiasm of character was of special
service in animating the chilled and timorous spirit of his
colleagues. Towards Dominic and his companions he was
ever a liberal benefactor.

And indeed there was need of some support in the
position in which the departure and death of Diego had
left his friend. He was not only alone, but alone just as
the difficulties of the cause to which he was bound were
about to be increased tenfold by the horrors of civil war.
This conflict, associated as it was with the religious
contest in which he was engaged, could scarcely fail to
entangle him in something of its confusion: so at least

it would seem, if we remember that the war was that
crusade against the Albigenses, which history has per-
sisted in linking with the name of Dominic. The reader
of his life who comes full of this prepossession, will turn to
the chapter of the Albigensian crusade with the natural
expectation of finding there the most striking details of
the man he has been accustomed to think of as its hero.
Whereas it is literally true that it is just during the ten
years of the Albigensian war that we find least record of
Dominic's life, so far as the world knew it. He had a life,
and a work, but one so wholly distinct from the conflict
that was raging around him, that it has hidden him from
sight. Here and there we find a trace of him, but in no
case are those scattered notices connected with any of
the warlike or political movements of the times. They
are the anecdotes of an apostolic life, whose course has
been thus briefly sketched by Blessed Humbert in a few
lines : "After the return of the bishop Diego to his diocese," he says, " S. Dominic, left almost alone with a few
companions who were bound to him by no vow, during
ten years upheld the Catholic faith in different parts of the
province of Narbonne, particularly at Carcassona and at
Fanjeaux. He devoted himself entirely to the salvation
of souls by the ministry of preaching, and he bore with a
great heart a multitude of affronts, ignominies, and sufferings for the name of Jesus Christ." And this is all.
The few details preserved of these ten years of suffering
and silent work will disappoint any who look for stirring
pictures of the crusade. Some trait of humility and
patience exhibited amid the insults of his enemies,—or,
it may be, a few words redolent with the spirit of prayer
and trust in God, which have come down in the tradition
of ages, or the record of miracles, worked, like those of
the Master whose steps he followed, as he went up and
down the hills of Narbonne, and among the towns and
villages, preaching the faith, and seeking for the sheep
that were lost,—this is all we find. There is an evangelical sweetness of simplicity about these broken notices
of his life, which, coming in the midst of the troubled and
bloody history of the period, sounds like the rich notes of

a thrush's song falling on the ear between the intervals
of a thunder-storm,—lost every now and then, and hushed
by the angry roll of the elements, then sounding sweetly
again in the stillness when the storm is over. We shall
give them as we find them, in their proper place, but it is
necessary first of all to notice very briefly some of those
events which followed on the departure of Diego of Azevedo,
and which plunged the southern provinces of France into
the bloody contest of which we have spoken.

It will be remembered, that among the legates and
missioners whom Dominic and Diego met at Montpellier,
on their first entrance on the mission, mention was made
of Peter de Castelnau, against whom the hatred of the
heretics had been so strongly evinced, that he had been
persuaded for some time to withdraw from the enterprise.
Something of severity and harshness in his character may
probably account for the peculiar vindictiveness of which
he was the object. He had often been used to say, that
religion would never raise its head in Languedoc till the
soil had been watered with the blood of a martyr; and
his constant prayer was, that he himself might be the
victim. It was even as he desired. Count Raymond of
Toulouse, the sovereign of the distracted provinces, had
been the constant but not always the avowed protector
of the Albigenses during the whole period of his government. Again and again, in reply to the pressing entreaties of the Holy See, he had promised to use his
authority to suppress their disorders, and to defend the
property and liberty of the Catholics; and again and
again, when the dread of excommunication was withdrawn, he had failed to fulfil his engagements. It is
no part of history to asperse its characters with epithets
of reproach. Count Raymond has been the hero of one
party, and the object of unlimited abuse from the other;
but we may well content ourselves with such conclusions
as may be drawn from facts which none have attempted
to dispute. He had bound himself by solemn oaths to
suppress those violent disorders, the frightful increase of
which had opened the eyes of his predecessor, and forced
from him the unwilling acknowledgment, that "the

spiritual sword was no longer enough; the material sword was needed also." These oaths were made, and as often violated; after incessant remonstrances, Peter de Castelnau, in his office of Papal legate, pronounced the final sentence of excommunication against him. The result was an earnest entreaty from the count to meet him at Saint Gilles, in order that by fresh submissions he might be once more reconciled to the Church. His request was agreed to, but it seemed impossible for Raymond to act with good faith. No sooner were the legates in his power, than he changed his tone of submission, and haughtily threatened them with imprisonment if they did not grant him the unconditional repeal of his sentence. Such threats were lightly felt by men who counted their lives as nothing in the cause in which they were engaged, and they answered him only with a stern reproof. Next day, as they stood by the rapid waters of the Rhone, on the banks of which they had passed the night, and which they were preparing to cross, two members of the count's household came up in pursuit of them, and one plunged his lance into the body of Peter de Castelnau. It was the death for which he had so often longed; he fell without a struggle, and summoned his departing strength to utter words worthy of a martyr. "May God pardon you," he said to his murderer; "as for me, I forgive you,—I forgive you;" then turning to his companion, "Keep the faith," he said, "and serve God's Church without fear, and without negligence;" and, with these words upon his lips, he died.

When the news of this murder reached the ears of the Pope and the Catholic potentates of Europe, there seemed a unanimous feeling that all time for further treating with the heretics was at an end. Let us remember, that the south of France had now been at their mercy for more than a century; that during that time these atrocious wretches, whom Protestants are not ashamed to boast of as their ancestors in the faith, had ravaged the country like bandits, setting fire to churches, torturing priests and nuns, trampling under foot the holy Eucharist, and committing every violence most shocking to human feeling; and that during this century of crime the Church had opposed only her censures and her entreaties, sending among them missionaries and preachers, but never unloosing the temporal sword. Nay, she had even interposed with peaceful measures when the civil arm was at length raised against them. Raymond of Toulouse, the predecessor of the present count, and himself a favourer of the heretics, had at length become aware of the danger threatened to his own government, and to the very existence of all law, by their continued excesses. Too late he strove to check the evil he had fostered, but he found the task was far beyond his strength. In his terror he wrote to the French king a memorable letter, which, as coming from his pen, may fairly be received as impartial testimony, "Our churches," he says, "are in ruins, penance is despised, the Holy Eucharist is held in abomination, all the sacraments are rejected—*yet no one thinks of offering any resistance to these wretches.*" He then makes an earnest appeal to the king for assistance, and would have obtained it had not the reigning Pontiff, Alexander III., interfered, and proposed once more to try the effect of an ecclesiastical mission before harsher measures were adopted.

But however well fitted a legation of monks and preachers might be for the suppression of theological errors, it scarcely had the strength necessary for delivering Languedoc from its swarms of bandits. The sufferings of the country were not simply doctrinal: Stephen, abbot of S. Genevieve, sent to Toulouse by the king, and an eye-witness of what he describes, gives us a picture of the state of things in his time in a few words which occur in one of his letters: "I have seen," he says, "churches burnt and ruined to their foundations; I have seen the dwellings of men changed into the dens of beasts." Is it any wonder, therefore, that after these terrible disorders had been endured for more than a century, and opposed only by the weapons of ecclesiastical censures, the murder in cold blood of the Papal

legate by the avowed leader of the Albigenses seemed
to fill the measure of their iniquity? War at once
burst out ; and surely if ever war is just, it must be
deemed so when waged to defend society from outrage,
and the faith from ruin. This at least we may affirm
without in any way binding ourselves to vindicate the
manner in which it was carried on, when men's passions
and personal interests were once irretrievably engaged ;
but we cannot think that the act which proclaimed the
crusade against the Albigenses, after a century of for-
bearance, can be condemned by any who will patiently
go over that century's most melancholy history.

— ✠ —

CHAPTER VI.

Proclamation of the Crusade.   Simon de Montfort.   Dominic
among the heretics.   His apostolic labours

THE death of De Castelnau took place in the February
of the year 1208. Early in the following month Pope
Innocent addressed letters to the kings of France and
England, and to the sovereign nobles of France, calling
on them to lay aside their private quarrels, and join
in an unanimous effort against " the rage of heresy."
The crime of the Count of Toulouse was declared to be
one which freed his subjects from their allegiance until
such time as he would return to his own allegiance to the
Church; and a new commission of bishops and abbots
was appointed to preach the crusade, and undertake the
ecclesiastical government of the country. In this commission Dominic's name does not occur; Arnold of Citeaux
is the man charged with the chief burden of the whole
undertaking, and his fiery and inflexible temper caused
him to fulfil his charge with an unrelenting severity,
which can never be excused. If indeed we had to make
any religious body responsible for the severities of the
crusade, it certainly seems as though the Cistercians had

done more to merit such a reproach than any other. We
find their leader, Arnold, eagerly and zealously engaged
in all the movements of the Catholic chiefs, often accompanying them to the field and rousing the country to
arms with the energy of his preaching. Every representation of the progress of the war which reached the Pope
came through him and his followers; and these representations seem, in more instances than one, to have been
coloured by partiality, and to have misled the Pontiff
whom they were intended to direct. For more than a
year after the war first broke out, Arnold was the only
acknowledged leader and director of the Catholic forces;
and the unfortunate plan of setting the two houses of
Montfort and Toulouse in rivalry one against the other,
as the means of destroying the latter by the vindictiveness of a personal quarrel, was the invention of his own
scheming brain.

Yet this man, who really played so conspicuous a part
in the history of his time, and who stands bound to every
detail in those proceedings of which he was the animating
spirit, is almost forgotten by Protestant historians and
their readers, so eager are they to heap terms of reproach
on one who had little or no share in them. Doubtless in
their own day, Dominic Gusman was a very insignificant
person compared to the legate, Arnold of Citeaux; but
the Church, in her unerring justice, has raised one to her
altars, and left the other to the mercy and indifference of
future ages; and this explains what would otherwise
be an unaccountable phenomenon. Arnold of Citeaux,
though a busy man in his time, is in no way a representative of the Catholic Church; she has not identified
herself with him, and so there is no good reason for
attacking him and his order, and holding up their names
for popular abuse, however deeply they were responsible
for the excesses of the crusade. But it is quite another
thing to vilify a Catholic saint. Dominic bears on his
brow the indelible seal of the Church's canonization, and
therefore no Protestant can touch on the history of the
Albigensian war without assuring us that it was " preached
by the infamous Dominic," with a thousand other like

expressions which would give us to understand that he was the foremost character in the whole affair, but which are simply inexplicable to any one who, in studying his life, finds it his chief difficulty to come on any trace of him during this period.

It must be acknowledged that the perpetual insincerities of the Count of Toulouse render it difficult to follow, with anything like clearness, a history which shows him to us submitting to public penance in the church of S. Gilles in 1209, and swearing at the same time, on holy relics and the very body of our Lord, to drive away the heretic insurgents, to repair the churches, and replace the lawful bishops in their sees; then a year afterwards, evading the demands of the council, held at the same place, which called on him to fulfil his engagements, and persisting in his refusal, even whilst he supplicates to be heard in justification of the accusations brought against him. A little while after, we find him at Toulouse, preparing to take up arms against the Catholic forces whom he had sworn to assist; and, in return for this breach of faith, we have a touching and affectionate letter from Pope Innocent, calling on him once more to stand to his plighted word. Then more conferences and more evasions. In 1211, at a meeting held at Montpellier, he seems about to yield, but suddenly leaves the city without a word of explanation. Then at length the thunder of excommunication falls on his head a second time; and the war begins in earnest.

Raymond had the powerful protection of his brother-in-law, the king of Arragon, together with many of the territorial lords of the south. The power of the crusaders under the leadership of Count Simon de Montfort was certainly in no overwhelming disproportion, and, we are told, more than a thousand cities and towns were in the hands of the heretics. Two of these towns, Beziers and Carcassona, had yielded to the Catholic confederates, after a bloody contest at the very commencement of the war, and before the final rupture with Raymond. The cruelties practised on the inhabitants of the former, and the pillage of the latter, gave a vindictive character to the very opening of the campaign. For the enormities perpetrated by the heretics had lashed the Catholics of Languedoc to fury; and when the day of retribution came, and vengeance was in the power of men who had so long suffered the worst injuries without redress, it broke out into the usual excesses. There is no temptation to justify such excesses, yet surely there is an astonishing unfairness, may we not say an astonishing hypocrisy, in those who can find no words to express their horror at the slaughter of Beziers, yet forget the tortures of helpless women, the profanation of holy things, the murders and oppressions of the century which had passed, the recollection of which was doubtless too terribly alive in the minds of the crusaders for them to find such mercy in their hearts for those who were in turn their victims.

Where was Dominic all this time? Some of his historians gave the year 1207 as the date of the foundation of his order; inasmuch as it was then that he took the command of that little company of missionaries who remained with him after the departure of Diego. But they were bound to him by no other tie than a common interest; and the only ground for the supposition seems to be, that they lived together in a kind of community-life, and were known by the name of the Preaching Brothers. It does not, however, seem that they had anything of the formation of a regular religious body, and probably no plan for such a formation had yet been clearly developed in Dominic's own mind. Of their manner of life we can form some notion from those scattered anecdotes which are all that are left us. Even amid the hottest period of the war, it was the same as it had ever been; they went about barefoot from village to village preaching the faith. The only commission which Dominic held, was the original one he possessed in virtue of that first legation to which he and Diego had been associated before the crusade began. It gave him the power of reconciling heretics, and receiving them to penance, an office which has acquired him the title of the first Inquisitor. If by this is meant that the office of the Inquisition, as afterwards constituted, was established at this time, such title is certainly an error; no such office existed before the Lateran Council of 1215, and it was not until 1230, nine years after the death of Dominic, that the Council of Toulouse gave it a new form, and intrusted a large share of its government to the recently instituted order of Friars Preachers. It is singular also, that the first commission for denouncing heretics to the civil magistrate was granted to the Cistercians. But, on the other hand, there is no doubt that the commission of reconciling heretics, held by S. Dominic, was the germ from which the Inquisition afterwards sprang; and so Dominic may be called the first Inquisitor, in the same sense as the Marquis of Worcester is called the inventor of the steam-engine, or Roger Bacon the discoverer of gunpowder; without supposing that the marvels of a cotton-mill, or the broadside of a three-decker, ever crossed the imagination of either.*

His chief residence was at Fanjeaux and Carcassona. Fanjeaux he chose for its proximity to Notre Dame de Prouille, and Carcassona for another reason. "Why do you not live in Toulouse, or the diocese?" was a question one day asked him. "I know many people in Toulouse," he replied, "and they show me respect; but at Carcassona, every one is against me." They certainly were: it was

---

* It is no part of the plan which we have laid down for ourselves, to enter at any length into the vexed question of the character of the Inquisition. But we cannot resist referring to one authority, quoted by Père Lacordaire, in his well-known " Memorial to the French People," whose partiality can scarcely be questioned. It is from the Report presented to the Cortes, on the character of that tribunal, which was followed by its suppression, and bears the date of 1812. Considering that it proceeded from the party most violently opposed to the Inquisition, and who — political successors, the Progressistas of Spain, have succeeded in abolishing all religious orders in that country, its testimony is of peculiar value. " The early Popes for," they say, "encountered heresy with no other arms than those of prayer, patience, and instruction; and this remark applies more particularly to S. Dominic, as we are assured by the Bollandists, with Echard and Touron. Philip II. was the real founder of the Inquisition." For a minute and careful account of the changes introduced into the character of the tribunal by the royal statesmen, we must refer the reader to the celebrated work of Balmez, on " Protestantism and Catholicity compared in their Effects on the civilization of Europe."

their diversion to treat the humble barefooted friar who
was to be seen about their streets as a fool; rather let us
say, they gave the truest testimony to his likeness to his
Lord by the likeness of their treatment of him. They
were wont to follow him, throwing dirt at him and spit-
ting in his face; tying straws to his cloak and hat, and
pursuing him with shouts of derisive laughter. He never
seemed to heed them, or to let the singular quietude of
his soul be once disturbed by these affronts. Sometimes
their insults were accompanied with blasphemous oaths
and threats of death: "I am not worthy of martyrdom,"
was the only answer they were able to draw from him.
He was warned once of a party of heretics who lay in
ambush in a certain place to assassinate him. He treated
the information with his usual indifference, and passed
by the place singing hymns with a joyful aspect. The
heretics, who were probably not prepared for the actual
execution of their threat, accosted him on their next
meeting in their usual style. "And so thou dost not
fear death? tell us, what wouldst thou have done if thou
hadst fallen into our hands?" Then the great and courageous spirit of Dominic spoke in a memorable reply:
"I would have prayed you," he said, "not to have taken
my life at a single blow, but little by little, cutting off
each member of my body, one by one; and when you had
done that, you should have plucked out my eyes, and then
have left me so, to prolong my torments, and gain me a
richer crown." It is said that this reply so confounded
his enemies, that for some time afterwards they left him
unmolested, being convinced that to persecute such a man
was to give him the only consolation he desired. The
place of the intended attempt on his life is still shown,
half-way between Prouille and Fanjeaux, and its name
"Al Sicari," in the dialect of the country, commemorates
the event.

On another occasion a great conference was appointed
to be held with the heretics, at which one of the neighbouring bishops (who, some writers tell us, was Fulk of
Toulouse) was to attend. He came in great pomp, to the
great displeasure of Dominic. "Then the humble herald

of God spoke to him, and said, 'My father, it is not thus
that we must act against this generation of pride. The
enemies of the truth must rather be convinced by the
example of humility and patience, than by the pomp and
grandeur of worldly show. Let us arm ourselves with
prayer and humility, and so let us go barefooted against
these Goliaths.'" *The bishop complied with his wishes,
and they all took off their shoes, and went to meet the
heretics singing psalms upon the way. Now, as they were
not sure of their road, they applied to a man whom they
met and believed to be a Catholic, but who was in truth a
concealed and bitter heretic; and who offered to be their
guide to the place of meeting, with no other design than
that of embarrassing and annoying them. He led them,
therefore, through a thorny wood, where the rough stones
and briers tore their naked feet, and caused them to dye
the ground with their blood. The bishop and his suite were
a little disconcerted at this, but Dominic encouraged them
to persevere. Joyous and patient as ever, he exhorted
his comrades to give thanks for their sufferings, saying,
"Trust in God, my beloved; the victory is surely ours,
since our sins are expiated in blood; 'is it not written,
'How beautiful are the feet of them who bring the gospel
of peace?'" Then he intoned a joyful hymn, and the
hearts of his companions took courage, and they also sang
with him; and the heretic, when he witnessed the patience
and courage of the saint, was touched to the heart, and,
falling at his feet, confessed his malice, and abjured his
heresy.

As we have said, these anecdotes of Dominic's apostolic
life in Languedoc can hardly be given in successive order
as they occurred: the most ancient writers tell us only in
general terms, that during this time he suffered many
affronts from his enemies, and overcame their wiles by
his patience, giving these disconnected stories without
anything to guide us as to the particular times when
they happened. One anecdote, however, in which the
miraculous powers of the saint are first exhibited to us,
is given with greater exactness. It was in 1211, whilst

* Theodoric of Apoldia.

D

the crusaders were under the walls of Toulouse, and just
after open hostilities had for the first time broken out
with Count Raymond, that the course of Dominic's
apostolic wanderings led him to the bank of the river
Garrone. Whilst he was there, a band of English pilgrims also arrived in the neighbourhood. They were
about forty in number, bound to the shrine of S. James
of Compostella. In order to avoid the town, which lay
under the Papal interdict, they took a boat to cross the
river; but the boat, being small and overladen, was upset,
and all those who were in it sank to the bottom. Dominic
was praying in a small church which stood near the scene
of the accident, but the cries of the sufferers and some of
the soldiers who saw their danger roused him from his
devotions. He came to the river's bank, but not one
of the pilgrims was to be seen. Then he prostrated himself on the earth in silent prayer, and, rising full of a
lively faith, " I command you," he cried, " in the name
of Jesus Christ, to come to the shore alive and unhurt."
Instantly the bodies rose to the surface, and with the help
of the soldiers, who flung them their shields and lances,
they all safely reached the bank, praising God and his
servant Dominic.

Several other miracles are related as having happened
at this period, they are the only footprints left us of his
apostolic journeys over Languedoc. At one time we hear
of him dropping his books into the river Ariege as he
forded it on foot, and after three days they are recovered
by a fisherman, and found perfectly dry and uninjured.
At another time he is crossing the same river in a little
boat, and being landed on the opposite shore, finds he has
no money to pay the boatman. The boatman insisted on
his fare: " I am," said Dominic, " a follower of Jesus
Christ; I carry neither gold nor silver; God will pay you
the price of my passage." But the boatman, being angry,
laid hold of his cloak, saying, " You will either leave your
cloak with me, or pay me my money." Dominic, raising
his eyes to heaven, entered for a moment into prayer;
then, looking on the ground, he showed the man a piece
of silver which lay there, which Providence had sent, and

said to him. My brother, there is what you ask, take it, and suffer me to go my way."

Cardinal Ranieri Capocci, who lived during the time of S. Dominic, in a sermon preached shortly after his canonization, relates the following fact which had come to his own knowledge. A certain religious chanced to be the companion of the saint on a journey of some days, but being of another country, and neither of them understanding the language of the other, they were unable to hold any conversation together. Desiring very much, however, to profit by the time he should spend in his society, this religious secretly prayed to God that, for the three days they should be together, they might be intelligible to one another, each speaking in his own tongue, and this favour was granted until they reached their journey's end. We read also that, after a night spent in long disputes with the heretics, Dominic left the place of conference in company with a Cistercian monk, and desired to retire into a neighbouring church, in order, according to his custom, to spend the remainder of the night in prayer. They found the doors locked, and were therefore obliged to kneel outside. But scarcely had they done so, than, without being able to say how, they found themselves before the high altar inside the church, and remained there until break of day. In the morning the people found them there, and crowding together, brought them the sick and infirm in great numbers to be healed. Among these were several possessed persons, whom the holy father was intreated to restore by his touch. He took a stole, and fastened it on his shoulders as if about to vest for mass; then throwing it around the necks of the possessed, they were immediately delivered.

These miracles, some of which are mentioned in the process of his canonization, were commonly known and talked of both by the crusaders and by the people of Toulouse. Among the latter their effect was sensibly felt, and in no small degree aided the success of his preaching. Yet the marvels produced by his simple eloquence were, perhaps, as great in their way as those directly supernatural gifts communicated to him by God.

One day, as he prayed in the church of Fanjeaux, nine women who until then had been of the heretical sect, came to him, and threw themselves at his feet in great anguish. "Servant of God," they cried, "if what you preached to us this morning is true, we have till now been living in horrible darkness; therefore have compassion on us, and teach us how we may be saved." The holy man looked on them with a bright and cheerful countenance, and comforted them with words of hope. Then he prayed awhile, and turning to them bade them be of good heart, and not be afraid of what they should see. Scarcely had he spoken, when they saw in the midst of them a hideous animal, of a ferocious and horrible aspect. It fled from among them, and seemed to escape from the church through the bell-tower. The women were greatly terrified, but Dominic spoke and re-assured them. "God has shown you, my daughters," he said, "how terrible is the devil whom till now you have served; thank Him, therefore, for the evil one has from this moment no more power over you." These women, who were all of noble birth, he afterwards caused to be instructed in the faith, and received into the monastery of Prouille. Miracles and preaching, however, are not the only means, scarcely the most powerful, by which the saints of God extend the kingdom of their Master. The silent eloquence of a holy life has a larger apostolate than the gifts of tongues or of healing; and we find some records of the harvest of souls which were gathered to the faith solely by the example of the servant of God. There were living, near Toulouse, some noble ladies who had been led to join the heretics, being seduced into this error by the show of pretended austerity which their preachers affected. Dominic, who had their conversion greatly at heart, determined to preach there that Lent; and, going thither with one companion, it chanced, by the providence of God, that they were received to lodge in the house occupied by these ladies. He remained there during the whole time of his stay, and they saw with wonder the reality of that life of penance which differed so widely from the empty professions of the heretics. The soft

beds which had been prepared for them were never used,
for Dominic and his companion slept upon the ground.
Their food was scarcely touched; until Easter time they
took only bread and water, and that in scanty measure.
Their nights were spent in prayer and austerities, their
days in labours for God; and so new and wonderful did
this life seem to those who beheld it, that it opened their
eyes to the truth of the faith which inspired it; and the
whole household made their recantation in his hands before the time of his stay was ended. In after days he
was often accustomed to exhort his brethren to this, as
the best method of preaching, reminding them that it was
by good works, and by the outward habit, even more than
by holy words, that we must let our light shine before
men to the glory of God.

It was this singular holiness of life which endeared him
so wonderfully to all those among whom he was thrown.
Three times the episcopal dignity was offered to him, but
he refused it with a kind of horror. He was used to say
he would rather go away by night with nothing but his
staff than accept any office or dignity. He could not,
however, succeed in avoiding a temporary appointment as
vicar to Guy, bishop of Carcassona, during the time that
the latter was absent from his diocese preaching the crusade, and gathering together fresh forces to join the army
of the Count de Montfort. He held this charge during
the Lent of the year 1213, during which time he resided
in the episcopal palace, and discharged all the duties of
the office, without, however, suffering them to interfere
with his customary occupation of preaching and instructing in the faith. During this Lent we again find him
spoken of as fasting on bread and water, and sleeping on
the ground. "When Easter came," says his historian,
"he seemed stronger and more vigorous than before, and
of a better aspect." We may remark in this appointment,
how entirely distinct Dominic's mission was from the
military or political affairs in which many other of the
Catholic clergy and prelates took their share. So far
from being himself the preacher of the crusade, we see
him taking the place and duties of another who is engaged

in that undertaking, as if the purely spiritual character
of his ministry were generally recognised. Once, and
once only, do we find his name in any way associated
with any of the judicial severities of the time; it is in an
anecdote given by Theodoric of Apoldia, but it will be
hard to draw from it the conclusion that Dominic was the
bloody persecutor represented in popular fiction; for as
we shall see, his part was to *release*, and not to *condemn*
the prisoner in question. "Some heretics," says the historian, "having been taken and convicted in the country
of Toulouse, were given over to secular judgment, because
they refused to return to the faith, and were condemned
to the flames. Dominic looked at one of them with a
heart to which were revealed the secrets of God, and said
to the officers of the court, 'Put that man aside, and see
well that no harm befall him.' Then, turning to the
heretic, he said with great sweetness, 'My son, I know
that you must have time, but you will at length become a
saint.' Wonderful to relate, this man remained for
twenty years longer in the blindness of heresy, till at
length, touched by the grace of God, he renounced his
errors, and died in the habit of the Friars Preachers, with
the reputation of sanctity."

The presence of Dominic at this execution will be understood, if we remember that, before the diliverance of
any heretic to the secular arm for punishment, every
effort was made, by the exhortations of persons appointed
for that purpose, to convince them of their errors, and
reconcile them to the Church; in which case their sentence was rescinded, and they were admitted to canonical
penance. This course was always followed in the later
proceedings of the Inquisition; the part of the Church
was to reconcile and convince, and not to condemn;
in the instance just quoted, we might call it to pardon.
This office was exercised by Dominic in virtue of the
powers he held from the Papal legates; two letters proving this fact are giving us by Echard, but have no date
attached, although there is little doubt they belong to this
period of his life. They are as follows: "To all the faithful in Christ to whom these presents may come, Brother

Dominic, canon of Osma, the humble minister of preaching, wishes health and charity in the Lord. We make
known to your discretion, that we have permitted Raymund William de Hauterive Pelaganira to receive into
his house of Toulouse, to live there after the ordinary
life, William Hugueccion, whom he has declared to us to
have hitherto worn the habit of the heretics. We permit this until such time as it shall be otherwise ordered
either to him or to me by the Lord Cardinal; and this
shall not in any way turn to his dishonour or prejudice."
If it seems singular to us in those days that a written
permission was necessary in order to allow any man to
receive into his house a reconciled heretic, we must remember the double character attaching to these people.
They were not merely heretics, but the disturbers of
the public peace; and, as the authors of every kind of
outrage against society, it is not singular that some kind
of pledge for their future good conduct was reasonably
demanded.

The other letter is of a severer character; it is as follows: "To all the faithful in Christ to whom these presents may come, Brother Dominic, canon of Osma, wishes
health in the Lord. By the authority of the Lord Abbot
of Citeaux, who has committed to us this office, we have
reconciled to the Church the bearer of these presents,
Ponce Royer, converted by the grace of God from heresy
to the faith; and we order, in virtue of the oath which
he has taken to us, that during three Sundays or feast-
days he shall go to the entrance of the village, bare to the
waist, and be struck with rods by the priest. We also
order him to abstain for ever from flesh, eggs, cheese, and
all which comes from flesh, except at Easter, Pentecost,
and Christmas, when he shall eat some to protest against
his former errors. He shall keep three Lents each year,
fasting and abstaining from fish, unless from bodily infirmity or the heat of the weather he shall be dispensed.
He shall dress in religious habit, as well in the form as
in the colour, to the ends of which shall be hung two
little crosses. Every day, if possible, he shall hear mass,
and he shall go to vespers on festival days. Seven times

a day he shall recite ten " Pater Nosters," and he shall say
twenty in the middle of the night. He shall observe
chastity, and once a month he shall, in the morning, present this paper to the Chaplain of the village of Céré.
We desire this Chaplain to have great care that his penitent lead a holy life, and observe all we have said until
the lord legate shall otherwise ordain. If he neglect to
do so through contempt, we will that he be excommuni-
cated as perjured and heretic, and be separated from the
society of the faithful."

Such was still the Church's discipline in the thirteenth
century. We who live in days when that discipline has
been gradually, though reluctantly, relaxed, because of
the relaxing love and faith of penitents, are amazed at
its severity: we are even disposed to lay the responsi-
bility of its seeming harshness on the head of him who
pronounced the sentence. But Dominic was in no way
the legislator in such a case as this: he was simply the
executor and dispenser of the Church's law. The above
diploma is one of those monumental records of canonical
penances which we occasionally find preserved in the
course of history, and which when so stumbled on are
almost invariably rocks of offence to those who are
accustomed to look on a litany, or a ' Salve Regina,' as
a reasonable penance for the sins of a life. The accumulation of indulgences in modern times ought surely
to have its significance to such minds. In those days,
men really *performed* the penances which are now dispensed. The rod which descends so gently on the head
of the wandering stranger in the Roman basilicas,—that
ghost of the ancient penitential discipline,—fell with a
hearty earnestness on the shoulders of our fathers; and
we cannot too often remind ourselves, by means of such
documents as that we have just read, of a difference
which should cover us with humiliation for the feeble-
ness of modern penitence, rather than send us to criticize
the severity with which the Church has ever looked on
sin.

CHAPTER VII.

The institution of the Rosary. The Council of Lavaur. The battle of Muret.

We have given a few anecdotes of the life led by Dominic during a time when war and bloodshed were raging around him. They are all that are left us to mark his course for many years. But it was during this time, though it would be difficult to affix the precise date, that he propagated that celebrated devotion which would alone entitle its author to our veneration, did we know him in no other way than as the first institutor of the Rosary. The universal voice of tradition affirms this devotion to have been revealed to him by the Blessed Virgin herself; and if we consider its almost supernatural character, combining as it does the simplest prayers with the profoundest meditations, or again if we remember the extraordinary power with which it has been blessed, and its adoption through the universal Church as the very alphabet of prayer, it is difficult for us not to believe it something more than a human invention, but rather as a gift which came to us as the most precious token of the love of our dear Mother. Although, however, there is ample ground for this belief, the details of any such revelation have not been preserved to us for the circumstantial accounts of the giving of the Rosary, which are so popular with later writers, are not to be found in any of the more ancient authors, who leave the date and the manner of its first institution in obscurity.* Dominic's life during these years was, for the most part, a lonely and hidden one:

* Local tradition declares the sanctuary of Notre Dame de Dreche, near Albi, to have been the scene of the vision of our Lady; it is certain that this sanctuary first attained celebrity during the Albigensian troubles, and was one of the favourite resorts of S. Dominic in the course of his apostolic labours.

his communications with heaven remained locked within
his own breast; for it was not with him as with so many
other saints, on whom a hundred busy eyes were always
fixed to mark every indication of supernatural grace, every
phenomenon, if we may so say, of their ecstacy and prayer:
his own lips were the only source from whence the secret
favours of God could ever have been made known, and
they certainly were the last which were ever likely to speak
of them to another.

We again remark in the institution of the Rosary
something of that characteristic feature of S. Dominic to
which we have before alluded. It was not altogether a
new devotion. There was nothing novel in the frequent
repetition of the "Angelical Salutation," or the "Pater
Noster;" such devotion had been common in the Church
from time immemorial, and we read of the hermits of the
deserts, counting such prayers with little stones, in the
same way as we use the beads. The novelty was the
association of mental and vocal prayer in those mysteries, which gather together, under fifteen heads, all the
history of the life of Christ. This working out of the
materials which lay before him, and which others had
used before him, is the peculiarity of which we have
spoken. It is the distinctive humility of our Saint. If
we reflect on the way in which all his greatest actions
were performed, we may safely say, that they came from
a soul in which the petty desire of personal reputation,
of making a noise in the world, of being known as the
founder of an institution, or the originator of a noble
thought, was never felt. Nay, if we may so say, there
is something which perpetually reminds us of our Lord's
own way of working; when He took His parables and
similitudes from the common things before His eyes, and
was content to let His Church grow out of the relics of
Judaism, as its visible temples may sometimes be seen
standing among the ruins of heathen fanes, converting
all their beauty to a sacred use. In all S. Dominic's
institutions we see this unconsciousness of self, which is
an evidence of the highest class of mind, and it is
probably from this cause that, in the commencement of

all of them, there is an obscurity and uncertainty of date which is rarely found to attach to the inventions of human genius.

We may, however, consider it as certain that the Rosary had begun to be propagated before the year 1213, as we are assured that it was used by the soldiers of the Count de Montfort's army before the battle of Muret, which took place in that year. Many stories are told of the wonders which followed on its first adoption. Some despised it, and ridiculed its use; among whom was one of the bishops of the country of Toulouse, who, hearing the Rosary preached by S. Dominic, spoke of it afterwards with contempt, saying it was only fit for women and children. He was soon convinced of his error; for shortly afterwards, falling into great persecution and calumnies, he seemed in a vision to see himself plunged into thick mire from which there was no way of escape. Raising his eyes, he saw above him the forms of our Lady and S. Dominic, who let down to him a chain made of a hundred and fifty rings, fifteen of which were gold; and laying hold of this he found himself safely drawn to dry land. By this he understood, that it was by means of the devotion of the Rosary he should be delivered from his enemies, which shortly took place after he had devoutly commenced its use. Another similar story relates how a noble lady opposed the new confraternities of this devotion with all her power, but was converted by the following vision, which was granted to her one night in prayer. Being rapt in ecstasy, she saw an innumerable company of men and women, surrounded by a great splendour, who devoutly recited the Rosary together; and for every "Ave Maria" which they repeated, a beautiful star came forth from their mouths, and the prayers were written in a book in letters of gold. Then the Blessed Virgin spoke to her and said, "In this book are written the names of the brethren and sisters of my Rosary, but thy name is not written; and because thou hast persuaded many not to enter it, there shall befall thee a sickness for a time, which yet shall turn to thy salvation." The lady was soon after seized with sickness, and, recognizing the truth of the

prediction, she caused herself, on her recovery, to be inscribed among the members of the confraternity. The
spread of this devotion was the most successful weapon
in the eradication of the Albigensian heresy. The child of
ignorance, it fled before the light of truth; and as the
mysteries of the faith were gradually brought back to the
minds and hearts of the people, the mysteries of falsehood
disappeared. The doctrine of the Incarnation, so specially
commemorated in the Rosary, became then, as ever, the
bulwark of the truth; and wherever the society was established, and the name of Mary was invoked, that name, as
the Church sings, "alone destroyed all heresies."

During the time that Dominic exercised the office of
vicar to the Bishop of Carcassona, the position of the
contending parties in Languedoc was considerably altered
by the arrival of Peter, king of Arragon, who joined the
forces of the Count of Toulouse with a powerful army.
He was allied to the count by marriage, but had hitherto
contented himself by negotiating in his favour with the
court of Rome. In the beginning of the year 1213,
however, a council was summoned at Lavaur, at which
the king formally demanded from the legates and Catholic
chiefs the restitution of the towns and lands which they
had taken in the course of the war from the Count of
Toulouse and the other nobles who had espoused his
cause, and their restoration to the communion of the
Church. The council consented to admit the others on
the terms proposed, but refused to include the Count of
Toulouse, whose repeated perjuries and evasions had
rendered him unworthy of trust. This answer was considered by the king as an evidence that there was a resolve to destroy the house of Toulouse, from motives of
personal ambition on the part of the Count de Montfort;
and he, therefore, declared the family of Raymond under
his protection, and appealed to the Holy See against the
decision of the council. The legates, on their part, represented to the Pope that the only chance of restoring peace
to the distracted country was by the entire removal of
the house of Toulouse, and the destruction of its hereditary power. The contradictory appeals and reports which

were sent him, rendered it difficult for Innocent to judge
in a cause involved every way in embarrassment. That
he was very far from advocating unnecessary or undue
severity towards Raymond and his family, we may gather
from his own letters to the Count de Montfort, in which
he urges him not to let the world think that he fought
more for his own interests than for the cause of the faith.
On the other hand, he complains, in a letter, that
the king of Arragon has misled him as to the state of
affairs, and enjoins him to proceed no further against the
Count de Montfort, until the arrival of a cardinal whom
he is about to despatch to the spot, to examine the whole
question as his delegate. It was too late. Before the
order arrived, the king had passed the Pyrenees, and,
joining the troops of the Counts of Toulouse, Foix, and
Comminges, prepared to advance against the army of the
crusaders. Their position seemed indeed but gloomy,
for the forces of the heretic leaders far outnumbered those
of the Catholics. A lay brother of the Cistercians, who
watched the progress of the war with painful interest,
went in company with Stephen de Metz, another religious
of the same order, to consult Dominic at this juncture,
well knowing that God often revealed to him the secrets
of coming events. "Will these evils ever have an end,
Master Dominic?" asked the afflicted brother. He repeated his question many times, but Dominic remained
silent. At length he replied, "There will be a time when
the malice of the men of Toulouse will have its end; but
it is far away; and there will be much blood shed first,
and a king will die in battle." Brother Stephen and the
Cistercian interpreted this prediction to allude to Prince
Louis of France, the son of Philip Augustus, who had
joined the army of the crusaders in the previous February.
"No," replied Dominic, "it will not touch the king of
France; it is another king whose thread of life will be cut
in the course of this war." This prophecy was very shortly
to be accomplished, and Dominic himself was destined to
be present on the spot where the decisive struggle took
place which witnessed its fulfilment.

Very shortly after uttering the prediction, he left Car-

cassona on the return of the bishop, intending to join a
congress of the Catholic prelates and legates which was
to be held at Muret. On the road thither he passed
through the city of Castres, where the body of the martyr
S. Vincent was preserved, for the veneration of the faithful. Entering the church, to pay his devotion at the
shrine of the saint, he remained so late that the prior of
the collegiate canons of Castres, who was his host for the
time, despatched one of the brethren to call him to dinner. The brother obeyed, but on going into the church,
he saw Dominic raised in the air in ecstasy before the
altar; and not daring to disturb him, he returned to the
prior, who himself hastened to the spot, and beheld the
spectacle with his own eyes. So forcible was the impression it left on his mind of the sanctity of the man of God,
that shortly after he joined himself to him, and was one
of those who formed the first foundation of the order.
This was the celebrated Matthew of France, afterwards
the prior of the convent of S. James in Paris, and the
first and last who ever bore the title of abbot among the
Friars Preachers. After this incident, Dominic proceeded
on his road to Muret.

It was on the 10th of September of the same year, that
the king of Arragon suddenly appeared before the walls of
this place, with an army, according to some writers, of
100,000 men, or, as others more probably state, of 40,000.
The intelligence of his approach reached De Montfort at
Fanjeaux. It seems probable that this hostile movement
took the Catholic chieftain by surprise; for only a few
weeks previously, he had been invited to a friendly conference by the king, and so little was he prepared for any
active measures at the time (owing to the pending negotiations with the Roman court), that he had no more than
800 horse, and a small number of men-at-arms with him,
with which to come to the relief of the besieged. To
oppose so contemptible a force to the army of the king,
seemed little less than madness, yet he never hesitated.
On the day following that on which the news reached
him, he set out from Fanjeaux, taking with him the
bishops and legates, amongst whom was Fulk, bishop of

Toulouse, with the intention of at least attempting a pacific settlement before the last appeal to arms. He stopped on his way at the Cistercian monastery of Bolbonne, and going into the church, laid his sword on the altar, as though to commend his cause to God, and remained for some time in prayer; then taking back his sword, as now no longer his, but God's, he proceeded to Saverdun, where he spent the night in confession and preparation for death. His little company of followers did the same, and on the morning of the following day they all communicated, as men who were about to offer their lives as a sacrifice. Some authors tells us that Dominic was present with the other legates and ecclesiastics in the army; others name him as being in their company only at Muret; but it seems probable that he had joined them previously, and if the current tradition is the correct one, that the crusaders ascribed their subsequent victory to the particular assistance of Mary, whom they had united to invoke in the prayers of the Rosary, we may well believe that this appeal to our Lady of Victories came from his counsel and exhortation. The army reached Muret on the side of the town opposite to that where the forces of the king of Arragon were drawn up; but, before entering the gates, the bishops were dispatched with propositions of peace to the enemy's camp. A contemptuous sarcasm was the only reply they received, and returning to the army they all entered Muret together. But they determined on one more effort, and very early in the morning dispatched another message to the king, to the effect that they would wait upon him barefoot, to bring about the terms of reconciliation. They were preparing to execute this design, when a body of cavalry attacked the gates; for the king had ordered the advance, without even deigning a reply to this second embassy.

The scene that morning within the walls of Muret was surely a religious one. Eight hundred devoted men, fortified by prayer and the sacraments of reconciliation, were about, as it seemed to human judgment, to lay down their lives as a sacrifice for the faith. There might be seen how the holy sacrifice was celebrated in the presence of them all; and how, when the Bishop of Uzès turned to say the last "Dominus vobiscum." De Montfort knelt before him, clad in armour, and said, "And I consecrate my blood and life for God and His faith;" and how the swords and shields of the combatants were once more offered on the altar; and when it was over, and the horsemen were gathering together, and the very sound of the attack was at the gates, these men all once more dismounted, and bent their knee to venerate and kiss the crucifix, extended to them by the Bishop of Toulouse. He had come to give them his parting words and blessing. Did his voice falter, or his eye grow dim at the spectacle before him? Something there certainly was of human emotion at that moment which history does not notice; for we are told it was not he, but the Bishop of Comminges who stood by his side, that spoke the last charge to the army, and, taking the crucifix from the hands of Fulk, solemnly blessed them as they knelt. Then they rode out to battle, and the ecclesiastics turned back into the church to pray.

Nothing more heroic is to be found in the whole history of chivalry, than this battle of Muret. It was a single charge. They rode through the open gates, and after a feigned movement of retreat, they suddenly turned rein, and dashed right on the ranks of their opponents, with the impetuosity of a mountain-torrent. Swift as lightning they broke through the troops that opposed their onward course, scattering them before their horses' hoofs with something of supernatural energy, nor did they draw bridle till they reached the centre of the army where the king himself was stationed, surrounded by the flower of his nobles and followers. A moment's fierce struggle ensued; but the fall of the king decided the fortune of the day. Terrified by the shock of that tremendous charge, as it hurled itself upon them, the whole army fled in panic. The voice and example of their chief might again have rallied them, but that was wanting; Peter of Arragon lay dead on the field, and Dominic's prophecy was fulfilled.

And where was he meanwhile? and what place has this page of chivalry in the annals of his apostolic life? The flash of swords, and the tramp of those galloping steeds, startle us strangely from the story of his quiet, lonely wanderings over the mountains, filling their echoes with the sound of his hymns and litanies, as he goes about to preach. Where are we to look for him in such a scene? Protestant writers are ready enough to tell us he was *at the head of the Crusaders,* carrying a crucifix, and urging them on to slaughter. We must be suffered to think, however, that neither in the schools of Palencia, nor in the canonry of Osma, could he have fitted himself for such a post as the leader of a cavalry charge whose equal is scarce to be found in history. Yet the battle of Muret forms part of the story of Dominic's life; he had his place there; for that one moment, and, so far as history gives us any token, for that one alone, he was brought in contact with the stormy scenes of the Crusade. He had his place; but, to find it, we must leave the battle-field, and go back to the church of Muret, where a different sight will greet us. When the Christian knights were ridden forth to the battle, the churchmen had gone before the altar to pray. They had sent their comrades, as it seemed, to certain death; and their prayer had in it the anguish of supplication. Prostrate on the pavement, which they bathed with their tears, they poured out their souls to God. F. Bernard, of the Order of Preachers, who lived in Toulouse at the beginning of the following century, and who wrote whilst the memory of these events was still fresh in the minds of the people, thus describes them: "Then going into the church, they prayed, raising their hands to heaven, and beseeching God for His servants who were exposed to death for His sake, with such great groans, and cries, that it seemed not that they prayed, but rather howled."*

---

* A very popular tradition has represented S. Dominic as ascending one of the towers on the wall, and displaying the crucifix for the encouragement of the Christian troops. This assertion has been supported by the exhibition, in later ages, at Toulouse, of a crucifix pierced all over with arrows, which is supposed to have been the

E

But from this agonizing suspense they were roused by
the shouts of the populace. The cry of victory sounded
in their ears; they hastened to the walls, and beheld the
plain covered with the flying companies of the heretics.
Some plunged into the waters of the Garonne and
perished in their armour; others trampled their own
comrades to death in the confusion of their flight; many
died under the swords of the Crusaders. It is computed
that no fewer than 20,000 of the heretic forces were
slain, whilst we are assured by all authorities that *eight*
only of the Catholics fell during the combat of that day.
As the Count de Montfort rode over that victorious field
he checked his horse by the bleeding and trampled body
of the king of Arragon. De Montfort had some of the
failings, but all the virtues, of his order: he was cast in
the heroic type of Christian chivalry. Descending from
his horse, he kissed the body with tears, and gave orders
for its honourable interment, as became a gallant enemy;
then, returning barefoot to Muret, he went first to the
church to return thanks to God, and gave the horse and
armour with which he had fought to the poor. It was a
true picture of the ages of faith.

We need scarcely be surprised that so wonderful a victory
was looked on as miraculous, and counted as the fruit of
prayer. De Montfort himself ever so regarded it; and

identical one used by him on the occasion. Polidori, who in all
things strictly adheres to the ancient authors, and is careful to
repudiate every modern addition of less authority, rejects this tale
as utterly unfounded, chiefly from the entire silence of F. Bernard
concerning the whole matter; and as he was Inquisitor of Toulouse
during fourteen years, if any such crucifix had been preserved by the
Institute in his day, he could hardly have failed noticing it. Père
Lacordaire, in his eloquent life of S. Dominic, has followed the
same argument On the other hand, in the chapel of our Lady in
the church of S. James at Muret, which was built as a memorial
of the victory in the course of the same year, we see a picture
representing the Blessed Virgin giving the Rosary to S. Dominic,
who holds in his right hand a crucifix pierced with *three arrows:*
on the other side of our Lady, kneel Simon de Montfort and Fulk
of Toulouse. A fac-smile of this picture, and of the same date,
was long kept in the Dominican church at Toulouse. Whether
this picture alluded to any circumstance which really took place,
or was itself the origin of the tradition, we do not pretend to
determine.

attributing his success, under God, to the intercession of
Dominic, his love and gratitude to the saint knew no
bounds. It has always been so associated in the traditions
and chronicles of the time with the institution of the
Rosary, as to make many affirm that the first propagation
of that devotion must be dated from this time.

The battle of Muret was a fatal blow to the cause of
the count of Toulouse. Very shortly after, Toulouse
itself opened its gates to the victorious arms of De Montfort; and a council,* which assembled at Montpellier in
the following year, decided that the sovereignty of the
country should be intrusted to him, until the general
council, about to assemble at Rome, should declare further. Cardinal Benvenuto, who reached Toulouse just as
the decisive blow had been struck, was commissioned to
receive the elder Raymond to absolution, and to put a
stop to further hostilities; but the question as to his
future enjoyment of the temporal rights he had forfeited by
breach of engagement, was still deferred.

Twice again Dominic's name occurs among the busy
scenes of De Montfort's career. He was called on to
baptize his daughter, and to celebrate the marriage of his
eldest son with the daughter of the dauphin of France.
But the favour of the victorious chieftain, and the distractions of the camp and court, were scarcely felt by him
at this moment. The shifting chances of the war, guided
by the hands of Providence, were opening to him, after
long waiting, the way to that design which had ever
floated before his mind's eye. The clouds which had so
long hung over that distant horizon rose at last; and
when Toulouse opened her gates, and the storm of the
combat was lulled, and the favour of man was at hand to
help on the will of God, Dominic, in his forty-sixth year,
prepared to lay the foundation of that order which was
to bear his name to future ages so long as the world and
the Church should last.

* In the Life of S. Francis we are informed, that the holy founder
of the Friars Minor was present at this council, being then on his
return from Spain. He had, however, no opportunity of meeting
S. Dominic, as the latter was then absent at Carcassona, and took
no part in the proceedings.

CHAPTER VIII.

Dominic commences the foundation of his order at Toulouse. The grant of Fulk of Toulouse. Dominic's second visit to Rome. The Council of Lateran. Innocent III. approves the plan of the Order. Meeting of Dominic and Francis

DOMINIC came to Toulouse soon after the Crusaders had entered it, and was joyfully received both by Fulk and by the count de Montfort. Neither of these distinguished persons were, however, destined to be the immediate co-operators with him in the foundation of the order. Peter Cellani, an opulent citizen of Toulouse, and another of the same rank, known to us only under the name of Thomas, presented themselves to him shortly after his arrival at Toulouse, and placed themselves and all they had at his disposal. Peter Cellani offered his own house for the use of the few companions whom Dominic had gathered together to commence his work. They were but six in all, and in after years Peter was accustomed to boast, that he had not been received into the order, but that it might rather be said he had received the order into his own house. With these six followers, whom he clothed in the habit of the Canons Regular, which he himself always wore, Dominic accordingly commenced a life of poverty and prayer under rules of religious discipline.

But this alone did not satisfy him; the first design which he had conceived, and which had never left his mind, had pre-eminently as its object the salvation of souls, by means of such a ministration of the Divine Word as should proceed from a knowledge of sacred science, large enough for the defence of the Christian dogmas against all the assaults of heresy and infidelity. The whole future scope of the Friars Preachers was in the mind of Dominic at the moment of their first foundation. That it was so is evinced by his first step after

assembling these six brethren in the house of Peter Cellani. He explained to them the extent and nature of his
design; and showed them that, in order to carry it out
and fit themselves for the task of teaching truth, they
must first learn it. Now it so happened that there was
then in Toulouse a celebrated doctor of theology, named
Alexander, whose lectures were greatly admired and frequented. It was to him that Dominic resolved to intrust
his little company. On the same morning Alexander had
risen very early, and was in his room engaged in study,
when he was overcome by an unusual and irresistible inclination to sleep. His book dropped from his hand, and
he sank into a profound slumber. As he slept he seemed
to see before him seven stars, at first small and scarcely
visible, but which increased in size and brightness, till
they enlightened the whole world. As day broke he
started from his dream, and hastened to the school where
he was to deliver his usual lecture. Scarcely had he
entered the room when Dominic and his six companions
presented themselves before him. They were all clad
alike, in the white habit and surplice of the Augustinian
canons, and they announced themselves as poor brothers,
who were about to preach the gospel of Christ to the
faithful and heretics of Toulouse, and who desired first of
all to profit by his instructions. Alexander understood
that he saw before him the seven stars of his morning
dream; and many years after, when the order had indeed
fulfilled the destiny predicted, and had covered Europe
with the fame of its learning, he himself being then at the
English court, related the whole circumstances with an
almost fatherly pride, as having been the first master of the
Friars Preachers.

These first steps of the brethren were marked by the
bishop, Fulk of Toulouse, with unmixed satisfaction. The
piety and fervour displayed by them, and their exact following in the footsteps of Dominic, for whom he had
ever entertained a peculiar reverence, determined him to
give the infant order the support of his powerful protection. With the consent of his chapter he assigned the
sixth part of the tithes of the diocese for their support,

and the purchase of the books necessary for their studies. The document in which he makes this grant will not be without its interest:—" In the name of our Lord Jesus Christ. We make known to all present and to come, that we Fulk, by the grace of God the humble minister of the see of Toulouse, desiring to extirpate heresy, to expel vice, to teach the rule of faith, and recall men to a holy life, appoint Brother Dominic and his companions to be preachers throughout our diocese; who propose to go on foot, as becomes religious, according to evangelical poverty, and to preach the word of evangelical truth. And because the workman is worthy of his hire, and we are bound not to muzzle the mouth of the ox who treadeth out the corn, and because those who preach the gospel shall live by the gospel, we desire that, whilst preaching through the diocese, the necessary means of support be administered to them from the revenues of the diocese. Wherefore, with the consent of the chapter of the church of S. Stephen, and of all the clergy of our diocese, we assign in perpetuity to the aforesaid preachers, and to others who, being moved by zeal for God and love for the salvation of souls, shall employ themselves in the like work of preaching, the sixth part of the tenths destined for the building and ornamenting all the parochial churches subject to our government, in order that they may provide themselves with habits, and whatsoever may be necessary to them when they shall be sick, or be in need of rest. If anything remain over at the year's end, let them give it back, that it may be applied to the adorning of the said parish churches, or the relief of the poor, according as the bishop shall see fit. For inasmuch as it is established by law, that a certain part of the tithes shall always be assigned to the poor, it cannot be doubted that we are entitled to assign a certain portion thereof to those who voluntarily follow evangelical poverty for the love of Christ, labouring to enrich the world by their example and heavenly doctrine; and thus we shall satisfy our duty of freely scattering and dividing, both by ourselves and by means of others, spiritual things to those from whom we receive temporal things. Given in the year of the Word Incarnate 1215, in the reign of Philip king of France, the principality of Toulouse being held by the Count de Montfort." Neither was De Montfort wanting in a like liberality towards the young order. He had already made many grants to the house of La Prouille, and in this year we find him making over the castle and lands of Cassanel to the use of Dominic and his companions.

In the autumn of the same year Fulk of Toulouse set out for Rome, to attend the approaching council of the Lateran, and Dominic was his companion. Eleven years had passed since his first visit in company with Diego; they had been years of hard and solitary labour, and the work, the plan of which had even then been formed within his mind, was now but just developing into actual existence. Most surely he had within his soul the principle of a far higher strength than mere human enthusiasm, or he might well have been daunted, as coming for the second time within sight of the eternal city, the forty-six years of his life lay before him, so full of patient work, and, as it seemed, blessed with so little fruit. And something more than human enthusiasm was needed, to look forward to the task of the future—the task of teaching and reforming a world; whilst all the materials which he had as yet gathered for the struggle were to be found in the six unknown and unlettered companions whom he had left behind him at Toulouse.

Innocent III. still filled the Papal chair, and the Council of Lateran formed almost the closing scene of a Pontificate which must be held as one of the greatest ever given to the Church. On the 11th of November, 1215, nearly 500 bishops and primates, above 800 abbots and priors, and the representatives of all the royal houses of Europe, met in that ancient and magnificent church, the mother church of Rome and of the world. Few councils, save that of Trent, have higher claims on our veneration; for in it were defined some of the highest articles of Catholic faith. The Albigenses, like so many other heretical sects, were the involuntary means of drawing forth an explicit declaration of the Church's doctrine and disci-

pline, and eliciting regulations of reform and Christian observance, which have probably contributed more than any
other to the well-being of the whole ecclesiastical body,
as well as to each individual member thereof. We allude
to the decrees concerning the nature of the Sacraments,
and in particular of the Holy Eucharist, and to the establishment of those two binding obligations of yearly confession and communion, which, whilst they do indeed
attest the lamentable decay from primitive fervour which
could have rendered such regulations necessary, yet placed
a barrier against farther relaxation which no future
age has been able to overstep. This council has always
called forth the bitterest rancour from the supporters of
heresy ; a result which was but natural, considering the
vigour and success with which it not only opposed itself
to the evils which existed at the time, but, with an astonishing spirit of discernment, provided defences for the
future, which have lost nothing of their power and stability even at the present day. In fact, the singular energy
displayed by this celebrated council, and the very nature
of its decrees, are a sufficient proof of the state in which
the world and the Church were then found. There was
everywhere a decay and a falling off. Old institutions
were waxing effete, and had lost their power; whilst indications were everywhere visible of an extraordinary activity and restlesness of mind, which was constantly breaking out into disorder for want of channels into which it
might be safely guided. Europe had taken some centuries to struggle through the barbarism which had fallen
on her after the breaking up of the Roman Empire. As
the waters of that great deluge subsided, life came back
by degrees to the submerged world, and just at this period
was quickening into a vitality which, in the succeeding
century, was manifested in what we might call a luxuriance of growth. It was just one of those junctures in
the world's history, when God is wont to raise up great
men who lay their hands on the human elements of confusion, and fashion them into shape. And it is not too
much to reckon among these the founder of the Friars
Preachers.

As yet the Church possessed only the more ancient forms of monasticism, with some institutes of later creation, which had, however, but a limited object, or a merely local influence; for the Friars Minor, though they preceded the Preachers by several years, could not as yet be said to have been formally established as a religious order. Dominic's idea included a much wider field than any of the more modern founders had attempted. He had designed an order for preaching and teaching; which for that purpose should apply itself to the study of sacred letters, with the express object of the salvation of souls. But preaching and teaching had hitherto been considered the peculiar functions of the episcopate, and one of the decrees of this very council of Lateran, after enumerating the evils flowing from the neglect or inability of the bishops in respect to these offices, empowers them to choose fit and proper persons in each diocese to discharge the "holy exercise of preaching" in their stead. This decree, however, in nowise contemplated the establishment of any body of persons exercising the office as an independent right, or in any other way than as deputies to the bishop, and the plan was, therefore, one full of novelty, and, as it seemed, of difficulty and even danger. But, apart from every other consideration, we may observe in it its admirable adaptation to the peculiar wants and feelings of the time. The world was like an untrained, untaught child, just rising into manhood, and ready to learn anything. It wanted teachers, and whilst the want was unsatisfied, it made them for itself. During the eleventh and twelfth centuries, one wild sect after another had risen, and counted its followers by thousands, with scarcely any other reason for its success than the favour which was ready to attach to a popular leader. Dominic determined on nothing less than to give them truth in a popular form, and from the mouths of popular teachers; he felt that it had too long been buried in the cloister or the hermit's cell, and that the time was come for the world also to have evangelists. In short whilst his idea was directly aimed at the guidance and taming of the wild spirit of the day, it had in it not a little of the

prevailing tone of enterprise and enthusiasm. It was the
very chivalry of religion.

His reception by the fathers of the council, and by the
Pope himself, was cordial and flattering. Met as they
were, in a great measure, to discuss the questions which
had arisen out of the state of the French provinces,
Dominic's name, and the part he had taken during the
last ten years, were not unknown and unappreciated by
them. Before the formal opening of the council, Pope
Innocent granted him an apostolic brief, by which he
received the convent of Prouille under the protection of
the pontifical see, and confirmed the grants made to it.
But when the plan for the foundation of the order was laid
before him, its novelty and the vastness of its design
startled him. It seemed to encroach on the privileges of
the episcopate, and its boldness seemed dangerous at a
moment when men's minds were so powerfully agitated.
The troubles of the Waldenses were fresh in his mind, a
sect which had grown out of the simple abuse of this
same office of preaching, when usurped by men without
learning or authority. The Church, in short, was jealous
of innovation, and had just ruled, in the council then
sitting, that no more new orders should be introduced or
allowed. In the face of this fresh regulation, it certainly required no small degree of boldness and confidence to present the scheme of a new foundation for approbation, and
to perseverve in the request; yet Dominic did so, and the
result proved not only the strength of his confidence, but
the source from whence it had been derived. Five years
previously, when Francis of Assisi had visited Rome to
solicit the approbation of his infant order from the same
Pope, the like objections and difficulties had been raised;
and we are assured that, on both occasions, they were removed by a similar interposition of Divine Providence.
Pope Innocent, doubtful as to the reply he should grant,
saw, in a vision of the night, the Lateran Basilica about to
fall, and Dominic supporting it on his shoulders. An
exactly similar dream had before decided him to listen to
the petition of S. Francis: and it is probable that the
coincidence of the two visions had an additional weight

in determining him on this occasion to favour that of Dominic.

Yet the language of the council was too strong to be entirely evaded; it was as follows:—" In order that the too great diversity of religious orders be not a cause of confusion in the Church of God, we strictly prohibit that any one do for the future form any new order; whoever desires to become a religious, let him do so in one of those already approved. In like manner, if any one desire to found a new religious house, let him be careful that it observe the rule and constitutions of one of the approved orders." Not, therefore, to act in positive contradiction to a principle so recently and distinctly laid down, Innocent sent for the servant of God, and, after commending his zeal, and assuring him of his approval of the design, he desired him to return to France, that, in concert with his companions, he might choose one out of the ancient rules already approved, which should seem to them the best fitted for their purpose. When the selection was made he was to return to Rome, with the assurance of receiving from the apostolic see that confirmation which he desired.

Besides this encouragement and promise of future protection, Innocent was the first who bestowed on the order the name it has ever since borne. The circumstances under which he did so were a little singular, and have been preserved with unusual exactness. Shortly after granting the above favourable answer to the prayer of Dominic, he had occasion to write to him on some matters connected with the subject, and desired one of his secretaries to despatch the necessary orders. When the note was finished, the secretary asked to whom it should be addressed. " To Brother Dominic and his companions," he replied; then, after a moment's pause, he added, " No, do not write that; let it be, 'To Brother Dominic, and those who preach with him in the country of Toulouse;'" then, stopping him yet a third time, he said, " Write this. *To Master Dominic and the Brothers Preachers.*" This title, though not at first formally given by his successor Honorius in the bulls of confirmation, was, as we shall see, afterwards adopted, and has always continued to be used. It was one to which Dominic himself was attached, and which he had always assumed. So early as the June of 1211, when he was in the midst of his solitary missionary labours in Languedoc, we find a document bearing his seal, attached to which are these words, " The seal of Brother Dominic, *Preacher*."

The object of his visit to Rome was now fully accomplished; yet he did not return to Languedoc until the spring of the following year. The council still sat, and it is probable that he was present at those deliberations concerning the future settlement of the French provinces, which terminated in the formal declaration that Raymond of Toulouse had forfeited his rights, and in the definitive transfer of them to the Count de Montfort. But we do not feel that these transactions require any further notice in a biography of S. Dominic. His connection with the history of the Albigensian struggle was now at an end; henceforth he was to belong, not to Languedoc or to France alone, but to the world. During his stay in Rome his first acquaintance with S. Francis was formed under the following circumstances. One night, being in prayer, he saw the figure of our Lord in the air above his head, with the appearance of great anger, and holding three arrows in his hand, with which he was about to strike the world in punishment of its enormous wickedness. Then the Blessed Virgin prostrated herself before him, and presented two men to Him whose zeal should convert sinners, and appease His irritated justice. One of these men he recognised as himself; the other was wholly unknown to him. The next day, entering a church to pray, he saw the stranger of his vision, dressed in the rough habit of a poor beggar, and recognising him as his companion and brother in the work to which both were destined by God, he ran to him, and, embracing him with tears, exclaimed, " You are my comrade, you will go with me; let us keep together, and nothing shall prevail against us." This was the beginning of a friendship which lasted during the remainder of their lives. From that time they had but one heart and one soul in God; and though their orders

remained separate and distinct, each fulfilling the work
assigned to it by Divine Providence, yet a link of fraternal charity ever bound them together: "brought forth
together," in the words of Blessed Humbert, "by our holy
mother the Church," they felt that "God had destined
them from all eternity to the same work, even the salvation of souls." In the following century the storm of
persecution bound these two orders yet closer together;
the blows aimed at the one fell on the other, and when
they eventually triumphed over their enemies, the defence which so successfully silenced all attacks came from
the lips of the two greatest doctors of either order,
S. Thomas and S. Bonaventure; men who revived in their
own day the friendship and the saintliness of their two
great patriarchs.*

In the Life of S. Francis it is said, that Angelus the
Carmelite, afterwards a martyr of his order, was likewise
in Rome at this time, and preached in the church of
S. John Lateran, in the presence of the two holy founders,

* The friendship between the two orders was not a mere matter
of sentiment. It was considered of sufficient importance to be
noticed in their very rule. In the Chapter of Paris, held in 1236,
the following was ordained, and still continues in the Constitutions
of the Friars Preachers:—
"We declare that all our Priors and Brethren should have a
diligent care that they always and everywhere bear, and heartily
preserve, a great love to the Friars Minor: let them praise them
with their lips, and by their works kindly receive and courteously
treat with them; and be solicitous as far as they can to be at peace
with them. And if any do contrary, let him be gravely punished.
And let the Brethren beware, lest they ever speak otherwise than
well of them, either among themselves or to any of their friends.
And if any one, under the show of friendship, shall report any evil
of the aforesaid Friars, our brethren must not be easy in believing
it: but shall rather endeavor as far as possible to excuse them.
And if it chance that the Friars Minors shall have provoked us by
speaking ill of us, nevertheless let us in nowise publicly contend
with them."
It is in the same spirit that we find it ordered, that there
shall always be made a commemoration of "Our holy father
S. Francis" in the little office of S. Dominic. (Such is the
affectionate title given by the Friars Preachers to the founder
of the order of Minors. Whilst within the last twelvemonth
(85) the entire office of both holy Patriarchs has been ordered
to be recited by the brethren of the two orders on their respective
feasts.

predicting their future greatness, and the extension of
their orders. Some of the Franciscan writers place this
meeting of Dominic and Francis in the following year,
when both were again present in Rome for the confirmation of their institutes, but the Dominican authorities are
generally agreed in giving it as occurring during this visit.
The difference is of no great consequence, and might easily
arise without throwing any discredit on the authenticity
of the circumstance itself, which rests on the authority of
one of S. Francis's constant companions, and has never
been called in question.

— ✄ —

CHAPTER IX.

Dominic's return to France. The brethren assemble at Prouille
to choose a rule. The spirit of the Order. Some account of
the first followers of Dominic. The Convent of S. Romain.

THE Council of Lateran lasted but three weeks, and
broke up at the end of November, 1215. In the early
spring of the following year, Dominic found himself once
more among his brethren at Toulouse. In the short
period of his absence their numbers had increased from
seven to sixteen, and we may well imagine the mutual
joy of their meeting. He explained to them the result
of his expedition to the Holy See, and the necessity
which now lay on them to apply themselves to the choice
of a rule. For this purpose he appointed Notre Dame
de Prouille as the place of meeting, where two other of
the brothers, Fr. William de Claret and Fr. Noel, who
had care of the religious of Prouille, were waiting for
them. It was April when they all gathered in this
mother-house of the order; and after earnest prayer
and invocation of the Holy Spirit, they agreed in
choosing the rule of S. Austin; a rule to which Dominic

himself had long been bound, ever since he had worn the
habit of Canon Regular, and which from its simplicity
was the better fitted for their purpose, as being susceptible of nearly any development which the peculiar
objects of their institute might require. In choosing
this rule, Dominic fulfilled the obligation imposed on
him by the Pope, and escaped the censure of the late
council, while at the same time he was left free to
expand the general principles of religious life laid down
by S. Austin into particular constitutions of his own.

He had not been the first who had made a singular use
of this rule. If we compare the plan and work of S.
Dominic with that of S. Norbert, who had preceded him
by nearly a century, we shall find a very striking similarity. S. Norbert's rule was a reformation of that of the
Regular Canons. In its design he departed from the ordinary line of the more ancient forms of monasticism, and
set before him as his object active missionary labours for
the salvation of souls. His work was preaching. He
himself preached all over the provinces of France and
Flanders, and obtained faculties from Pope Gelasius II.
enabling him to preach wherever he choose. A mere cursory glance would induce us to judge the spirit of these
two orders identical; and there can be no doubt that, in
many points of interior discipline, Dominic took the Premonstratensian rule as his guide. Yet we see clearly,
that, whatever similarity existed between them, they were
not the same; they were called to different works, and
were to fill a different place in the Church of God. Religious orders, we must never forget, are the result of
Divine vocation, not the mere creations of human intelligence; and those vocations they accomplish in an infinite
variety of ways, which human intelligence could never
have planned or executed: they are like the varieties of
plants and animals in nature, whose mingled distinctions
and similarities, multiplied in so many thousand forms,
attest the authorship of an infinite Creator. We cannot
but be struck by this supernatural element in the formation of the order of Friars Preachers. As a mere human
work, critics might find so much to say against it. If

Dominic only wanted to join the active and contemplative
lives together, S. Norbert had done it before him; why
could he not be a Premonstratensian? They followed the
same rule, and wore the same habit. Or if he and S. Francis
really had the same thoughts, and were raised up for the
same purpose, why did they not amalgamate, and then their
strength would have been concentrated, instead of being
divided? These seemed reasonable objections; they were
doubtless some of those which encountered the holy
founder at his first outset, for it is the way in which the
world is wont to criticize the Church. It is certainly the
way in which in our own day we do so, as though she
were a vast piece of ingenious machinery, which we have
a right to take to pieces and improve, as we like best.
We often loose sight of the fact, that great men and great
institutions, popes and councils and religious orders, are
but instruments in the hands of God, who works them
like puppets without their will, for the accomplishment of
His own designs. The order of Friars Preachers had a
place to fill in the Universal Church, never yet filled by
any religious body, and in which it has since had no rival,
even in the period of its decay. Only a hundred years
from its first foundation, an Emperor* who was its avowed
enemy, and who during his whole life had persecuted it
to the last extremity, witnessing its remarkable contest
against the alleged errors of a Pontiff,† whom it had been

* Louis of Bavaria

† John XXII. This pontiff was reported to have given utterance,
as a private individual, to some opinions of doubtful orthodoxy,
concerning the state of souls previous to the day of judgment. He
himself, in a brief which death alone prevented him from publishing
in the consistory he had summoned for the purpose, made the most
distinct and formal protest of his entire and hearty accordance with
the doctrine of the Church. (Rohrbacher, _Histoire de l'Eglise Catho-
lique_, tom. xx. p. 227.) Whether or no he ever did hold the opinions
in question, the subject gave rise to a controversy, in which the
Friars Preachers took a distinguished part; particularly an Englishman, by name F. Thomas Walent, who is described as " a man of
great zeal, great heart, and great learning:" with daring courage
he preached in the very presence of the Pope, denouncing the
supposed error in no measured terms, and suffered for his boldness
by a long imprisonment. The favourers of the disputed point had

foremost to defend when the aggressions of an Antipope divided the allegiance of the faithful, pronounced this celebrated verdict, wrested from him, as it were, against his will: "The order of Preachers is the *order of truth*."

This is the place which it has ever filled; which in God's Providence, we trust it ever will fill; and it was the place for which Dominic determined it should be fitted from the very first. His plan was threefold. The first and primary idea of the order was labour for the salvation of souls: but in setting this before him as his principal aim, he was not willing to abandon anything of the religious character which attached to the elder institutes of the Church. In short, the whole of his design is expressed in that passage of the constitutions where it is said that "the Order of Preachers was principally and essentially designed for preaching and teaching, in order thereby to communicate to others the fruits of contemplation, and to procure the salvation of souls." Dominic well knew that to sanctify others the teachers should first be sanctified themselves, and he was content to follow the guidance of antiquity in choosing the means of that sanctification whose fruits were to be imparted to the world. Those means had ever been considered as best found in the rigorous discipline of the cloister: in silence and poverty, prayer, fasting, and a life of penance, and the secret and magical influences of community life. He therefore included in his rule all the essential characteristics of monasticism, whilst at the same time a certain freedom and expansiveness was mingled with the strictness of its discipline, which enabled it ever to bend and mould itself so as to meet its great and primary intention, the salvation of souls. In the constitutions of the order, accordingly, we find, mixed with the usual enactments of regular discipline, certain powers of dispensation, to be used when a literal and unbending adherence to the letter of the rule would embarrass and impede the brethren in their more active duties. There are also express constitutions, both for the ordering of

sufficient influence to cause considerable suffering and disgrace to the order, which, however, never relaxed an inch in its obstinate defence of the teaching of the Catholic Church.

F

their own studies, and the regulation of such schools as
they might open for the teaching of others; so that all
their active and apostolic undertakings, instead of being
departures from the rule, should be provided for in it, and
partake of its own spirit and discipline. We may, therefore, consider contemplation, apostolic labour for souls,
and the especial cultivation of theological science, as the
three objects which Dominic sought to unite in the constitution of his order.

With what success he laboured, and with what fidelity
his children have adhered to the character first imprinted
on their institute by the hand of its founder, it is for history to show. The order of Friars Preachers has never
lost anything of the monastic spirit, whilst at the same
time it has never so exclusively adhered to it as to lose
sight of the active duties imposed on it by its vocation to
apostolic labour. The two characters have ever been preserved entire, and it has presented to the world, throughout six centuries, the spectacle of a body acting in the
most perfect unity of government and design, producing
at one and the same time the highest examples of contemplative saints, apostolic missionaries, and theological
writers. If we are dazzled by the fame of its doctors, we
have but to turn over the page of the Dominican chronicles, and, in exchange for the successes of a university
contest, we shall find some tale of saintly life, redolent
with the sweetness of evangelic simplicity. Its saints are
not all great men in the world's reckoning; they are
gathered from all ranks; from the shepherds of the
Spanish mountains, the blind beggars of Italy, or the
slaves of America, as well as from princes and doctors of
the church. Or if, whilst dwelling on this side of the vast
scene which it unfolds to us, absorbed, it may be, in the
seraphic revelations of S. Catherine, or the sweet mys-
ticism of the German Suso, we are tempted to think that
its genius grew to be contemplative only, and that in time
it shrank from close contact with the world for which it
was called to labour, other pages lie open before us rich
with tales of the strife of martyrs. Poland, Hungary,
Ethiopia, America, and China—these, and many other

countries, have the children of Dominic evangelized by
their preaching and watered with their blood. Nor is this
all; it has constantly been true to its vocation as the
organ of popularizing truth. It has borrowed from the
spirit of the age to supply the wants of the age. When
the world was accustomed to gather science from the lips
of living orators, it gave out its companies of preachers
and lecturers. When books became more popular vehicles
of teaching, there was no want of Dominican writers.
Nay, it knew how to use other and lighter kinds of instruction, and laid a strong hand upon the magic of the
arts. How many a sermon has Angelico left us in the
colours which still charm us on the walls of his convent;
and after him, painting still remained the heritage of the
order which gave him birth, and in its hands has never
ceased to be Christian. And if we cannot say of the
greatest poet of the middle ages, that he was himself a
child of Dominic, it must at least be confessed that he
found means to clothe his verse in the spirit of a theology
whose master and teacher was S. Thomas. Pre-eminently
the order of the church, it has shared her destinies, as it
has clung to her teaching. Like her, it has never lost its
unity: we do not indeed pretend to say of either, that
time has never seen their children waxing cold and un-
faithful; but with both, the power of reformation has ever
been found to exist within their own bosoms. The only
occasion when the order of Preachers can ever be said to
have endured a divided government, was the unhappy
period when it shared in a schism which rent the allegiance of the church herself; when one regained unity of
obedience, it was restored also to the other. After all its
sufferings we constantly see it renewing its strength like
the eagle; and even in our day, we can scarcely fail to
observe that astonishing vitality and power of fresh development, which after six centuries bursts out as vigorous as
ever, attesting its principle of eternal youth.

Before closing this chapter, we must give a brief account of those brethren who joined with S. Dominic in
the deliberations of Prouille, and who with him may be
considered the first founders and propagators of the order.

They were, as we have said, sixteen in number. Matthew of France we have before mentioned in relating the circumstances of his first acquaintance with S. Dominic, when prior of S. Vincent's church at Castres; Bertrand of Garrigues, a little village in the province of Narbonne, was the constant companion of the holy father in all his journeys, and a most faithful imitator of his life and austerities. It is of him that it is related, how, being constantly weeping for his sins, S. Dominic reproved him, and enjoined him rather to weep and pray for the sins of others. This circumstance throws light upon another story, very commonly repeated, but which we venture to think has not always been fully understood. It is thus related by Surius:—"This Brother Bertrand, a holy man, and, as we have said, the first prior provincial of Provence, was accustomed every day to celebrate mass for sins; and being asked by one Brother Benedict, a prudent man, why he so rarely celebrated mass for the dead, and so frequently for sins, he replied, 'We are certain of the salvation of the faithful departed, whereas *we* remain tossed about in many perils.' 'Then,' said Brother Benedict, 'if there were two beggars, the one with all his limbs sound, and the other wanting them, which would you compassionate the most?' And he replied, 'Him certainly who can do least for himself.' 'Then,' said Benedict, 'such certainly are the dead, who have neither mouth to confess nor hands to work, but ask our help; whereas living sinners have mouths and hands, and with them can take care of themselves. And when Bertrand was not persuaded in his mind, on the following night there appeared to him a terrible figure of a departed soul, who with a bundle of wood did in a wonderful manner press and weigh upon him, and waking him up more than ten times that same night, did vex and trouble him. Therefore on the following morning he called Benedict to him, and told him all the story of the night; and thence religiously, and with many tears, going to the altar, he offered the holy sacrifice for the departed, and from that time very frequently did the same. This is the same Brother Bertrand, a most holy and venerable man, to whom S. Dominic

enjoined that he should not weep for his own, but for
others' sins; for he well knew that he was wont to do
excessive penance for his sins. And this charge of the
Blessed Dominic had such an effect on the soul of Brother
Bertrand, that from that time, even if he wished, he was
not able to weep for his own sins; but when he mourned
for those of others, his tears would flow in great
abundance."

The next of S. Dominic's companions whom we find
noticed, are the two whom we have before mentioned as
residing at Prouille, where they had care of the nuns;
William de Claret of Pamiers, and Brother Noel, a native
of Prouille. The former of these had been one of the
first missioners among the Albigenses, in the time of
Diego of Azevedo. After remaining in the habit of the
Friars Preachers for twenty years, he left the order and
joined the Cistercians. Not content with this, he even
attempted to induce the nuns to follow his example, but,
it is unnecessary to say, without success. Then there
was Brother Suero Gomez, a Portuguese of noble birth,
who left the royal court to join the army of De Montfort against the Albigenses. He was one of those who
witnessed the deliverance of the fourteen English pilgrims, and who assisted in bringing them to shore,
and shortly afterwards passed to the company of Dominic; he is said to have been distinguished for many
virtues, and was the founder of the order in Portugal.
Michael de Fabra, a Spaniard of noble blood, was
the first lecturer on theology in the order, and held
that office in the convent of S. James, at Paris. He
was also a celebrated preacher, and accompanied King
James of Arragon in his expedition against Majorca,
where it is said, "So great was the esteem had of him,
that during the fifteen months that the siege lasted
nothing was done in the camp, either by soldiers or
captains, save what was by him ordered."[*] Such was
the reverence in which he was held, that after the
conquest of the island he was looked on as the father
and ruler of it; and his name was always invoked next

[*] Michaele Pio Uomini—illustri.

after God and the Blessed Virgin. Divers stories of his apparitions and supernatural assistance to the Christian soldiers are to be found; and the Moors were themselves accustomed to say, that it was Mary and Brother Michael, not the Spaniards, who conquered the island.

Another Michael, called De Uzero, was afterwards sent by Dominic to establish the order in Spain. Brother Dominic, called sometimes the little, on account of his stature, or by others, Dominic the second, (and confused by some writers with Dominic of Segovia,* or the third,) had also been one of the holy patriarch's first companions in the missions of Toulouse. "He was," says his historian, "little of body, but powerful of soul, and of great sanctity." He too was a wonderful preacher, and cleared the court of king Ferdinand, "as it were in a moment," of all buffoons, flatterers, and other evil company.

Next comes Lawrence the Englishman. He is said to have been one of the pilgrims whom Dominic saved from death, as before related. By many he is called Blessed Lawrence, a title he seems to have deserved by his sanctity and his gifts of prophecy and miracles. Then there was Brother Stephen of Metz, a Belgian, "a man of rare abstinence, the frequent macerator of his own body, and of burning zeal for the eternal salvation of his neighbour;" and Brother John of Navarre, whom S. Dominic had brought with him to Toulouse from Rome, and there given the habit. He it was to whom S. Dominic gave the celebrated lesson on holy poverty, which we shall notice in its proper place. "He was then imperfect," says his biographer, "but afterwards made many journeys with S. Dominic, and by familiar conversation with him learnt how to be a saint, which indeed he became." He was one of those who gave his evidence on the canonization of the holy father. Peter of Madrid

---

* Many authors tell us, that "Dominic the little" was the first Provincial of Lombardy, and afterwards of Spain: and that he was likewise called "Dominic of Segovia. It is clear, however, from the account of Michaele Pio, that the two Dominics were distinct persons, and that Dominic of Segovia," the Provincial of Lombardy, was *not* the same as the early companion of the holy patriarch of his order.

is the next name, but we find no particulars of his life.
The two citizens of Toulouse, Peter Cellani and Thomas,
have already been mentioned. Oderic of Normandy was
a lay brother, and accompanied Matthew of France to
Paris, where he was known and reverenced for his
"perfection of sanctity." Lastly, there was Manez
Gusman, S. Dominic's own brother, "a man of great
contemplation, zealous for souls, and illustrious for
sanctity;" the only one of the sixteen who has received
the solemn beatification of the Church. He had a great
gift of preaching, although his attraction was wholly to
contemplation. Michaele Pio gives us his character in a
few expressive words: "Above all things he loved quiet
and solitude, taking most delight in a contemplative life,
in the which he made marvellous profit; and in living
alone with God and himself, rather than with others. He
had the government of the nuns who were established
at Madrid. Sincerity and simplicity shone in him above
all things; and many miracles declared to the world how
dear he was to heaven."

As soon as the little council of Prouille had concluded
its deliberations, Dominic returned to Toulouse. There
fresh demonstrations of the friendship of Fulk awaited
him. With the consent of his chapter he made him the
grant of three churches: Saint Romain at Toulouse, and
two others; one at Pamiers, and another, dedicated to
our Lady, near Puy-Laurens. These in time had each a
convent attached to them; but that of S. Romain was
commenced immediately, for Peter Cellani's house was
no longer adapted to their increased numbers. A very
humble cloister was therefore built contiguous to the
church, and over it were placed the cells of the brethren.
This was the first monastery of the order. The friars left
it in 1232, in order to remove to a larger and more
magnificent building. The convent of S. Romain was
poor enough, and soon completed; the brethren went
into it in the summer of the same year, 1216; and the
house of Peter Cellani became the future residence of the
Inquisitors.

Previous to his last departure to Rome, Dominic had,

with the concurrence of his brethren, made over all the
lands and property granted to him and his brethren, to
the nuns of Prouille. Afterwards he had accepted, as
it seems a little reluctantly, the revenues provided by
the generosity of Fulk of Toulouse. But though he
himself felt attracted towards the entire observance of
poverty in its strictest form, the mendicity which was
afterwards made a law of the order was not among those
constitutions drawn up at Prouille and immediately
adopted. It was reserved for the test of experience,
and for future deliberations. Nevertheless poverty was
scarcely less dear to Dominic than it was to Francis; he
honoured it in his own person, and was vigorous in seeing
it observed by those he governed; and we are assured that
every detail of the convent of S. Romain was executed
from his orders, and under his own eye, so as to insure
its conformity to the strictest requirements of his favourite
virtue.

— ✠ —

CHAPTER X.

Dominic's third visit to Rome.   Confirmation of the Order by
   Honorious III.   Dominic's vision in S. Peter's   He is appointed
   master of the Sacred Palace.   Ugolino of Ostia.

As soon as the convent of S. Romain had been taken
possession of by the brethren, Dominic prepared to return
to Rome, to lay the result of his consultation with the
other brethren before the Sovereign Pontiff. Before he
did so, the news arrived of the death of Innocent III.,
which took place at Perugia on the 16th of July, and of
the election on the day following of Cardinal Savilli as his
successor, under the title of Honorious III. This seemed indeed a severe blow to the hopes of the young order, for Innocent had been a sure and faithful friend, and it might well
cause no small anxiety to have to treat with a new Pontiff
for the confirmation of an unknown and untried institute.
He, however, set out, leaving Bertrand of Garrigues to

govern the convent in his absence, whilst he himself made
his third visit to the Roman capital. He arrived there in
the month of September, and found the Pope still absent
at Perugia; this caused him some delay, and during the
interval he lived a poor and unknown life, having no other
lodging at night than in the Churches. It seemed at first
as if many difficulties would stand in the way of the success of his enterprise; for the new Pontiff was engaged
in various troublesome negotiations, and his court was full
of dissensions. Dominic's resource was constant prayer;
and in spite of all obstacles, he obtained the two bulls
confirming the foundation of the order of the 22nd of
the following December. The confirmation of the Order
of Friars Minor was made at the same time, S. Francis
being at that time in Rome; and by very many the
meeting between him and Dominic is said to have taken
place at this period, and not on the occasion of their
former visit.

The first bull given by Honorius is of considerable
length: it grants a variety of privileges and immunities,
and confirms the order in the possession of all the lands,
churches, and revenues with which it had been endowed
by Fulk and other benefactors. The second bull is much
shorter, and we insert it for the sake of a remarkable
expression which it contains prophetic of the future destinies of the order:—" Honorius, bishop, servant of the
servants of God, to our dear son Dominic, prior of S.
Romain at Toulouse, and to your brethren who have
made or shall make profession of regular life, health and
apostolic benediction. We, considering that the brethren
of the order *will be the champions of the faith and true
lights of the world*, do confirm the order in all its lands
and possessions present and to come, and we take under
our protection and government the order itself, with all its
goods and rights."

It was at Santa Sabina, then the apostolic palace, that
these two bulls were given on the same day. In neither
of them, however, did the new order receive the title
which had been originally given to it by Innocent III.,
and which was so dear to Dominic, that of Preachers. In

a third bull, however, dated the 26th of January, 1217,
the omission is made up. It begins as follows:—"Honorius,
bishop, servant of the servants of God, to his dear son the
prior and brethren of S. Romain, *Preachers* in the country
of Toulouse, health and apostolic benediction." Meanwhile Dominic, whose mission at Rome was accomplished
as soon as the two first bulls had been granted, was
anxious to return to Toulouse, but was detained at Rome
by the command of the Pontiff, who had conceived a high
esteem and affection for him. Day and night, therefore,
he commended his children and their work to God, and
specially in those watches which he still continued to
keep in the churches, which were his only lodging. That
of the Holy Apostles was the one he loved the best, and it
was whilst fervently praying for his order at their tomb,
that he was granted a second vision to encourage and
console him. This was the appearance of the apostles
S. Peter and S. Paul, the first of whom gave him a staff,
and the second a book, saying these words: "Go and
preach, for to this ministry thou art called." Then he
seemed to see his children sent forth two and two into
the world, preaching to all nations the word of God.
Some writers add that the Holy Spirit was seen to rest
on his head in the form of a fiery tongue, and that from
that time he was singularly confirmed in grace, and freed
from many temptations; others, that he ever afterwards
bore about with him the book of the Gospels and of the
Epistles of S. Paul. In all his journeys, too, he constantly carried a stick, an unusual thing which he probably did in memory of this vision. His delay at Rome, if
tedious to himself, was greatly profitable to others. Lent
found him still there; and during that holy season he
took occasion frequently to exercise his office of preaching.
His success induced the Pope to appoint him to explain
the Epistles of S. Paul in the sacred palace, before the
court and cardinals. An ancient author of the noble
house of Colonna, himself a Dominican, tells us that
" Many came from all parts to hear him, both scholars
and doctors, and all gave him the title of Master." Other
authors, among whom is Flaminius, relate that the origin

of the appointment of S. Dominic was as follows He was, they say, greatly displeased, on the occasion of his visits to the palace, to see the followers of the cardinals idling about the ante-chambers, playing at games of chance, whilst their masters were engaged on the business of the Church; and that he suggested to the Pope whether some means could not be devised for entertaining them religiously and usefully, by the explanation of the Scriptures. The Pope, agreeing to his views, laid the charge on himself, and instituted the office of Master of the Sacred Palace, which continues even to our own day, and is always conferred on one of the Dominican order. This office is not simply a titular one; its duties are considerable, and of no small importance, including the censorship of all books published in Rome; and its possessor has been described as the Pope's theologian, acting as his domestic adviser in all matters of a theological character.

Another of those dear and honourable friendships which so embellish the life of Dominic, was formed during this visit to the Roman capital. Ugolino Conti, cardinal bishop of Ostia, and afterwards successor to Honorius, under the title of Gregory IX., already the friend and protector of Francis and of the Friars Minor, now first made the acquaintance of his brother and rival in sanctity. He was advanced in age, but a man of warm and enthusiastic feelings, who ever counted the close personal ties which bound him to those two great men as among the greatest privileges of his life. It was at his house that Dominic met another younger friend, William de Montferrat, who was spending Easter with Ugolino. The charm of the saint's intercourse, which indeed seems to have been of a very peculiar and winning kind, so captivated him that he was induced to take the habit of his order. He has left us the account of the whole matter in his own words:—

"It is about sixteen years," he says, "since I went to Rome to spend Lent there, and the present Pope, who was then Bishop of Ostia, received me into his house. At that time Brother Dominic, the founder and first master of the order of Preachers, was at the Roman court, and often visited my lord of Ostia. This gave me an opportunity of knowing him; his conversation pleased me, and I began to love him. Many a time did we speak together of the eternal salvation of our own souls, and those of all men. I never spoke to a man of equal perfection, or one so wholly taken up with the salvation of mankind, although indeed I have had intercourse with many very holy religious. I therefore determined to join him, as one of his disciples, after I had studied theology at the university of Paris for two years, and it was so agreed between us; and also, that after he had established the future discipline of his brethren, we should go together to convert, first, the pagans of Persia or of Greece, and then those who live in the southern countries." Once more we find here the key-note of Dominic's soul, the salvation of souls, which "wholly took him up;" and how large and magnificent was that thought of going *first* to convert Persia and Greece, and then on to the southern world! He had the very soul of chivalry under his friar's tunic; and we can well imagine the charm which such vast and glowing thoughts, clothed in the eloquence which was all his own, must have exerted over the minds of those who listened to him. He endeavoured also to persuade Bartholomew of Clusa, archdeacon of Mascon and canon of Chartres, one of his own penitents, to enter the new order, for he clearly discerned that such was God's vocation to his soul. Bartholomew, however, turned a deaf ear to all he said, and Dominic predicted that many things would befall him in consequence of his resistance to grace, which things, he himself assures us, did really afterwards happen to him; but what they were does not appear

Among the incidents of his life at Rome during this visit, we find mention of several active works of mercy, both spiritual and corporal. Outside the walls of the city there resided at that time certain recluses, commonly called *Murati* from their habitation. They were a community of hermits; each lived in a poor little cell separate one from the other; in which they were inclosed, never leaving them; being moved to this singular life by a particular spirit of mortification and solicitude. Almost every morning, after celebrating mass and reciting the Divine office, Dominic went to visit them, conversing with them on holy subjects, and exhorting them to perseverance. He was also accustomed to administer to them the sacraments of penance and the eucharist, and was, in short, what would be now called their director. When not engaged in these duties, or in the public exercise of preaching, he was to be found in the churches, where he spent his nights.

—✼—

CHAPTER XI.

Dominic returns to Toulouse. He disperses the Community of S. Romain. His address to the people of Languedoc. Future affairs of the Order in that country.

IT was not until the May of 1217, that Dominic was able to return to Toulouse. His return was very welcome to his children; yet their joy was, if we may so say, a little sobered, when, almost immediately on his arrival, after gathering them together and addressing to them a fervent exhortation on the manner of life to which they now stood pledged, he announced his intention of breaking up the little community as yet but just formed, and scattering its members to different countries. The plan seemed the height of imprudence; all joined in blaming it, and endeavouring to dissuade him from it. But Dominic was inexorable; the vision which he had seen beside the tomb of the apostles was fresh in his eye; their voice yet sounded in his ear. Fulk of Toulouse, De Montfort, the archbishop of Narbonne, and even his own companions, urged him to pause, but nothing would stir him from his purpose. "My lords and fathers," he said, "do not oppose me, for I know very well what I am about." He felt that their vocation was not to one place, but for all nations; not for themselves alone, but for the Church and the world. "The seed," he said, "will fructify if it is sown; it will ut moulder if you hoard it up." Some little time he gave them to consider if they could submit to his determination, with the alternative otherwise of abandoning the order. But his followers, whatever had been their feelings on the subject, had too profound a veneration for his person and character to oppose their judgments to his, and soon yielded the point. The event showed how entirely his resolution had been guided by the spirit of God.

Meanwhile, in the preparation which he made for this dispersion of his children, he showed how great was his anxiety for the preservation among them of the observance and spirit of their rule. The convent of Toulouse he designed to be the model which was to be followed in all later foundations, and made several regulations to render it more perfect in its arrangements. He thought it well that the brethren should from time to time meet together for mutual counsel and encouragement. With this idea he caused two large additional rooms to be built, one for containing the habits of the community, the other for the brethren to assemble in; for until now they, like the Cistercians, had had no rooms but their cells and the refectory. These two additions to their little convent added materially to the comfort of those who were to be left to inhabit it, and were doubtless the more welcome to them as proofs of the watchful thoughtfulness of their father. He was very earnest in enjoining upon them the strict observance of that part of S. Austin's rule which forbids all private appropriation of the smallest article. Even in the church itself he desired that the spirit of holy poverty should never be forgotten : and though he constantly insisted on its being kept a mirror of cleanliness, yet he forbade all elegancies and curiosities, and even ordered that the sacred vestments should not be made of silk. As to the cells of the brethren, the poverty he enjoined was absolute : a little cane bedstead, and a miserable bench were the only furniture he allowed. They had no doors, in order that the superior might always be able to see the brethren as he passed along; the dormitory resembled, as closely as possible, that of an hospital.

Blessed Jordan tells us, that it was whilst engaged in these regulations, that the holy father had the vision which foretold to him the death of the Count De Montfort. He seemed to see an immense tree, in whose branches a great quantity of birds had taken refuge; the tree was luxuriant and beautiful, and spread out its arms over the earth; suddenly it fell, and the birds all took flight, and Dominic was given to understand, that this represented the fall of him who had been known in a special manner as the protector and "father of the poor." This was accomplished in the following year, when the two Raymonds regained possession of Toulouse, and the Count de Montfort fell at the siege of that city. It is probable that his knowledge of the approaching return of war hastened Dominic in the execution of his designs. He fixed the feast of the Assumption for the assembly of all his brethren at Notre Dame de Prouille, previous to their departure for their different missions; and these missions were to include Paris, Bologna, Rome, the two convents of Toulouse and Prouille, and Spain; whilst he himself was letting his beard grow, with the intention, when things were fairly put in train in Europe, of setting out to the countries of the infidels. And all this was to be accomplished with sixteen followers! such was the largeness of Dominic's confidence in God.

On the appointed day, the little company all met to keep the festival of the Assumption with an unusual solemnity in the church of their mother-house of Prouille. It must have been a deeply touching spectacle to all present, and to Dominic himself one of profound and singular emotion. Great numbers of persons from the surrounding country, who knew the circumstances which had gathered the brethren together, came to witness the ceremony of the day; among them was De Montfort himself, and several prelates, all anxious to ascertain the final determination of S. Dominic as to the destination of his little flock. It was he himself who offered the Holy Sacrifice, and who, still habited in the sacred vestments, preached to the assembled audience in language some of which is still preserved to us. We are compelled,

from the severity of his tone, to draw conclusions un-
favourable to the people of Languedoc; for it was them
whom he thus addressed: "Now for many years past,"
he said, "have I sounded the truths of the Gospel in
your ears, by my preaching, my entreaties, and my
prayers, and with tears in my eyes. But, as they are
wont to say in my country, the stick must be used when
blessings are of no avail. Lo! princes and rulers will
raise all the kingdoms of this world against you; and
woe be unto you! they will kill many by the sword, and
lay the lands desolate, and overthrow the walls of your
cities, and all of you will be reduced to slavery; and so
you will come to see, that where blessings avail not, the
stick will avail." These dismal announcements were too
truly fulfilled when the army of the French king was
sent against the people of Toulouse; and they seem to
indicate that the evils under which the unhappy country
had so long laboured had produced an effect which not
even the twelve years labour of an apostle had been able
to counteract: it was a solemn farewell which framed
itself, almost unintentionally, into words of prophetic
warning. He then turned to his own brethren, and
reminded them of the first origin of their order, the end
for which it was instituted, and the duties to which they
stood pledged. Above all, he exhorted them to confidence
in God, and a great and unflinching courage, always to
prepare for wider and wider fields of labour, and to be
ready to serve the Church, in whatever way they might
be called to work for the conversion of sinners, heretics,
or infidels. His words had an extraordinary effect on
those who listened; any lingering feelings of dissatis-
faction they might have felt were dispelled by this
appeal to the heroism of their natures. Like soldiers
harangued by a favourite leader on the battle-field, they
seemed all kindled with a spark of his own chivalrous
ardour, and were impatient to be led on to the enterprise
which awaited them.

But another ceremony yet remained to be performed.
When Dominic had concluded his address, the sixteen
brethren knelt before him, and made their solemn vows

in his hands, binding themselves to the three obligations
of the religious state; for until then they had been bound
to him by no other tie than their own will. The nuns
of Prouille, in like manner, all made their profession on
the same day, adding the fourth vow of inclosure. When
this ceremony was over, he declared to each of them the
quarter to which they were destined. The two fathers,
who had until then had the direction of the convent of
Prouille, were to remain there as before, whilst Peter Cellani and Thomas of Toulouse were to continue at S. Romain. A large section of his little company were appointed
for the establishment of the order in Paris; these were
Matthew of France, Bertrand, Oderic, Manez the saint's
brother, with Michel Fabra and John of Navarre, the
last of whom had but just received the habit, and our
own countryman Lawrence. Stephen of Metz he reserved
as his own companion, and the four remaining Spaniards
were sent to Spain. Before they separated to their different parts, Dominic determined to provide for the future
government of the order in case of his death or removal,
for he still cherished the secret design of himself departing for the countries of the infidels, and finding perhaps
a martyr's crown among them. It was the old dream
planned so long ago with Diego of Azevedo, and never
laid aside. He therefore desired them to make a canonical election among themselves of some one who should
govern the order in his absence, or in case of his death.
Their choice fell on Matthew of France, who received the
title of *Abbot*, a designation never continued in the order;
after his death the brethren were content with the title
of *Master* for him who held the chief authority, whilst
the other superiors were called priors and sub-priors,
names chosen as best befitting the humility of their state.
This election being finished, Dominic committed the bull
of confirmation to the keeping of the new abbot, that it
might be solemnly published in the capital of France, and
gave them a parting exhortation to keep their vows, and
be diligent in founding convents, preaching God's word,
and following their studies; and so dismissed them with
his blessing.

G

One of them, and one only, showed evident signs of reluctance to obey. This was the newly-clothed brother, John of Navarre. He strongly shared in the sentiments of those ecclesiastics who solemnly condemned the holy patriarchs for imprudence. He ventured, before departing, to ask for a little money for his expenses on the way. The request seemed reasonable; but Dominic's discernment saw clearly the secret feelings of distrust and discontent which prompted it. He sharply reproved him, and set before him the example of the disciples whom their Lord sent forth, "having neither scrip nor purse;" then, quickly exchanging severity for the paternal tenderness which was more natural to him, he threw himself at his feet, and with tears in his eyes besought him to lay aside his cowardly fears, and to arm himself with a generous trust in God's Providence. But John still continuing stubborn in his view, and unconvinced of the practicability of travelling two hundred miles without funds, Dominic desired them to give him twelve pence, and then dismissed him.

We are told that some Cistercians who were present expressed their surprise in no measured terms, that he should send out these ignorant, unlettered boys to preach and teach; their criticism was something more than free, it was even contemptuous. Dominic bore the officious remarks with the equanimity which he never failed to exhibit on such occasions, the virtue for which the Church has so worthily designated him "the rose of patience." "What is it you say, my brothers," he replied with his accustomed sweetness; "are you not a little like the Pharisees? I know, nay I am certain, that these 'boys' of mine will go and come back safe, but it will not be so with yours." As for himself, when his little flock was dispersed, he still lingered awhile at Toulouse, and, before he left, he gave another token of his disinterestedness and magnanimity. The two brethren of S. Romain became entangled in some disputes with the procurators of the bishop's court, about the portion of tithes granted to the order by Fulk of Toulouse. Dominic settled the matter by causing an instrument to be executed in accordance with the views of the procurator, without further controversy: this paper is dated the 11th of September, 1217. He left for Italy soon after its execution, but not till he had received several new sons into his order; amongst these were Poncio Samatan, afterwards the founder of the convent of Bayonne; Raymond Falgaria, a noble of the neighbourhood, and successor to Fulk in the bishopric of Toulouse; and Arnold of Toulouse, first prior of the convent of Lyons. From this time we shall not have much occasion to speak of Languedoc; for, in following the future course of S. Dominic's life, we shall be led forward to other countries; the bright star which had risen in Spain, and spent its long meridian in France, was to shed its setting splendour over the fields of Italy.

Simon de Montfort perished the following year under the walls of Toulouse, as foreseen by Dominic. His death, like his life, was that of a brave and Christian knight. The victorious arms of the two Raymonds had stripped him of the greater part of the provinces with which he had been invested; and, urged to a last effort for their recovery, he laid siege to Toulouse with a force wholly unequal to the enterprise. It was sunrise on the 25th of June, when word was brought him of an ambuscade of the enemy. He received the message with tranquillity; and arming himself with his usual composure, he went to hear mass before going to the field. Another despatch arrived in the middle of the ceremony; they had attacked his machines of war, would he not hasten to their defence? "Leave me!" was his reply, "I stir not till I have seen the sacrament of my redemption!" Yet once again another messenger rushed into the church; the troops could hold out no longer; he would surely come to their aid. He turned to the speaker with a stern and melancholy air: "I will not go," he said, "till I have seen my Saviour." He knew his last hour was at hand; the sadness of deep disappointment was in his heart, but he surely made that day a solemn offering and resignation to God of the life whose human hopes had failed. When the priest elevated the sacred host, De Montfort knelt, and uttered the words "Nunc dimittis." Then he went out to the scene of

combat. His presence had its wonted effect on his followers, as well as on his enemies. The men of Toulouse
fled back to the city, pursued by the victorious crusaders;
but a stone from the wall struck their gallant leader to
the ground; and smiting his breast with his hand, he
expired, recommending his soul to God, and with the
name of Mary on his lips.

His friendship towards the order of Friars Preachers
survived in his family. One of his daughters, Amice, or,
as the Italians sweetly name her, Amicitia, the wife of
the Seigneur de Joigny, bore so peculiar a love to the
children of Dominic that she used all her endeavours to
induce her only son to take the habit. He, however, followed the army of S. Louis to the Holy Land; but whilst
detained in the island of Cyprus, he was taken with a
mortal sickness, and on his death-bed, remembering his
mother's prayers, he sent for the friars and received the
habit from their hands. When the tidings were brought
her, she gave thanks to God, and on the death of her
husband resolved to enter the order herself. She was
constantly repeating the words, "If I cannot be a Friar
Preacher, I will at least be one of their sisters;" and she
succeeded, after much opposition, in founding the convent
of Montaign, where she herself took the habit, and died
in odour of sanctity about the year 1235.

Toulouse, the nursery of the Dominican order, continued to be closely linked with its history for many a
year, though after the death of De Montfort we hear less
of the triumphs of its champions than of the sufferings of
its martyrs. Among these we find some hardly to be
passed over without notice, such as the blessed Francis
of Toulouse, one of the first who received the habit, and
whom Taegius calls one of the most intrepid preachers of
his time: he fell into the hands of the heretics, who tormented him in every way that more than pagan barbarity
could suggest; but he preached through it all, and proclaimed the Catholic faith. Then they plaited a crown of
thorns, and placed it on his head; and Francis received it
joyfully, counting himself unworthy to be made partaker
in one of the sufferings of his Lord; and still, as the blood

streamed down his face, "he confessed and denied not,"
but boldly preached the word of God, and the faith of
His Church. Then they shot him to death with arrows;
and so, standing like Sebastian with his face to his enemies, and with that glorious crown upon his brow, he
went to Christ. This was in 1260; a few years previously
Toulouse had witnessed the confession of others of the
order, among whom was William of Montpellier and his
companions. They were all of the convent of Toulouse,
and Count Raymond, the successor to the dominions and
the heresy of the Raymond of Dominic's time, enraged at
their boldness and success among his subjects, tried first
to starve them into submission. He gave orders that
none, under pain of death, should bring any meat or drink
to the convent, or hold any communication with it, and
posted guards about its boundaries to see his orders enforced. But angels set his guards at defiance, and were
seen going to and fro with provisions, so that no man
durst hinder them. Then he drove them from the town,
stripped them of all things they possessed, and condemned
their houses to be burned: this did not disturb them; they
went on their way, singing the Creed and the *Salve
Regina* with joyful countenances as they left the city
gates. But though forced to retire, they soon returned to
the province, and everywhere carried, as before, the light
of truth among the people; so that in 1242 Raymond
determined on yet more violent measures. Being then
at his country house of Avignette, and seated at his ease
at the window of his private room, William, with ten other
companions, some of his own order, some of that of the
Friars Minors, were brought before him, and severely tortured in various ways; Raymond looking on and enjoying
the scene. And whilst his eyes were satisfied with the
spectacle of their sufferings, there was not wanting music
for his ears, if indeed it were of a kind that such a soul
as his could understand. Under the very knives of their
torturers, the dying martyrs raised a sweet harmony with
their failing breath; they sang clear and loud the canticle
Te Deum, and taught their murderers, even with their
expiring voices, that the triumph of that hour **belonged**

to their victims, and not to them. This happened on the vigil of the Ascension, 1242.

—※.—

CHAPTER XII.

Dominic's fourth visit to Rome. His mode of travelling.

The October of the year 1217 saw Dominic crossing the Alps on foot, for the fourth time, on his way to Rome, in company with Stephen of Metz. A considerable obscurity hangs over this journey. According to an account sent to Rome by the fathers of the convent of SS. John and Paul at Venice, it was at that city that he first stopped, having, as it is said, the intention of carrying out the design already spoken of, namely, to embark for the East, and preach the Gospel to the Saracens in the Holy Land. Whilst there he preached publicly on several occasions, with such effect that several of the inhabitants demanded the habit, and the authorities of the Republic granted to him and these new brethren the little oratory of S. Daniel. The words of this document are as follows:—"In the year of our Lord 1217, the holy father Dominic came to Venice with a few other brethren, and received from the Republic the oratory then called S. Daniel, but which after his canonization was called the chapel of S. Dominic, and since the year 1567, down to the present day, has been called the chapel of Rosary. In this oratory, which was at first very small, S. Dominic erected a little convent for his brethren, and in the place now called the novitiate may still be seen, in the windows and walls, the remains of this ancient fabric." Whether indeed this relation may be trusted, in so far as concerns the foundation of the convent at Venice, seems a matter of doubt; yet there appears every probability that the saint did visit the city at that time with the intention of embarking for the Holy Land; an intention which, it is well known, he entertained whilst yet at Toulouse. What the circumstances were which induced him to abandon it does not appear; nor is there any certain account preserved of his manner of passing the months which intervened between his departure from Toulouse and his arrival at Rome at the close of the year 1217. We find, however, that he stopped at Milan on his way, and was there courteously entertained by the Canons Regular of San Nazario, who received him as one of their own order, for he and his brethren still wore the Augustinian habit; nor did they change it until after the vision granted to Blessed Reginald, of which we shall speak further on.

In default of exact details concerning this fourth journey to Rome, we will present our readers with the picture which has been so faithfully left us of Dominic's mode of performing all his journeys, and leave them by its means to fill up the blank, and to follow him thus in their mind's eye as he crossed the Alps on foot and made his way through the plains of Lombardy, and, as some have not hesitated to add, through the valleys of Switzerland and the Tyrol, preaching as he went. It will help us to a more intimate acquaintance with him, and set him before us with a more personal reality, as we enter on the most important period of his life.

Dominic always travelled on foot, with a little bundle on his shoulder and a stick in his hand. As soon as he was a little out of the towns and villages through which he passed, he would stop and take off his shoes, performing the rest of his journey barefoot, however rough and bad the roads might be. If a sharp stone or thorn entered his feet, he would turn to his companions with that cheerful and joyous air which was so peculiar to him, and say, " This is penance," and such kind of sufferings were a particular pleasure to him. Coming once to a place covered with sharp flints, he said to his companion, Brother Bonvisi, " Ah! miserable wretch that I was, I was once obliged to put on my shoes in passing this spot." " Why so ?" said the brother. " Because it had rained so much," replied Dominic. He would never let his companions help to carry his bundle, though they often begged him to suffer them to do so. When he looked down from the heights which they were descending, over any country or city which they were about to enter, he would pause,

and look earnestly at it, often weeping as he thought of
the miseries men suffered there, and of the offences they
committed against God.   Then, as he pursued his journey
and drew nearer he would put on his shoes, and, kneeling down, would pray that his sins might not draw down
on them the chastisement of Heaven.   For there was in
his character a singular mixture of that frank and joyous
bonhomie, so invariably to be found in a high and
chivalrous mind, with the tenderness of a melancholy
which had in it nothing morose, but was rather the consequence of a profound reverence for the purity of God,
the outrages against Whom, as they hourly came before
him, were felt with an exquisite sensibility.   He seldom
looked about him, and never when in towns or other
places where he was not alone.   His eyes were generally
cast down, and he never seemed to notice anything
curious or remarkable on the way.   If he had to pass a
river he would make the sign of the cross, and then enter
it without hesitation, and was always the first to ford it.
If it rained, or any other discomfort disturbed him on the
road, he encouraged his companions, and would begin
singing in a loud voice his favourite hymn, the *Ave
Maris Stella*, or the *Veni Creator*.   More than once at his
word the rain ceased, and the swollen rivers were passed
without difficulty.

   He constantly kept the fasts and abstinences of his
rule, and the silence prescribed by the constitutions
until prime; and this silence he insisted on being also
observed by the others; though, as regarded the fasts
and abstinences he was indulgent in dispensing with
them for the brethren whilst they were travelling; an
indulgence he never extended to himself.   Then, as they
went along, he would beguile the way with talking of the
things of God, or he instructed his companions in points
of spiritual doctrine, or read to them; and this kind of
teaching he enjoined on the other brethren when travelling with younger companions.   Sometimes, however,
he was used to say, " Go on before, and let us each think
a little of our Divine Lord."   This was the signal that
he wished to be left to silent meditation.   At such times

he would remain behind, to escape observation, and
would very soon begin to pray aloud, with tears and
sighs, losing all thought of the road he was following, or
the possible presence of others. Sometimes they had to
turn back and search for him, and would find him kneeling in some thicket or lonely place without seeming to
fear wolves or other dangers. The dread of personal
danger indeed formed no part of Dominic's character.
His courage, though always passive, was essentially
heroic. Over and over again he had been exposed to
the assaults of his enemies, and warned of their intentions against his life; but such things never so much
as made him change his road and alter the plan of his
journey in any particular: he always treated the subject
with silent indifference. When his prayers were ended,
his brethren, who often watched him on such occasions,
would see him take out his favourite book of the gospels,
and, first, making the sign of the cross, pursue his road,
reading and meditating to himself. However long and
fatiguing was the day's journey, it never prevented him
from saying Mass every morning whenever there was
a church to be found; and most frequently he would
not merely say but sing it; for he was one who never
spared his voice or strength in the divine offices. We
are constantly reminded of the heartiness of the royal
psalmist, in the character left us of Dominic's devotion.
"I will sing to the Lord with all my strength," was the
language of David; "I will sing to the Lord as long as
I have any being." And Dominic had no indulgence for
any indolence or self sparing in the praises of God. He
always rendered Him the sacrifice, not of his heart only,
but of his lips; and called on all his companions to do
the same, for he felt it a good and joyful thing to praise
the Lord.

It must be acknowledged, that his wonderful bodily
constitution was no little assistance in this matter to the
fervour of his soul. In his animal nature, no less than
in the cast of his mind, there was much of the gallant
spirit of a soldier; he never felt that fatigue, or in-
disposition, or other little ailments and difficulties, could

be an excuse for doing less for God. Therefore when he stopped for the night at some religious house, which he always preferred doing when it was possible, he never failed to join them in the singing of matins; and he gave it as his reason for choosing to stop at a convent, in preference to other lodgings which he might have accepted, saying, " We shall be able to sing matins to-night." At such times he generally chose the office of waking the others. These passing visits to the convents, either of his own or of other orders, were always full of profit to their inmates. They made the most of the few hours of his stay, and Dominic never thought of pleading for the privilege of a weary traveller. If the convent were under his own government, his first act was to call together the religious, and make them a discourse on spiritual things for a "good space;" and then if any were suffering from temptations, melancholy, or any kind of trouble. he never was tired of comforting and advising them till he had restored them to the quiet and joy of their souls. Very often these little visits were so delightful to the religious who entertained him, that on his leaving them in the morning they would accompany him on his way to enjoy a little more of his discourse; for the fascination of his conversation was universally felt to be irresistible. But if there were no such houses to receive him, he left the choice of the night's lodging to his comrades, and was all the better pleased if it chanced to be incommodious; he made it a rule, before entering. always to spend some time in the nearest church. When people of high rank entertained him, he would first quench his thirst at some fountain, lest he should be tempted to exceed religious modesty at table, and so give occasion of scandal; a prudence which, in a man of such austerity of life, gives us a singular idea of his humility. When ill, he would eat roots and fruit rather than touch the delicacies of their tables; and even when canon of Osma he never touched meat; he would take it and hide it in his plate, not to be observed. Sometimes he begged his bread from door to door, thanking his benefactors for their scanty alms on his knees, and with uncovered head. His sleep was taken on the floor, and in his habit; and very often those who slept near him could hear that the night was spent in prayers and tears, and "strong crying" to God for the salvation of souls.

Thus journeying, he would stop and preach at all the towns and villages in his way: what kind of preaching this was, we may easily guess. "What books have you studied, father," said a young man to him one day, "that your sermons are so full of the learning of holy Scripture?" "I have studied in the book of charity, my son," he replied, "more than in any other: it is the book which teaches us all things." "With all his strength," says blessed Jordan, "and with the most fervent zeal, he sought to gain souls to Christ without any exception, and as many as he could; and this zeal was marvellously, and in a way not to be believed, rooted in his very heart." His favourite way of recommending to man the truths of God, was the sweetness of persuasion; and yet, as his parting address to the people of Languedoc shows us, he knew (according to his own expression) "how to use the stick." Finally, to cite once more the words of the writer just quoted, "Wherever he was, whether on the road with his companions, or in the house with the guests or the family of his host, or among great men, princes or prelates, he always spoke to edification, and was wont to give examples and stories whereby the souls of those who heard him were excited to the love of Jesus Christ, and to contempt of the world. Everywhere, both in word and deed, he made himself known as a truly evangelical man." The same testimony was borne by those who were examined on his canonization: "Wherever he was," they say, "whether at home or on a journey, he ever spoke *of* God or *to* God; and it was his desire that this practice should be introduced into the constitutions of his order." We must, however, conclude these brief notices, so precious in the personal details they have preserved to us of some of his characteristic habits, and once more take up the thread of his story, which finds him for the fourth time under the walls of the eternal city.

CHAPTER XIII.

DOMINIC was received at Rome with renewed evidences of affection and favour from Pope Honorius, who showed every disposition to forward the view with which he had returned thither, namely, the foundation at Rome of a convent of his order. The church granted to him by the Pontiff for this purpose was chosen by himself; it was one already full of ancient and traditionary interest, which its connection with the rise of the Dominican order has certainly not lessened. There is a long road that stretches out of Rome, following the course of the ancient Via Appia, which, deserted as it now is by human habitation, you may trace by its abandoned churches and its ruined tombs. In the old days of Rome, it was the patrician quarter of the city; the palace of the Cæsars looks down upon it, and by its side stand the vast ruins of Caracalla's baths, with the green meadows covering the site of the Circus Maximus. This circumstance of its being formerly the place of popular and favourite resort, accounts for the abundance of Christian remains which mingle with the relics of a pagan age, and share their interest and their decay. For here were formerly the houses of many of noble and some of royal birth; and when their owners confessed the faith, and died martyrs for Christ, the veneration of the early church consecrated those dwellings as churches, to be perpetual monuments of names which had else been forgotten. But in time the population of Rome gathered more and more to the northern side of the Cælian Hill, and the Via Appia has long been left to a solitude which harmonizes well enough with its original destination, for it was the Roman street of tombs. There, mixed with the ruined towers and melancholy pagan memorials of death, where the wild plants festoon themselves in such rich luxuriance, and the green lizards and snakes enjoy an unmolested home, stand these deserted Christian churches, never open now, save on the one or two days when they are places of pilgrimage for the crowds who flock to pray at shrines and altars which at other times are left in the uninterrupted silence of neglect. Among these is one dedicated to S. Sixtus, pope and martyr, and the tomb of five others, popes and martyrs like himself. If the English traveller visit it now, on one of those days of which we speak, when its doors are opened to the devotion of the faithful, and should chance to address himself to any of the white-robed religious whom he may find there, and who seem to be its masters, he will be startled with the sound, so sweet, and alas! in a place of holy association, so strange to his ears, the accent of his own English tongue. The church of San Sisto is, in fact at this time, the property of the Irish Dominican convent of San Clemente a circumstance not without its interest to ourselves.

This was the church chosen by Dominic for his first foundation at Rome, and Honorius did not hesitate to grant it to him, together with all the buildings attached. These had been erected by Innocent III., with the intention of gathering together within their walls a number of religious women who were at that time living in Rome under no regular discipline. The design had never been carried out, and Dominic was ignorant of it when he applied for and obtained the grant of the church. His first care was to reduce the house to a conventual form, and to enlarge it so as to be capable of receiving a considerable number of brethren. To do this he was obliged to solicit the alms of the faithful, which were indeed abundantly supplied; the Pope himself liberally contributing to a work in which he felt no common interest. Meanwhile Dominic laboured at his usual trade of preaching. Whilst the walls of his convent were daily rising above the ground and growing into shape, he was busy forming a spiritual edifice out of the hearts and souls of those whom his eloquence daily won from the world to join themselves to God. In our own day we are often tempted to talk and think much of our great successes, and the extraordinary impulse given to our religious life. It is a style known only to those among whom that life is still but feeble, and would doubtless have sounded strange in the ears of our fathers; and nothing is better fitted to humble and silence our foolish boasting, than a glance at the results of a religious impulse in the ages of faith. It is nowhere painted to our eyes in more vivid and magnificent colours than in the period of this Church's history.

Many influences certainly paved the way for what in these days would be called the "success" of Dominic and Francis. As we have before said, they were wanted by their age: the world was restlessly heaving with the excitement of new feelings, which stirred men with emotions they neither understood nor knew how to use. We need not therefore wonder at the enthusiasm with which they flung themselves into the ranks of the two leaders whom God had sent them. For, after all, great men are not the exponents of their own views or sentiments. Be they saints, or heroes, or poets, their greatness consists in this, that they have incarnated some principle which lies hidden in the hearts of their fellow-men. All have felt it; they alone have expressed and given it life; and so when the word is spoken which brings it forth to the world, all men recognize it as their own; they need no further teaching and training in this thought, for unconsciously to themselves they have been growing into it all their lives; and the devotion with which they follow the call of him who guides them is, perhaps, the strongest sentiment of which human nature is susceptible; made up not merely of admiration, or loyalty, or enthusiasm, but in addition to all these, of that gratitude which a soul feels towards that greater and stronger soul whose sympathy has set its own prisoned thoughts at liberty, and given them the power and the space to act. Then like some pent-up and angry waters, that have long vexed and chafed themselves into foam, and beaten aimlessly against the wall that kept them in, when the free passage is made, how impetuously they rush forth! At first agitated and confused, but gathering majesty as they flow, till the torrent becomes a river, and the river swells into a broad sea, the dash of whose long united waves no barrier can resist. This is what we call a popular movement. Europe has seen such things often enough, as well for good as for evil; but she never saw one more universal or more extraordinary than the first burst into existence of the mendicant orders. Francis had been first in the field, and the first chapter of his order saw him in the midst of five thousand of his brethren. But the fields were white with the harvest, and the Friars Minor were not to be the only gatherers of it. In three months Dominic had assembled round him at Rome more than a hundred religious with whom to begin his new foundation. His convent of S. Sixtus had to be even yet more enlarged; and here he may now be said to have carried out for the first time the entire observance of that rule of life which was commenced at S. Romain.

This period of his life is every way remarkable; it sets him before us in a new character. Hitherto we have caught but broken and imperfect glimpses of him in his life of solitary and unappreciated labour. But now at length we see him manifested to the world, ruling over a numerous community, and sending them out to be in their turn the apostles of their day. Many details of his character come out to our view which till now have lain concealed; and as if to make him known in the eyes of men in an especial manner, God was pleased at this time to confirm his teaching and authority by many supernatural signs. The first of these was on the occasion of an accident which happened during the erection of the convent. A mason, whilst excavating under part of the building, was buried by a mass of the falling earth. The brethren ran to the spot too late to save him, but Dominic commanded them to dig him out, whilst he betook himself to prayer. They did so, and when the earth was removed, the man arose alive and unhurt. This miracle, however much it confirmed the faith and devotion of his own followers, was little known or talked of beyond the

walls of his convent; but it was followed by another of
more public notoriety. Dominic was accustomed at this
time to preach in the church of S. Mark, where he was
listened to with enthusiasm by crowds of all ranks who
flocked to hear him. Among them one of his most constant
auditors was a certain Roman widow, Guatonia or Tuta
di Buvalischi; and one day rather than miss the preaching, she came to S. Marks, having left her only son at
home dangerously ill. She returned to her house to find
him dead. When the first anguish of her grief was over,
she felt an extraordinary hope rise within her that by
the mercy of God, and the prayers of His servant Dominic, her child might yet be restored to her. She therefore determined to go at once to S. Sixtus; and firm in
her faith she set out on foot, whilst her women servants
carried the cold and lifeless body of the boy behind her.
S. Sixtus was not yet inclosed, on account of the unfinished state of the convent, and she therefore entered
the gates without difficulty, and found Dominic at the
door of the chapter-house, a small building standing separate from the church and convent. Kneeling at his
feet, she silently laid the dead body before him, whilst her
tears and sobs of anguish told the rest. Dominic, touched
with compassion, turned aside for a few moments, and
prayed; then, coming back, he made the sign of the cross
over the child, and taking him by the hand, raised him,
and gave him back to his mother, alive, and cured of his
sickness. Some of the brethren were witnesses of this
miracle, and gave their evidence in the process of canonization. Dominic strictly charged the mother to keep the
fact a secret, but she disobeyed him, as the woman of Judea
had before disobeyed One greater than *him*. Her joy was
too abundant, and out of its abundance her heart and lips
were busy, and so the whole story was quickly spread
through Rome, and reached the ears of Honorius, who
ordered it to be publicly announced in the pulpits of the
city. Dominic's sensitive humility was deeply hurt: he
hastened to the Pontiff, and implored him to counter-
mand his order. "Otherwise, Holy Father," he said, "I
shall be compelled to fly from hence, and cross the sea to

preach to the Saracens; for I cannot stay longer here."
The Pope, however, forbade him to depart; he was obliged
to remain and receive what is ever the most painful portion
of the saints, the public honour and veneration of the
populace. And certainly they evinced it with a warmth
which English hearts may find it difficult to understand.
They were Catholics and Romans, and so thought little
of human respect, or of anything save the giving free vent
to that almost passionate devotion which is the hereditary
characteristic of their race. So great and little, old and
young, nobles and beggars, "they followed him about"
(to use the words of contemporaneous authors) "wherever
he went, as though he were an angel, reputing those
happy who could come near enough to touch him, and
cutting off pieces of his habit to keep as relics." This cutting of his habit went on at such a pace as to give the
good father the appearance of a beggar, for the jagged and
ragged skirt scarcely reached below his knee. His brethren
on one occasion endeavoured somewhat harshly to check
some of those who crowded round him, but Dominic's
good-nature was hurt when he saw the sorrowful and disappointed looks of the poor people. "Let them alone," he
said; "we have no right to hinder their devotion." A memorial of these circumstances may still be seen in that
same church of S. Mark of which we have spoken. Once a
year, on the festival of its patron saint, there is an exhibition in that church of saintly treasures, which few sanctuaries can rival and none surpass. There, amid the relics
of apostles and martyrs in jewelled and crystal shrines
and elaborate carvings, you may see, inclosed in a golden
reliquary, a little piece of torn and faded serge. Priests
are there holding up these precious objects one by one for
the veneration of the kneeling crowd, and they hold this
also for you to look at and to kiss, whilst they proclaim
aloud, "This is part of the habit of the glorious Patriarch S. Dominic, who in the first year of his coming to
Rome, was wont to preach in this church." And fancy
is quick to suggest that this precious morsel may be one
of those so unceremoniously torn from him by the crowds
who flocked about him on that very spot.

Other miracles are related as having occurred during the time of his residence at S. Sixtus, and we give them here, as no more exact date is assigned. Giacomo del Miele, a Roman by birth, and the syndic of the convent, was attacked by sickness, which increased so rapidly that he received extreme unction, and was desired by the physician to prepare for death. The brethren were greatly afflicted, for he was a man of singular ability for his office, and much beloved. Dominic was overcome by the tears of his children: desiring them all to leave the cell, he shut the door, and, like Elias when he raised the Sunamite's son, extended himself on the almost lifeless body of the dying man, and earnestly invoked the Divine mercy and assistance. Then, taking him by the hand, Giacomo arose entirely recovered, and Dominic delivered him to his companions, who knew not how to contain and express their joy.

Among the "Murati," whom we mentioned in a former page, and whom he still continued to visit and direct, there were some who lived a life of extraordinary mortification, and were entirely enclosed in little cells built in the walls, so as that none could enter, or communicate with their inhabitants; food and other necessaries being given to them through a window. One of these recluses was a woman named Buona, who lived in a town near the gate of S. John Lateran; another, Lucy, in a little cell behind the church of S. Anastasia. Both of them suffered from incurable and most terrible diseases, brought on by the severity of their mode of life. One day, after Dominic had administered the sacrament of penance and the holy Eucharist to Buona through her little window, and exhorted her to patience under her dreadful sufferings, he blessed her with the sign of the cross, and went away; but at the same instant she felt herself perfectly cured. Lucy was likewise restored in a similiar manner, as Brother Bertrand, who was present on the occasion, attested.

But perhaps the most interesting of all these miraculous events is one still daily commemorated in every house of the Dominican order. We are assured that a similar event happened *twice* during the period of his residence

at S. Sixtus; but we shall only give the account of one
of these circumstances, as related at length in the narrative of Sister Cecilia:—" When the Friars were still
living near the church of S. Sixtus, and were about one
hundred in number, on a certain day the blessed Dominic
commanded Brother John of Calabria and Brother Albert
of Rome to go into the city to beg alms. They did so
without success from the morning even till the third hour
of the day. Therefore they returned to the convent, and
they were already hard by the church of S. Anastasia,
when they were met by a certain woman who had a great
devotion to the order; and seeing that they had nothing
with them, she gave them a loaf; " For I would not," she
said, " that you should go back quite empty-handed." As
they went on a little further they met a man who asked
them very importunately for charity. They excused
themselves, saying they had nothing themselves; but the
man only begged the more earnestly. Then they said one
to another, " What can we do with only one loaf? Let us
give it to him for the love of God." So they gave him
the loaf, and immediately they lost sight of him. Now,
when they were come to the convent, the blessed father,
to whom the Holy Spirit had meanwhile revealed all that
had passed, came out to meet them, saying to them with
a joyful air, " Children, you have nothing?" They replied, " No, father;" and they told him all that had happened, and how they had given the loaf to the poor man.
Then said he, " It was an angel of the Lord; the Lord
will know how to provide for His own; let us go and
pray." Thereupon he entered the church, and, having
come out again after a little space, he bade the brethren
call the community to the refectory. They replied to him
saying, " But, holy father, how is it you would have us
call them, seeing that there is nothing to give them to
eat?" And they purposely delayed obeying the order
which they had received. Therefore the blessed father
caused Brother Roger the cellarer to be summoned, and
commanded him to assemble the brethren to dinner, for
the Lord would provide for their wants. Then they prepared the tables, and placed the cups, and at a given

signal all the community entered the refectory. The
blessed father gave the benediction, and every one being
seated, Brother Henry the Roman began to read. Meanwhile the blessed Dominic was praying, his hands being
joined together on the table; and, lo! suddenly, even as
he had promised them by the inspiration of the Holy
Ghost, two beautiful young men, ministers of the Divine
Providence, appeared in the midst of the refectory, carrying loaves in two white cloths which hung from their
shoulders before and behind. They began to distribute
the bread, beginning at the lower rows, one at the right
hand, and the other at the left, placing before each brother one whole loaf of admirable beauty. Then, when they
were come to the blessed Dominic, and had in like manner
placed an entire loaf before him, they bowed their heads,
and disappeared, without any one knowing, even to this
day, whence they came or whither they went. And the
blessed Dominic said to his brethren: " My brethren,
eat the bread which the Lord has sent you." Then he
told the servers to pour out some wine. But they replied, " Holy father, there is none." Then the blessed
Dominic, full of the spirit of prophecy, said to them, " Go
to the vessel, and pour out to the brethren the wine which
the Lord has sent them." They went there, and found,
indeed, that the vessel was filled up to the brim with an
excellent wine, which they hastened to bring. And Dominic
said, " Drink, my brethren, of the wine which the Lord
has sent you." They ate, therefore, and drank as
much as they desired, both that day, and the next, and
the day after that. But after the meal of the third day,
he caused them to give what remained of the bread and
wine to the poor, and would not allow that any more of
it should be kept in the house. During these three days
no one went to seek alms, because God had sent them
bread and wine in abundance. Then the blessed father
made a beautiful discourse to his brethren, warning them
never to distrust the Divine goodness, even in time of
greatest want. Brother Tancred, the prior of the convent,
Brother Odo of Rome, and Brother Henry of the same
place, Brother Lawrence of England, Brother Gandion,

and Brother John of Rome, and many others were present at this miracle, which they related to Sister Cecilia, and to the other sisters, who were then still living at the monastery of Santa Maria on the other side of the Tiber; and they even brought to them some of the bread and wine, which they preserved for a long time as relics. Now the Brother Albert, whom the Blessed Dominic had sent to beg with a companion, was one of the two brethren whose death the blessed Dominic had foretold at Rome. The other was Brother Gregory, and a man of great beauty and perfect grace. He was the first to return to our Lord, having devoutly received all the sacraments. On the third day after, Brother Albert, having also received the sacraments, departed from this darksome prison to the palace of heaven. Allusion is made in the concluding part of this narrative to a circumstance which took place a little later. One day, Dominic being full of the Holy Spirit, was holding chapter, and was observed by all present to be very sad. "Children," he said, "know that within three days, two of you now present will lose the life of your bodies, and two others that of their souls." Within the time described, the two brothers named above died, as we have related; and two others, whose names are not given, returned to the world.

We said that the circumstance of the angel's visit to the refectory of S. Sixus, so beautifully related by Sister Cecilia, is still daily commemorated in the houses of the order. And it is so; for from this time the custom was adopted of beginning to serve the lowest tables first, and so going up to the table of the prior; a custom which was afterwards made a law of the order, being introduced into the constitutions.

CHAPTER XIV

SOME mention was made in the last chapter of a design entertained by Pope Innocent III., to appropriate the church of S. Sixtus to a number of religious women then living in Rome without inclosure, and some even in the private houses of their relations. The design of collecting them together under regular discipline had been found fraught with difficulty, and had failed; even the papal authority, aided by the power and genius of such a man as Innocent, had been unable to overcome the wilfulness and prejudice which opposed so wise a project. Honorius, who no less than his predecessor ardently desired to see it carried out, resolved to commit the management of the whole affair to Dominic. He could not refuse; but aware of the complicated obstacles which lay in the way, he made it a condition that three other persons of high authority might be united with him in a business which, he probably felt, was far harder than the foundation of many convents, namely, the reform of relaxation, and the union under one head and into one body of a number of individuals who owned no common interest or authority

These religious had for a considerable time been badly governed; perhaps, we should rather say, they had not been governed at all. They claimed exemption from the ordinary rules, were members of powerful families, and their relatives, among whom many of them lived, urged them on to resist every encroachment on their liberty as an act of tyranny. And indeed, in the then existing state of things, they could not be said to be absolutely compelled to obedience: the matter was one rather demand-

ing address than authority. But if ever man possessed
the art of persuasion it was the blessed Dominic, whom,
as it is said. "none did ever resist;" or rather persuasion
with him was not art, but nature. It was the effect of
that admirable union of patience, prudence, and firmness,
tempered with the charm of a sweet and tranquil gaiety,
which gave so wonderful a magic to his intercourse; and
his powers were never more severely tested than on this
occasion. The coadjutors given him by the Pope were
the cardinals Ugolino, Bishop of Ostia, the venerable
friend of S. Francis; Stephen of Fossa Nuova; and Ni
cholas Bishop of Tusculum. The very first steps which the
cautious commissioners took raised a storm of obloquy.
The cardinals had enough to do to quiet the nuns, and
bring them to listen to the Pope's proposals. But those
who held out had a strong party in their favour. The
gossip of Rome was on their side; and there was a tempest of busy angry tongues all declaiming against tyranny
and aggression, and talking great things about innovation
on an ancient custom. "And truly," says Castiglio, with
a touch of Spanish humour, "the custom was so very ancient, that it could scarce keep its legs. Moreover," he
adds. "we know well, that for relaxation and liberty there
will always be ten thousand persons ready to do great
things, but for virtue not one willing to stir a step."
However, as we have said, the nuns had the popular cla-
mour on their side, and they used their advantage with
considerable address. They had but to receive visitors
all day long, and keep up the excitement of their friends
by perpetual talking, and the Pope and cardinals would
be held at bay.

The most refractory of these religious were some who
were living at that time in the monastery of Santa Maria
in Trastevere, in which was kept a celebrated picture of
our Blessed Lady, said to have been painted by S. Luke.
This picture was a particular favourite with the Roman
people. Tradition said that it had been brought to Rome,
many centuries before, from Constantinople; that it was
the same that had been borne processionally by S. Gregory in the time of the plague, on that Easter-day when

the words of the *Regina Cœli* were first heard sung overhead by the voices of the angelic choirs. After that Sergius III. had caused it to be placed in the Lateran Basilica, but in the middle of the night it found its own way back to the majestic old church which seemed its chosen resting-place. The possession of this picture was no inconsiderable addition to the power and popularity of the nuns; without it they were determined never to stir, and there seemed great difficulties in the way of removing it. Dominic's plan was simply to carry out that previously designed by Pope Innocent, and collect all the nuns of the different convents that had no regular discipline, as well as the others living out of inclosure, into one community, to whom he proposed giving up his own convent of S. Sixtus, receiving instead that of Santa Sabina on the Aventine Hill. His first visit was a failure; the very mention of inclosure and community life was received by a very intelligible assertion that they neither were nor would be controlled by him, the cardinals, or the Pope. But Dominic was not so easily daunted. He used all the skill and address of manner with which God had endowed him; and on his second visit he found means to win over the abbess, and after her all the community, with one solitary exception, to the wishes of the Pope. There were, however, conditions proposed and accepted. These were, that they must be suffered to carry their picture with them to S. Sixtus, and should it come back to the Trastevere of itself, as in the days of Pope Sergius, that they should be held free to come back after it. Dominic consented; but, saving this clause, he induced them to profess obedience in all else to himself; and they having done so, he gave them as their first trial a prohibition to leave their convent in order to visit any of their friends or relatives; assuring them that in a very short time S. Sixtus should be ready to receive them.

After this it seemed as though the affair were pretty well settled; "but" (to use the words of the grave and judicious Polidori) "the instability of human nature, and especially of the female sex, easy to be moved by whatsoever wind may blow, did very soon make the contrary to

appear." The wise regulation which Dominic had made
was evaded, and the vituperating tongues were busier
than ever. There were no terms too strong to use in
denouncing the proposed migration to S. Sixtus. It
would be the destruction of an ancient and honourable
monastery; they were about blindly to put themselves
under an intolerable yoke of obedience, and to whom?
— to a *new man*, a "*frate*," whose order nobody had ever
heard of before—a scoundrel (*ribaldo*), as some were
pleased to term him: they must certainly have been be-
witched. The nuns began to think so too, and many
repented of their too hasty promise. Whilst this new
disturbance was going on, Dominic was relating the success of his mission to the cardinals. But the fresh disorders which had arisen were revealed to him by the Holy
Spirit even at the moment that they occurred. He resolved to let the excitement exhaust itself a little before
taking any new measure; and a day or two afterwards
proceeded to the convent, where, having said mass, he
assembled all the religious in chapter, and addressed them
at considerable length. He concluded with these words:
" I well know, my daughters, that you have repented of
the promise you gave me, and now desire to withdraw
your feet from the ways of God. Therefore, let those
among you who are truly and spontaneously willing to go
to S. Sixtus make their profession over again in my
hands." The eloquence of his address, heightened by
that strange and wonderful charm of manner to which all
who knew him bear witness, whilst none can describe it,
was victorious. The abbess instantly renewed her profession (with the same condition respecting the picture),
and her example was followed by the whole community.
Dominic was well satisfied with their sincerity; nevertheless he thought it well to add one precaution against
farther relapse. It was a simple one, and consisted of
taking the keys of the gate into his own custody, and appointing some of his own lay brothers to be porters, with
orders to provide the nuns with all necessaries, but to
prevent their seeing or speaking with relatives or any
other person whatsoever.

On Ash Wednesday, which fell that year on the 28th of February, the cardinals assembled at S. Sixtus, whither the abbess and her nuns also proceeded in solemn procession. They met in the little chapter-house before mentioned, where Dominic raised to life the widow's child. The abbess solemnly surrendered all office and authority into the hands of Dominic and his brethren; whilst they, on their part, with the cardinals, proceeded to treat concerning the rights, government, and revenues of the new convent. Whilst thus engaged, the business of the assembly was suddenly interrupted by an incident which is best told in the language of one of the eye-witnesses:—" Whilst the blessed Dominic was seated with the cardinals, the abbess and her nuns being present, behold! a man entered, tearing his hair and uttering loud cries. Being asked the cause, he replied, 'The nephew of my lord Stephen has just fallen from his horse, and is killed!' Now the young man was called Napoleon. His uncle, hearing him named, sank fainting on the breast of the blessed Dominic. They supported him; the blessed Dominic rose, and threw holy water on him; then, leaving him in the arms of the others, he ran to the spot where the body of the young man was lying, bruised and horribly mangled. He ordered them immediately to remove it to another room, and keep it there. Then he desired Brother Tancred, and the other brethren to prepare everything for Mass. The blessed Dominic, the cardinals, friars, the abbess and all the nuns, then went to the place where the altar was, and the blessed Dominic celebrated the Holy Sacrifice with an abundance of tears. But when he came to the elevation of our Lord's Body, and held it on high between his hands, as is the custom, he himself was raised a palm above the ground, all beholding the same, and being filled with great wonder at the sight. Mass being finished, he returned to the body of the dead man; he and the cardinals, the abbess, the nuns, and all the people who were present; and when he was come, he arranged the limbs one after another with his holy hand, then prostrated himself on the ground, praying and weeping. Thrice he touched the face and limbs of the deceased, to put them in their place, and thrice he prostrated himself. When he was risen for the third time, standing on the side where his head was, he made the sign of the cross; then with his hands extended towards heaven, his body raised more than a palm above the ground, he cried with a loud voice, saying, 'O young man, Napoleon, in the name of our Lord Jesus Christ, I say unto thee, Arise.' Immediately, in the sight of all those who had been drawn together by so marvellous a spectacle, the young man arose alive and unhurt, and said to the blesssed Dominic, 'Father, give me to eat;' and the blessed Dominic gave him to eat and to drink, and committed him, joyful and without sign of hurt, to the cardinal, his uncle.'* It must be acknowledged, there is a wonderful grandeur in this narrative. We realize at once the alarm and emotion of the bystanders, and the supernatural calm and tranquillity of the saint, who was acting under the Spirit of God. Never, perhaps, was any miracle better attested, or more accurately described; and, as we shall hereafter see, it bore abundant fruits.

Four days after, on the first Sunday in Lent, the nuns took possession of their convent. They were forty-four in all, including a few seculars, and some religious of other convents. The first who spontaneously threw herself at Dominic's feet, and begged the habit of his order, was the same sister Cecilia whose narrative has been just quoted. She was then but seventeen, of the house of Cesarini, and distinguished for the great qualities of her soul, even more than for the nobility of her birth. Meagre as is the account left us concerning her, we scarcely feel the want of further details, for her character is sufficiently evidenced in the little which is preserved. She had a soul large enough to appreciate that of Dominic. Child as she was, she had been quick to recognize, and value at their true worth, the qualities of that mind which had brought into order the tempestuous and disorganized elements of the community of

Narrative of Sister Cecillia.

the Trastevere. Then she became an eye-witness of that great miracle which we have just related in her own beautiful language; and the admiration which she had already felt for him was raised to a devotion as fervent as it was lasting. We are told that Dominic communicated to her the most hidden secrets of his heart; and we feel in reading the narrative which she has left, so noble and touching in its biblical simplicity, that she was worthy of such confidence. Her example was followed by that of all the nuns; all received the habit of the rew order, and took the vow of inclosure.

Dominic waited until night-fall before he ventured to remove the picture so often named; he feared lest some excitement and disturbance might be caused by this being done in broad day, for the people of the city felt a jealous unwillingness to suffer it to depart. However, at midnight, accompanied by the two cardinals, Nicholas and Stephen, and many other persons, all barefoot and carrying torches, he conducted it in solemn procession to S. Sixtus, where the nuns awaited its approach with similar marks of respect. It did not return; and its quiet domestication in the new house completed the settlement of the nuns. They were soon after joined by twenty-one others from various other houses, and thus was formed the second house of religious women living under the rule of S. Dominic.

---:/:---

CHAPTER XV

Affairs of the Order in France. First settlement of the brethren at the convent of St. James at Paris. Foundation at Bologna Character of the religious houses of the Order. Settlement of the Friars in Spain and Portugal. Brothers Tancred and Henry of Rome.

BEFORE we proceed to give any account of the settlement of S. Dominic at the convent of Santa Sabina, whither he removed after that of S. Sixtus had been given up to the nuns, as just related, it will be necessary

for us to speak of several events which had taken place
since his departure from Toulouse in the autumn of the
preceding year. Various were the discouragements and
difficulties which had attended the first outset of the
missionaries sent from Prouille. Dominic of Segovia
and Michel de Uzero had returned from Spain without
having been able to succeed in establishing themselves
in that country; and had joined their brethren in Rome.
The little community destined for the French capital had
scarcely fared better, and might possibly have abandoned
their project in a similar manner, had it not been for the
presence of the Englishman Lawrence. "For as they
drew near to that great city, they went along in great
doubt and affliction, because in their humility they
greatly feared to preach in so celebrated a university,
where there were so many famous doctors and masters
versed in sacred science; but God, in order to encourage
them, revealed to his servant Lawrence all that should
hereafter happen to this mission, and all the favours
which God and the Blessed Virgin would show them
in the house of S. James, and all the bright stars, as
well of sanctity as of learning, that should rise from
thence, to illuminate not the order only, but the entire
Church; which revelation, as it greatly comforted the
soul of brother Lawrence, so he in like manner declared
it to his companions, to animate them also; and they
believing it, for the opinion which all had of the sanctity
of that servant of God, conceived a lively faith. Wherefore they joyfully entered into the city where all things
happened as he had predicted."*

Notwithstanding this "joyful entry," they spent ten
months in extreme distress. None of them were known
in Paris except Matthew of France, who in his youth had
studied at the university; and Lawrence very shortly
after was summoned to Rome, where he was present, as
we have seen, before the removal of the Friars from
S. Sixtus. It was not until the August of 1218, nearly
a year after their departure from Prouille, that John de

* From a short notice of blessed Lawrence in Marchese's, "*Diaro
Domenicano*," drawn from ancient writers

Barastre, one of the king's chaplains and a professor of
the university, having been struck by the singular effects
of their preaching, and their patient endurance of so much
poverty and suffering, persuaded his colleagues to grant
them the little church of S. James, then attached to an
hospital for poor strangers, afterwards the most celebrated
house of that order. But besides the missionaries whom
he had already sent from Prouille, Dominic had not been
long in Rome before he began to dispose of some of the
followers who had so soon been gathered there about his
standard. It seems certain that it was whilst still inhabi-
ting S. Sixtus, that John of Navarre (who had returned
with Lawrence from Paris), Brother Bertrand, Brother
Christian, and Peter, a lay brother, were despatched to
lay the first foundation of the order in Bologna. Their
preaching soon attracted general attention ; they are said
to have been the first religious who had ever been heard
to preach publicly in Bologna, and the astonishment and
admiration felt for their eloquence was increased when it
was understood that they were the children of Dominic,
whose name was not unknown to the Bolognese. Two
houses were soon given to them, with the accompanying
grant of a neighbouring church, called Santa Maria della
Mascarella. They were soon after joined by the two
brethren who had returned from Spain and a few others
whom Dominic despatched from Rome ; but they had to
struggle with many difficulties. As soon as they could,
they began to arrange their house into a conventual form,
building a very humble refectory and dormitory ; for it
seems to have been always felt as a first and indispensable
requisite in these early foundations of the order to have
a religious house, in order to carry out their rule in a religious spirit, and this even at a time when the community consisted of no more than four or five persons. That
this was done from a deep conviction of the utility and
necessity of such external observances, and not from a
love of show, or a desire to build great establishments, is
evident if we look at the way in which it was done. " As
well as they could" (we are told in the account of this
Bolognese foundation), " considering the confined space,

they made a dormitory and refectory, with other necessary
offices; their cells were so small, that they were not more
than seven feet long and four feet two inches wide, so that
they could scarce contain a hard and narrow bed and a
few other things; but they were more content with this
poor habitation than if they had possessed the largest and
most magnificent palaces."* Here they led "a life of
angels;" and "so wonderful was their regular observance,
and their continual and fervent prayer; so extraordinary
their poverty in eating, in their beds and clothes, and all
such things, that never had the like been seen before in that
city." They continued to live in this way, without making
much progress, and, in spite of their first favourable reception, enduring many affronts and persecutions, until the
end of the year 1218, when, as we shall see, a fresh impulse
was given to their enterprise by the arrival among them of
one man, the celebrated Reginald of Orleans.

Certainly, if we wish to form an idea of the true spirit
of the order, we cannot do better than dwell on what is
preserved to us concerning the manner of these first foundations. Throughout all of them we shall find the same
characteristics. The great missionary work of preaching
and saving souls was the first thing thought of; everything gave way to that. They were scattered abroad right
and left, as soon as they had given themselves to the work,
for Dominic never departed from the inflexible law which
he had laid down at Prouille:—"We must sow the seed,
and not hoard it up." Doubtless there must often have
been hard sacrifices and struggles with nature in this;
his children were separated from him as soon as they had
learnt to love him; and, to use the expression of blessed
Jordan, in speaking of his departure from Bologna on a
late occasion, "they wept to be so soon taken from their
mother's breast." "But all these things," he adds,
"happened by the will of God. There was something
marvellous in the way in which he was wont to disperse
the brethren here and there through all parts of the
Church of God, in spite of all the representations often
made to him, and without his confidence being once dis

* Michel Pio of Bologna.

quieted by a shadow of hesitation. One might have said he knew beforehand their success, and that the Holy Spirit had revealed it to him; and indeed who would dare to doubt it? He had with him to begin but a small number of brethren, for the most part simple and illiterate, whom he sent through the world by twos and threes; so that the children of the world, who judge according to human prudence, were wont to accuse him of destroying what he had begun, rather than of building up a great edifice. But he accompanied those whom he sent forth with his prayer; and the power of God was granted to them to multiply them."

But though this was the first thought, it was never so followed out as to induce the neglect of the fundamentals of religious observance. The Friars Preachers were to sacrifice all comfort, and all human ties for the work of God; they were to endure poverty, humiliation, and detachment of heart in its most painful form; but one thing they were not to sacrifice, and that was the character of religious, and the habits of regular observance. Whilst they begged their bread, and lived on alms, the first thing on which those alms were expended was the rude and imperfect conversion of their poor dwellings into a religious shape. We feel at once how different such a plan of proceeding is from our modern notions; and the difference is more important than appears at first sight. "Let us have essentials," is the favourite expression of our own day; "let us only do our work; the external forms are of secondary importance." But the language of the saints and the men of faith was rather, "Let us have the religious spirit, for without it our work will be of no avail;" and in their deep and living humility they acknowledged that they were powerless to retain this spirit, made up as it is of prayer and recollection and continual self-restraint, without certain external helps and hindrances which modern theorists feel themselves privileged to despise. Every part of the Dominican rule and constitutions breathes of this principle; whilst the salvation of souls is ever placed before us as the end and object of the order, the formation of the religious man

himself is provided for by regulations of the most astonishing minuteness; and as a part, and an essential part,
of these, there is given us the beautiful ordering of the
religious house.

We do not mean to assert that this necessary connection between the outward form and the inward spirit
is anywhere stated in express terms, for there was not
much talk about theories and general principles among
men in the Middle Ages; yet, perhaps unconsciously to
themselves, they ever acted under a deep prevailing
sense of this sacramental character of our being. They
believed that not in soul alone, but also in body, the
whole nature was to be made subject to Christ; and with
the simplicity of antique wisdom, they condescended to
provide for this by making laws, not only for their work
and their prayer, but even for their houses and their
dress. The religious man was ever to be surrounded by
an atmosphere redolent with sanctity; he was to reflect
a light of holiness cast on him by the very walls of his
dwelling. Nothing, therefore, was neglected by which
they could be invested with this peculiar character.
They were the mould in which souls were insensibly
to receive a shape that separated them from the world.
The amateurs of ecclesiastical architecture tell us that,
in its purest form, no ornament will ever be found
introduced for ornament's sake; there was always a
use and significance in the most fanciful and grotesque
of those elaborate designs. And so in the conventual
house, common and necessary things were not exchanged
for what was fanciful or extraordinary; but a religious
form and colouring was given to the whole. Thus the
man who was being trained to the life of religion was
placed where he saw nothing that did not harmonize
with that one idea. His refectory was as unlike a
dining-room as possible; it was as much a room to
pray in, as to eat in. There, ranged in a single row
behind the simple wooden tables that stood on either
hand, sat the same white robed figures beside whom he
stood in the choir, and with an air scarcely less modest
and devout. At the top was the Prior's seat; there

I

were neither pictures nor ornaments on the wall, only
a large crucifix above that seat, to which all were to bow
on entering; for even in hours of relaxation the religious
man was to be mindful of the sufferings of his Lord.
There was no talking or jesting as in the feasting of the
world, for the refectory was a place of inviolable silence;
but from a little pulpit one of the brethren read aloud
(as we have seen brother Henry represented doing in
the scene of S. Sixtus), that, to use the words of the old
rule of S. Austin, "whilst the body was refreshed, the
soul also might have its proper food." The house was
to be poor and simple, having "no curiosities or notable
superfluities, such as sculpture, pavements, and the like,
save in the church," where some degree of ornament was
allowed to do reverence to the presence of God. The
dormitory too had its own character; the cells were all
alike in size and arrangement, for here all were equal.
They were separate, that every one might be silent and
alone with God; yet partly open, that the watchful eye
of the superior might never be shut out. Even the
dormitory-passage itself had something holy; for it was
ordained, that "to promote piety and devotion to the
Blessed Virgin, the especial Patroness of the order, an
altar with her image should be erected in the dormitory
of every convent," and here the lamp was kept burning
through the night. Each of these places had its own
sweet tradition. Angels, as we have seen, have before
now served in the Dominican refectories; nor, as we
gaze on such a scene, do we feel they were out of place;
and the dormitories have been blessed no less than the
choir with the sweet presence of Mary, who through
those open doors has given her benediction to the
sleeping brethren, and sprinkled them with her dear
maternal hand. Surely these houses were as the gate
of heaven. All about them were holy sentences, preaching from the walls; poverty reigned everywhere, but
clad in the beauty and majesty of that spirit of *order*,
which has been fitly termed, "the music of the eye."
All things were in common, and common things were
made to speak of God; yet there was neither gloom nor

melancholy, but rather a glad and cheerful aspect, tempered
by the pervading tone of silence and recollection; so that
the beholder might well exclaim, "How good and joyful a
thing it is for brethren to dwell together in unity!"

At the risk of being tedious on a subject which may
not perhaps be felt to be of general interest, we would
but suggest how often we must feel, in reading the
earlier devotional writers, that many of their most
charming passages could only have been inspired in a
house of this character. The author of the following
sentences had certainly caught their spirit nowhere but
in a religious refectory: "He that reads words of holy
wisdom to his brother, offers choice wine to the lips of
Jesus.—He that at table gives up to his brother the
better portion, feeds Jesus with the honey of charity. --
*He that during refection reads to his brethren correctly
and distinctly*, serves up a heavenly cup to the guests of
Jesus; but if he reads ill, he takes away the relish of
the food; and if he stammers, he stains the cloth which
covers the table of Jesus.—He that goes to the common
refectory with his brethren to hear spiritual reading,
eateth and drinketh with Jesus and His disciples; and if
he lay up in his heart the word of God which he hears,
he reposes with S. John, during supper, on the breast
of Jesus." Writing in a day, and in a country where
our holy and beautiful houses have long ago been swept
away, and the ideas that raised them have become lost
like historical antiquities, we well know how difficult it
is to realize the true significance of the monastic rules.
They and all their accompaniments are looked on as, at
best, but dreary fancies which have had their day, but
could never stand the test of utility. "To what purpose
is this waste?" is the continual cry of England over the
relics of her old religion. Nevertheless our fathers had
their purpose, and did not deem it waste; and we are
desirous of directing our reader's attention to the
particular care evinced in this matter by the founder
of the Dominican order, because, if we do not mistake,
it illustrates one prominent characteristic of his own

Thomas à Kempis, Garden of Roses, ch. xvii.

I 2

mind, as well as of the institution which was its off-
spring, and which bore and ever retains the likeness of
its father.   The life of a saint like S. Dominic is not
made up alone of journeys and foundations and the dates
of his birth and death; his living soul is to be found in
the rule whose most striking features were the impression of his own hand: and it is not a little remarkable that, together with that free and pliable spirit which
is one of its distinguishing characters, there should be
this invariable adhesion to the externals of monastic and
community life.   The same rule was observed in all the
foundations of the order, and this of course by the
particular direction of its founder; and the fact reveals
more of his mind and feeling than whole volumes of
commentary.   It exhibits him to us in that mixed character of contemplation and action, the union of which is
the basis of the Dominican life: we see him at once,
"the Jacob of preaching and the Israel of contemplation;" and we see also what in his eyes constituted the
essentials of such a life, and the indispensable means for
attaining it.

In Spain blessed Peter had succeeded in founding
a convent at Madrid, of which foundation, however, no
particulars are preserved.   Two of his companions, as we
have seen, returned to rejoin Dominic at Rome, whilst
the third, Suero Gomez, went on to his native country of
Portugal, where he became known to the Infanta Donna
Sancha, who gave him a little solitary oratory on Monte
Sagro, about six miles from Alancher, dedicated to Santa
Maria *ad Nives*.   Here he built a miserably poor convent, or rather hermitage, formed of stones and straw
cemented together with mud, "according to the manner
of those first days of fervour in the order."   He lived in
this singular dwelling alone for some time, but very soon
numbers of all ranks flocked to him to receive the habit
from his hands; and "though they were so many, and
of such character and nobility as might have done
honour to any order in the Church, yet did he not
bate one iota in the rigours which he had learnt from
his holy master, and which were established as laws in the

stitutions." Every day he preached in the city, which soon became renowned for its sanctity of manners. He was a true son of Dominic, "thinking only how to sow the Divine word, and caring nothing for his own body;" and so, little by little, the mud hermitage was frequented like a place of pilgrimage, and the crowds who thronged there to see and hear one whom they reckoned rather as an angel or apostle than as a common man, compelled him to enlarge his dwelling in order to receive them; so that in the following year, when Dominic himself visited the spot, he found a spacious and well-ordered convent, the mother-house of the order in Portugal. Suero was in every way a remarkable man: his adherence to the rule, even in the minutest particular, was almost a proverb. In 1220, when he went to Bologna to attend the first general Chapter, he performed the whole journey on foot, carrying only a stick and his breviary, and so begged his way the entire distance. He became afterwards the first Provincial of Spain.

It only remains for us to add a few words concerning some of the brethren whose names have already been mentioned as having joined the order at Rome. Tancred, the prior of S. Sixtus, had been called in a singular way. He was a German, and a courtier of the Emperor Frederic II. Being at Bologna when the first brethren arrived there, he was one day made sensible of a singular and powerful impression on his soul, urging him to reflect on the great question of eternity in a manner wholly new to him. Disturbed and agitated, he prayed to the Blessed Virgin for direction; and in the night she appeared to him, saying these words: "Go to my household." He awoke in doubt as to their meaning, but in a second dream there appeared to him two men dressed in the habit of the order, the elder of whom addressed him, saying, "Thou hast asked of Mary to be directed in the way of salvation; come with us, and thou shalt find it." In the morning he begged his host to direct him to the nearest church, that he might hear mass. **As he**

Michel Pio

entered, the first figure he met was that of the old man he
had seen in his vision; the church was in fact Santa
Maria, in Mascarella, and the friar was none other than
the Prior Roger. Tancred's mind was soon made up as to
his future course; and, abruptly severing his engagements
with the court he proceeded to Rome, where he took the
habit. Henry of Rome, who has also been mentioned,
entered the order against the earnest remonstrances of
his family. As they expressed a determination to carry
him back by force if he would not return, Dominic sent
him out of Rome, with some companions, by the Via
Nomentana. His relatives pursued him as far as the
banks of the Anio. Seeing there was no chance of escape,
Henry raised his heart to God, and invoked His help
through the merits of His servant Dominic; and the
waters of the little stream suddenly increased to so large
and rapid a torrent, that the horses of his pursuers were
unable to pass. After this he returned undisturbed to
S. Sixtus.

After the sisters had removed to that convent, thirty of
the friars were left there under the government of Tancred,
but in a distinct and separate house; for the convent at
Santa Sabina was not yet able to contain them all. Brother
Otho, also a Roman by birth, was appointed the prior and
director of the nuns.

—⟨⟩—

CHAPTER XVI.

Dominic at Santa Sabina. The Vocation of S. Hyacinth. Reginald of Orleans. The Blessed Virgin bestows on him the habit
of the order.

IT is said that all lives have their chapter of poetry;
if so, the poem of Dominic's life is now opening before
us. No period of his history is at once so rich in
legendary beauty, and so full of ample and delightful
details, as that of his residence at Santa Sabina—the
church which, as we have already said, had been granted

to him; and his brethren by Pope Honorius when they
abandoned S. Sixtus to the nuns of the Trastevere. It
was attached to the palace of the Savelli, of which family
Honorius was a member; and we are told that the
change of residence was particularly welcome to the
friars, inasmuch as the neighborhood was at that time
more thickly populated than that of S. Sixtus, and the
church was one of popular resort. This character has
long since departed from it; and the tide of population,
retreating every year further and further to the west,
has left the Aventine hill once more to its silent and
solitary beauty. Built on the brow of that hill, as it
rises abruptly above the Tiber, the convent of Santa
Sabina stands between the ancient and the modern city.
On one side it looks over a long vista of churches and
palaces, until the golden glow of the horizon above Monte
Mario is cut by the clear sharp outline of that wonderful
dome which rises over the tomb of the apostles. Turn
but your head, and you gaze over a different world.
Heaped all about in fantastic confusion, there are the
arches of gigantic ruins, and the broken walls and
watch-towers standing among the vineyards; and beyond
them is the wide Campagna stretching like a sea into
the dim horizon, spanned by the long lines of the
aqueducts, that seem as though they reached the very
base of those distant mountains which stand round the
Eternal city as "the hills stand about Jerusalem." S.
Sixtus is not far off, you may find your way down to
it through the green and pleasant lanes that wind among
the almond-trees; everything here seems full of Dominic;
and when the story of his life has become dear and familiar
to us, the whole of the Aventine seems consecrated as his
shrine.*

The convent of Santa Sabina remains little altered since the
time of S. Dominic, and many memorials of him are still preserved
within its walls. Among others is an orange-tree said to have been
planted by his hand, which is shown in the quadrangular inclosure.
A few years since, this tree sent out a young and vigorous sucker,
which grew and flourished, and in the course of the year 1834
produced flowers and fruit. It was remarked that this took place
during the noviciate of Père Lacordaire and his companions, to

It was here, then, that the friars removed as soon as the nuns had taken possession of their formcr residence; and they had not long settled in their new convent when some very remarkable additions were made to their numbers. Ivo Odrowatz, the Polish Bishop of Cracow, was at that time in Rome, having in his company his two nephews, Ceslaus and Hyacinth, both of them canons of his cathedral, and men of singular virtue. They had all been present in S. Sixtus on the occasion of the raising of the young Napoleon to life, and when, by means of Cardinal Ugolino, they became personally acquainted with Dominic, the deep impression made on their minds by that scene was increased by his saintly and winning manners. Ivo urged him to send some of his brethren to the northern countries, but the difficulties of the language seemed to offer an insuperable obstacle to this plan; Dominic, however, suggested that were some of his own followers to take the habit, it would be the best way of carrying out his wishes. A few days after this Hyacinth and Ceslaus, with two others, Henry

whom is due the restoration of the French province; and the little incident was hailed as significant of that universal restoration and return to youthful vigour and the beauty of regular discipline whose impulse since that period has been manifested throughout the entire order.

A singular discovery has recently been made within the inclosure of this convent. ' About three months ago" (says Cardinal Wiseman in his lecture on " Rome, Ancient and Modern," delivered January 31, 18 6,) "the good religious wished to make an alteration in their garden, and reduce it more into the English style. They were, of course, their own workmen, and it was not long before their industry was repaid. They met with an opening, into which they entered, and found an ancient Christian hall elegantly painted in arabesque. Having cleared it out, they found an entrance into another chamber. In this way they went forward from room to room; so that when I last heard, about a fortnight ago, they were arrived at the tenth apartment. The discovery has excited immense interest, no suspicion having been entertained of such a monument existing there. One room is covered with names of about the third or fourth century, only one of which had then been deciphered. But this excavation is further important in another way. For the first piece of antiquity discovered was a portion of the wall of Tullius, the early king of Rome; and this recurring at a distance from a portion found, a few years ago, in the Jesuit's neighbouring vineyard, in planting new vines, decides the direction of the wall, and the boundary of the primitive city."

of Moravia, and Herman, a noble German, presented
themselves at Santa Sabina, and, throwing themselves
at the feet of the saint, begged to be allowed to enter
the order. They were joyfully received, and their progress was as rapid as it was extraordinary. Doubtless
in those days of early fervour, the growth of souls planted in a very atmosphere of sanctity was quicker and
more vigorous than now : and we are led to exclaim,
" There were giants in those days," when we find these
four novices, within six months after their first admission,
ready to return to their own country to be the founders
and propagators of the order. They travelled back with
the bishop of Cracow, preaching as they went. Separation, that law of the Dominican institute, was the lot
that awaited them also. Hyacinth and Ceslaus pursued
their way to the north, where they divided the land between them. Ceslaus planted the order in Bohemia,
whilst the apostolate of Hyacinth extended over Russia,
Sweden, Norway, Prussia, and the Northern nations of
Asia. Dominic's old dream of a mission to the Cumans
became realized in the labours of this the greatest of his
sons, and in him the order of Friars Preachers took
possession of half the known world. Henry proceeded
to Styria and Austria, and founded many convents, especially that of Vienna. An account of singular beauty
is left of his death. He fell sick in the convent of
Wratoslavia ; and finding his last hour draw near, he
fixed his eyes on a crucifix before him, and sang sweetly
while he had strength. After a little space he was silent,
yet smiled, and put his hands together, and showed
in his eyes and his whole face a great and inexplicable
joy. Then, after a brief time he spake and said, " The
demons are come, and would fain disturb and trouble my
faith, but I believe in God the Father, and the Son, and
the Holy Ghost ;" and with these words on his lips he
gently expired. Herman, the fourth of this society, was
left at Friesach to govern a convent founded in that
place. He was a man of extraordinary devotion, though
of small learning. In consequence of his simplicity and
ignorance he was often despised and ridiculed by his

companions; and, seeking comfort from God in prayer, he obtained the gift of so much understanding of the holy Scriptures that, without study of any kind, he was enabled to preach not only in German, but also in Latin, with extraordinary eloquence and success.

But another disciple was to be gathered into the order during this same year, whose career, if shorter than any of those we have mentioned, was scarcely less brilliant; and who was destined to exercise a considerable influence over some of the most important of the early foundations. Indeed, there were singular marks of a Providential ordering of things, in what seemed the accidental assembling at Rome that year of so many men whose hearts were ready for the work which was preparing for them there. Among these he of whom we are about to speak was not the least distinguished. Reginald, deacon of the church of Orleans, had come there, in company with the bishop, with the intention of visiting the holy place, and thence passing on in pilgrimage to Jerusalem. He was already known as a profound doctor in canon law, and held the chair of that science in the University of Paris. But brilliant as was his intellect, and the renown which it had procured him, it did not satisfy him; for he had within him something greater than genius, and a thirst which the world's applause could not satiate. Whilst the world of Paris was busy with his fame, there had come upon him a desire to abandon all things for Christ, and to take refuge from popular applause in some state where he could spend his life for the souls of others, while his own should be made a sharer in the very poverty and nakedness of the crucifix. His pilgrimage to Rome and Jerusalem was undertaken under this idea: it formed part of his plan for breaking loose from the ties of his present life, and searching for the better part to which he felt he was called and chosen. The result must be told in the words of blessed Humbert: "He prepared himself for this ministry, therefore, though he knew not in what way he was to carry it out; for he was ignorant that the order of Friars Preachers had as yet been instituted.

Now it chanced that in a confidential discourse with a certain cardinal he opened to him his whole heart on this matter, saying to him that he greatly desired to quit all things in order to go about preaching Jesus Christ in a state of voluntary poverty. Then the cardinal said to him, 'Lo! there is an order just risen up, whose end is to unite the practice of poverty with the office of preaching; and the master of this new order is even now present with us in the city, who also himself preaches the word of God.' Now when Master Reginald heard this, he hastened to seek out the blessed Dominic, and to reveal to him the secret of his soul. Then the sight of the saint, and the graciousness of his words, captivated his heart, and he resolved to enter into the order. But adversity, which proves so many holy projects, failed not in like manner to try his also. He fell sick, so that the physicians despaired even of saving his life. The blessed Dominic, grieving at the thought of losing a child ere as yet he had scarcely enjoyed him, turned himself to the Divine mercy, earnestly imploring God (as he himself has related to the brethren) that He would not take from him a son as yet but hardly born, but at least to prolong his life, if it were but a little while. And even whilst he yet prayed, the Blessed Virgin Mary, Mother of God, and Mistress of the World, accompanied by two young maidens of surpassing beauty, appeared to Master Reginald as he lay awake and parched with a burning fever; and he heard the Queen of Heaven speaking to him, and saying, 'Ask me what thou wilt, and I will give it to thee.' And as he considered within himself, one of the maidens who accompanied the Blessed Virgin suggested to him that he should ask nothing, but should leave it to the will and pleasure of the Queen of Mercy, to the which he right willingly assented. Then she, extending her virginal hand, anointed his eyes, ears, nostrils, mouth, hands, reins, and feet, pronouncing certain words meanwhile appropriate to each anointing. I have heard only those which she spake at the unction of his reins and feet : the first were, 'Let thy reins be girt with the girdle of

chastity;' and the second, 'Let thy feet be shod for
the preaching of the Gospel of Peace.' Then she showed
to him the habit of the Friars Preachers, saying to him,
'Behold the habit of thy order,' and so she disappeared
from his eyes. And at the same time Reginald perceived
that he was cured, having been anointed by the Mother
of Him who has the secrets of salvation and of health.
And the next morning, when Dominic came to him, to
ask him how he fared, he answered that nothing ailed
him, and so told him the vision. Then both together did
render thanks to God, who strikes and heals, who wounds
and who makes whole."

Three days after this Dominic again came to his room,
bringing with him a religious of the Hospitallers of
S. John. And as they sat all three together, the same
scene was repeated in the sight of all. We are told by
some that on her former appearance the Blessed Virgin
had promised this repetition of her previous· visit, and
that Reginald had mentioned this fact to S. Dominic.
He now conjured him and his companions to keep the
whole of the circumstances secret until after his death ;
and he did this out of humility. Dominic complied with
his request ; and in announcing to his brethren his intention of changing the form of their habit, he did not
give the reason which had caused the change until after
Reginald's death. Until this time the habit of the regular canons had continued to be worn by all the brethren ;
it was now changed for that which had been shown by
Mary to Reginald, and which Dominic had himself seen
on the second occasion of her appearance. The linen surplice was laid aside, and in its place was used the long
woollen scapular, which was the particular part of the
habit she was seen holding in her hands. Thenceforward
this has been the distinctive sign of religious profession
among the Friars Preachers; and the words with which
it is accompanied in the ceremony of the giving of the
habit, mark at once its origin, and the reverence with which
its wearers are accustomed to regard it : " Receive the
holy scapular of our order, the most distinguished part of
our Dominican habit, the maternal pledge from heaven

of the love of the Blessed Virgin Mary towards us." This
especial love of Mary for the order of Friars Preachers is
indeed a claim which we do not wonder at their making,
when we consider the many ways in which it has been
evinced. In those early days of the order one of the
popular names by which the brethren were known, was that
of "the Friars of Mary;" a title which reveals to us how
vivid was the devotion which they felt for the Mother
who had clothed them with her own hands; and we shall
find, among the traditions of Santa Sabina, other tales
which show us the singular and tender nature of the protection she gave them.

Some of these traditions, illustrating as they do this
period of Dominic's life, we will give in the following
chapters, together with that sketch of what we may term
his conventual habits, which has been left us by blessed
Jordan and other early writers; and they will probably
render us more familiar with his personal character than
any other portion of his history. Meanwhile Reignald of
Orleans departed for the Holy Land, whence he did not
return until the conclusion of the year.

CHAPTER XVII.

Dominic's Life at Rome.   The rule of the Order.   Description of
his person and appearance.   His prayer, and manner of life.

WHEN Dominic was fairly settled at Santa Sabina, he
saw himself surrounded by a multiplicity of cares and
occupations, any one of which would have demanded the
whole strength and time of an ordinary man. There
was the government of two communities; that of his own
convent, a company of novices gathered from all ranks
and ages, unused to rule and discipline, and who had to
learn the whole science of religion from his lips alone;
while the training of the nuns of S. Sixtus was even a

harder task, for with them there were long habits of
negligence and relaxation to eradicate, before the spirit of
fervour and observance could possibly be infused. How
hard and difficult a thing it was, we may judge, from the
unwearied assiduity with which Dominic laboured at his
task. He visited them daily, instructing them in the
most minute particulars of their rule; and sent to Prouille
for eight of the more experienced religious of that house,
one of whom, Sister Blanche, was appointed prioress.
His long and patient care was not thrown away. Inclosure and the observance of a holy rule produced their
usual marvels, and transformed the undisciplined nuns of
the Trastevere into mirrors of sanctity and grace. These
two undertakings, carried on at the same time, called for
a genius of government which few have ever possessed in
a more remarkable degree than S. Dominic. But within
his soul there lay vast resources, and a certain fullness of
spiritual light which never failed to guide him in the
guidance of others; so at least we are led to affirm if we
contemplate him alone and unaided in his gigantic tasks.
And if we are curious to know the means whereby he
achieved them, we must seek for them in that rule which,
if we mistake not, exhibits to us more of the character of
his mind than we can gather from any other source.
" The Christian perfection which he taught " (to use the
admirable words of Castiglio) " consisted primarily indeed
in the love of God and of our neighbour; but secondarily
and accidentally in that silence and solitude, and in those
fasts, mortifications, disciplines, and ceremonies, which
are the instruments whereby we reach unto that high and
most excellent end." It would seem indeed as if these
" ceremonies " he speaks of formed no insignificant part
of Dominic's great idea of spiritual training. We read of
his " diligent training of the nuns in the rules and ceremonies;" and again S. Hyacinth is said to have become
a perfect master in " all the ordinances and ceremonies of
the order during his short noviciate." And if we examine
the rule itself, we find in it very much of this outward
training so deep and significant in its intention, and so
great in its results. This arose partly from the sagacity

which perceived how large an influence is exerted over
the inner man by the subjugation of his external nature;
partly also from a characteristic feature in Dominic's mind,
the love of order. Whilst wholly free from the narrowness
of mere formalism, his soul yet delighted in that harmony
which is a chief element of perfection; it was as though his
eagle eye had gazed on the ordering of the heavenly courts,
and, drawing from the image pictured on his soul, he strove
to reflect something of their beauty in his convent choirs.
And so, perhaps, those bowings and prostrations of the
white robed ranks, which, when exactly performed, give so
unearthly and beautiful an appearance to the worship of a
religious choir, may, at the same time as it harmonized the
souls of the worshippers into recollection, have been intended
to recall and symbolize those scenes on which doubtless his
own spiritual vision had so often rested, and the repeated
foldings of those many wings, and the casting of the golden
crowns upon the ground.

Let us now see what was the rule of his own life at this
period, and the impression which his intercourse and example left on the minds of those who observed him; and
first we will give the portrait they have delineated of his outward appearance. It must have been very noble, if we may
judge from the description of Sister Cecilia: " He was about
the middle stature, but slightly made; his face was beautiful,
and rather sanguine in its colour; his hair and beard of a
fair and bright hue, and his eyes fine. From his forehead,
and between his brows, there seemed to shine a radiant light
which drew respect and love from them that saw it. He
was always joyous and agreeable, save when moved to compassion by the afflictions of his neighbours. His hands
were long and beautiful, and his voice was clear, noble, and
musical. He was never bald, and he always preserved his
religious crown or tonsure entire, mingled here and there
with a very few white hairs." Next we find an equally
minute and interesting description of his dress. Gerard de
Frachet, who wrote by command of blessed Humbert so
early as 1256, speaks thus: " Everything about the blessed
Dominic breathed of poverty; his habit, shoes, girdle, knife,
books, and all like things. You might see him with his

scapular ever so short, yet did he not care to cover it with
his mantle, even when in the presence of great persons.
He wore the same tunic summer and winter, and it was
very old and patched, and his mantle was of the worst."
It was the same spirit of poverty that induced him never
to have any cell or bed of his own. He slept in the church.
If he came home late at night from his expeditions drenched
with rain, he would send his companions to dry and refresh
themselves, but himself would go as he was to the church.
There his nights were passed in prayer; or if overcome with
fatigue, he would sleep leaning against the altar steps, or
lying on the hard stones. On one part of the pavement of
the church of Santa Sabina there is still preserved an inscription indicating one of the stones as that whereon he
was accustomed to lie at night If, when he travelled, they
stopped where there was no church, he slept anywhere, on
the floor, or on a bench, or sitting in his chair, and always
dressed in his habit as during the day. Thrice every night
he disciplined himself to blood; the first time for himself,
the second for sinners, the third for the souls in purgatory.
His prayer was in a manner continual. There was neither
place nor time in which he did not pray, but especially in
those night hours which he spent alone with God in the
church. Very often they watched him unknown to him,
and saw the way in which, when he believed himself entirely
alone, he poured out all the fervour of his soul without control. After compline, when the others were dismissed to rest, he remained behind, visiting each altar
in turn, and praying for his order and for the world. Sometimes his tears and prayers were so loud as to wake those
who slept near; and though very often these exercises
lasted until the hour of matins, he never failed to
assist at the office with the spirit and alacrity which
were so remarkable in him. He was most zealous for the
exact performance of what he considered the primary
duty of a religious, and would go through the choir from
one to another, calling on them to sing with attention
and devotion, and in a loud and distinct tone. He never
passed an altar whereon was the figure of our Lord
without a profound inclination, to recall the sense of

his own nothingness. He taught his brethren to do the
same by the repetition of the *Gloria*, as a homage to the
Most Holy Trinity, and was wont to quote the words of
Judith, "The prayer of the meek and humble shall ever
please Thee." He was accustomed likewise to pray, in
imitation of Christ in the garden, with his face on the
ground; and in this posture he would remain for a long
space, repeating passages from the Psalms of the most
profound abnegation, and accompanied with many tears, so
that the place was often wet where his face had leaned.

Some of his favourite ejaculations are preserved. "O
God, be merciful to me a sinner!" he was heard exclaiming. "I have sinned, and done amiss." Then, after a
little space, "I am not worthy to behold the height of
heaven, because of the multitude of my iniquities, for
Thy wrath is irritated against me, and I have done evil
in Thy sight. Yea, my soul cleaveth to the ground;
quicken me according to Thy word." To move his disciples
to a similar mode of prayer, he would cite the example of
the holy kings throwing themselves at the feet of Christ,
and would say, "Come let us adore, and fall down before
God, and weep before the Lord who made us." "If you
have no sins of your own to weep for," he would say to the
younger novices, "weep after the example of the prophets
and apostles, and of the Lord Jesus; and grieve for the
sinners who are in the world, that they may be brought
back to penance." Another of his favourite devotions was
to keep his eyes fixed on the crucifix, and meanwhile to
genuflect a hundred times or more; and so he would pass
many hours, uttering ejaculations from the Psalms; or he
would kneel silently, as if unconscious of aught save the
presence of God; and then his face, and his whole person,
and his very gestures, seemed as though he would penetrate
the distance that separated him from his beloved; now
beaming with a holy joy, and now sorrowfully bathed in
tears. At other times he was seen to start up upright
before the altar, with his hands clasped before his breast,
as though holding a book, out of which he had the air of
reading; then he would press them over his eyes, or
raise them above his shoulders. In these postures he

had the appearance of a prophet, now listening or speaking with God and the angels, now thinking within himself on what he had heard. He would stand also with his arms stretched out in the form of a cross, and would so pronounce steadily and at intervals sentences like these:—" O Lord God of my salvation, I have cried before Thee day and night. I have cried unto Thee, O Lord; all the day long have I stretched out my hands to Thee. I have stretched out my hands unto Thee; my soul graspeth to Thee as a land where there is no water." This was when he prayed for any special grace or miracle, as on the raising of Napoleon; and at such times his face breathed an air of indescribable majesty, so that the bystanders remained astonished, without daring to question him of that which they beheld with their own eyes: often in rapture, he was seen raised above the ground; his hands then moved to and fro as though receiving something from God, and he was heard exclaiming, " Hear, O Lord, the voice of my prayer, when I cry unto Thee, and when I hold out my hands to Thy holy temple." As soon as the hours and the grace after dinner were ended, he would retire alone to some secret place, where sitting down and making the sign of the cross, he would meditate on those things which he had heard read. Then taking out that book of the Gospels, which he always carried, he would kiss it reverently and press it to his breast; and those who observed him could mark how, as he read, he would seem to fall into arguments with another, smiling or weeping, beating his breast, or covering his face with his mantle, rising and again sitting and reading, as the passing emotions of his soul sought for expression. Nor must we fail to notice the singular devotion with which he daily celebrated the holy sacrifice of the Mass, which he almost always sang. At the Canon and the Lord's Prayer his tears fell in abundance; those who served his Masses noticed this, and bore witness that it was always the case, and that with a tenderness of devotion which moved them also to weep with him.

Of his manner towards his subjects, we read that its undeviating rule was charity. He was their loving

father, even whilst he knew how to reprove and correct
them. The following are the words of Rodolph of Faenza: "He was ever kind, cheerful, patient, joyful, merciful, and the consoler of his brethren. If he saw any
of them fall into a fault, he would seem as though he
did not at the time observe it, but afterwards, with a
serene countenance, and with gentle speech, would say,
'Brother, you have done wrong, but now repent;' and
so did he bring all to penance. And yet though he
told them of their faults with such humble words, he
could gravely punish them." "He punished transgressors
of the rule with severity, and yet with mercy," says
John of Navarre, "and greatly did he grieve when he
had to punish any." Brother Frugerius, another of the
eye-witnesses of his life, says, "He was rigid himself in
the observation of the rule, and would have it observed
also by others; yet did he punish transgressors with
meekness and sweetnesss. He was kind and patient in
trouble, joyful in adversity, loving, merciful, and the consoler of his brethren, and of all men." To which testimony Brother Paul of Venice adds, "So sweet and
just was he in correction, that none could ever be troubled
by a punishment or reproof received from him." Another of his disciples adds, "Although like a father,
he could use the rod of correction; yet also as a
mother he could give the breast of consolation; and
so sweet and efficacious was his way of comforting
those who came to him, that none went away without
solace and relief. And if he saw his brethren at any
time sad or afflicted, he would call them to him, and
condole with them, and ofttimes deliver them by his
prayers."

We may draw the reader's attention to the striking
similarity of the character sketched by so many different
hands. Indeed, when we read over "the Acts of Bologna, as these evidences for his canonization are entitled,
we are immediately struck with the exact resemblance
they bear to one another. We see, as it were, the
portrait of one whose features were too marked not
to be instantly caught by the painter; they were the

outlines of the most perfect form of charity. And the mother of his charity was a profound humility. " Never did I see a man so humble in all things as was Brother Dominic," is the language of one of the witnesses on his canonization ; " he dispised himself greatly, and counted himself as nothing; he was the example to his brethren in all things—in words, gesture, food, clothing, and manners. He was generous, too, and hospitable, and gladly gave all he had to the poor. He passed his nights without sleep, praying for the sins of others." And blessed Jordan, on the last-mentioned quality (zeal for souls), says, " It was the trait in which he most desired to resemble his Lord." With the beautiful eulogy which is given by this holy writer, the worthy successor and biographer of his great patriarch, we must conclude this chapter : " The goodness of his soul, and the holy fervour with which he acted, were so great, that none could doubt him to be indeed a chosen vessel of honour adorned with precious stones. He had a particular firmness of spirit, always equal, save when moved to pity or compassion. The peace and quietude of his heart was manifest in his gentleness and his cheerful looks. And he was so firm and resolute in the determinations he had taken after just reflection, that never, or almost never, did any succeed in making him change his mind. The holy joy which shone in him had something singular about it, which drew all men's affections to him so soon as they had looked upon his face. He embraced all in great charity, and so was loved of all ; and his rule was to rejoice with them that rejoiced, and to weep with them that wept. He was all love for his neighbour, all pity for the poor ; and the simplicity of his conduct, without a shadow of insincerity either in word or deed, made him dear to all."

With this portrait in our mind, sketched by the very eye-witnesses of his daily life, we shall now proceed to give some of those legends attached to the period of his residence at Rome, to which we have before referred.

CHAPTER XVIII.

ON the second Sunday in Lent, being the first after
the settlement of the nuns at S. Sixtus, Dominic preached
in their church, standing, as it is said, " at the grating,"
that is, so as his discourse should be heard both by them
and by the congregation assembled in the public parts of
the church. As he did so, a possessed woman who was
in the midst of the crowd interrupted the sermon. " Ah,
villain !" cried the demon, speaking through her voice,
" these nuns were once all mine own, and thou hast robbed
me of them all. This soul at least is mine, and thou shalt
not take her from me, for we are seven in number that
have her in our keeping." Then Dominic commanded her
to hold her peace, and making the sign of the cross, he
delivered her from her tormentors in the presence of
all the spectators. A few days after this she came to
him, and, throwing herself at his feet, implored to be
allowed to take his habit. He consented to her request,
and placed her in the convent of S. Sixtus, where he gave
her the name of Amata, or, as we used to call her, Amy :
to signify the love of God displayed in her regard.
She afterwards removed to Bologna, where she died
in the odour of sanctity, and lies buried in the same tomb
with Dominic's two other holy daughters, Cecilia and
Diana, the latter of whom was foundress of the convent of
women in that place.

In speaking of this and other examples of the malice
of the demon, which are narrated in the history of
S. Dominic, we cannot but observe something perhaps
a little distinctive about them. Never do we find one
instance in which Satan was permitted the least power
to vex or trouble him. Never, as with so many other

saints, was he suffered to do him bodily harm, or to
assault him with grievous temptations. The evil one
appears to us always baffled and contemptible, as in the
power of one who is his master, the very Michael among
the saints. Yet though always petty, and as it were
ridiculous, he ceased not in his efforts to thwart and
disturb him, and chiefly directed his malice against the
friars and sisters of S. Sixtus, grievously trying them
by perpetual distraction, as though he hoped thereby at
least to diminish something of the fervour of their devotions. Once indeed he made a more serious attempt
against Dominic's life. One night, as he prayed in the
church of Santa Sabina, a huge stone was hurled at him
by an invisible hand from the upper part of the roof,
which all but grazed his head, and even tore his hood,
but falling without further injury to the saint, was
buried deep in the ground beside him. The noise was
so loud that it awoke several of the friars, who came
in haste to the spot to inquire the cause; they found
the fragments of the broken pavement, and the stone
lying where it fell; but Dominic was kneeling quietly
in prayer, and seemed as if unconscious of what had
happened.

Another story, of a similar character, is told as follows :
" The servant of God, who had neither bed nor cell
of his own, had publicly commanded his children in
chapter, that in order that they might wake the more
promptly, to rise to matins, they should retire to bed at
a certain hour, in which he was strictly obeyed. Now,
as he himself abode before the Lord in the church, the
devil appeared before him in the form of one of the
brethren, and though it was past the prohibited time, yet
did he remain in the church with an air of particular
devotion and modesty. Wherefore the saint, judging
it to be one of the friars, went softly up to him, and
desired him to go to his cell, and sleep with the others.
And the pretended friar inclined his head, in sign of
humble obedience, and went as he was bid; but on each
of the two following nights, he returned at the same hour
and in the same manner. The second time the man **of**

God rose very gently (although, indeed, he had reason to be somewhat angry, seeing he had at table during the day remarked all of the observance of that which had been enjoined), and again desired him to go away. He went; but, as we have said, returned yet a third time. Then, it seemed to the saint that the disobedience and pertinacity of his brother was too great, and he reproved him for the same with some severity; whereat, the devil (who desired nothing else, save to disturb his prayer and stir him unto wrath, and move him to break the silence) gave a loud laugh, and, leaping high into the air, he said, 'At least I have made you break the silence, and moved you to wrath!' But he calmly replied, 'Not so, for I have power to dispense, neither is it blameworthy wrath when I utter reproofs unto the evil-doers.' And the demon, being so answered, was obliged to fly."

On another occasion, as he was by night walking about the convent of S. Sabina, guarding his flock with the vigilance of a good shepherd, he met the enemy in the dormitory, going like a lion seeking whom he might devour; and recognizing him, he said, "Thou evil beast, what doest thou here?" "I do my office," replied the demon, "and attend to my gains." "And what gains dost thou make in the dormitory?" asked the saint. "Gain enough," returned the demon. "I disquiet the friars in many ways: for first, I take the sleep away from those who desire to sleep in order that they may rise promptly for matins; and then I give an excessive heaviness to others, so that when the bell sounds, either from weariness or idleness they do not rise; or, if they rise and go to choir, it is unwillingly, and they say their office without devotion." Then the saint took him to the church, and said, "And what dost thou gain here?" "Much," answered the devil; "I make them come late and leave soon. I fill them with disgusts and distractions, so that they do ill whatsoever they have to do." "And here?" asked Dominic, leading him to the refectory. "Who does not eat too much or too little?" was the reply; "and so they either offend God or injure their health." Then the saint took him to the parlour, where the brethren were allowed to speak with seculars, and to take their recreation. And the devil began maliciously to laugh, and to leap and jump about, as if with enjoyment, and he said, " This place is all mine own; here they laugh and joke, and hear a thousand vain stories ; here they utter idle words, and grumble often at their rule and their superiors ; and whatsoever they gain elsewhere they lose here." And lastly they came to the door of the chapter-room, but there the devil would not enter. He attempted to fly, saying, " This place is a hell to me ; here the friars accuse themselves of their faults, and receive reproof and correction, and absolution. What they have lost in every other place they regain here." And so saying, he disappeared, and Dominic was left greatly wondering at the snares and nets of the tempter ; whereof he afterwards made a long discourse to his brethren, declaring the same unto them, that they should be on their guard.

But if, at the risk of wearying the reader, we have given these instances of the infernal malice, it is time for us to present him with other and more lovely pictures, as they are left us in the relation of Sister Cecilia. The first, as is fitting, shall be of the maternal love of Mary. Before reading it, we must remember that Dominic never had cell or bed of his own, and slept, when he slept at all, in the church or the dormitory. " One night, Dominic having remained in the church to pray, left it at the hour of midnight, and entered the corrider where were the cells of the brethren. When he had finished what he had come to do, he again began to pray at one end of the dormitory, and looking by chance towards the other end, he saw three ladies coming along, of whom the one in the middle appeared the most beautiful and venerable. One of her companions carried a magnificent vessel of water, and the other a sprinkler, which she presented to her mistress, and she sprinkled the brethren, and made over them the sign of the cross. But when she had come to one of the friars, she passed him over without blessing him ; and Dominic having observed who this one was, went before the lady, who was in the middle of the dormitory, near to where the lamp was lit. He fell at her feet, and though he had already recognised her, yet he besought her to tell him who she was. At that time the beautiful and devout anthem of the *Salve Regina* was not sung in the convents of the friars or of the sisters at Rome; it was only recited, kneeling, after compline. The lady who had given the blessing said therefore to Dominic, ' I am she whom you invoke every evening, and when you say ' *Eia ergo advocata nostra,*' I prostrate before my Son for the preservation of this order.' Then the Blessed Dominic inquired who were the two young maidens who accompanied her, and she replied, ' One is Cecilia, and the other Catherine.' And the blessed Dominic asked again why she had passed over one of the brethren without blessing him ; and he was answered, ' Because he was not in a fitting posture ;' and so, having finished her round, and sprinkled the rest of the brethren, she disappeared. Now the Blessed Dominic returned to pray in the place where he was before, and scarcely had he begun to pray when he was wrapt in spirit unto God. And he saw the Lord, with the Blessed Virgin standing on His right hand ; and it seemed to him that our Lady was dressed in a robe of sapphire blue. And, looking about him, he saw religious of every order standing before God ; but of his own he did not see one. Then he began to weep bitterly, and he dared not draw nigh to our Lord, or to His Mother ; but our Lady beckoned him with her hand to approach. Nevertheless, he did not dare to come until our Lord also in His turn had made him a sign to do so. He came therefore, and fell prostrate before them, weeping bitterly. And the Lord commanded him to rise ; and when he was risen, He said to him, ' Why weepest thou thus bitterly ?' And he answered, ' I weep because I see here religious of all orders except mine own.' And the Lord said to him, ' Wouldst thou see thine own ?' And he, trembling, replied, ' Yes, Lord.' Then the Lord placed His hand on the shoulder of the Blessed Virgin, and said to the blessed Dominic, ' I have given thine order to my Mother.' Then He said again, ' And

wouldst thou really see thine order?' And he replied,
' Yea, Lord.' Then the Blessed Virgin opened the
mantle in which she seemed to be dressed, and extending
it before the eyes of Dominic, so that its immensity
covered all the space of the heavenly country, he saw
under its folds a vast multitude of his friars. The
blessed Dominic fell down to thank God and the Blessed
Mary, His Mother, and the vision disappeared, and he
came to himself again, and rang the bell for matins ; and
when matins were ended, he called them all together, and
made them a beautiful discourse on the love and veneration they should bear to the most Blessed Virgin, and
related to them this vision. It was on this occasion that
he ordered his friars, wherever they might sleep, always to
wear a girdle and stockings."

Another story we give in the words of the same writer :
" It was the constant habit of the venerable father to
spend the entire day in gaining souls, either by continual
preaching, or hearing confessions, or in other works of
charity. And in the evening he was accustomed to come
to the sisters, and give them a discourse or a conference
on the duties of the order, in presence of the brethren;
for they had no other master to instruct them. Now,
one evening, he was later than usual in coming, and the
sisters did not think he would come at all, they having
finished their prayers and retired to their cells. But, lo!
suddenly they heard the little bell, which the friars were
used to ring to give the sisters a signal of the approach
of the blessed father. And they all hastened to the
church, where, the grating being opened, they found him
already seated, with the brethren, waiting for them.
Then he said, ' My daughters, I am come from fishing,
and the Lord has this night sent me a great fish.' He
spoke of Brother Gandion, whom he had received into the
order; he was the only son of the Lord Alexander, a
Roman citizen, and a man of consequence. Then he
made them a long discourse, which gave them great consolation. After which, he said, ' It will be well, my
children, if we drink a little.' And calling Brother
Roger, the cellarer, he bade him go and bring a cup and

some wine. And the friar having brought it, the blessed
Dominic desired him to fill the cup to the brim. Then
he blessed it, and drank first, and after him also the other
friars who were present. Now they were of the number
of twenty five, as well clerks as laies; and they drank as
much as they would, yet was not the wine diminished.
When they had all drunk, the blessed Dominic said, 'I
will that my daughters drink also.' And calling Sister
Nubia, he said to her, 'Come in thy turn, and take the
cup, and give all the sisters to drink.' She went therefore, with a companion, and took the cup, full up to the
brim, without a drop having been poured out. And the
prioress drank first and then all the sisters, as much as
they would, the blessed father saying to them, 'Drink
at your ease my daughters.' They were a hundred and
four, and all drank as much as they would; nevertheless
the cup remained full, as though the wine had just been
poured into it; and when it was brought back, it was
still full. This done, the blessed Dominic said, 'The
Lord wills me now to go to Santa Sabina.' But Brother
Tancred, the prior of the brethren, and Odo, the prior of
the sisters, and all the friars, and the prioress with the
sisters, tried to detain him, saying, 'Holy father, it is
near midnight, and it is not expedient for you to go.'
Nevertheless he refused to do as they wished, and said,
'The Lord wills me to depart, and will send His angel
with me.' Then he took for his companions Tancred and
Odo, and set out. And being arrived at the church-door,
in order to depart, behold! according to the words of the
blessed Dominic, a young man of great beauty presented
himself, having a staff in his hand, as if ready for a
journey. Then the blessed Dominic made his companions go on before him, the young man going first, and
he last, and so they came to the door of the church of
Santa Sabina, which they found shut. The young man
leaned against the door, and immediately it opened; he
entered first, then the brethren, and then the blessed
Dominic. And the young man went out, and the door
was shut; and Brother Tancred said, 'Holy father, who
was the young man who came with us?' And he

replied, ' My son, it was an angel of God, whom He sent to guard us. Matins then rang, and the friars descended into the choir, and were surprised to see there the blessed Dominic and his companions, for they knew that the door had been left shut."

Such are some of the legends of these times. Traces of them may yet be found on the spots they have enriched with their associations. Over the door of Santa Sabina, a half-defaced fresco commemorates this visit of the angel; within, is still preserved the fragment of the stone which was hurled at Dominic in prayer; and the spot on the pavement where he was wont to take his scanty rest is marked by a Latin inscription. The room, too, where Hyacinth and Cestaus received the habit is yet shown, and the picture that hangs over the choir tells the story of their singular vocation. This church and convent have never passed from the hands of the order, and the freshness of their association with the legendary history of its founder is unimpaired.

S. Sixtus is no longer inhabited, though still the property of the order. The malaria drove the nuns from its walls so long ago as the year 1575; since which time they have been established at a new house on the Quirinal, bearing the name of "San Dominico e Sisto." But amid its desertion and ruin one monument of its ancient history yet remains. That little chapter-house, on whose threshold the widow's son was raised to life, and where Dominic and the sisters were assembled when the news came of the death of young Napoleon, yet stands; one of the very few buildings in the ancient ecclesiastical style which are yet left in Rome. A fate has awaited this almost solitary relic of Christian architecture which we cannot but trust may have results worthy of its historic interest. In it has been made the first attempt to restore the early ecclesiastical style, which has been seen in Rome for three centuries. It has been recently arranged as a chapel, and its walls decorated with frescoes, in the antique manner, descriptive of the life of Dominic. It may have been nothing but a chance; yet one feels it was a happy and appropriate

eh   a t the first steps towards a revival of Christian
   a d have been made in this monument of the
D   n order, and by the hands of a Dominican
art. [*]

In 1667, the two convents of S. Clement and S. Sixtus
were granted to the Irish Dominicans, driven out of their
own land by the persecutions of the times. "Inasmuch
as our province of Ireland," says Father Anthony Monroy,
the master general of the order at that time, "has
endured long and cruel persecutions, so that its sons have
neither house nor place where they may lay their head,
we judge them worthy of all commisseration." The brief
continues by formally ceding to them these two convents
"as a refuge for the miserable province of Ireland," and
also as a place of education; and they have ever since been
assigned to the brethren of that nation.

Some years ago the church and buildings of S. Sixtus,
were covered with paintings and inscriptions commemo-
rative of the many miracles and incidents of S. Dominic's
life which had taken place within their walls; and the
pulpit was shown from which he was accustomed to
preach and propagate the Rosary among his audience;
but many of these are now destroyed or removed. No
lapse of years or injury of time could however efface the
memory of the saint on that spot, and in the diploma
wherein Clement VIII. restored the locality to the
Dominican order, after it had for some time been alien-
ated, he prefaces the donation by a long summary of
those wonderful events which have made it worthy to be
enumerated among the holy places of Rome. The
diploma is dated the 19th of January, 1611.

* Pere Hyacinth Besson

CHAPTER XIX.

It was in the autumn of 1218 that Dominic prepared
to leave Rome, in order to visit the places where his
children had been forming so many new settlements
during the short year which had passed since their first
dispersion at S. Romain. That memorable year had seen
them well-nigh planted throughout Europe; and he felt
that the rapid increase of the order rendered his own
presence and inspection of the young houses a thing no
longer to be delayed. It is said also, that a feeling of
humility was one of the motives which urged him to leave
Rome; his preaching and the fame of his miracles had
gained him a reputation from which he shrank. We
therefore find him, in the month of October, leaving the
city gates, with his stick, his little bundle, and his copy
of the Gospels, in company with a few of his own religious,
a Franciscan, Brother Albert, soon after joining them on
the road; whilst Hyacinth and his three companions set
out at the same time for the north. Dominic's steps
were directed towards Bologna, where the brethren were
still in their first convent of Santa Maria della Mascharella,
suffering many inconveniences and discouragements, against
which they continued to struggle until the month of
December following, when, as we shall have occasion to
show, the arrival of Reginald of Orleans gave a fresh spirit
to their undertaking.

Dominic's visit lasted but a few days; yet we can
easily imagine the joy and comfort which it diffused
among them. In the course of his stay the same miracle
which had previously taken place in the refectory of S.
Sixtus was here renewed; the brethren were fed by

angels, and the story is told with such a peculiar quaint-
ness by the good Father Ludovico Prelormitano, that we
cannot resist inserting the account in his own words :—
" After that our most sweet father S. Dominic had
finished the arduous business committed to him by the
Holy Pontiff at Rome, he came to Bologna, and lodged
at the Mascharella, where the friars still abode, not being
yet able to go to S. Nicholas by reason of the rooms being
yet too fresh and damp. And it happened on a day that
by reason of the multitude of the brethren, there was no
bread, except a few very little pieces; and the blessing
being given, the good father raised his eyes and his heart
to God; and lo! (*januis clausis*) the doors being closed,
there appeared two beautiful youths with two baskets of
the whitest loaves, and giving one thereof to each friar,
they so multiplied, that abundantly (*ad saturitatem*) there
remained enough for three days. And this great miracle
happened twice at Rome and twice at Bologna. The
second time, after the loaves, they gave a good handful of
dried figs. And the brother who made oath of the same
to Pope Gregory IX. added and said, ' That never had he
eaten better figs.' Then replied the Pontiff, ' Grammercy
to Master Dominic, for they were not gathered in your
garden;' as though he had said, ' God did at that time
produce them.' And the number that ate was more than
a hundred friars. *Benedictus Deus!*" He adds, " I
have been in the cells which the said friars built, and
accurately measured them, in the year 1528; they were
four feet and a half wide, and scarcely six long. And
the rector of Santa Maria Mascharella, my very dear
friend, told me that every year, on the same day when
the holy angels brought the heavenly bread, most sweet
odours were perceived in the space then occupied by the
refectory, which lasted forty hours." The table on which
the miraculous loaves were placed was left at Santa
Maria when the friars removed to S. Nicholas, and was
still to be seen, guarded by iron bars in the wall, at the
time when Father Prelormitano wrote.

But Dominic soon left Bologna: his journey being
now principally directed towards that native country

which he had not seen for sixteen years. Two anecdotes alone are left us of his journey. It is said that on quitting Bologna in company with the Franciscan before mentioned, they were attacked by a fierce dog, who tore the poor friar's habit, so that he was unable to proceed on his journey, and sat down by the wayside in some dispair. Dominic applied a little mud to the rent garment, and this new kind of mending perfectly succeeded; when the mud dried, the habbit was discovered perfectly joined together. The other story is thus amusingly told by Castiglio :—"Having, one day, come to an inn with several companions, the hostess was much disturbed at the small gains she saw herself likely to make by them; for they being many, and eating little, she saw herself put to much trouble to little purpose. Wherefore, as the servants of God conversed together on spiritual things, as was their wont, she went about grumbling and blaspheming, saying all the evil words that came into her mind; and the more the holy father S. Dominic sought to appease her with fair speeches, the more violent she became, not being willing to hear reason. At length, being wholly disturbed by the noise of this virago, S. Dominic spoke to her and said, 'Sister, since you will not leave us in peace for the love of God, I pray Him that He will Himself silence you:' the which words were no sooner uttered than she lost the power of speech, and became entirely dumb. She continued so until the saint's return from Spain, when, as he stopped at the same inn, she threw herself at his feet to implore his pardon, and he restored her to the use of her tongue, with a warning that she should use it in future to the praise of God."

It was probably in the course of this journey that the following incident occurred at the city of Faenza, as given in the ancient memoirs preserved in the convent of that place. Albert, the bishop of Faenza, was so charmed by his eloquence and the fascination of his discourse, that he would not allow him to lodge anywhere but in the episcopal palace. This did not, however, prevent Dominic from pursuing his ordinary course of life;

every night he rose at the hour of matins, as was his
custom, and proceeded to the nearest church to assist at
the divine office. The attendants of the bishop noticed
this; and on watching him secretly to observe how he
was able to leave the palace without rousing the inmates,
they observed two beautiful youths who stood by the
door of his chamber with lighted torches, and so led the
way for him and his companions, every door opening for
them as they went along; and in this way they were
every night conducted in safety to the church of S.
Andrew, whence, after the singing of matins, they returned in like manner. When this was made known
to Albert, he himself watched and became an eye-witness
of the fact; and in consequence he procured the above
church to be the foundation of a convent of the order.
A memorial of the circumstances is preserved in the name
given to the ground lying between the palace and S.
Andrew's church, which is still called "The Angels'
Field."

Doubtless many cities of northern Italy received like
passing visits from Dominic, but no certain traditions
concerning them have been preserved. We can, therefore, but follow him in imagination, as he made his
way over the plains of Lombardy, and crossing the Alps,
found himself once more in the convent of S. Romain
at Toulouse. The number of the brethren was greatly
increased, but their prospects, together with those of the
Church generally in those parts, had received a serious
check by the death of the Count de Montfort, and the
renewed persecutions of the heretics. Dominic remained
a while with them to encourage them, and nominated
Bertrand of Garriga, who had just returned from Paris,
their superior. He then continued his journey to Spain;
and we find that before Christmas he was at Segovia, in
Old Castile. One circumstance occurred on his way
which must not be omitted. The brethren who travelled
in his company, discouraged perhaps by the hardships of
the journey, and yet more by those which they witnessed
in the young houses of Bologna and Toulouse, broke out
into murmurs, and even determined to quit the habit

and return to the world. Some writers tell us that
these religious were not those who came from Italy
with the saint, but some young Castilian novices, who
had been attracted to him by the fame of his eloquence
and miracles, and whose fervour cooled as soon as they
made a closer acquaintance with the austerity of his rule ;
and this seems the more probable conjecture. However
that may be, their discontent was soon discovered by
Dominic : he did his best to deter them from their purpose, but in vain; three only remained with him, the
others, having put their hand to the plough, looked back
and left him. Turning sadly and gently to those who
remained faithful, Dominic addressed them in the words
of our Lord on a like occasion, " Will ye also go
away ? " And the memory of this incident has been
preserved in a touching passage of the Constitution of
the order, introduced at a later period with an evident
allusion to these circumstances. " Whenever novices,"
it is said, " wish to return to the world, we command
all the religious freely to let them go, and to return
them all that they have brought. Nor must they
give them any vexation on this account, after the example of Him, who, when some of his disciples went
back, said to those that remained, ' Will ye also go
away ? ' "* The greater number of those who had
abandoned him, shortly afterwards returned to their
obedience.

The city of Segovia, where Dominic first stopped, is
not far from Osma. His return to those familiar scenes,
so thick with memories of his friendship with the bishop
Diego, and the long quiet years of his early life, before
the call of God had drawn him before the world, must
have been full of singular emotion to a heart so tender
and sensitive as his own. Perhaps it was something of
this natural affection for old scenes, linked to such dear
associations, that made him fix on this neighbourhood
for his first foundation on his return to his native land.
Only a few particulars of his residence there have been
preserved. He lodged at the house of a poor woman, who

* Const. F. F. Præd. d. i. c. 14.

contrived to get possession of a coarse hair shirt which
he had worn, and had laid aside to exchange it for one of
softer material. Some time afterwards, the house
caught fire, and everything was burned excepting the
box which contained this precious relic. This hair shirt
was long preserved among the relics of the monastery of
Valladolid. Dominic had not been long in the city
before he began his usual work of preaching, and with
more than usual success. Possibly the familiar language of his mother-tongue, and the sight of those
Spanish Hills, after the long years of exile and separation,
gave a fresh inspiration to his words. It seemed, too,
that God was willing, that special tokens of His miraculous power should accompany the preaching of His
servants. A long drought had afflicted the country of
Segovia, and reduced the inhabitants to the utmost distress. One day, as they gathered together outside the
walls to hear the preaching, Dominic, after beginning his
discourse, as if suddenly inspired by God, exclaimed,
" Fear nothing, my brethren, but trust in the Divine
mercy. I announce to you good news, for to-day even
God will send you a plentiful rain, and the drought shall
be turned into plenty." And shortly after, his words
were fulfilled, for such torrents of rain fell, that scarcely
could the assembled crowd make their way to their own
homes. The spot where this took place is still shown,
and the event is commemorated by a little chapel which
has been erected in his honour. On another occasion,
as he preached before the senate of the city, he spoke
thus: " You listen to the words of an earthly king, hear
now those of Him who is eternal and divine." One of
the senators took offence at the freedom of his words,
and mounting his horse, rode off, exclaiming contemp-
tuously, "A fine thing, forsooth, for this fellow *cirrla-
tire* to keep you here all day with his fooleries. Truly,
it is time to go home to dinner!" Dominic looked at
him sorrowfully: " He goes as you see," he said,
addressing the others, " but within a year he will be
dead." And, indeed, not many months after this occur-
rence, he was slain on that very spot by his own nephew.

Dominic's preaching soon rendered him very popular
among the Segovians. They were proud of him as a
fellow-countryman, and flocked together to listen to him
wherever he appeared. We are told, that he never spoke
in public without first prostrating in prayer before a little
image, and repeating the versicle, " *Dignare me laudare
te, Virgo sacrata,*" &c. It is with him also, according to
Pere Croiset, that the custom among preachers of intro-
ducing the *Ave Maria* at the beginning of their sermon,
first arose. In a short time a number of new disciples
were gathered together at Segovia, the foundations of a
convent were laid, under the title of the Holy Cross ; and
one of his followers, named Corbolan, and known as
" Blessed Corbolan the Simple," was appointed prior.
This convent was erected close by the little river Eresma,
on whose banks Dominic was accustomed to address the
multitudes. Close by may still be seen another spot
consecrated by the memory of his presence. It is a
grotto deep sunk in the rock, where he was wont nightly
to retire from the presence of his followers, to give himself up to the free exercise of prayer and the presence of
God. Its walls (as those testified who secretly watched
him at these times) were often wet with his tears and
his blood. This grotto now forms part of the chapel
erected in his honour, and is attached to the church. It
was visited by S. Theresa, who declared that she received
such grace and consolation in her visit to it, that she
could have desired to spend her life within its recesses.

As soon as the convent of Segovia was founded,
Dominic proceeded to Madrid. The house already
founded there by Brother Peter, originally sent thither
from Toulouse, was without the town. It was very poor,
having a little church like a hermitage, and a narrow
dormitory without division. Dominic resolved to convert
it into a monastery of women, for he considered its
revenues and endowments unsuitable for his brethren.
This, therefore, was the third convent of sisters which he
founded. Nor was his care of them inferior to that he
had before bestowed on Prouille and S. Sixtus. A beautiful letter is still preserved, in which he addresses them on

their duties and vocation. We give part of it as another
illustration of the importance he evidently attached to
the external aids whereby the strictness and entireness
of the rule should be perfectly observed : " Brother
Dominic, Master of the Preachers, to the Mother Prioress,
and all the convent of the Sisters of Madrid, health
and amendment of life by the grace of God. We
rejoice, and thank God for your spiritual progress, and
that He has drawn you from the mire of the world.
Combat still, my daughters, against your old enemy by
prayer and watching; for he only shall be crowned who
has striven lawfully. Hitherto you have had no house
suitable for following all the rules of our holy religion,
but now there will be no excuse ; since now, thanks
be to God, you have a building where regular observance
can be exactly kept. Therefore I desire that silence
may now be kept in all the places enjoined by the Constitutions, in the choir, refectory, dormitories, and
wherever you live according to rule . . . . . We send
our dear brother Manez, who has laboured so much for
your house, and has fixed you in your holy state, to order
all things as shall seem good to him, to the end that you
may live holily and religiously." The people of Castile
received Dominic with extraordinary marks of honour ;
Castiglio gives us a long list of donations granted by the
magistrates of Madrid to his order, bearing the date of
May, 1219. His sermons were listened to by crowds
of the inhabitants, among whom a wonderful change was
effected in a short time. This change was so great and
striking that, in the words of Castiglio, " he could not be
satisfied with weeping, by reason of the marvellous and
heavenly contentment which he felt for the clear and
manifest favours of God, and his tenderness towards
sinners." The preaching of the Rosary, as usual, was his
great instrument for the conversion of the people, and
many wonders were wrought by the extension of its
devotion. When at length he prepared to return to
Toulouse, the regret of the citizens knew no bounds ;
" for his manner and conversation," continues Castiglio,
" had marvellously captivated the souls of all, and they

felt themselves raised on high to great and heavenly desires, whilst their affections were likewise drawn to him by a singular tenderness." There must, indeed, have been something peculiarly sweet and familiar in the intercourse between him and these converts of Madrid; for we find him writing to the Pope to declare their fervent and devout dispositions; and Honorius in consequence sent a brief conveying his special benediction both to them and the people of Segovia.

Several other convents were already founded in Spain, but it is uncertain what share S. Dominic himself had in their establishment. Nor is there any universal agreement among authors as to the cities he visited, though it seems certain that he made some stay at the Palencia, the scene of his early university life. We have an interesting memorial of this visit in the will of Anthony Sersus, who leaves a certain sum for candles for the confraternity of the Holy Rosary, founded in that place by " the good Dominic of Gusman," as he terms him. We find by this how very early a date may be claimed for the confraternities of the Rosary, which indeed were founded in almost every city wherein Dominic preached, especially in the north of Italy. For still, as he passed from place to place, his work was ever the same: he preached without rest and intermission, and many of the miracles attributed to him by popular tradition are given to us associated with stories of the propagation of the Rosary. His time was never his own : he had long since made it over to God for the salvation of souls: his idea of the vocation of a Friar Preacher was one of utter self-abandonment, and so whenever he appeared abroad he was followed by crowds, attracted by the odour of his sanctity, who were accustomed to say that penance was easy when preached by Master Dominic.

Yet though never alone, his life of prayer was uninterrupted : the secret of that perpetual communion with God in the midst of exterior distractions, so admirably displayed in the life of the great spiritual daughter of his order, S. Catherine of Siena, when she spoke of the interior cell of the heart wherein she

... went to retire, was well known to him; it was there he found his rest; and the habit of prayer had knit his heart so close to God, that nothing had the power of separating him from that centre, "wherein," says Castiglio, "he reposed with a marvellous quiet and tranquillity. Never did he lose that repose of soul which is essential to the spirit of prayer; but in all his labours and disquiets, in the midst of hunger, thirst, fatigue, long journeys, and continued interruption from others, his heart was free and ready to turn to God at all hours, as though it were conscious of none else but Him. Therefore many consolations were granted to him that are not given to others; and of this we have evidence in his words, his zeal, and all his actions, wherein there appeared a certain grace and sweetness of the Holy Ghost, showing how dearly favoured was his soul." In fact S. Dominic was pre-eminently a man of prayer; it is the feature above all others which we find traced upon his life. By night or by day, whether alone or with others, silent in contemplation, or surrounded by the distractions of an active apostolic vocation, his heart never stirred from the true and steady centre it had so early found in God; and in this one fact lay the secret of all the graces which adorned his most beautiful soul. It was the source of that interior tranquillity which fitted him to be called "the rose of patience," as well as of the exterior and gracious sweetness to which all have borne testimony, and which with him was nothing else than the fragrant odour proceeding from the abiding presence of God.

CHAPTER XX.

WE find Dominic once more among the brethren of S. Romain in the April of the year 1219. His presence was joyfully welcomed, nor was it among his own brethren only that his coming always seemed to diffuse a spirit of gladness; if we may credit an ancient writer, " even the Jews and Gentile Saracens, whereof there were so many in Spain, held him dear, all save the heretics, whom he was wont to conquer and silence by his preachings."[*] And now, once more, Toulouse heard for awhile the mighty eloquence of that voice which had before carried the Gospel of peace over the hills and villages of Languedoc. Such crowds flocked to hear him, that S. Romain could not contain them; it was in the cathedral church of S. Stephen, before the bishop and chapter, that he was obliged to deliver his sermons ; and their fruit was an abundance of conversions. Here again he gave himself without reserve to all the labours of his apostolic calling. All day long he was in the city, or in the surrounding country, preaching and instructing the people; and the night was devoted to prayer and sharp austerities. Here, too, all his care and devotion was lavished on his brethren and children, whom he strove to form to sanctity. Prouille and S. Romain were to him now, what S. Sixtus and Santa Sabina had already been at Rome ; and another miracle of the multiplication of the loaves is said to have taken place in the refectory of S. Romain.

Bertrand of Garrega was his companion in the journey to Paris, which next lay before him. Some of his younger disciples were also with him, and it was in

* John of Spain.

tenderness to their weakness and fatigue that he is said to have miraculously changed some water into wine, a trait of his characteristic thoughtfulness and compassion; "for," says Gerard de Frachet, "they had been tenderly nurtured in the world."

On the road they turned aside to visit the sanctuary of Roquemadour, near Cahors, where they spent the night praying in the church of our Lady. The next day, as they journeyed along, singing litanies and reciting the Psalms of the divine office, two German pilgrims overtook them; and being greatly attracted by the devotion of their exterior, they followed closely behind them. When they came to the next village, their new friends begged them to sit down and dine with them; and they continued this conduct for four consecutive days. On the fifth day Dominic said to Bertrand, "Brother Bertrand, it grieves me to reap the temporal things of these pilgrims, without sowing for them spiritual things; let us kneel down and ask God to grant us the understanding of their language, that we may speak to them of Christ." They did so; and during the rest of their journey were able to converse with them without difficulty. When they drew near Paris, they separated, and Dominic charged Bertrand to keep the matter secret till his death, "lest," as he said, "the people should take us for saints, who are but sinners." Jordan of Saxony tells us another anecdote of this journey, which he heard from the lips of Bertrand himself: it was that being threatened with a violent tempest of rain, they walked on in the midst of it, Dominic making the sign of the cross as he went along, and none of them were touched by the floods of water that fell around them. On another occasion, when the rain had drenched them through and through, they stopped for the night at a little village, and his companions went to the inn fire to dry their clothes, whilst Dominic, as usual, made his way to the church, where he spent the night before the altar. In the morning the habits of the others were still wet, but his were perfectly dry; the fire of charity that burned within had communicated itself also to his exterior.

We have already noticed the foundation of the convent of S. Jacques, at Paris; in spite of all obstacles, the numbers of the brethren had now increased to thirty, and the presence of Dominic was a fresh encouragement to them. His stay among them was very short, but marked by two characteristic proceedings. His first act was to " set in order a regular house, with cloisters, domitory, refectory, and cells for study;"* for it must be remembered that the brethren were in close connection with the university, where they followed the course of divinity and philosophy with the other students. Dominic's next step was to carry out his usual law of dispersion; Limoges, Rheims, Poitiers and Orleans, were all chosen as the scenes of new foundations; and the little band, so hardly gathered together, were no sooner collected than they were scattered abroad.

Peter Cellani, the citizen of Marseilles who had been the first benefactor and disciple of the order, was chosen for Limoges; but he ventured to plead his ignorance, and incapacity for preaching. " Go, my son." was the heroic answer of his leader, " go, and fear nothing : twice every day will I remember thee before God, and do not thou doubt. Thou shalt gain many souls to the Lord, and He will be with thee." Peter obeyed with the simplicity so natural to him, and was used afterwards to say that in all his difficulties he had never invoked God and S. Dominic without obtaining relief. Whilst at Paris, Dominic had the happiness of giving the habit to his old friend William of Montferrat, whose two years of study at the university were now complete. His first acquaintance was also made with Jordan of Saxony, then also a young student of the university. The story of his vocation to religion is of singular beauty. He was accustomed every morning to rise for the matin service of Notre Dame; and whatever might be the season or the weather, nothing ever detained him in his bed. One

---

* These words are from Martene's history, and are an additional evidence of what we have before alluded to as one of the primary conditions of a religious community, according to the system of S. Dominic; namely, the " *regular house.*"

morning, fearing he was late, he left his lodging in great haste, and hurried to the church-door, which he found shut, for the hour was still early. As he stood waiting to enter, a beggar solicited an alms, and Jordan felt about him for his purse, but in haste he had left it in his room, and he had nothing to give. Sooner, however, than refuse an alms for the love of God, he stripped off a rich belt mounted in silver, which he wore after the fashion of the times, and gave it to the poor man. As he entered the church, and knelt for a moment before the great crucifix, he saw the same belt hanging round the neck of the figure, and at that moment a voice within him called him powerfully to the closer service of God. This call, and the desires to which it gave rise, pursued him without rest, and when he heard of the fame of Dominic, he resolved to lay the whole state of his soul before him. His counsel and direction restored his peace; but he did not take the habit until Reginald of Orleans finally won him to the order by his eloquence.

Another interesting incident of Dominic's visit to Paris, as connected with the history of the order in our own island, is his interview with Alexander II., king of Scotland. This monarch was then at the French capital for the purpose of renewing the ancient alliance of his crown with the royal house of France. The Princess Blanche, mother to St. Louis, had a particular esteem for S. Dominic, and often invited him to her court, and there probably the Scottish king first met with the Patriarch of the Friars Preachers. We know nothing of the particulars of their interview; but we are assured that he eagerly pressed the saint to send some of his brethren to Scotland, and promised them his fatherly and royal protection. At what exact period this request was granted seems a little doubtful;* but it is certain that Alexander did build several convents for the fathers in his kingdom, and always bore a singular love to the order. Eight religious were sent into Scotland, headed by one Father Clement, afterwards bishop of Dublin; and no less than

---

* The Melrose Chronicle assigns the year 1230 as the earliest date of the establishment of the order in Scotland.

eight monasteries were founded in that country during the
the reign of this prince.

The period of his short visit being expired, Dominic
once more took the road to Italy, accompanied only by
William de Montferrat, and a lay brother who had come
with him from Spain. All these long journeys were performed on foot, in the fashion of poor pilgrims ; and their
rapidity, and the short rest he allowed himself, fill us
with admiration for the energy and courage which they
evince. His joyous and manly temperament of spirit
bore him on in spite of all fatigues and dangers, and in
those days foot-travelling over wild and uncultivated
countries must have been plentiful in both. Passing
through Burgundy, he arrived at Chatillon on the Seine,
where he was charitably lodged by a poor ecclesiastic ;
but Dominic richly repaid his kindness, for whilst he was
yet in the house, the news was brought him that his host's
nephew had fallen from a high roof, and was being brought
home dead. Dominic went to meet him, and restored him
to his parents alive and well. Other miracles of healing
also marked his stay in the place, from whence he proceeded
on to Avignon, where a little trace of his sojourn may
yet be seen in a well, bearing an inscription to the effect
that in 1219 the founder of the Friars Preachers blessed
this water, which has since restored health to many sick
persons.

All Dominic's companions were not quite such good
travellers as himself. We find that as they were making
their way through the passes of the Lombard Alps, the
strength and courage of poor Brother John, the Spanish
lay brother, entirely failed him: overcome with hunger
and fatigue, he sat down, unable to proceed further. The
good father said to him, "What is the matter, my son,
that you stop thus?" And he replied, "Because, father,
I am dying of hunger." "Take courage, my son," said
the saint, "yet a little further, and we shall find some
place in which we may rest." But as Brother John
replied again that he was utterly unable to proceed any
further, Dominic had recourse to his usual expedient of
prayer. Then he bade him go to a spot he pointed out,

and take up what he should find there. The poor brother
dragged himself to the place indicated, and found a loaf of
exquisite whiteness, which, by the saint's orders, he ate,
and felt his strength restored. Then, having asked him if
he were revived, Dominic bade him take the remains of the
soft loaf to the place where he found it; and having done
this, they continued their route. As they went on, the
marvel of the thing seemed to strike the brother for the
first time. "Who put the loaf there?" he said; "I was
surely beside myself to take it so quietly! Holy father,
tell me whence did that loaf come?" "Then," says the
old writer, Gerard de Frachet, who has related this story,
"this true lover of humility replied: 'My son, have you
not eaten as much as you needed?' And he said, 'Yes.'
'Since, then,' replied the saint, 'you have eaten enough,
give thanks to God, and trouble not yourself about the
rest.'"

And now Dominic was once more on the Italian soil,
which thenceforth he never quitted to the day of his death.
It was the summer of 1219; only eight months had
elapsed since he had quitted Rome, and within that space
he had spread his order through the whole extent of Spain
and France. His road was literally marked by new foundations; we may trace it on the map by the convents that
date their origin from this time. Asti, Bergamo, and
Milan, all received him with marks of honour; at Bergamo
he was detained by a severe illness, which even compelled
him to discontinue his abstinence and fasting—a fact
noticed as almost unexampled in his life. At Milan he
was welcomed as the messenger of God; the canon of S.
Nazaire, in particular, received him with singular marks of
affection, and three celebrated professors, all citizens of that
place, received his habit. In company with these new
brethren he set out for Bologna, where he arrived about
the month of August; but it is time for us to give some
brief account of the progress of that convent since the
period of his last visit to it in the preceding year.

CHAPTER XXI.

The Convent of Bologna. Effects of Reginald's preaching and government. Fervour of the Community of S. Nicholas. Conversion of Fathers Roland and Moneta. Dispersion of the brethren through the cities of Northern Italy. Reginald's novices. Robaldo. Bonviso of Placentia. Stephen of Spain. Rodolph of Faenza. Reginald is sent to Paris. Jordan joins the Order. Reginald's success—and death.

THE progress of the brethren of Bologna at their little convent of La Mascharella had been slow, and their difficulties and discouragements very great, up to the time of the arrival amongst them of Reginald of Orleans. As soon as he returned from the Holy Land, he set out for Bologna, according to his previous agreement with S. Dominic, and arrived there on the 21st of December, 1218. His presence caused an immediate change in the position of the friars; he held the authority of vicar-general in Dominic's absence, and his extraordinary powers of government, added to the brilliancy of that eloquence which so remarkably distinguished him, infused a fresh spirit into the community, whilst crowds of those who had before treated them with contempt now crowded about their church in hopes of catching the words of the celebrated preacher. There was a certain vehemence of spirit about Reginald that carried all before him; very soon the church was too small to contain his audience, and he was compelled to preach in the streets and public piazzas; the people came from all the surrounding towns and country to hear him, and the age of the apostles seemed to have returned. The fire of his words produced an astonishing effect on the hearts of all who listened; and whilst a general change of manners was observed among all ranks, a vast number were kindled with a holy and impetuous enthusiasm, and feeling the call of God in their hearts, they turned their backs on the world, and early displayed the habit of religion. "He was filled with a burning and vehement eloquence," says Brother Jordan, "which kindled the hearts of his hearers, as though with a lighted torch." Within six months Reginald received more than a hundred persons into the order; among them were several of the most distinguished doctors and students of the university; and it came to be a common saying, that it was scarce safe to go and hear Master Reginald, if you did not wish to take the friar's habit

This rapid increase of the brethren soon rendered their habitation too small for them. Early in the spring of 1219, they removed to the church and convent of S. Nicholas delle Vigne, situated without the walls. Many miraculous signs had betokened the future sanctity of this place; angels had been heard singing over it by those who worked in the vineyards; and a kind of universal tradition had pointed it out as some day to be a place of prayer and pilgrimage. The life led within its walls, under the government of Blessed Reginald, was a worthy fulfilment of these auguries. It was the strictest and most fervent realization of the rule of Dominic which has ever been seen. Many of the brethren closely imitated him in their nightly watchings and disciplines, and in the devotions which were dear and peculiar to himself. At no hour of day or night could you enter the church without seeing some of the friars engaged in fervent prayer. After compline they all visited the altar, after the manner of their holy founder; and the sight of their devotion, as they bathed the ground with their tears, filled the by-standers with wonder. After singing matins very few returned to bed; most of them spent the night in prayer or study, and all confessed before celebrating the Holy Sacrifice. Their devotion to the Mother of God was of the tenderest kind. Twice every day they visited her altar, after matins and again at compline, walking round it three times, as they sang canticles in her honour, and recommended themselves and their order to her love and protection. They held it a matter of conscience never to

eat till they had first announced the word of God to some
soul. They also served in the hospitals of the city,
adding the corporal to the spiritual works of mercy; and
in spite of the excessive austerity of their lives, it is said
such was the joy of their hearts, shining out in their
countenances, that they seemed none other than angels
in the habit of men. The strict observance of the rule
of silence practised among them is illustrated by the
following anecdote. One night a friar, being in prayer
in the choir, was seized by some invisible hand, and
dragged violently about the church, so that he cried aloud
for help. These disturbances, arising from diabolic
malice, were very frequent in the beginning of the order;
and at the sound of the cry more than thirty brethren,
guessing the cause, ran into the church and endeavoured
to assist the sufferer, but in vain; they too were roughly
handled, and, like him, dragged and thrown about without pity. At length Reginald himself appeared, and,
taking the unfortunate friar to the altar of S. Nicholas,
he delivered him from his tormentor. And all this while,
in spite of the alarm and horror of the circumstances,
not one of those present, who amounted in all to a considerable number, ventured to speak a single word, or so
much as to utter a sound. The first cry of the vexed
brother was the only one uttered during the whole of
that night.

This admirable discipline was certainly attained and
preserved by the practice of a somewhat rigid severity;
yet its very sharpness attests the perfection which must
have been reached by those who could have inflicted or
accepted it. In the following anecdote, as given by
Gerard de Frachet, the supernatural and passionless self-
command exhibited by the chief actor, robs the story of
that austere character which might make an ordinary
reader shrink, and clothes it with a wonderful dignity and
sublimity. A lay brother had committed a slight in-
fringement of the law of poverty, and on conviction of
his offence, refused to accept the penalty imposed.
Reginald perceived the rising spirit of insubordination,
and at once prepared to extinguish it. Causing the

delinquent to bare his shoulders, he raised his eyes
to heaven, bathed in tears, and calmly and gently, as
though presiding in choir, pronounced the following
prayer:—"O Lord Jesus Christ, who gavest to thy
servant Benedict the power to expel the devil from the
bodies of his monks through the rod of discipline, grant
me the grace to overcome the temptation of this poor
brother through the same means. Who livest and
reignest, with the Father and the Holy Spirit, for ever
and ever, Amen." Then he struck him so sharply that
the brethren were moved to tears, but the penitent was
reclaimed, nor did he ever again relapse into a similar
fault. This sort of chastisement was a very ordinary
means which he used to deliver them from the assaults of
the devil; yet we should err if we attributed to him a
harsh or tyrannical spirit. It was a severity wholly
compatible with the sweetness which formed a peculiarity
of his character; for the very tenderness of his love
towards his children was the cause of that severity he
showed against the enemy of their souls. They certainly
never looked on it in any other light, for he was beloved
as a father, and the fame of his strict discipline did not
keep multitudes from embracing it as their surest guide
to heaven.

The first who joined the order after the arrival of
Reginald, was Roland of Cremona, the public Reader of
Philosophy at the University. His coming was most opportune, for the brethren were then still suffering from the
old spirit of discouragement; and in spite of the presence
of Reginald among them, some had even resolved on
quitting the order. They were assembled in Chapter,
engaged in earnest and sorrowful conference, when the
door suddenly opened, and Roland appeared among
them and impetuously demanded the habit. Reginald,
yielding to a sudden inspiration, took off his own
scapular and flang it over his shoulders. The incident
seemed to restore the spirit and courage of the whole
assembly, and the fame of Roland's conversion was the
means of inducing many of his former companions to take
a similar step. Another remarkable conversion was that

of Brother Moneta, also a professor of the University,
but a man who, until the coming of Reginald, had been
wont to ridicule all religion, and to live without any of
its restraints.   Hearing of the wonderful effects of the
new preacher's eloquence, he feared to expose himself to
its influence, and kept away.   One day, however, being
the feast of S. Stephen, some of the scholars endeavoured
to carry him with them to hear the preaching.   Not
liking to refuse, and yet unwilling to comply, Moneta
proposed that they should first hear Mass at S. Procolus.
They went, and stayed during three Masses, till, unable
to delay longer, Moneta was obliged to accompany the
others to Santa Maria, where Reginald was then delivering his sermon.   The doors were so crowded that
they could not enter, and Moneta remained standing on
the threshold.   But as he stood there he could command a
view of the whole scene, and every word reached his ear.
A dense mass of people filled the church, yet not a sound
broke the words of the preacher.   He was speaking on the
words of S. Stephen, the saint of the day: "Behold, I see
heaven open, and Jesus standing at the right hand of
God."   "Heaven is open to-day also," he exclaimed; "the
door is ever open to him who is willing to enter.   Why do
you delay?   Why do you linger on the threshold?   What
blindness, what negligence is this!   The heavens are
still open!"   And lo! as he listened, Moneta's heart was
changed and conquered.   As Reginald came down from
the pulpit, he was met by his new penitent, who abandoned
himself to his direction, and after remaining in the world
under probation for a year, he was received to the habit,
and became himself the founder of several convents.
His after holiness equalled the irregularity of his former
life.   He died full of years and of merit, and, it is said,
blind from his constant weeping.   It was in his cell
that the great patriarch breathed his last, as we shall
hereafter relate.

Such was the position of the community of Bologna,
when Dominic again appeared among them.   His first
act was to make a renunciation of certain endowments
which had been made over to the convent by a citizen of

the p... Dominic tore the contract in pieces with his
own hands, declaring they would rather beg their bread
than depart from their law of poverty. His next step
was one which perhaps a little moderated the joy caused
by his presence; it was another dispersion of the society
so newly gathered together. Religious were sent to every
one of the towns where, as he passed through on his late
journey, he had prepared the way for their reception;
and in a few weeks, Milan, Bergamo, Asti, Verona, Florence, Brescia, Faenza, Placenza, and other cities of Tuscany
and Lombardy, received little companies of the new apostles.
There was, doubtless, a reason for this very extensive dispersion of the order throughout the north of Italy, it may
be found in the fact that that country was at the time
overrun by the self-same destructive heresy of the Manicheans
which had produced such desolating effects in France. This
was the great enemy against which the Order of Friars
Preachers had been raised to combat; and wherever it
showed its head, Dominic knew that he and his faithful
soldiers had a call to follow. If the community of Bologna
was greatly reduced by these colonies sent to other cities,
its numbers were soon made up by fresh acquisitions.
Among those clothed by the holy father was Brother
Robaldo, who afterwards became distinguished for his success against the heretics in the city of Milan. A somewhat
amusing story is told of him when preaching there. The
Manicheans then filled the city in great numbers, and
treated the Catholic missionaries with the utmost insolence.
As Robaldo was one day in prayer before the high altar of
the church, a band of these miscreants determined to divert
themselves at his expense, and sent one of their number in
to practise a joke upon him. "Father," said the heretic,
"I well know you are a man of God, and able to obtain
whatever you wish by prayer; I pray you, therefore, to
make over me the sign of the cross, for I suffer from a
great fever, and I would fain receive my cure from your
hand." Robaldo knew well the malice of his enemy, and
replied, "My son, if you have this fever, I pray God to
deliver you; if you have it not, but are speaking lies, I
pray Him to send it to you as a chastisement." The man

instantly felt the approach of the malady he had feigned, and cried, impatiently, "Sign me with the cross, I say, sign me; it is not your custom to send curses upon men, but cures." But Robaldo replied again, "What I have said, I have said; if you have it, may He deliver you: if not, you will surely have it." Meanwhile, the others stood at the door, laughing to see the saint, as they thought, made a fool of; but their merriment was soon silenced, when they saw their companion return to them with every symptom of the fever he had before pretended. The result of these circumstances was his own conversion, and that of his entire family; and Robaldo, on his sincere penitence, restored him to health, and received him and all his children into the communion of the church.

Bonviso of Placentia, was another of the novices clothed at Bologna by the great patriarch. Before he was professed he was sent to preach in his own country, and very unwillingly he went, for his humility made him fear lest he should fail, and bring disgrace on the order. Dominic, however, encouraged him, and said, "God's words will be in your mouth, my son; go without fear, and do my will:" and Bonviso never felt afterwards any difficulty in preaching. He was one of those who gave their evidence on the canonization of the saint, and says that so long as he knew him he never slept save on benches or on the ground, and never in any particular place; but sometimes in the church, sometimes in the dormitory, and often in the burial-place of the convent. Stephen of Spain was another of the new disciples of the order; his conversion was remarkable. He has himself described it, being at the time a student at Bologna. "Whilst I was there," he says, "Master Dominic arrived and preached to the students and others, and I went to confession to him, and I thought he loved me. One evening, I was sitting down to supper with my companions, when two of the friars came to me, and said, 'Master Dominic is asking for you,' and I replied that I would come as soon as I had supped. But they repeating that he expected me at once, I rose, and, leaving everything as it was, I came to S. Nicholas, where I found Master Dominic in the midst of a number of the friars.

He turned to them, and said, 'Show him how to make the prostration,' and they having shown me how to do it, I made it, and he instantly gave me the habit of a friar preacher. I have never thought of this without astonishment, reflecting by what instinct he could thus have called and clothed me, for I had never spoken to him of the matter; wherefore I doubt not he acted by some divine revelation." Stephen was another of the witnessess on the canonization, whose evidence is preserved among the other "Acts of Bologna."

Another very distinguished member of the family of Bologna was Rodolph of Faenza, whom we notice here, though he entered the order at an earlier period. Some affirm that he acted as confessor to S. Dominic, and it is said that the saint, being at one period afflicted on account of the withdrawl of some who had at first given themselves to God, Rodolph was granted a vision, wherein he saw our Lord and His Blessed Mother, who laid their hands on his head and comforted him; after which they led him out to the shores of the river, and showed him a great ship as it were, laden with brethren dressed in the habit, and said to him, "Seest thou all these, Brother Rodolph! They are all of thy order, and are going forth to fill and replenish the world." Rodolph acted as procurator to the convent; and on one occasion, he made some trifling addition to the two dishes allowed by the rule; this greately displeased Dominic, who himself never tasted but one; and calling the procurator to his side, he whispered, "Why do you seek to bribe the brothers with these pittances?" And yet we are assured the addition to their ordinary fare was of the plainest kind. "Dominic's own dinner," adds Rodolph, "was so spare, and so quickly finished, that often, as he waited whilst the others despatched their meal, he fell asleep for weariness, after his long vigils."

Such were some of the brethren of the convent of S. Nicholas. Its reputation for sanctity came to be so great that men spoke of it as a kind of harbour of salvation; as may be illustrated by the following beautiful story which is given us by Taegius and others. There was a certain

cleric in Bologna of great learning, but devoted to worldly
vanity, and to other than a holy life. Now, one night he
seemed suddenly to be in the midst of a vast field, and
above him the sky was covered with clouds, and rain fell
in great abundance, and there was a terrible tempest.
He, therefore, desiring to escape from the hail and lightning, looked all around him to see if by any means he
might find a place of shelter, but he found none. Then
at the last he perceived a small house, and going to it
he knocked, for the door was fast shut. And a voice
spoke to him from within saying, "What wantest thou?"
And he said "A night's lodging, because of the great storm
that is raging." But the keeper of the house answered
him, saying, "I am Justice, and this is my house; but
thou canst not enter here, for thou art not just." Then he
went away sad, and presently he came to a second house,
and he knocked there likewise; and the keeper answered
and said, "I am Peace, but there is no peace for the
wicked, but only to them of good will. Nevertheless, because my thoughts are thoughts of peace, and not of affliction, therefore I will counsel thee for what thou shalt do.
A little way from hence dwelleth my sister, Mercy, who
ever helpeth the afflicted : go, therefore, to her, and do even
as she shall command thee." So he, continuing on his way,
came to the door of mercy, and she said to him, "If thou
wouldst save thyself from this tempest, go to the convent
of S. Nicholas where dwell the Friars Preachers; there
thou shalt find the food of doctrine, the ass of simplicity,
the ox of discretion; Mary who will illuminate, Joseph
who will make perfect, and Jesus who will save thee." And
he, coming to himself, and thinking well on the words of
Mercy, went quickly and with great devotion received the
holy habit.

The great talents and success of Blessed Reginald
determined Dominic to remove him to Paris, in the hopes
that he would do as much for the convent there established as he had done for that of Bologna. His departure
was a severe grief to his brethren; they wept as though
torn from the arms of their mother; but the expectations
of their founder were fully realized in the short but

brilliant career which awaited Reginald in the French
capital. That marvellous eloquence, whose vehemence
was so irresistible, while at the same time so far removed
from mere human impetuosity, soon drew all to hear
him. When he preached, the streets were deserted; his
holy life, too, so corresponded to his words, that men
looked on him as an angel of God. "All judged him to
be one come down from heaven," says an old writer;
and indeed the students and citizens of Paris were best
able to appreciate the worth of one whose sacrifice to the
cause of religion they had witnessed with their own eyes.
Matthew of France, the superior of the convent of S. James,
who had himself been a student at Paris in former years,
when Reginald was professor in the same university,
asked him once how he, who had been used to so luxurious and brilliant a life in the world, had found it
possible to persevere in the severe discipline of their order.
Reginald cast his eyes humbly to the ground. "Truly,
father," he said, "I do not think to merit anything for
that before the tribunal of God. He has given me so
much consolation in my soul, that the rigours of which
you speak have become very sweet and easy." And this,
indeed, appeared in all he did: for whilst he was constantly
distinguished for the exceeding austerity of his life, he did
all things with such a ready and joyful spirit that he
taught men the sweetness of the Cross by the very light-
ness with which he bore it.

Among the disciples whom he drew into the order, and
who received the habit at his hands, was Jordan of
Saxony. We have already spoken of his first vocation to
religion, but he did not finally determine on taking the
habit until overcome by the persuasions of Reginald.
He brought with him a near and dear friend, Henry of
Cologne, then canon of Utrecht. "A man," he says,
"whom I loved in Christ, with an affection I never gave
to any other; a vessel of perfection and honour, so that
I remember not in all my life to have seen a more
gracious creature." They lodged in the same house, and
followed their studies together; and Jordan, whose mind
was always full of the thoughts of that vocation which

he himself had not as yet obeyed, often spoke of it to his friend, and endeavored to persuade him to form a similar determination. Henry constantly rejected the idea; Jordan as constantly persevered in his arguments and persuasions. He has left us an account of the result, given in his most beautiful style:—"I made him go to Blessed Reginald to confession, and when he came back, opening the prophet Isaiah by way of taking counsel, I fell on the following passage:—'The Lord made me to hear His voice, and I did not resist him: I went not back.' And as I interpreted the passage, which answered so well to the state of my own heart, we saw a little further on the words, 'Let us keep together,' which, as it were, warned us not to separate from one another, but to consecrate our lives to the same object." "Where are now those words 'Let us keep together?'" wrote Henry some years after, in a letter to his friend. "You are at Bologna, and I at Cologne!" But this was the Dominican law of dispersion. A vision completed the conquest of Henry. He saw Christ sitting in judgment, and one by his side cried to him, and said:—"You who stand there, what have you ever abandoned for God?" Filled with trouble at this saying, his soul was torn by a short and agonizing struggle. He desired, yet he could not resolve on the sacrifice. At length, he sought Reginald, and, yielding to the powerful impulse with which God was drawing his heart in spite of himself, he made his vows in his hands. When he returned to Jordan, "I saw," says the latter, "his angelic countenance bathed in tears, and I asked where he had been; he answered, 'I have made a vow to God, and I will perform it.'" They were both clothed together at the close of Lent; but a singular revelation had previously declared to Jordan the death of Reginald, and something of his own future destiny in the order. On the night that blessed man departed to God, towards the commencement of the month of February, he saw in his sleep a clear and sparkling fountain suddenly spring up in the church of S. James, and as suddenly fail; and as he grieved, understanding the vision to predict the untimely death of Reginald, a clear stream of water took the place of the fountain, and flowed on in immense waves till it filled the world. It was a fit emblem of his own future career, so abundant in its fecundity that he is said to have clothed a thousand novices with his own hand.

Among Reginald's disciples, during his life at Paris, may also be mentioned, Robert Biliber Kilward, an Englishman, who afterwards became archbishop of Canterbury under Edward I., and cardinal of the Roman Church. He was reckoned one of the greatest theologians of his age, as well as a distinguished minister of state; yet in all his dignities he never laid aside his religious dress or character, made his journeys on foot, and lived in the utmost simplicity of holy poverty, reckoning his profession, as a friar preacher, the greatest of all dignities lavished on him by fortune.

Reginald's death took place in the early part of the March of 1220. When the physicians declared the hopelessness of his case, Matthew of France came to announce their decision to him, and to propose that he should receive the sacrament of Extreme Unction: "I do not fear the assault of death," he replied, "since the blessed hands of Mary herself anointed me at Rome. Nevertheless, because I desire not to make light of the Church's sacraments, I will receive it, and humbly ask that it may be given to me." His body was laid in the church of Sainte Marie-des-Champs, and though he has never been solemnly beatified, the veneration which was paid him may be gathered from the prayers and hymns in his honour which may be found in the ancient office-books of the order. He was undoubtedly one of its greatest men, to whom there has hardly been done sufficient justice. In him might be seen the rare union of human genius and heroic sanctity; and even when the supernatural element had taken possession of every capacity of his soul, it consecrated them without destroying any of his fervour and richness of imagination, or the force and impetuosity by which it manifested itself in his preaching, and which gave him such a magical power over the hearts of his hearers. These dazzling gifts once placed the world at his feet, but he was happy above so many of his fellows, in that he made no other use of its homage and its smiles than to offer them to God. None, perhaps, ever made a nobler sacrifice, or felt that it cost him less ; and he may stand to all ages an example of the rarest of all the miracles of grace, a soul of consecrated genius.

The spirit of a saint may be said to multiply itself, and to survive in his disciples ; and in the distinctive graces exhibited to us in them we have another means of estimating the character of their founder, besides what is afforded us by the study of his own life. Or rather we might say the truest judgment will be formed by a comparison of the founder and his disciples; and when we find any one trait of the former caught up and repeated over and over again in those who came after him, and whose supernatural life was formed on the model of his own, we may safely conclude that the similarity is no accident, but the result of some great principle which had struck deep root in his soul, and spread its branches far and wide over his followers. Now if this be so, we can scarcely fail to be struck with one peculiarity in the history of these early companions of Dominic which will surprise us, if we have any share in the popular prejudice which attaches to his name. We might have expected, along with much zeal and fervour, to have found some traces of that stern fanaticism which is attributed to him and his order, betraying itself like a hereditary malady in the ranks of the Friars Preachers. But as we search for illustrations of bigotry or gloom, or of a fierce and bloody vindictiveness, we lose ourselves, as it were, in a garden of sweetness. Gathered from all states of life— knights, courtiers, professors, men of the world, peni- tents, and saints—the novices of Dominic, so soon as his spirit has breathed over them, display to our gaze amid many varieties, one trait of which has the indescribable peculiarity of a family likeness. It is sweetness : that quality of which it is said, in the Book of Ecclesiasticus, "Accomplish your works with sweetness, and you shall

draw the love and esteem of men." We see i first in the
great founder himself, of whom it is said, "None did ever
resist the charm of his intercourse, or went away from him
without feeling himself the better." It spoke in his low
sonorous voice; nay, it might be seen in the very splendour
of his starry forehead, and in the beauty of that countenance, which every one who gazed on it described as full of
joy and hilarity. And yet, we are told, he often and easily
wept, but only when moved by the sufferings of others;
nay, so tender was his heart that he could not think of
human misery as he gazed over a distant city without
being touched to tears.

This tenderness of spirit was the hereditary birthright of
his children. There was Reginald of Orleans, winning
men to penance against their will; and Henry of Utrecht,
that "gracious creature," as Jordan calls him, with the
joy of God painted on his angelic countenance, and whose
voice breathed the odour of a childlike innocence. There
was Jordan himself, whose simple *bonhomie* of character is perhaps as delightful as any of them; who could
tranquillize disturbed consciences by a look, who was
severe only to those who were severe to others, and whom
we find taming and playing with the wild ferrets on
the road as he journeyed, in the overflowing tenderness
and kindness of his heart. Of another we read, that as
he prayed in the garden, his looks were so gentle, that
timid birds would come and perch on his outstretched
arms. And whole volumes might be written of their
deaths. Of numbers it is related that they died singing.
In the convent of Vincenza we find a brother who, after
"singing versicles to the Blessed Virgin, with wondrous
delightsomeness, signed to his companion to rejoice also
with him, saying, 'Brother, do not think it strange, but
it is impossible for me not to sing of the love of Mary.'
Then after a while he opened his eyes again, and said
three times with much jubilation, 'Let everything that
hath breath praise the Lord;' and so, with a smile,
expired." Father William of Aniey, as he lay dying,
was visited by the angels, who visibly appeared to the
bystanders; and one of them bent over his bed and

kissed his rorchead, a grace he had deserved by his angelic life and conversation. There was John of Gascony, "a very marvel of sanctity, who, like the swan, sang as he was a-dying; sweetly repeating with his last breath, 'Into Thy hands, O Lord, I commend my spirit. Alleluia! For Thou hast redeemed me O God of truth! Alleluia! Alleluia!'" Then again we find other stories of their special earnestness in the work of peace. F. Robaldo, for instance, seemed to have a vocation for the healing of quarrels and feuds. He worked miracles to make men forgive one another; but perhaps his own angelic temper had a greater magic in it than his miracles. A young Milanese noble had been slain by his feudal enemy, and the two surviving brothers had vowed revenge. Robaldo, after having in vain endeavoured to appease one of them, took him by the hand and commanded him not to move till he had promised peace. He instantly lost the power of motion, and whilst he stood thus his other brother came to the spot, uttering curses and imprecations, and binding himself by oaths never to rest till he had steeped his sword in the blood of the murderer. And yet neither of them could resist the sweetness of Robaldo, and it ended by his sending them to the house of their enemy to dine with him, and bringing all three next day to the convent church, to bury all their differences at the foot of the altar. Then there was our own Lawrence; called blessed because of his blessed temper, and known through Spain and France as the reconciler of enemies. In short, turn where we will, we find the feet of these true preachers "shod with the preparation of the gospel of peace." They were all shaped after one likeness, even that of their holy patriarch: "benign, merciful. patient, and sober, not giving cursing for cursing, but rather blessing those that cursed." Such are the words of Bonviso of Placentia.

These we repeat were no fanatics; the pages of our own history will furnish us, in the followers of Cromwell, or Argyle, with a portrait of fanaticism never to be found among these Friars Preachers; and when we have been compelled to grant them the character of saints, it will perhaps startle us to know that many of these very men bore also the dreaded title of Inquisitors.

We must not close this chapter without noticing the foundation at Bologna of a convent of women, which was begun through the means of Diana of Andala, one of S. Dominic's spiritual daughters. Her extraordinary constancy and resolution overcame all the obstacles opposed by her friends; and eventually her own father became one of the most liberal supporters of the new house. Cecilia and Amy, the two sisters of S. Sixtus before named, were removed from thence to Bologna in 1223, and all three lie buried in the same grave, where their remains have been twice discovered, and honourably translated.

CHAPTER XXII.

AFTER Reginald's departure from Bologna, Dominic remained a while in the place, chiefly occupied in quieting the dissensions among the inhabitants which arose from the jealousy subsisting between the nobles and the citizens. Nor were his efforts unavailing: the Bolognese recognized him as their mediator of peace, and this was the first origin of that singular affection with which he was ever afterwards regarded in the city. Their confidence in him was increased by their conviction of his entire disinterestedness in the whole matter; for when their gratitude sought to show itself by gifts and donations, he constantly and inflexibly refused to receive the smallest

offering beyond the pittance of daily alms which was
begged from door to door. Indeed, his rigid regard of
poverty was in no degree inferior to that observed by
S. Francis: if there was food enough in the convent to
suffice for the day, he never allowed more alms to be
received for the next day; and very often he himself
would undertake the office of begging in the streets, which
he practised with a peculiar pleasure. He left Bologna in
the October of the same year, and, crossing the Appennines,
proceeded to Florence, whither some of the brethren had
already been despatched, and had commenced their
foundation. Here again the malice of the devil was
overcome and made the means of extending the order.
A woman named Benita, who had been grievously tormented by the evil spirit, and had led an irregular and
irreligious life, being converted, and delivered from her
possession, by the prayers of Dominic, took the veil,
and the name of Sister Benedicta. From Florence, he
came to Viterbo where the Pope was then staying, who
received him with open arms. The recital of the progress
which he and his brethren had made, since his departure
from Rome, filled the Pontiff with delight. He testified
his renewed affection and esteem by briefs, addressed
to the prelates and ecclesiastical superiors throughout
all the countries of Christendom, recommending the order
of Friars Preachers to their protection and respect. These
briefs are dated the November and December of 1219.

Soon after their publication, Dominic returned for the
fifth time to Rome, where he arrived in the commencement of the year 1220. A trifling circumstance is
recorded, connected with his return, which may seem
scarce worthy of notice, and yet discloses to us whole
volumes of the character and disposition of this great
man. He had brought with him, we are told, from Spain,
certain spoons of cypress-wood for the nuns of S. Sixtus.
Sister Cecilia thus describes this beautiful little incident:
" Upon a certain time S. Dominic, returning from Spain,
brought the sisters, as an affectionate little gift, some
spoons of cypress, for every sister one. And upon a day,
having finished his preaching and other works of charity,

in the same evening he came to the sisters, that he might
deliver to them these spoons from Spain." Amid all his
journeys and fatigues, he had time and room enough in
his heart for so simple a thought as this; and the comfort and pleasure of his children was still present to his
mind. One of those spoons, carried over the hills of
Spain and Italy in the little bundle of the saint, during
the long foot journeys of so many months, was surely a
precious relic.

He was soon busy in his old quarters at Santa Sabina
and hard at work again, preaching to the Roman people.
A great number of miracles and miraculous conversions
are recorded as taking place at this time; and many of
them we find spoken of as effected through the instrumen-
tality of the Rosary. The stream of novices continued
to flow as abundantly as ever into the cells of Santa
Sabina, and the care of the saint was bestowed on them
with all his usual vigilance and tenderness. Their fervour,
according to the testimony of Theodoric of Apoldia, was
truly admirable. "When they looked on the beauty and
purity of their institute," he says, "all their regret was
not sooner to have embraced it." A great care was ever
taken of the novices, both as to their instruction and their
health, for their zeal always had to be moderated. Instead
of its being necessary to wake them for the midnight office,
it was rather needful to seek for them in retired places,
where they had hidden themselves to pray, and oblige them
to take some rest. The abstinence they practised was
remarkable: many passed eight days without drinking,
and mixed their food with cold water. They ever looked
on preaching for the salvation of souls as the essential
part of their institute. When they went to preach,
according to Dominic's direction, they took with them
only the Bible or the New Testament. When it was
proposed to send missions among the barbarian nations,
or wheresoever there was a certainty of suffering, crowds
offered themselves for the service; they had a holy
eagerness for the salvation of souls and the chance of a
crown of martyrdom

It was at this time, according to the most probable

conjecture of historians, that the interview took place between Dominic and Francis, in the palace of Cardinal Ugolino, which the Franciscan writers give as occurring at Perugia, in the year 1219. After a spiritual conference of some duration, the cardinal asked them whether they would agree to their disciples accepting ecclesiastical dignities. Dominic was the first to reply : he said that it was honour sufficient for his brethren to be called to defend the faith against heretics. The words of S. Francis were equally characteristic ." My children," he said, " would no longer be Friars Minors if they became great; if you would have them bring forth fruit, leave them as they are." Edified by their replies, Ugolino did not, however, abandon his own views; when he was elevated to the papacy, he promoted a great number of both orders to the episcopate, as many as forty-two of whom were of the order of Friars Preachers.

We shall not pause to notice at any length the renewed favours of the Holy See, so liberally poured out in the shape of briefs and letters at this period, one of which, published in the commencement of this year, constituted Dominic the Superior or Master-General of the entire order ; an office he had hitherto only held by tacit consent, and which was doubtless formally given him at this time with a view to the assembling of the brethren in the first general chapter, which was now in contemplation. Whilst the preparations for this event were in hand, the friars were every day making further advances in Lombardy, and the great convent of S. Eustorgia was founded at Milan. The church had been granted to the order through the intervention of Cardinal Ugolino; and before their coming, a certain hermit had been wont to declare to the people, saying. " Before long this church will be inhabited by friars called Preachers, who shall give light to the whole world; for every night I see bright lamps shining over it which illuminate the entire city." The canons also heard the sweet music of angelic choirs singing round the walls, and a great devotion had attached to the sanctuary in consequence. This convent became the head-quarters of the order of Lombardy, and it was ever foremost in its attacks on the heretics of the day.

The general chapter had been fixed for the Pentecost of 1220, just three years from what may be deemed the commencement of the order. Its astonishing progress in that brief period seems to our eyes truly miraculous; perhaps the coldness of later days, could they have beheld it in vision, might have seemed as hard of credit or comprehension to the men of that heroic era. To ourselves the comparison can bring nothing but humiliation, whilst we contemplate a vigour, and, if we may so say, an impetuosity, in the religious life of those days, which seems like the giant verdure of the forests of the New World beside our own stunted and degenerate growth. And what is perhaps as worthy of our admiration, is the simplicity and unconsciousness with which the facts of this extraordinary progress are given to us; we scarcely find a word, among those who were the eye-witnesses of what had been going on during those three years, expressive of any sense of success. The work was the work of God, and for their own share in it, each one, with a sincere humility, could have joined in the words of their holy founder, as he stood in the midst of that first assembly of his children: "I deserve only to be dismissed from among you, for I have grown cool and relaxed, and am no longer of any use."

CHAPTER XXIII.

First general Chapter at Bologna. Law of poverty. The Order
spreads through Europe. Dominic's illness at Milan. Visit to
Siena. Tancred. Apostolic journeys through Italy. Return
to Bologna, and conversion of Master Conrad. John of Vicenza.
Anecdotes.

IT was on the 27th of May that the fathers of the
order met in the convent of S. Nicholas at Bologna.
Jordan of Saxony, who has left an account of their
proceedings, was himself present, having come from Paris
three weeks before. But so little was there among any
of them of a desire to seem great in men's eyes, that
very few details have been left regarding it, and many
things are passed over in silence which would have been
interesting to know. The number of friars present at the
first chapter of his order held by Francis have been carefully preserved; but no similar reckoning was made of
the Friars Preachers: we know only that France, Spain,
Italy, and even Poland, had their representatives in that
assembly. Dominic was then fifty years of age, having
lost nothing of that manly vigour of mind and body
which ever distinguished him : if we seek amid the
scanty materials which history has left us, to find some
token which may reveal to us the secret feelings of his
heart at a moment so deep in its interest, we shall find
that power, and success, and a government over other
men which gave him a personal empire of souls extending over half Christendom, had produced no change in
the simplicity and humility of his heart. It tended
Godward as it had ever done; and his first act was to
implore permission to renounce a superiority of which
he accounted himself unworthy. Some, perhaps, may be
tempted to look on this as an easily assumed modesty,
and to doubt how far he hoped or expected his resignation would be accepted. But the evidence of blessed

Paul of Venice shows that even at this time the darling hope of his soul had never been abandoned; he still cherished the thought, so soon as the order was firmly established of carrying the light of the Gospel among the heathen. "When we shall have fully instructed our order," he was wont to say, "we will go to the Cumans and preach the faith of Christ; and, doubtless, this secret and deeply-rooted idea was in his mind when he made the effort to rid himself of the government of his order.

It is needless for us to say this resignation was unanimously rejected, and Dominic was compelled to retain an authority none other could have accepted in his lifetime. Yet he made it a condition, that his power should be limited and controlled by the appointment of definitors whose office extended over all the acts of the chapter, and even to the correction and punishment of the Master himself, in case of necessity.

Many of the laws, still forming part of the constitutions of the order, were now established—those relating to abstinence and fasting, and many regarding the titles and authority of the local superiors. But the principal object of this chapter was the entire adoption of the rule of poverty, which had not been formally laid down by any statute. A renunciation was made of all lands and possessions until then retained, and it was resolved that nothing should be accepted in future save the daily alms on which they depended for support. The property of the monasteries of Toulouse and Madrid was respectively made over to the convents of women; and the order was reduced to the severity of the apostolic standard. If in the revolution of six centuries the change which has passed over the whole surface of society has necessitated a repeal of what, at the time, seemed a fundamental law, it need neither scandalize nor surprise us. Dear as was the rule of poverty to Dominic's heart, he never put it forth as the *end* of his order; he judged it but a means, and at that age a chief and essential means, for the one unchanging object of the institute of Preachers, the salvation of souls. And when the living authority of the Church in a later day dispensed the observance of

N 2

the letter of a rule no longer adapted to that object, she adhered strictly to the spirit, and explained the principle on which this change was made in words* so luminous and conclusive that they leave nothing to be added on the subject. Dominic was anxious to provide for the preservation of another essential of his institute, the pursuit of sacred learning; and for this purpose proposed that all the temporal affairs of the convent should be left in the hands of the lay brothers, so as to set the others entirely at liberty for the purposes of prayer and study. This was overruled by the other fathers, experience having shown the danger of this custom in other orders; and Dominic did not press the proposal. Some regulations were added about the cells, in respect to size and arrangement, and it was ordered that a crucifix and an image of the Blessed Virgin should be in each. The chapter was to be held yearly, at Paris and Bologna in turn: this regulation was afterwards done away, as the extension of the order rendered so frequent an assembly impossible, and made it desirable to fix it at other cities according to circumstances. The arrangement was made at this time in consequence of the neighbourhood of the two universities, a connection with which was held to be of the first importance.

We do not know what length of time was taken up by the proceedings of the chapter; but we find that early in the summer Dominic's attention was once more wholly given to the foundation and settlement of new convents. Brethren were sent also to Morocco and several of the infidel countries, as well as to Scotland, as some historians tell us. Luke, bishop of Galicia, speaking of this period, says, "At that time one saw nothing but foundations of the Friars Preachers and Friars Minors springing up everywhere; and wherever heresy appeared, the children of Dominic," he adds, "were at hand to combat and subdue it." The Ghibeline influence of the German Emperors was doubtless

---

* See Const. F. Praed, d. ii. c. 1; where the principles of religious poverty as professed by the order are laid down with great exactness.

a chief cause of that heretical tendency so widely diffused in the north of Italy, and there Dominic's chief efforts were directed. His residence at Bologna was constantly broken by excursions to the various cities of Lombardy, though we have no certain guide as to the exact order in which these visits were made. We find him again at Milan, in company with Brother Bonviso, in the course of the summer, and here he was again taken ill. Bonviso has left an account of this illness, and remarks upon the patience and cheerfulness he displayed in the extremity of fever: "I never had reason to complain of him" (he says; "he seemed always in prayer and contemplation, to judge from his countenance; and so soon as the fever subsided, he began to speak to the brethren of God; he praised God and rejoiced in his sufferings, as was his custom." He caused them to read to him, as he lay on his rough wooden bed, those Dialogues of Cassian and the Epistles of S. Paul, which had ever been his favourite books; and we feel that it is not fanciful to detect in this persevering attachment a token of that tranquil stability of mind, which formed so distinctive a peculiarity of his nature.

It would be scarcely interesting to the reader to be detained with the mere names of foundations, or of the new disciples daily admitted to the order. We shall endeavour to select a few among those which may be most worthy of our notice. The date of Dominic's visit to Siena has not been exactly preserved, though it may probably be referred to the present year. As he preached in one of the churches of that city, Tancredo Tancredi, a young noble of high birth and renown for learning, stood amid the crowd. As he listened and gazed at the celebrated preacher, he saw another figure standing beside him in the pulpit, and whispering in his ear: it was the Blessed Virgin, who was inspiring the words of her faithful servant. The sight filled Tancred with admiration, but as the saint descended the pulpit-stairs, that same glorious vision of Mary floated nearer and nearer to the spot where he stood. It pointed with its hand to the figure of the Preacher, and a low sweet voice

uttered in his ear, " Tancred, follow after that man, and
do not depart from him." From that time Tancred became
what he had been so sweetly called to be, a close and
faithful follower of his great master. Many very beautiful records are left us of his life. He had a strange
familiarity with the angels, who stood by him as he
prayed. Once, as he was earnestly interceding in prayer
for an obstinate sinner, the angelic friend beside him
whispered, " Tancred, your prayer for that soul will be
in vain." But the zeal and charity of this true Friar
Preacher was not to be checked even by such a word as
this ; he only prayed the harder, as though he would be
heard ; and, lo ! three days after, he saw the soul for
whom he laboured flying up safe to heaven. We can
scarce find a more beautiful or instructive anecdote of
the might of prayer than this.

Immense numbers of all ranks were attracted by the
ever-increasing fame of the new institute ; many were
men of learning and sanctity, many doubtless very
imperfect and uninstructed ; yet we are told S. Dominic
did not hesitate to employ the latter equally with the
former in the work of teaching, in the firm conviction
that, when so engaged, God would speak by them as
readily as by those better fitted, according to human
judgment, for the task ; and also, as it would seem,
because such work formed a part of his method of training them. This labour of training went on incessantly,
for it was his own hand that formed and directed all of
those new disciples. We can scarcely estimate aright
the prodigious labour which he assigned himself ; we see
him, as it were, in every city of Italy ; and we find him
in the same year busy at this engrossing work at
Bologna, which was now his head-quarters ; and never
did he relax, for all his engagements, that public office of
preaching to which he held himself so solemnly bound.
Very strange must have been the scenes which were often
witnessed in the churches where those discourses were
delivered. Every day, and sometimes more than once, he
preached whilst at Bologna. The people crowded round
his pulpit, and often the multitude were forced to adjourn

t the open air. They followed him afterwards to his
own out-door that they might still gaze at him, or speak
with him. On one of these occasions two young students
addressed him, and one said, "Father, I am just come
from confession: I pray you obtain from God the pardon
of my sins." The saint, after a moment's thought,
replied, "Have confidence, my son, for your sins are
already pardoned." Then the other made the same
request, but the answer was different: "Thou hast not
confessed all," said Dominic; and the young man, entering into himself, discovered indeed a secret sin which had
escaped his memory.

On another occasion, he had been preaching in one of
the public places of the city, when, the sermon being
ended, a nobleman, the governor of S. Severino, who had
been among the audience, pushed his way through the
crowd, and waited on his knees to receive his blessing as
he came down from his pulpit. Nor did his admiration
end here; that one sermon had gained for the order the
grant of a church and convent, and established the Friars
Preachers in the marches of Ancona.

Every part of the country between the Alps and the
Appennines was trodden by the unwearied feet of this
great apostle. At Cremona he met once more his
friend and fellow-labourer S. Francis, who was there,
together with his spiritual daughter S. Clare. The
three saints lodged in the same house, and an anecdote
of their meeting has been preserved. The water of a well
belonging to the house had become unfit for use, and the
people of the place, bringing some of it in a vase, begged
one of the two saints to bless it that it might recover its
sweetness. A graceful contest arose, each wishing the
other to undertake the miracle, but the humility of
Francis conquered. Dominic blessed the water, which
was immediately restored to its clearness and sweet
savour.*

Such of our readers as are familiar with the Franciscan history will doubtless be surprised at the omission in these pages
of many other interviews between the two great patriarchs, noticed
by those writers; but although far from wishing to decide on

In the course of his wanderings, Dominic found himself one night before the gates of S. Colomba, a Cistercian house, but the hour was late, and he would not disturb the inmates. "Let us lie down here," he said to his companion, "and pray to God, who will surely care for us." They did so, and both immediately found themselves transported to the interior of the convent. Thus we see it was ever with the same simplicity that Dominic journeyed; it was the poor mendicant friar, with his wallet on his back, and nothing save the light that gleamed on his noble forehead to distinguish him from other men, who went barefoot up and down the hills and valleys of Italy, where we may now mark the magnificent foundations of S. Eustorgio of Milan, or SS. John and Paul of Venice, and that other convent which lies amid the wooded hills of Como, and a thousand others, all nurseries of saints.

The festival of the Assumption saw him once more at Bologna, where, on his return, he found matter for both sorrow and displeasure ; for Rodolph of Faenza, the procurator of the convent, had in his absence made some additions to the building which the saint judged inconsistent with the profession of holy poverty. Before his departure he had himself left directions for the proposed alterations, and even a kind of plan or model to insure the preservation of that rigorous observance of poverty which was so dear to him, and which he conceived to be the indispensable condition of religion. He gazed at the new building with tears flowing down his cheeks. "Will you build palaces whilst I am yet living," he said, "after such a fashion as this ? Know then that if you do, you will bring ruin on the order ; you have pierced my very heart." Such words did indeed pierce the hearts of those who listened ; and during the remainder of his life none dared speak of finishing the building, on which not another stone was laid. And yet the cells he

these as being wholly fictitious, we feel ourselves obliged to pass them over in silence, as they are not given by Dominican authorities, and are often difficult to reconcile with the chronology of the order.

found so luxurious and unsuitable were after all but poor and narrow, and not much superior to those which had been before erected. How rigid indeed was the poverty and humility of the structure, we may judge from a other circumstance which occurred about this time.

Francis also came to Bologna on a visit to the religious of his order recently established in the city, but when he found them living in a large and spacious house, he was so indignant that he ordered them every one to quit it, and he himself took up his dwelling in the convent of the Friars Preachers, "which," says Father Candidus Cha-lippus, "he found more to his taste, and where he passed some days with his friend S. Dominic."

Shortly after the return of the latter to Bologna, a remarkable addition was made to the number of his disciples, in the person of Conrad the German. He was a professor of the university, whom the brethren had long and ardently desired to have amongst them. On the evening of the Assumption Dominic was in familiar conversation with a certain Cistercian prior, and said to him, "Prior, I will tell you a thing, which you must keep secret till my death. Never have I asked anything from God, but He has granted it to me." "Then, father," said the prior, "I marvel that you do not ask the vocation of Master Conrad, whom the brethren desire so greatly to have among them." "The thing is difficult," answered Dominic; "nevertheless, if you will pray with me this night, I doubt not God will incline to our request." That night the prior kept watch in the church by his friend's side; and at the hour of prime, as they intoned the hymn, *Jam lucis orto sidere*, Conrad entered the choir, and demanded the habit from the hands of the saint.

Another of the disciples of this year was John of Vicenza, who deserves a more particular notice. Martin Sillo, his father, intended him for the law, and sent him with this intention to Padua, then the great legal univer-sity. There, however, a more sublime vocation awaited him. Dominic passed through the city, and no church in the place being large enough to hold the crowds who

flocked to hear him, he preached in the great piazza
known as the Piazza della Valle. John was there, and
that day's preaching put all thoughts of law out of his
head. As soon as the sermon was ended, he went to find
the preacher, and begged to be instantly admitted among
his followers, and to receive the habit of his order. He
made his noviciate at Bologna, but afterwards returned to
the convent of Padua, where he became one of the most
famous preachers of his time. He was called the apostle
of Lombardy, and indeed Lombardy needed an apostle in
those unhappy days, torn as it was by the wars, and
desolated by the cruelties, of Frederick II. and the tyrant
Ezzelino. John was a preacher of peace amid all the
terrible calamities of those times. He left one memorial
of himself in the salutation "God save you," which he
introduced among the citizens of Bologna during a time
of public commotion, to excite them to gentler and more
courteous treatment of their opponents, and which soon
spread through Europe, and has lasted to our own day.
The angels were seen whispering in his ear as he preached,
and his words had ever the same burden, purity and peace.
He was a fervent lover of the Rosary, and sometimes, as
he preached this devotion, a bright rose would appear on
his forehead, or a golden sunny crown would glitter over
his head. He had a marvellous power over the fiercest
animals; eagles were obedient to him, and a wild un-
tamable horse became tractable at his bidding. His devotion to the memory of Dominic was very remarkable, and
Father Stephen of Spain assures us that 100.000 heretics
were converted by only hearing the account of his life
and miracles as narrated by his devoted follower. The
Pope at length appointed him on a mission of pacification
to the north of Italy, and such was the success of his
labours, especially after a discourse addressed to the
populace on that very Piazza della Valle where he had
first heard the eloquence of his holy father, that all the
contending parties agreed to abandon their differences
and accept of peace. Ezzelino alone held out; and concerning him John had an awful vision. He saw the
Almighty seated on His throne, and seeking for a scourge

for the chastisement of Lombardy. Ezzelino was chosen
as the instrument of his wrath, and surely a more terrible
one was never found. At that time John had never seen
him, and when first they met, and he cast his eyes on
him, he wept, recognising him as the man he had seen in
his vision, and cried aloud, "It is he whom I saw—the
scourge of Lombardy. Woe! woe to thee, unhappy
country! for he shall execute judgment on thee to the
uttermost." Nevertheless, even this monster was in
some degree touched and softened by the preaching of
Blessed John. We can scarcely imagine a more wonderful and beautiful sight than that presented on S.
Augustine's day in the Campagna of Verona, when the
banks of the Adige saw 300,000 people met together,
with the princes and prelates of half Italy, to swear a universal peace. There, by the river-side, rose an enormous
pulpit sixty cubits high, that John, who stood in it to
harangue and bless the vast assembly, might be seen by all.
Ezzelino himself was there. A few weeks before, he had
been burning and laying waste everything that was before
him, and Mantua, Brescia, and Bologna had all united
in besieging the unhappy city of Verona. But one
powerful and impassioned appeal of blessed John had
changed the entire scene; and now the sun rose on that
vast assembly, ranged in order according to their dignities,
and in the midst of a profound silence he addressed them
again from the words of our Lord, "Peace I give you,
my peace I give unto you;"* and such was the power of
his eloquence that even Ezzelino hid his face and wept.
Then was heard a cry that rose from that great multitude
as from one man. "Peace, peace," they cried, "and
mercy!" And then, when they had given vent to their
emotion, John spoke again, and blessed them in the name
of the Pope, and all swore to peace and unity, and Ezzelino and his brother Alberic were proclaimed citizens of
Padua. And in the evening there were rejoicings - the
first that land had seen for many a day - fires and illuminations, music and happy laughter, all the hours of that

* These words are engraved on the foot of his image in the church
of ... Holy Crown, at Vicenza.

summer's night, to celebrate "The Festival of Peace."
It was of short duration; yet, short as it was, and soon
disturbed by the unquiet spirits of evil men, there was a
harvest of glory won that day that was worth a thousand
battle-fields of victory.   Ezzelino soon added heresy to
his other crimes, and while he deluged Lombardy with
blood, he let loose on it the poison of false doctrine.
The cities of Italy at length banded against him, and in
1259 he was taken prisoner; and refusing to be cured of
his wounds or to receive any food, he died a miserable
death of despair.   An obscurity hangs over the last days
of John of Vicenza.   By some he is said to have died
in the prisons of Ezzelino; whilst others affirm him to
have found a martyr's death among the Cumans.   But,
however this may be—and the uncertainty of his fate is
but one among many examples of the indifference of the
order to historical fame—the acclamations of Italy declared
him "Blessed;" a title from time immemorial allowed
by the Sovereign Pontiff, though never ratified by any
formal process of beatification.

To return, however, to Dominic and his novices.   The
vocations of which we have spoken were certainly very
remarkable, and were often the result of what we should
call a mere chance, directed by the providence of God.
Thus, a certain priest, greatly drawn to the person of
Dominic, yet still uncertain how to act, had recourse to
a favourite custom of those days, and opening the Bible
after prayer, beheld the words addressed to the centu-
rion, "Arise, and go with him, nothing doubting, for I
have sent him."   The same means were adopted by
another, Conrad, bishop of Porto, who was a Cistercian
monk, and entertained grievous and perplexing suspi-
cions as to the character of the order.   He opened his
missal, and read the words, "*Laudare, benedicere, prae-
dicare;*" and embracing the saint the next time he met
him, he exclaimed, "I am all yours: my habit is Cistercian,
but in heart I am a Friar Preacher."   Sometimes the
sudden vocations of some caused violent opposition from
their friends.   A young student, just received to the
habit, was beset by all his relations and companions, who

the stead, if he would not return to the world, to carry him off by violence. Dominic's friends advised him to ask the protection of the magistrates. " Trouble not yourselves, my good friends," he replied, " we have no need of magistrates; even now I see more than two hundred angels standing round about the church, and guarding it from our enemies."

These threats of violence were sometimes, however, carried into execution. There was among the novices a youth whose singular gentleness and sweetness of disposition greatly endeared him to Dominic. His name was Thomas of Paglio ; and shortly after his reception his relatives forcibly carried him off by night, and dragging him to a neighbouring vineyard, stripped off his habit, and clothed him in his former worldly garb. Dominic, hearing what had happened, immediately betook himself to his only arms, of prayer ; and as he prayed, Thomas was seized with a strange and unendurable heat. " I burn, I burn," he cried ; " take these clothes from me, and give me back my habit ; " and having once more gained possession of his woollen tunic, he made his way back to the convent in spite of all opposition, and at the touch of that white robe of innocence the fiery anguish was felt no more. The same author who relates this circumstance tells us that other miraculous signs, besides those of the efficacy of his prayers, were noticed as attaching to the person of Dominic. A student of the university who served his Mass, attested, that as he kissed his hand, a divine fragrance was perceptible, which had the power of delivering him from grievous temptations with which he was tormented ; and that a certain usurer, whom the saint communicated, felt the Sacred Host burning against his mouth like hot coals, whereupon he was moved to penitence, and making restitution of all his ill-gotten gains, became sincerely converted to God.

CHAPTER XXIV.

Heretics of northern Italy. Foundation of the third order. Last visit to Rome Meeting with Fulk of Toulouse. Second general chapter. Division of the order into provinces. Blessed Paul of Hungary. S. Peter Martyr.

THE heretics of Northern Italy, of whom frequent mention has already been made, were not less violent in their attacks on the rights and property of the Catholics than their brethren of Languedoc. Protected as they were in many cases by the secular princes, who in their constant feuds one with another made use of them as political instruments, even when no way sharers in their opinions, they availed themselves of every opportunity for seizing the lands of the Church, so that the clergy were in many places reduced to the same state of degradation and dependence which had already produced such frightful effects in Languedoc. It was to oppose this abuse, and to place a barrier against that social corruption which everywhere followed on the track of the Manichean heresy, that Dominic founded his third order. Intimately entering into the needs of his age, his quick and sagacious eye perceived that his institute was imperfect so long as it aimed at the salvation of souls only through the ministrations of preaching, or the discipline of convent rule. The world itself was to be sanctified; therefore, out of the world itself should be formed the instruments of sanctification. The " Militia of Jesus Christ," as the new institute was called, ranked under the standard of the Church those of either sex who had received no call to separate themselves from the ordinary life of seculars, and yet desired to shelter it under the skirts of the religious mantle. The first object contemplated in its institution was the defence of ecclesiastical property ; but this was a very small part of the work to which, in God's providence, it was afterwards called.

The third orders of Dominic and Francis completed the
conquest of the world.   They placed the religious habit
under the breastplate of warriors and the robes of kings.
They were like streams, carrying the fertility of Paradise
to many a dry and barren region, so that the wilderness
blossomed like a rose.   Something of the barrier between
the world and the cloister was broken down ; and the
degrees of heroic sanctity were placed, as it were, within
the grasp of thousands, who else, perhaps, had never
risen above the ordinary standard.

These third orders have given us a crowd of saints,
dearer to us, perhaps, and more familiar than any others,
in so far as we feel able to claim their close sympathy
with ourselves; and the more so, that they are a perpetual witness to us, that no path in life is so busy, or so
beset with temptations, but that God's grace may cover it
with the very choicest beauty of holiness.   As time
went on, and the circumstances of its first institution
had passed away, the Militia of Jesus Christ exchanged
its name for that of " the Order of Penance of S. Dominic," and by degrees assumed more and more of the religious character ; particularly after S. Catherine of Siena
had by her example given a new shape to the order,
in so far as regarded its adoption by her own sex; and in
her life, and that of the numberless saints who have trodden in her steps, we see the final triumph and vindication
of what we may venture to call the primary Dominican
idea ; namely, that the highest walks of contemplation
are   not   incompatible   with   the   exercises   of   active
charity, and the labour for souls; but that a union of
both is possible, which more nearly fulfils our conception
of the life of Christ than the separated perfections of
either.

The circumstances attending the first establishment of
this order are unknown to us; many authors are of
opinion that it is to be referred to a much earlier date,
and that it was even the first of the three founded by
S. Dominic, having been originally instituted in Languedoc for the resistance of the Albigenses.   It is very
probable that some kind association had been formed

by him among the Catholic confederates, and afterwards developed into a more regular shape, when the renewed encroachment of the heretics in Lombardy rendered a similar means of protection desirable ; for such a supposition would harmonize very much with S. Dominic's general method of action. It is certainly not a little remarkable, that an uncertainty hangs over the foundation both of this institute, and even of the first regular establishment of his greater order, which shows how little the thought of human praise or celebrity found its way into the soul of their author—like the silence in the Gospels on the life of Mary, which tells us more of her sublime humility than many words could do—and this humility and simplicity of action forms also, if we mistake not, a large feature in the portraiture of Dominic. It is without doubt, however, that to him must be ascribed the first origin of this form of the religious life ; for the third order of S. Francis, which so long divided with its sister institute the favour of Christendom, was not founded until 1224, three years after S. Dominic's death.

The December of 1220 saw Dominic once more in Rome. This, his last visit to a city which had been the scene of so many labours and miracles, is marked by the date of various fresh briefs and privileges granted to his order by its faithful friend and benefactor, Pope Honorius. The first of these briefs was for remedying some irregularities which had taken place in the ordinations of the brethren ; others were addressed to the bishops and prelates of the Church, recommending the order to their protection in terms of the warmest eulogy ; and one dated April 1221, had reference to the nuns of S. Sixtus, to whom it secured the possessions formerly enjoyed by the community of the Trastevere. This visit to Rome was the occasion of a meeting that must have been full of the tenderest interest to the heart of Dominic. Fulk of Toulouse was then at the pontifical court ; little more than three years had elapsed since that dispersion of the sixteen brethren of S. Romain, which had taken place in his own presence, and now he witnessed the triumph of an order to which he had been so true a nursing father. Three years had converted the prior of Prouille, the leader of that devoted little band whose destinies, to every eye but his, seemed then so hopeless and obscure, into the master-general of a great order, whose convents were spread through the length and breadth of Christendom. All things in their respective positions were changed, save Dominic himself: but Fulk could have detected no difference between Dominic the apostle of Languedoc, and Dominic the master of the Friars Preachers, save in the adoption of a yet poorer habit, and those few silver hairs which, we are told, his long labours, and not his years, had begun to sprinkle over his tonsured head. But the heroic heart, the patient gentle spirit, the simple hearty joyousness of his friend, were still the same; and so, too, was the disinterestedness of his soul, of which Fulk had proof in a transaction whose acts are still preserved. This was the renunciation, on Dominic's part, of that grant, formerly made by the bishop, of the sixth part of the tenths of his revenues for the support of the order when it was yet young and friendless. The principle of poverty had since then been more strictly developed in the institute, and Dominic believed he could no longer in conscience accept this revenue, even though given, in the very terms of the grant, as an alms to the poor of Christ. Fulk, on his part, confirmed the donation of the church of Notre-Dame-de-Fangeaux to the religious of Prouille; for it will be observed that the rigid law of poverty which he enforced on the rest of his order, he relaxed in favour of the communities of women, for whose state he judged a moderate revenue was requisite to be secured.

It were to be wished that more particulars had been left us of the great patriarch's last appearance in the Roman capital. Rome had witnessed the *épopée* of his life: henceforward S. Sixtus and Santa Sabina were to become classic names among his children; and if, as we have reason to believe, a prophetic knowledge had been granted him that the period of his death was not far off, there must have been a peculiar charm in his parting

visits to these familiar scenes. As usual, every day saw
him at the grating of S. Sixtus, renewing his exhortations
to the sisters to keep fast to the holy rule under whose
power they had been transformed into the saintly life.
The affection which he so faithfully preserved for these
spiritual children is illustrated by one of the miracles
related to us by Sister Cecilia as happening at this time.
Upon a certain day he stopped at the gate, and, without
entering, asked of the portress how Sister Theodora,
Sister Tedrano, and Sister Ninfa were. She replied they
were all three ill of fever. " Tell them," said Dominic,
"from me, that I command them all to be cured ;" and
at the delivery of the message they all three arose in
perfect health.

Dominic's presence was always peculiarly welcomed in
Rome, where he was well known to many of the cardinals
and others attached to the Pontifical court ; and these
vie one with another in the diligence with which they
sought his companionship ; for as it was well expressed in
the bull of his canonization, " none ever spoke to him and
went away without feeling the better." But popularity
was the last thing that he sought ; and it is to be believed
that the celebrity he enjoyed at Rome was one of the
principal motives for his formerly removing his residence
from thence to Bologna, whither he now returned early
in the month of May, to meet the second chapter of the
order, which was about to assemble in that city. On his
way he passed through Bolsena, where he was often
accustomed to stay, being at such times always hospitably
entertained by a certain citizen, who, to prove his friendship for his guest, left it as an obligation to his heirs
that they should always receive and lodge all the Friars
Preachers who should pass through Bolsena in time to
come, a condition still faithfully observed at the end of
the thirteenth century, as Theodoric of Apoldia narrates.
This particular mark of esteem was probably a token of
gratitude, for it happened that in one of his visits to this
house, Dominic had preserved the vines of his host in the
midst of a violent storm which devastated all the surrounding vineyards.

The second chapter of Bologna opened on the 30th of May, 1221. Dominic, at the commencement of their proceedings, addressed the brethren at considerable length, laying before them the state of the order in the countries wherein it was already established, and proposing its still farther extension. It appeared that sixty convents were already founded, and yet a greater number in course of erection. For the more perfect government, therefore, of the order, it was now divided into eight provinces, and a prior provincial appointed to each of them; namely, to Spain, Toulouse, France, Lombardy, Rome, Germany, Hungary, and England. These two latter countries were yet to be colonized by the Friars Preachers; and the appointment and despatch of their first missioners formed one of the undertakings of this chapter. Of the foundation of the English province we shall presently speak more at length; that of Hungary was placed under the government of a native of the country, named Paul, who had recently been received into the order by Dominic, and had previously filled the chair of canon law in the university of Bologna. Immediately after his reception, Paul was despatched to his new province with four companions, of whom one was Blessed Sadoc of Poland, the tale of whose martyrdom, with his forty-eight companions, is among the most interesting incidents recorded in the annals of the order.[*] The crown of martyrdom was reserved for Paul also. He received it the following year, together with ninety of his brethren, from the hands of the Caman Tartars, who infested the borders of Hungary, and whose conversion to the Christian faith had so long formed the cherished day-dream of S. Dominic. It would seem, indeed, as though this nation, whose barbarity exceeded that of any of the savage hordes that still hung round the boundaries of Christian Europe, was destined, if not to be converted by his order, at least to fill its ranks with an army of martyrs. Another of Paul's earliest companions, Blessed Berengarius of Poland, the archbishop of Cracow, was slain by them a few years afterwards, and in 1260 seventy more were sent to join

[*] See No. 2. of "Catholic Legends," in this series.

their company; all of whom, it is said, were children and disciples of the glorious S. Hyacinth

The extraordinary manner in which these first founders propagated the order in the countries whither they were sent, may be estimated by the number of these martyrs: the ninety who died in company with blessed Paul must all have been gathered into the ranks of the institute within a year from the period of his departure from Bologna. If this may be taken as anything like a fair proof of the stimulus to religion which everywhere followed on the appearance of the Friars Preachers, it may perhaps dispose us the more readily to believe an incident which is said to have occurred just before the meeting of this second chapter. Two of the brethren who were travelling towards Bologna, were met on the road by a man who joined himself to their company and fell into conversation with them. He inquired the object of their journey, and being informed of the approaching chapter, "What," he asked, "is the business which is likely to be discussed?" "The establishment of our brethren in new countries." replied one of the friars; "England and Hungary are amongst those proposed." "And Greece also," said the stranger, "and Germany, is it not so?" "You say truly," returned the friar; "it is said that we shall shortly be dispersed into all these provinces." Then the stranger uttered a loud cry as of great anguish, and exclaiming, "Your order is my confusion," he leapt into the air, and so disappeared; and the friars knew that it was the voice of the great enemy of man, who was thus compelled to bear witness to the power which the servants of God exercised against him.

The convents of the Friars Preachers in the new province of Hungary may be said to have been planted in blood, that seed of the Church which has never failed to bring forth the hundredfold. "In blood were they sown," says Marchese, "and in blood did they increase; so that the more they were slain, so much the more numerous did they become, till within a brief space a province was erected of vast extent, including the countries of Molda-

viz. Transylvania, Croatia, Bosnia, and Dalmatia;" and
this was afterwards divided into two, the second of which,
being the name of Dalmatia, contained a great number
of convents, illustrious for the names of many saints and
martyrs who flourished in them

In his address to the assembled fathers, Dominic gave
them an earnest exhortation to the pursuit of the sacred
learning, that they might be the better fitted for the
charge laid on them by their vocation as Preachers.   He
reminded them that the briefs granted so liberally by the
Vicar of Christ, recommended them to the favour of the
universal Church, inasmuch as they were therein declared to be labourers for God's honour, and the salvation
of souls, and that this end could never be attained without a diligent application to the divine Scriptures ; he
therefore enjoined all who should be engaged in the
sacred office of preaching to apply without ceasing to
the study of theology, and to carry always with them
a copy of the Gospels, and the seven canonical Epistles.
The letter commonly attributed to S. Dominic, and pur-
porting to be addressed by him to his religious in the
province of Poland, after the conclusion of the second
general chapter, has been questioned by some as of
doubtful authenticity.   Without venturing to decide the
disputed point, we may refer to the peculiar force with
which the study of the divine Scriptures is recommended
in this letter, as exactly harmonizing with the tone of his
address to the chapter : it is given by Malvenda and
Bzovius as undoubtedly the work of S. Dominic, nor
was its authorship ever called in question until the time
of Echard.   Touron, in his life of the saint, has entered
into the critical examination of the question, and decides
that the evidence is all in favour of its authenticity ;
while the letter itself is, as he says, not unworthy of
him.   It breathes a noble spirit throughout, exhorting
the brethren to a fervent observance of their rule, and a
life worthy of the angelic ministry with which they were
charged.   " Let us apply ourselves with energy," he adds
in the concluding paragraph, " to the great actions which
God demands of us ;" a word of heroic exhortation which

has rung for centuries in the ears of his children, and led
them on to aim at something of that greatness in the
paths of holiness which it points out to them as the object
of their vocation.

It was probably whilst the chapter was still sitting
that Dominic gave the habit to one who was eventually
to become one of the brightest ornaments of the order.
Peter of Verona, the son of heretical parents, but himself destined to die a martyr in defence of the faith, was
at that time a student in the university of Bologna, and
though a mere youth of sixteen, his learning and holiness
had already made his name respected among his fellows.
Dominic did not live to see the glory of his future career,
yet even now there were sufficient indications of it to
make him peculiarly dear to the heart of the saint, who
felt himself drawn by a powerful attraction to the youth
whose angelic innocence of life had been united, even
from infancy, to an extraordinary courage in the profession of the Catholic faith.   " The hammer of the
heretics," as he was commonly termed, he died by their
hand, writing on the ground in his blood the word
Credo; and among all the disciples whom S. Dominic
left behind him to continue his work, we may single out
S. Peter Martyr as the one on whom his mantle may most
surely be said to have fallen.

Leaving for awhile the course of S. Dominic's life, we
will proceed to say a few words concerning the foundation
of the order in our own island, trusting that the digression,
if it be one, may be pardoned on a subject so full of interest
to the English reader.

CHAPTER XXV.

GILBERT DE FRESNOY was the person appointed by Dominic to undertake the foundation of the new province of England ; the establishment of which was, it is said, resolved on in compliance with the earnest entreaties of certain distinguished persons of that nation. Previous to the period of this second chapter, we can find no mention of Brother Gilbert ; but we are told he immediately set out with twelve companions, travelling in the suite of Peter de Roche, bishop of Wincester, whose presence at Bologna, on his return from the Holy Land, may probably have hastened the dispatch of the English mission. They arrived at Canterbury some time in the month of June, where the archbishop, Stephen Longton, was then residing. He received the new comers with extraordinary kindness, and insisted on Gilbert's addressing a sermon to the people on that very day. It must have been a somewhat hard tax on the preacher's powers, the more so as he probably felt the future success of his enterprise, in so far as it depended on the favour of the archbishop, was in no small degree likely to hang on the good or bad opinion he might form of his sermon. Happily it was received with universal applause. It was declared to be grave, elegant, and full of wisdom ; and Stephen promised both him and his companions that they should never fail to find in him a friend and a protector. They proceeded on their journey to London, and thence to Oxford, where they arrived on the feast of the Assumption ; and having settled in the parish of S. Edward's, they immediately erected a little oratory dedicated to our Lady, and opened schools, which from the name of the parish were called S. Edward's schools.

Thus the children of S. Dominic found themselves at length in connection with the three great universities of Europe—Bologna, Paris and Oxford ; although, indeed, it was not until the famous struggle which took place seven years afterwards at Paris, that any of their numbers were raised to the professors' chairs. But from the very first, the character they aimed at as a teaching order was universally avowed, as the very letter of their constitutions, and the provisions they assign for the carrying out of their system of study, and receiving degrees, evidently show. Yet it is worthy of notice, that the first occasion on which we find any formal mention of their schools is in the account of those opened at Oxford ; for hitherto, at both the other universities, they are rather spoken of as students than as having yet assumed the office of teachers, except in the pulpits. They continued to reside in the parish of S. Edward's till the king granted them a site of ground outside the walls ; but this place proving inconvenient for their purpose, owing to its distance from the city, they betook themselves to prayer that they might find favour in the eyes of the university authorities. Nor were their prayers in vain ; for they soon after obtained a settlement in the Jewish quarters in the town, " to the intent," says Wood, " that they might induce the Jews to embrace the Christian faith, as well by the sanctity of their lives as by preaching the word, in which they excelled." Shorly after this the canons of S. Frideswide let them some lands at a low rate ; and aided by further benefactions from the countess of Oxford, and Walter Malclerk, bishop of Carlisle, they built themselves a house and church, which stood partly in the parish of S. Aldate, on the ground belonging to the canons before mentioned. The composition entered into between the canons and themselves in regard to this ground still exists, and seems to bear a little hardly on the friars ; nevertheless, we are assured they were in favour with

the a as with the citizens, "being as acceptable to the
latter for their piety, as they were to the former for
their learning." Forty years afterwards, their houses
being too small to accommodate the immense number
of scholars who flocked to hear them, they removed to
an island in the river, "in the south suburbs, and most
delightful for situation," where they continued to reside until the general destruction of religious houses in
the time of Henry VIII. The first who taught in the
schools of S. Edward was one John of S. Giles, "a man,"
says Matthew Paris, "skilful in the art of medicine, a
great professor of divinity, and excellently learned and
instructing." They were there greatly cramped for room,
but in their island house, we read, they had larger space;
and that the acts of divinity were given in the church
and chapter house, whilst the lectures on philosophy were
delivered in the cloister. They became in time the greatest
ornaments of the university, eminent, as it is said, for all the
learning of the time.

Of the great men whom they gave to England it would
be impossible to recount all the names; yet some we
should not pass over without a word of notice. Walter
Malclerk, their first benefactor, became afterwards a
member of their community, and resigned his bishopric,
and every other dignity he possessed, to assume their
humble habit. His history is a remarkable one. His noble
birth, attractive manners, and extraordinary genius, raised
him to the highest favour at the court of Henry III.,
who, besides elevating him to the bishopric of Carlisle,
made him lord high treasurer of the kingdom. In this
position many years were spent in a life of brilliant state
services; but, as it would seem, the taint of worldly
ambition for a time obscured his better qualities and his
religious character. After a brief period of disgrace at
court, we find him again at the head of affairs in 1234;
and when, eleven years later, the king marched from
London against his revolted subjects, he left Walter
Malclerk to govern the kingdom during the period of his
absence in the field. But God had destined the conclusion of his life to present us with another of those

many singular conversions whose stories crowd the annals
of the Dominican order. We are not told what was the
immediate cause which wrought the change in his views
and desires, and disgusted him with the very career
which he had hitherto so ardently pursued; but as soon
as grace had effectually touched his heart, he resolved on
a generous and entire sacrifice ; and, resigning his
bishopric and distributing all he possessed to the poor,
he took the habit of the Friars Preachers at Oxford,
where he gave himself wholly to a life of penance and
religious fervour. This act of heroic renunciation filled
all England with surprise, whilst the friars themselves
were forced to admire the marvel which had transformed
a courtier and a minister of state into the humble novice
of a mendicant community. He died two years afterwards, and left behind him several learned works. Another
renowned member of the order was Robert Bacon, the
brother, or as some say, the uncle, of the yet more
celebrated Roger Bacon. He joined the friars when
an old man, out of the great love he bore S. Dominic.
Together with him we must notice his dear and bosom
friend, Richard Fishacre, whom Ireland calls "the most
learned among the learned." He was a great admirer
of Aristotle, whose works he ever carried in his bosom.
"He was," says Wood, "renowned both as a philosopher
and as a divine, for which reason he was so dear to
Bacon that he became his inseparable companion ; and
as they were most constant associates in life, so neither
could they be separated in death. For as the turtle-
dove, bewailing its lost mate, dies, so, Bacon being dead,
Fishacre neither could nor would survive." He was the
first English preacher who commented on the "Book of
Sentences."

Other convents of the order were soon affiliated to the
parent house, the Black Friars in London being one of
the earliest of these foundations. Indeed, they seem to
have been deservedly popular among the English, who
were then, as now, a sermon-loving people; and so great
were the crowds that flocked to hear the new preachers
that the sermons were generally delivered out of doors

and we find frequent mention of the "portable pulpit-" they used, convenient to be set up in the public streets.

From England they soon found their way to Ireland: Father Ronald, an Irishman by birth, and one of the first missionaries from Bologna, being sent over there very shortly after the settlement of his companions at Oxford. He died archbishop of Armagh, having lived to see the order spread through almost every province of the island. The spectacle exhibited in the example of Walter Maleclerk was again and again repeated in a long list of eminent men of both countries, who, in the succeeding centuries, laid aside every dignity to become children in the noviciates of the Friars Preachers.

The Franciscans soon followed in the track of their sister order, and an interesting account is given us of their first arrival at Oxford, where they were generously and hospitably received by their Dominican brethren. Two of the Friars Minors, ignorant of the country, and perfectly friendless, had first begged at the door of the Benedictine monastry of Abingdon, and being unknown, and mistaken for " mimics or disguised persons," were driven away with bad usage. They would have passed the night in the road, if a young monk, touched with compassion, had not secretly hid them in a hayloft ; and the next morning they pursued their way to Oxford, praying as they went, that "God would dispose some goodwill for them among the men of Oxford. Nor were their prayers in vain; for being come to the city, and going directly to the house of the Dominicans in the Jewry, though they durst scarce hope for it, they were by them entertained with extraordinary care and charity, and having found them as friendly as the Abingdonians had been merciless, they had the benefit of the refectory and dormitory till the eighth day."* This mutual exchange of hospitality forms one of the most beautiful features in the history of the two orders, and might be illustrated by innumerable examples of a similar kind.

It will be seen that both at Oxford and Paris, and also

Steven's Dugdale, from the MS. of A. Wood.

at Bologna, the order immediately assumed a position in
connection with the universities. In fact, this connection
was one of the principal objects contemplated by these
foundations in those cities. The constitutions of the
order were drawn up with a view of providing for a
regular system of study; and at the same time things
were so arranged that the student was still under religious discipline, and study was made only a part of his
religious training. They were not cast abroad on the
great world of university life to shift for themselves: but
the idea was, that in all the great centres of learning
there should be a religious house, to which the students
of the order were bound as members of its community
during the period of their university course; and so the
university and community life were woven together, and
the intellectual advantages of the one laid under the
restrictions of the other. The nature of their studies
was regulated and limited so as, if not exclusively theological, at least to bear more or less on theology. Merely
secular and honorary distinctions and degrees, granted
by the university authorities, were not recognized, the
order reserving a system of graduation in its own hands;
and so by means of very minute and most sagacious legislation, one of the great Dominican ideas was gradually
given an active and practical existence, namely, the
Christianizing of the intellect, the cultivation of human
science as a handmaid to the science of divine things,
and the pursuit of learning under the safeguard of that
subjection and spiritual bondage which secured humility.
This was the system which, founded by Dominic himself,
in the succeeding age produced S. Thomas. We say,
founded by S. Dominic himself, for it is in the very year
following that of his first visit to the brethren of S. James,
before spoken of, that we find that community described
by Pope Honorious as " The brethren of the Order of
Preachers, studying in the Sacred Page at Paris." Doubtless it was the peculiar adaptation of this system to
the wants of the day which produced the surprising
effects we observe in the period immediately succeeding
Dominic's death. The learning and the piety of Europe

these flowed into the order of Preachers like a great wave. Blessed Jordan, his successor in the government is said to have clothed more than a thousand novices with his own hand; and Martene, before quoted, says of him, " There entered under his rule at Paris, into the order of Preachers, so many masters in theology, doctors in law, doctors and masters of arts, and such a countless multitude of others, that the whole world stood amazed at the grace which attended their preaching, and at the wonderful things that they did."*

Before resuming the thread of Dominic's personal history, we cannot pass without notice the foundation of the German province, which took place at the same time as those of England and Hungary. The provincial appointed for Germany by the chapter of Bologna was that same Master Conrad who had been gained to the order in so extraordinary a manner by the progress of Dominic; and when, soon after his arrival in his new government, the people of Cologne demanded a foundation of the friars among them, Henry of Utrecht was chosen as superior of the new house destined to be so celebrated in the Dominican annals. Since his profession at Paris in company with Jordan of Saxony, as related in a former chapter, he had remained in that city, where the charm of his character no less than of his preaching had obtained him universal applause. But popularity had no power to change or disturb the perfect calm and humility of his soul. " Never was there seen in him," says Blessed Jordan, " any trouble, emotion or sadness; the peace of God and the joy of a good conscience were so painted in his countenance, that you needed but to see him to learn how to love God." It is said that when the news of his entrance into the order reached Utrecht, the canon who had educated him from boyhood, and two other of his friends, were greatly grieved; and before setting out

* Those few readers who may be curious for a more particular notice of the Dominican system of study, and its happy blending of intellectual and monastic training, we may refer to an article in the Tablet ..... (Sept. 1 45), on "the Ancient Irish Dominican Schools," and another, from a well-known writer in the Rambler ..... (Jan. 1843) on " Dante and the Catholic Philosophy."

for Paris to persuade him to return, they spent a night in earnest prayer to obtain light from God on the subject. As they prayed, a voice sounded through the church, saying, " It is the Lord who has done this, and He does not change." Relieved from their anxiety, they abandoned their first purpose, and exhorted him instead to a faithful perseverance.

In 1224 the convent of Cologne was at length founded. Henry went there alone; but his talents, and the singular attractiveness of his virtues, soon gathered many about him; his influence over the people was extraordinary. The besetting vice of the nation at that time was blasphemy—one, perhaps, the most difficult to eradicate from the inveterate force of habit; yet such was the power of Henry's eloquence that he inspired the whole city with a horror of every kind of imprecation.

Cologne became in the succeeding century the nursery of the Dominican order. Within its walls S. Ambrose of Siena and S. Thomas of Aquin studied together under Albert the Great; names to which might be associated a crowd of others who illustrated their age with the splendour of their learning and the saintliness of their lives; and when, in the succeeding age, the violence of heresy laid waste so many a sanctuary, and the children of Dominic were the foremost to suffer for a cause they had ever been foremost to defend, there were not wanting those who, by the generous sacrifice of their lives, gave a crowning splendour of martyrdom to the glories of Cologne.

CHAPTER XXVI.

Dominic's last missionary journey. His return to Bologna, and
His death. Revelations of his glory. His canonization, and the translation of his relics.

THE career of Dominic was now fast drawing to a close;
but five years had been granted him to reap the harvest of
his long and solitary labours, and yet short as the time
might seem, it was enough; he had lived to see that little
seed, planted in the fields of Languedoc, grown into a
mighty tree, whose branches might now be said to cover the
earth, and his work was accomplished.

The chapter had broken up in the latter part of May;
on the 30th of the same month, Dominic received an
unusual mark of honour from the magistrates of Bologna,
who by a solemn act admitted him to the rights of a citizen,
with the privilege of entering their council and voting
on all public questions. Nor did they confine this expression of their gratitude to his person alone, but declared
it to be henceforth granted to all his successors in the
supreme government of the order. When we remember
that it was through his means that peace had been restored to the city after it had been for years the victim of
cruel civil dissensions, we feel that this was but a fitting
and natural testimony of their affection from the citizens to
their deliverer.

In the following month Dominic left Bologna on his
last missionary journey. At Venice he met Cardinal
Ugolino, and laid the foundation of the great convent
of SS. John and Paul; some say that this visit was
undertaken with the idea that some opportunity might
still present itself which should enable him to pass to
the countries of the infidels, a plan he had nearly laid
by. And there is little doubt that even before he
left Bologna he had received from God an intimation of

his approaching release. Blessed Jordan tells us, that being one night in fervent prayer, an unusually powerful emotion overwhelmed him with the desire to be with God ; and suddenly a youth of dazzling beauty appeared before him, and, calling him by name, said to him, " Dominic, my well-beloved, come to the nuptials, come." And there seemed after this time a certain change about him, as though he knew the end of all sadness was at hand. As he sat in familiar conversation with some of the students and clergy of the university, he spoke with his usual cheerfulness and sweetness for some time, then, rising to bid them farewell, he said. " You see me now in health, but before the next feast of the Assumption I shall be with God." These words surprised those who heard them ; for indeed there were no signs of approaching sickness, or of the failure of that vigorous and manly spirit for which he had been ever distinguished. Nevertheless, when he returned to Bologna after a few weeks, a marked change was visible. His hair was thinning on his temples, the excessive heat of the summer appeared to render him languid and exhausted ; and yet, for all he was evidently suffering, he never relaxed in any of his usual labours. It was the 6th of August : he had travelled from Venice to Bologna, on foot as usual, stopping at Milan, and preaching as he went ; nay, there was even a more than ordinary zeal observable in his conduct, as if he felt the time was shortening, and desired that the last hour should find him watching and at work. As he approached Bologna, the extraordinary heat affected him painfully. It was evening when he reached the convent of S. Nicholas ; in spite of his fatigue, he remained until past midnight conversing with the procurator and prior, and then proceeded to the church, where he continued in prayer until the hour of matins, notwithstanding their earnest entreaty that for once he would consent to rest during the office. As soon as it was finished, he was obliged to give way to the violence of the fever, the advances of which he had hitherto disregarded ; they begged him to allow himself a little repose on a bed, but he gently refused, and desired to be laid on a sacking which was stretched upon the ground. His head was swimming with the pain and . . . . of his malady; but even then he would not . . . himself, but desired the novices to be called round . . . that he might speak to them, for what he felt would be the last time; and all the time his patience and sweetness were never interrupted; nor, spite of the pallor of death that fast overspread his noble features, was the joy and cheerfulness of their expression for a moment changed.

The brethren were overwhelmed with affliction; and hoping that some relief might be afforded by a change of air, they took him to Santa Maria dei Monti, situated on a hill just outside the city. He himself, however, well knowing that no human skill could avail for his recovery, called the community around him that he might leave them his last testament. "Have charity in your hearts," he said, "practise humility after the example of Jesus Christ, and make your treasure and riches out of voluntary poverty. You know that to serve God is to reign; but you must serve Him in love, and with a whole heart. It is only by a holy life, and by fidelity to your rule, that you ever do honour to your profession." It was thus he continued to speak as he lay on the ground, whilst F. Ventura and the other brethren stood weeping around him. "He did not even sigh," says Ventura in his evidence; "I never heard him speak a more excellent and edifying sermon." The rector of Santa Maria made a rather unsuitable interruption to this scene, by suggesting that, should the saint die in that convent, he would certainly not wish to be carried elsewhere for burial. This obliged the brethren to refer the question to himself, and he immediately replied, with some energy, "Look well to it that I am buried nowhere but under the feet of my brethren. Carry me away from here, and let me die in that vineyard; then no one will be able to . . . . . my being buried in our own church." And although they almost feared that he would expire on the road, they nevertheless fulfilled his command, and brought him back to S. Nicholas, carrying him through the fields and vineyards wrapped in a woollen sacking, weeping as they went. Having no cell of his own, he was taken to that of Brother Moneta, and there laid on his bed. He had already received Extreme Unction at Santa Maria ; and after remaining quiet for about an hour, he called the prior to him, saying. "Prepare," (meaning for the recommendation of a departing soul); but as they were about to begin, he added, "you can wait a little;" and it was perhaps during these moments that, according to the revelation made to S. Bridget, the Mother of God, to whom he had ever shown himself so loyal and loving a servant, visibly appeared to him, and promised that she would never withdraw her patronage and protection from his order.

He was now sinking so rapidly, that they saw a very short time would rob them of the father to whom their hearts cleaved with so overflowing a tenderness; all were bathed in tears. Rodolph held his head, and gently wiped the death-sweat from his forehead ; Ventura bent over him, saying, "Dear father, you leave us desolate and afflicted; remember us, and pray for us to God." Then the dying saint summoned his fast-failing strength, and, raising his hands and eyes to heaven, he said in a clear and distinct voice ; " Holy Father, since by Thy mercy I have ever fulfilled Thy will, and have kept and preserved those whom Thou hast given me, now I recommend them to Thee. Do Thou keep them: do Thou preserve them." Then, turning to his children, he added tenderly, " Do not weep, my children; I shall be more useful to you where I am now going, than I have ever been in this life." One of them again asking him to tell them exactly where he would be buried, he replied in his former words, " Under the feet of my brethren." He seemed then for the first time to perceive that they had laid him on a kind of bed, and obliged them to remove him, and place him on ashes on the floor: the novices left the room, and about twelve of the elder brethren alone remained beside him. He made his general confession to Father Ventura, and when it was finished, he added, addressing himself to the others,

"Thanks be to God, whose mercy has preserved me in perfect virginity until this day: if you would keep chastity, guard yourselves from all dangerous conversations, and watch over your own hearts." But, an instant afterwards, a kind of scruple seemed to seize him, and he turned to Ventura with a touching humility, saying, "Father, I fear lest I have sinned in speaking of this grace before our brethren." The recommendation of his soul now began, and he followed the prayers as well as he could: they could see his lips moving; and as they recited the words, "*Subvenite, Sancti Dei; occurrite, angeli Domini, suscipientes animam ejus, offerentes eam in conspectu altissimi,*" he stretched his arms to Heaven, and expired; being in the 51st year of his age.

His weeping children stood for awhile around the body, without venturing to touch the sacred remains; but as it became necessary to prepare for their interment, they began to strip off the tunic in which he died, and which was not his own, but one belonging to Brother Moneta: and having done so, their tears of tenderness flowed afresh, for they discovered an iron chain tightly bound round his waist, and from the scars and marks it had produced, it was evident that it had been worn for many years. Rodolph removed it with the utmost reverence, and it was afterwards delivered to blessed Jordan, his successor in the government of the order, who kept it as a precious relic. It was a singular and appropriate circumstance that the funeral obsequies of this great man should be performed by one who had ever during life shewn himself his truest and most faithful friend. Cardinal Ugolino Conti came from Venice to Bologna to preside at a ceremony which, in spite of their orphanhood and desolation, his children could scarcely feel a melancholy one. Ugolino claimed this office as his right, and it was he who celebrated the funeral mass. The people of Bologna, who had shown an extraordinary sympathy with the friars during the last days of Dominic's illness, and had made continual prayers for their benefactor's recovery, followed the procession in a dense body. Patriarchs,

bishops, and abbots from all the neighbouring country
swelled the train. Among them was one who had been a
dear and familar friend of the departed saint, Albert,
prior of the convent of S. Catherine in Bologna, a man
of great piety and warm affections. As he followed,
sorrowful, and bathed in tears, he observed that the friars
chanted the Psalms with a certain joyfulness and calm of
spirit; and this had such an effect on him, that he too
stayed his tears and began to sing with them. And then
he began to reflect on the misery of this present state,
and the folly of mourning it as an evil, when a holy soul
was released from bondage and sent to the presence of
his God. With this thought in his heart, he went up, in
an impulse of devout affection, to the sacred body, and
bending over it and conquering his grief, he embraced
his dead friend, and congratulated him on his blessedness.
When he rose, an emotion of wonderful happiness was
observable on his countenance. He went up to the prior
of S. Nicholas, and taking him by the hand, " Dear father,
rejoice with me," he said; " Master Dominic has even now
spoken to me, and assured me that before the year is ended
we shall be both re-united in Christ." And the event
proved his words, for before the close of the year Albert
was with his friend.

Nor was this the only revelation of the blessedness of
Dominic which was granted to his friends. At the same
hour in which he expired, Father Guallo Romanoni, prior
of the convent of Friars Preachers in Brescia, fell asleep,
leaning against the bell-tower of his church, and he
seemed to see two ladders let down from an opening in
the sky above him. At the top of one stood our Lord,
and His blessed Mother was at the summit of the other.
Angels were going up and down them, and at their foot
was seated one in the habit of the order, but his face was
covered with his hood, after the fashion in which the
friars were wont to cover the face of the dead when they
are carried out for burial. The ladders were drawn up
into heaven, and he saw the unknown friar received into
the company of the angels, surrounded by a dazzling
glory, and borne to the very feet of Jesus. Guallo

awoke, not knowing what the vision could signify; and
hastening to Bologna, he found that his great patriarch
had breathed his last at the very moment in which it had
appeared to him, namely, six in the evening; and he
judged it as a certain token that the soul of Dominic had
been taken up to heaven. Moreover, on that same day,
the 6th of August, Brother Raoul had gone from Rome
to Tivoli in company with Tancred, the prior of Santa
Sabina, and at the hour of Sext he celebrated mass, and
made an earnest memento for his holy founder, whom he
knew to be then lying in the extremity of sickness at
Bologna. And as he did so, he seemed to see the great
road reaching out of that city, and walking along it was
the figure of Dominic between two men of venerable
aspect, crowned with a golden coronet, and dazzling with
light. Nor was this the last of these visions. A
student of the university, warmly attached to the saint,
who had been prevented by business from assisting at
his funeral, saw him on the following night in a state of
surpassing glory, as it seemed to him, seated in a particular spot in the church of S. Nicholas. The vision was
so distinct that, as he gazed on it, he exclaimed, "How,
Master Dominic, are you still here?" "Yes," was the
reply. "I live, indeed, since God has deigned to grant
me an eternal life in heaven." When he went to S.
Nicholas on the following morning, he found the place of
sepulture was the same indicated in his dream.

We shall not attempt the task of transcribing the
miracles which rendered the place of his rest glorious;
they already fill volumes entirely devoted to the purpose
of recording them. His brethren of Bologna have been
severely blamed by many authors, because in spite of
this accumulation of prodigies and Divine favours, they
allowed the body to remain under the plain flag-stone
where it had been placed by the care of Rodolph of
Faenza, without any sign of honour to distinguish it to
the eye. And what is more, in spite of the crowds who
flocked thither day and night on pilgrimage, and whose
gratitude for the graces poured out on them with such
abundance was attested by a very forest of waxen images,

and other similar votive offerings which they hung over
the spot, no move was made by the authorities of the
order to obtain the canonization of the saint. This
conduct has, we have said, been censured as a culpable
neglect; but we may perhaps be permitted to instance it
as an example of that simplicity and modesty which
Dominic left behind him as a heritage to his children.
The answer of one of the friars, when questioned on the
subject, may be taken as a sample of the spirit of the
whole body. "What need for canonization?" he said;
"the holiness of Master Dominic is known to God: it
matters little if it be declared publicly by man." A
feeling similar to this has been hereditary in the order,
and has been the cause why the early annals of many of
their most illustrious saints are so barren of details.
They never thought of providing for the applause of man;
and brilliant as is the renown of the Dominican institute
in the history of the Church, it may perhaps be said that
its greatest works have never been made manifest.

It was chance, or rather necessity, that at length
obliged the religious of S. Nicholas to undertake the first
translation of the sacred relics. The convent had to be
enlarged on account of the ever-increasing size of the
community, and the church stood in need of repair and
alteration. The tomb of Dominic had, therefore, to be
disturbed, and to do so, the Pope's permission was first
required. Honorius III. was dead, and his successor in
the papal chair was none other than Ugolino Conti, who
had been consecrated Pope under the name of Gregory IX. He acceded to the request with joy, sharply
reproving the friars for their long negligence. The
solemn translation accordingly took place on the 24th of
May, 1233, during the Whitsuntide chapter of the order,
then assembled at Bologna under blessed Jordan of
Saxony, who had succeeded his great patriarch in the
government. The Pope wished to have attended in person at this ceremony, but, being prevented doing so,
deputed the archbishop of Ravenna to represent him, in
company with a crowd of other distinguished prelates.
Three hundred Friars Preachers, from all countries, were

assembled to assist at this function, not without a secret
fear lest the sacred remains should be found to have
suffered change; and this doubt as to the result of the
translation agitated many of them during the day and
night preceding that on which it was appointed to take
place, with a painful emotion.   Among those who showed
the greatest disturbance was one named Brother Nicholas
of Giovenazzo; but it pleased God to reassure him, and
all who shared his timidity, by a special revelation.   For,
as he prayed, there appeared to him a man of majestic
appearance, who spoke these words in a clear and joyous
tone: "*Hic accipiet benedictionem a Domino, et miseri-
cordiam a Deo salutari suo.*"   And he understood them
to signify the blessedness enjoyed by S. Dominic, and to
be a pledge of the honour which God would cause to be
shown to his relics.

On the 24th of May the ceremony of translation took
place.   The general, and all the chief fathers of the
general chapter then assembled at Bologna, together
with the bishops, prelates, and magistrates, who had come
to be present on the occasion, stood round in silence
whilst the grave was opened.   Rodolph of Faenza, who
still held the office of procurator, and who had been so
dear a son to the great patriarch, was the first to commence raising the stone.   Hardly had he begun to
remove the mortar and earth that lay beneath, when an
extraordinary odour was perceptible, which increased in
power and sweetness as they dug deeper, until at length,
when the coffin appeared, and was raised to the surface
of the grave, the whole church was filled with the perfume, as though from the burning of some precious and
costly gums.   The bystanders knelt on the pavement,
shedding tears of emotion as the lid was raised, when
there were once more exposed to their eyes, unchanged,
and with the same look of sweetness and majesty they
had ever worn in life, the features of their glorious father.
Cantipratano, in his second book *De Apibus*, relates a
singular circumstance, which has been repeated by Malvenda.   He says that among the fathers present at the
ceremony was John of Vicenza, whose singular zeal and

sanctity had always rendered him specially dear to S. Dominic. As he stood by the body, he made way to give place to William, bishop of Modena; but immediately the sacred remains were seen to turn in the direction in which he stood. His humility moved him to change his place again, and the same thing was observed; and it seemed as though, on this the first day when the public honour of the Church were about to be paid to the holy patriarch, he was willing by this token to show that he counted his chiefest glory to be less in such honours than in the sanctity of his children.

It was blessed Jordan who raised the body of the beloved father from the coffin, and reverently laid it in a new case. Eight days afterwards, this was once more opened to satisfy the devotion of some nobles and others who had been present on the previous occasion; then it was that Jordan, taking the sacred head between his hands, kissed it, while tears of tenderness flowed from his eyes; and, so holding it in his arms, he desired all the fathers of the chapter to approach and gaze at it for the last time: one after another they came, and kissed the features that still smiled on them like a father; all were conscious of the same extraordinary odour: it remained on the hands and clothes of all who touched, or came near the body; nor was this the case merely at the time of the translation. Flaminius, who lived 300 years afterwards, thus writes in 1527: " This divine odour of which we have spoken, adheres to the relics even to this present day."

We shall not pause to give a detail of those abundant miracles which every day shed fresh glory round the sepulchre of S. Dominic. They were scarcely needed, one may say, as attestations of his sanctity; it seemed the universal feeling, both of prelates and people, that his canonization should be no longer deferred. The bull to that effect was published in the July of 1234; and it was the singular happiness of Pope Gregory IX., who had been bound in such close ties of friendship to the founders of the two orders of the Friars Minors and Friars Preachers, that both should be raised to the

... ... the Church by his means, and during his pontifi-
... His well known expression with regard to Dominic
... so preserved to us by Stefano Salanco: "I have no
doubt of the sanctity of this man, than I have of that
S. Peter or S. Paul."

Three festivals have been consecrated to the memory
Dominic: the 4th of August, on which his death is
celebrated instead of the 6th, already occupied by the feast
the Transfiguration; the 24th of May, in memory of
the translation of his relics; and lastly, the 15th of September, in honour of the miraculous picture of Suriano.
An obscurity rests over the origin of this picture: or perhaps
we should rather say that the Church, whilst granting the
festival, and bearing her willing testimony to the extraordinary Divine favours shown to the devotion of the
pilgrims of Suriano, has been silent as to the history of the
painting itself. It first appeared in the convent in the year
1530, and did not attract much popular regard until the
beginning of the following century, when the miracles and
conversions wrought at Suriano made it a place of pilgrimage
to the whole world. After a number of briefs granted by
successive pontiffs, and a severe examination of the facts,
Benedict XIII. at length appointed the 15th of September
to be observed through the whole order, in commemoration
of the graces received before this remarkable picture.

A second translation of the relics of S. Dominic took
place in 1267; but the beautiful sculptures which now
adorn his place of burial, and which are probably the first,
both in design and execution, among similar works of art,
were not placed over his tomb until 1473, being the *chef-
d'œuvre* of Nicholas de Bari.

CHAPTER XXVII.

"WE should have wished," says Polidro in the concluding chapter of his life, "to have been able to put before the eyes of our readers all that S. Dominic ever wrote in defence of the Catholic religion, for the instruction of his disciples, in order that they might collect from these writings yet greater and more copious illustrations of his virtues. But there remains to us nothing, except the constitutions of his order (added to the rule of S. Austin), the sentence of reconciliation to the Church of Pontio Rogerio, and the faculty granted to Raymond William of Altaripa, to entertain the heretic William Uguccione in his house. It is, however, certain that he wrote many letters to his brethren, especially exhorting them to the study of the Sacred Scriptures, but none of these now remain ; that addressed to the Polish friars, and bearing his name, not being genuine." We have already spoken of the letter here alluded to, and, as may be remembered, have mentioned that many of the best and most cautious writers have taken a more favourable view of its claims to authenticity. We shall not, therefore, again enter on the question in this place. The commentaries of S. Dominic on the Epistles of S. Paul were still extant in the time of Giovanni Colonna ; and when we remember how these Epistles formed the constant and favourite reading of the Saint, we shall know how to regret the loss of their exposition from the hand of one who followed so closely in the footsteps of S. Paul, and seemed in a special manner to have borne his mantle and received his spirit.

The lectures he gave in the apostolic palace on the e *** Epistles, together with the conferences given at B**** on the Psalms and the canonical Epistles, and on the Gospel of S. Matthew, are also referred to by L***aire as still existing in his day; but all have since been lost, and it is the misfortune of the order and of the Church that, with the exceptions mentioned above, nothing of the writings of this great man now remains.

There is one book, the mention of which occurs in one of the most striking anecdotes of his life, and which, could it be restored to us, would naturally be held in peculiar veneration, not merely for the sake of its author, but also for that token of the Divine approbation which gave to its doctrines and contents even more than the authority of a saint. We refer to the book written by Dominic in confutation of the Albigensian heresies, and which, thrice cast into the fire remained uninjured, and was even flung out of the burning heap by the flames which refused to touch it. Although this book is lost to us, together with the other writings of S. Dominic, there exists a tradition concerning its contents which is of particular interest to us at this time; and which, without passing any judgment as to its authenticity, we will give, as it is to be found alluded to by several writers. The following extract is from a letter of Father Alessandro Santo Canale, of the Society of Jesus, published in a collection of letters on the Immaculate Conception, at Palermo, in the year 1742. He says, "All the regular orders, following the inclination of the Holy Church their mother, have always shown a courageous zeal in defence of the Immaculate Conception. And I say *all*, because one of the most earnest in favour of the Immaculate Conception has been the most learned and most holy Dominican order, even from its very first beginning. I mean even from the time of the great patriarch S. Dominic, in the dispute which he held with the Albigenses at Toulouse, with so much glory to the Church and to himself. Almost from the time of S. Dominic down to the present day, there has been preserved in the public archives of Barcelona a very ancient tablet, whereon

is inscribed the famous dispute of the saint with the
Albigenses, and the triumph of the truth, confirmed by
the miracle of the fire, into which, at the request of the
heretics, the saint having thrown his book, when that of
the Albigenses was destroyed, his remained uninjured."
Of which book this inscription thus speaks:—"Against
these errors S. Dominic wrote a book on the Flesh of
Christ. And the Albigenses, rising up furiously against
the said blessed Dominic, said that the Virgin was conceived in original sin. And blessed Dominic replied,
even as it is contained in his book, that what they said
was not true; because the Virgin Mary was she of whom
the Holy Ghost says by Solomon, 'Thou art all fair, my
beloved, and there is no stain in thee.'" In this book of
S. Dominic's on the Flesh of Christ, chap. xvii., there are,
among other passages, the following words, quoted from the
Acts of S. Andrew:—"Even as the first Adam was made
of virgin earth, which had never been cursed, so also was
it fitting for the second Adam to be made in like manner."* It would seem, therefore, that the book was still
extant at the time of this inscription, and that the above
passages were quoted from it. Nor is it in any way surprising or difficult for us to believe, that Dominic,
educated in the schools of Palencia, should have been a
firm and undoubting defender of that doctrine which was,
so to speak, the heritage of Spanish theologians.

Two men have been given to the world, each of them
foremost in the ranks of genius, who have in different
ways left us the living portraits of S. Dominic. The first
is his own son Angelico, who, steeped in the spirit of his
order, drew its founder, not indeed according to the
material likeness of flesh and blood,—for *that* he had not

---

* "According to creditable opinion," says Monseigneur Parisis,
"S. Dominic professed in very express terms his belief in the
Immaculate Conception. It is even said that he committed it to
writing in a certain book, which the heretics required him to cast
into the flames, &c. . . . . It contained (it is said) in the following
terms the precious text of the Acts of the Martyrdom of S. Andrew." And he proceeds to quote the words given above.—*De-
monstration de l'Immaculatée Conception de la B. Vierge Marie, Mère
de Dieu.*

... but according to that truer portraiture which is
the type of the spiritual man. The idea of S. Dominic as
it rose before the eye of Angelico in hours of prayer and
mystic contemplation, has been left us on a thousand
panel walls, in every attitude and under every variety.
Amidst them all, we see it is the same idea, the same
man; he is there in his joyousness, his majestic beauty,
and his life of prayer. Always noble, always simple,
with his bright star upon his forehead, and the lily in his
hand, he stands among a crowd of saints and angels,
beneath the Redeemer's Cross, or by the side of the
Madonna's starry throne; and everywhere we recognize
in him our old familiar friend : him who drew all men to
him by his winning courtesy, and from whose brow there
went out that mystic splendour which attracted all who
gazed upon it.

The other painter is a poet : *the* poet of Italy and of
the middle ages. If Dante drew his inspiration from
the fount of human imaginations, it was to the order of
S. Dominic that he owed the religious character in which
it has been clothed. The poetry of Dante is to poetry
what the paintings of Angelico are to art : and indeed
the new impulse his writings gave to the early Christian
poets, exhibits the close harmony that exists between
their works and his. And if he might thus claim brotherhood with the Angelic painter, to the Angelic doctor he
was bound by yet stricter ties. His theology is that of
S. Thomas ; and to understand the *Divina Commedia*, we
must first read the *Summa*. Thus we may understand
how it is that when he comes to draw the portrait of
"the holy athlete for the Christian faith," as he terms
S. Dominic, his words flow forth with such a power of
vivid and inspired delineation.

Do we not feel that some one greater than the herd of
common men is drawing near us, when the great master
prepares us for his coming by those few low tones of
sweetest harmony which he draws from his lyre when he
bespeaks of the founder of the Friars Preachers. "There,"
he says, "where the gentle breeze whispers and waves
among the young flowers that blossom over the fields of

Europe,—not far from that shore where break the waves behind which the big sun sinks at eventide, is the fortunate Calarego; and there was born the loyal lover of the Christian faith, the holy athlete, gentle to his friends and terrible to the enemies of truth. They called him Dominic; and he was the ambassador and the friend of Christ; and his first love was for the first council that Jesus gave. His nurse found him often lying on the ground, as though he had said, ' It was for this I came.' It was because of love of Divine truth, and not for the world, that he became a great doctor in a short time; and he came before the throne of Peter, not to seek dispensations, or tithes, or the best benefices, or the patrimony of the poor; but only for freedom to combat against the errors of the world by the word of God. Then, armed with his doctrine and his mighty will, he went forth to his apostolic ministry, even as some mountain torrent precipitates itself from its rocky height. And the impetuosity of that great flood, throwing itself on the heresies that stemmed its way, flowed on far and wide, and broke into many a stream that watered the garden of the Church."

We must apologize to our readers for giving the glorious poetry of Dante in weak and ineffective prose; yet perhaps less weak and less ineffective than the attempt to render it into such verse as a translator can give. We have but reminded them of the passage, that they may turn to it in the original; for a sketch of the character of S. Dominic seems incomplete without an allusion, at least, to the writer who has perhaps drawn him best.

We should be departing from the plan we have proposed to ourselves, if we detained our readers with any summary and critical examination of the character of S. Dominic's virtues, which is usual in lives of more pretension, and written with a different object to this. But we have sought only to place this great saint before our readers in a popular light, trusting that he might speak to them himself in the story of his life; and that something of that charm of gracious joyousness on which his old biographers are so eloquent, might win them to a closer study of one whose order has been termed so

emphatically, "The Order of Truth;" and whose spirit
is, even in our own day, as young and vigorous as ever.
If there be one saint who has greater claims than another
on the love and veneration of the Church, struggling as
she is in our own country against the high tide of heresy,
it is S. Dominic. And if we would learn the way to
fight her battles, we can scarcely do better than sit at the
feet of one who knew so well how to be at the same time
the enemy of heresy and the lover of souls. That wonderful intelligence, which was able to unite so rigid a discipline with the flexibility which is to be found in what his
great daughter S. Catherine calls "the free and joyous
spirit of his order,"* had it been engaged in prescribing for
the wants of England in our own day, could scarcely have
devised a fitter rule for those who would labour in
her cause.

The austerity of S. Dominic was for himself and his
own children; but wherever there was the question of
saving souls, we find only the gay sweet manner that
men called magic, because they could not resist it; the
familiarity that mixed with the people, and would let
them cut his very habit to pieces sooner than drive them
from his side; the tenderness that never wept but for
the sufferings or the sins of others, and which, as the
Castilians said, made even penance itself seem easy, when
it was preached to them by Master Dominic. All
hours come alike to him, and the rule that at other times
of such an iron grasp upon its subjects, relaxed in a
moment when the work of God was to be done. Then,
too, how wonderful it is to find, along with all this popularity and preaching, the theological spirit never separated
from any part of his design, building up every word on the
foundation of Catholic truth, and aiming yet more at
instruction than either eloquence or exhortation. The
Friars Preachers were pre eminently to be Friars Teachers;
and from the mysteries of the Rosary up to the *Summa*
of S. Thomas, we may see the same principle of
a sound knowledge of Christian truth the ground-

* Treatise on
Obedience.

work of Christian devotion.   Thus the most popular order
was at the same time the most learned; and whilst
their portable pulpits were erected in the streets of London
and Oxford, and surrounded by the sermon-loving English
crowds of the thirteenth century, and the men who filled
them, and knew how to win the ear and rouse the conscience
of their rude and ignorant audience, were the same who
filled the chairs of the university with so briliant a renown,
that they may be said to have commenced a new era in
theological studies.

This mixed character, which is so distinctive a feature
of the Dominican rule, gives it peculiar capabilities in
a country crowded with population, and crying aloud to be
taught.   It has its sermons and rosaries for the poor, and
its theology for the learned; for sin and suffering of all
kinds, and in all shapes, there is the tenderness of that most
gentle and fatherly heart of its great founder, who when he
sold his books for his starving countrymen, and was ready
to sell his own life also, left to his children in those two
actions the rule of charity which he would have them follow as their guide.

Of all the founders of religious orders, it may be said that
they live again in the history of their institutes : but with
S. Dominic this perpetual presence among his followers in
all ages was the last legacy of his dying lips.   And we can
scarcely close this notice of his life with fitter words than
those which the Church places on our own, when she
teaches us to invoke him :—

"Thou didst promise after death thou wouldest be help-
ful to thy brethren.   Fulfil, O father, what thou hast said,
and assist us by thy prayers."

—§—

PART II.

THE DOMINICAN ORDER.

— —%. —

CHAPTER I.

Progress of the Order after the death of S. Dominic. Mis-ion.
Rise of the Dominican School of theology. Albert the Great
and S. Thomas. The universities. Influence of the Order on
language, poetry, and society. S. Raymund Pennafort. Influence on other religious bodies,

WE should scarcely be completing the work we proposed to ourselves in these pages, were we to leave our
readers without some account of the after-destinies of
the Order of Preachers. The life of a founder must
be necessarily imperfect without some notice of that
institute, which is, perhaps, the clearest expression of his
own mind and character. Whether consciously or not,
the germ of all that followed must have lain within his
own soul; and much that it is difficult for us to bring
out in the portraiture of his single life, may be more
easily studied in the general history of his order.
The rapid progress of the Friars Preachers even during
the lifetime of S. Dominic, and the position they so soon
assumed as the great teaching order of the Church, may
indeed seem to render this glance into their after-history
less necessary with them than with many other orders
that might be named. Still, though the main features of
their mission were traced out and recognized by the
world, before their founder's death, time was needed to
call forth all their resources, and to exhibit them answering to the demands of different ages, and bringing out of
their treasure house " things new and old," as they
shaped themselves to the wants of every fresh exigency.

Q

And as we watch them in their work, and see them jealously preserving the unity of their government, and adhering to the laws as well as to the spirit of their first institution, we cannot but admire at the same time their wonderful adaptation of that spirit to the needs of the times, and their aptitude in the office of teachers to the people, as they successively occupied every avenue to the popular intelligence and heart.

We are aware that in treating this subject we can do little more than present our readers with what has already been so eloquently given in the celebrated "Memorial to the French people;" but originality forms no part of our pretensions. History itself can be but the repetition of the same facts from different points of view; and whilst the view of the Père Lacordaire has been that of a nationalist and an apologist, we conceive that neither a national nor an apologetic tone would be suitable to our own circumstances. In the same way, therefore, as we have attempted to give the life of S. Dominic, we shall now add a few words on the history of his order, whose triumphs, whilst they doubtless form part of his accidential glory in heaven, unfold to us, century after century, something more of the character of his own soul.

We have before observed that the most remarkable feature in the Dominican order has been the variety of ways in which it has been allowed to act on the destinies of the Church and of the world. As apostles, as theologians, as men of science, as bishops, or as simple ascetics, in every branch of human learning, and every form of the religious life, the world has felt the influence of the children of S. Dominic. Two only, however, of these characteristics had perfectly developed themselves during the life of the founder; namely, the apostolic labours of the order, and its cultivation of theological science, which last was expressly enjoined on the order by its very constitutions, and with a view to which the Friars Preachers had already fixed their residence in the neighbourhood of the three great universities of Europe. During S. Dominic's life, however, although the theological element had been

d.... .... y reco..nized and provided for, the apostolic cha-
r..... ....atly preponderated. And this was only natural;
wh... theologians were being slowly and painfully formed
in the schools of Paris and Bologna, a fervent noviciate
under the guidance of the saint was education enough
for the preacher, whose power lay not so much in the
depth of his science, as in the magic of his eloquence,
and the holiness of his life. We have but to recall some
of these wonderful conversions, to which we have referred in the foregoing pages, and of which the early
annals of the order are so full, and then to remember
the power of that deep religious enthusiasm which
follows on the death of human passion, and inherits all
its intensity, to understand how an ardent apostolic zeal
was sure to be the first spirit developed in an order
devoted to the salvation of souls. As time went on,
it seized on other means for the advancement of the
same object, and claimed science and the very arts as
instruments for saving souls; but in the fresh fervour of
their institute there was not time for this, and the first
fathers of the order were necessarily, and almost exclusively, preachers and apostles of the faith. It was in
this apostolic character that the order spread itself with
such rapidity over Europe during the first twenty years
of its foundation. The second chapter of Bologna, over
which S. Dominic had presided just before his death, had
witnessed the establishment of eight provinces, including
more than sixty convents— fruit enough for the labours
of six short years; before seven more had elapsed, four
new provinces had been added, under the government of
Blessed Jordan of Saxony, whilst the convents and the
numbers of the brethren had multiplied, we had almost
said, miraculously. Jordan is said to have clothed more
than a thousand novices with his own hand; and we are
told that the first thing done on his arrival at any of the
houses was to supply cloth for the habits of the crowd
of postulants who were sure to apply for admission.
This extraordinary expansion of the order did not show
i.... i.. .... direction more than another; for athletes
o.. ...g.. ties and early associations of Jordan hi... .f

naturally turned to the Holy Land, which was the country
of his birth, yet this attraction to the east did not prevent an equal growth in other and opposite directions,
so that whilst Greece and Palestine formed two of the
new provinces, others were established in Poland and
Dalmatia.

During the brief space granted to S. Dominic after the
establishment of his order, he was permitted to clothe
with his own hands two men destined to be among the
greatest of his children, and, like himself, to be enrolled
by the church among the catalogue of her saints. The
first of these was S. Hyacinth, of whose extraordinary
vocation and subsequent career we have before spoken.
And whilst he is reverenced in his order as her greatest
apostle, the name of S. Peter of Verona stands as the
glorious first-fruits of her martyrs. We shall not attempt,
in our limited space, anything like a sketch of the labours
of S. Hyacinth, and of the other great missionaries who
followed in his steps. In later ages, infidelity has well
nigh swept away the traces of their apostolate, so that
the very names of the countries through which they
preached are lost to Christendom; and we are apt to be
startled at the notices which we find in history, exhibiting
to us the vast extent of the empire of the Cross during
the middle ages. These accounts, which we are often
tempted to treat as mere fable and romance, receive
singular confirmation from the discoveries of our own
times; and the vestiges of Christian doctrine and Catholic ceremonial among the Tartars of the present day
may possibly seem less unaccountable, when we remember
that not only did S. Hyacinth preach the faith in those
distant regions of Asia, as far as the northern boundaries
of China, but that with a success which is evidenced by
the distinct notices we have of embassies from Christian
princes of these countries to various European courts so
early as the middle of the thirteenth century. The exact
detail of S. Hyacinth's labours has never been preserved;
he alone could have chronicled them; but, as one of
his historians* justly observes, "his only thought was to

*Touron.

... ... to tell us what he did for their Nation. And whilst the fruits of his prodigious toils have
in other places been utterly swept away, we cannot but
refer to what the same writer remarks as among the
greatest miracles, one ever fresh, and subsisting even,
as to this day,—we mean the preservation of the faith
with so much of its first fervour in the unfortunate country
which gave him birth. Nowhere has the Catholic faith
sustained ruder shocks than in Poland; heresy and schism,
and infidelity, and the tyranny of a foreign yoke, have
done their best to root it from her soil; yet still she
gives her martyrs to the torture and the sword, and
the Order of Preachers, to whom she owes her great
apostle, still finds a cherished home in her torn and
afflicted bosom.

If S. Hyacinth and his followers sustained the apostolic character of the order in the northern countries, a
long succession of great men might be cited, who were
for centuries the chief supporters of the faith throughout
the East. In 1330, under the pontifiate of John XXII.,
we find the Friars Preachers established in Armenia,
and one of their number, the blessed Bartholomew of
Bologna, governing the Church of that nation as archbishop of Naksivan. By his labours the Greek schism
was well nigh exterminated out of the land,* and the
Armenians returned to the Church in crowds. He also
made a successful resistance to the progress of Mahometanism, then beginning to extend its baneful influence
through the East; and we may gather some idea of the
position of the order in Armenia from the tradition of
the Christians of that country, who affirm that seven
distinct churches were founded at that time, whose
bishops were all taken from the ranks of the Friars
Preachers. These dioceses were established in Persia,
Caffa, Georgia, and the countries on the shores of the

* Clement Galanus tells us of a certain Brother John, an Englishman and companion of blessed Bartholomew's, who assisted him
in the translation of a vast number of theological books into the
Armenian dialect, and adds, that many copies of these translations
were to be found in the Armenian convents of the order still existing in his time.

Black Sea; and even after the triumph of Mahometanism in these regions, the Dominicans stood their ground, and their houses were still existing in Armenia up to a late period. The archbishopric of Naksivan, first filled by blessed Bartholomew, still exists : and his orthodox successor rules in our own day over a widely-extended diocese, in which the free exercise of the Catholic faith has been tolerated under the successive rules of the Tartars, the Saracens, and the Persians. So late as the date of Touron's history, the archbishops were still nominated by the superiors of the order, and chosen from its ranks.

In Persia the success of the Dominican missions was scarcely less brilliant. Under the same Pope, Franco of Perugia was appointed archbishop and metropolitan of Sultana, while six religious of his order were named to other sees. Nor were these empty titles. We have abundant proof of the rapid extension of the Church in these new provinces from the Papal briefs, which grant power to the archbishop to consecrate other bishops as necessity might require, and give the charge of all the churches, left without a sufficient number of pastors, to the community of the Friars Preachers. And here we may again observe the special blessing which seems to rest on the missionary labours of the order; for the primate of Armenia being won over to recognize the primacy of Rome by the zeal of Father Franco, his successors have ever since continued in the orthodox communion, and enjoy the title of "the Catholic."*

Our readers would perhaps smile were we to include among the missionary conquests of the order the dominions of Prester John; and quote the romantic pages of Uretta with their wonderful tales of the convents of Plurimanos and Alleluia, each inhabited by many thousand religious, and more than four leagues in circuit, with their eighty dormitories, each one with his own church and offices, and their refectories a mile in length. But though the extraordinary legends of the Spanish writer belong rather to poetry than to history, it can scarcely be

*Touron.

believed, but that some ground existed for his narrative; and that the Dominican Order had at one time made so extraordinary a progress in Abyssinia and Ethiopia that, while no authentic records are left of their achievements, their memory has been retained in the exaggerated fables of romance. The merest glance into the history of these countries, now overspread by Mahometanism, astonishes us with the idea it presents of the extent to which Christianity had spread in the south and east; and in the annals of the order we have indications of the countless martyrs who fell in the defence of these almost unknown churches. For everywhere the apostolate of the Friars Preachers was sown and sealed in blood; and throughout Poland, Hungary, Armenia, and Tartary, the first century of their labour yielded to the Church a glorious addition to her white-robed company of martyrs.

Meanwhile, the other element of which we have spoken, that of theological science, was developing itself in an equal degree. The very year that was marked by the death of S. Dominic witnessed the admission into the order of one who may be called the first-fruits of its theology. This was the stupid Swabian novice, driven to despair during his noviciate because he was too dull to learn, but who, receiving the gift of a profound intelligence from the very hands of Mary, has been known to all succeeding ages by the title of Albert the Great.[*] Albert may be taken as the very type of a doctor, or master of those times, and as such, his name, under the mythological guise of poetic fable, has been made as well known as that of Faust or Cornelius Agrippa. It need scarcely be said that the poetical and the historical Albert are two very different personages; yet a man's learning must needs be something wonderful to admit it to legendary fame. Perhaps, in few ages but the thirteenth would learning alone have gained him such a distinction; but that singular century presents us with the romance of science. We are accustomed to talk much of the taste for knowledge exhibited in our own day, yet it may be questioned whether, with all our education, we can in

any degree comprehend the enthusiasm with which our
fathers of the middle ages entered into the arena of
philosophy and scholastic learning. One great cause of
the popularity of science in those days may doubtless be
found in the method by which it was taught. The press
was then unknown, and men learnt everything from the
lips of their teachers ; the teaching came to them with
all that living, personal charm which ever gives so far
more powerful an influence to the spoken than to the
written word ; and so philosophy and grammar, the
logic of Aristotle, and the sentences of Peter Lombard,
which would seem but dull "reading for the million" in
the nineteenth century, were popular in the thirteenth,
and excited an extravagant enthusiasm when dressed in
the witchery and grace of rhetoric. We are surely right
in speaking of this age as the romantic era of learning,
when it furnishes us with such a scene as that given in
the life of the Great Albert on his first visit to Paris in
the year 1248. He came there to lecture on the sentences, as he had previously done in all the cities of
Germany. His fame preceded him, and no school in
the University was large enough to contain the crowds
who flocked to listen to his words ; so they and their
lecturer were forced to adjourn to the great square outside, and the subtle discourse of the great master was
delivered on the spot since called the "Place Maubert,"
a corruption of the words, "Place Maître Albert."

The variety of Albert's learning is indicated in the sentence by which his contemporaries describe him, "*Magnus
in magia, major in philosophia, maximus in theologia ;*"
but whatever his distinction of these branches of learning,
we may safely say that his crowning glory was in the
disciples whose minds were formed under his own. His
prodigious intellect was the morning star of Dominican
science, but a very galaxy followed : and at one time he
numbered among his pupils in the University of Cologne[*]

* Among other pupils of Albert the Great, and fellow-students
of S. Thomas, we may mention blessed Thomas Joyce, an Englishman, who joined the order with his five brothers, and was afterwards
created cardinal of Santa Sabina by Clement V.

There - Cantipratano, S. Ambrose of Siena, S. James of
B........, B. Augustine of Hungary, and, above and
...... and others, S. Thomas Aquinas, whose fame soon
..... first of his master and companions in the shade.
Happy indeed is it for an age, and an order, when, in
giving a list of their learned men, we give one only of
c......ized or beatified saints. The children of S. Dominic
..... will look back to that era with something of pride,
and something yet more of humiliation; for in those days
the men who earned for their order its highest claims in
the ranks of intellectual greatness, if, like Albertus Magnus,
they were "great in magic," greater in philosophy,
greatest in theology," were greatest of all in another and
profounder science, and that was the "supereminent science
of Divine love."

It would of course be quite unnecessary to enter here
on any analysis of the claims by which S. Thomas holds
his rank among the first doctors of the Church. His name
is enough to thousands who never read a line of his work,
and are content with knowing that the Church has accepted
.......ost as the definer of her faith. When the Tride-
.... fathers had laid on their council-table, as their only
.. h....ies, the Holy Scriptures, the decrees of the Pope,
.... the works of the angelic doctor, they completed his
.... fia......... as a theologian. Yet, whatever may be the
..... of reputation accorded to S. Thomas by the
v.... of the six centuries that have elapsed since he formed
t.... crate materials of dogmatic, moral, and speculative
te......gy into one grand and finished structure, we c...
r... certainly rightly estimate his merit without some
k.....ge of the dangers from which science and phil
..... were rescued by his teaching. During the 12th an
t..... c......, the revival of learning had led to dangers.
.... and men pursuing their philosophic inquiri
.... the check of authority, and with the ardour o.

an unbridled passion, had plunged into the very vortex of
scepticism.   The universities were as often schools of infidelity as of faith ; the philosophers of the age owned but
one master. and he had the misfortune to be a heathen.
"Aristotle," says Lacordaire. " was taken as the representative of wisdom; and, unfortunately, Aristotle and the
gospel did not always agree."

But, besides the natural consequences of taking a
Pagan philosopher as the infallible guide and teacher of
thought to Christian students, the very enthusiasm of
the age constituted its great danger.   "As soon as we take
our first glance at this epoch," says Balmez,* "we observe that in spite of the intellectual rudeness which
one would imagine must have kept nations in abject
silence, there was at the bottom of men's minds an
anxiety which deeply moved and agitated them. The
times were ignorant. but it was an ignorance, conscious
of itself, which longed for knowledge.   We find in different parts of Europe a certain germ and index of the
greatest disasters ; the most horrible doctrines arise
amidst the heaving masses ; the most fearful disorders
signalize the first step of the nations in the career of life:
rays of light and heat. indeed, have penetrated the shape-
less chaos, presaging the new future which is reserved for
humanity. but at the same time the observer is seized
with alarm, for he knows that this heat may produce
excessive fermentation, and engender corruption in the
field which promises soon to become an enchanting
garden. . . . . . The world was in danger of being abused
and deceived by the first fanatic who came ; and at such
a moment the fate of Europe depended on the direction
given to the universal activity."   This intellectual "fermentation." to use the expressive term of the Spanish
writer, gave rise to the most astonishing extravagances.
Perverting the *will*, we see it breaking out in the wild
and criminal excesses of the Manichees, and other fana-
tical sects ; whilst in the schools the *understanding* was
darkened and led astray by innumerable subtleties : and

* "Protestantism and Catholicity compared in their effects on
the civilization of Europe," chap. 43.

... the Christian philosophy had been reduced to
system, may, entering on the unexplored sea of thought
without a guide, made hopeless shipwreck of their faith.
In the same chapter of his great work on civilization
which we have quoted, Balmez, after presenting us with
a striking sketch of the confusion and excitement of the
times, does not hesitate to attribute the salvation of
Europe from the chaos into which it was about to plunge,
to the influence exerted on society by the mendicant
orders; nor was that influence anywhere more powerfully felt, nor the danger itself more imminent, than in
the schools of the Universities. For the peculiarity in
the mode of teaching of those times, when the chair of an
illustrious professor drew together crowds who had
travelled from distant countries to listen to the famous
master of the day, while it gave a wonderful vivacity and
interest to the pursuit of science, fostered a danger which
has ever been the nurse of false doctrine. It was hard
for a man who saw himself the object of such popular
enthusiasm, to resist the seductions of vanity ; and vanity
would often tempt him to sacrifice truth to novelty, to
seek the reputation of being the founder of a new
system, and to affect what was bold and original in theory
in matters where original speculation is seldom friendly
to the faith. It was amid the confusion of these new
opinions that S. Thomas was given to the world to mark
out the limits of Christian philosophy ; he did not attempt
to silence the strife of tongues by an antagonism of terms,
but skilfully adapted the language of Aristotle, and forced
it into the service of the Church. To use the expression of
a modern writer, "he recaptured his writings by giving
them a Christian sense." Thus the work which S. Dominic had begun by directing the enthusiasm of the will into
a religious channel, was completed by his great follower,
who laid the chains of faith on the enthusiasm of the
... A broad highroad, safe and visible to all, was
by his master hand over the quicksands of opinion;
... those who had preceded him as champions
of Christianity had, for the most part, advocated the sup-
... of the intellectual power whose erratic excesses

were beyond their control. S. Thomas boldly advocated
its claims, and did but bring the haughty rebel to the
servitude of the faith. "His leading idea," says Balmez,
"was to make the philosophy of the time subservient to
the defence of religion." For this reason he used the
language and system of Aristotle rather than those of the
fathers, to whom the master of the sentences had closely
adhered; he won men from the dangers of philosophy
by availing himself of its charms; and in the words
of the writer just quoted, "finding the schools in anarchy,
he reduced them to order, and on account of his angelic
intellect and eminent sanctity was looked up to as their
sublime dictator."[*]

In his own time, however, this bright luminary rose on
the world amid the storm of controversy and persecution.
The twin orders of S. Francis and S. Dominic had already
taught theology publicly in their schools, although
excluded from the chairs of the Universities. If, however, the University professorship were jealously guarded
by the secular authorities, these had sometimes the
mortification to see them resigned by their most illustrious occupants, in order to embrace the institute of
their despised rivals. It is interesting to ourselves to
know that the two first of either order who publicly
taught theology in the schools of Paris were English-
men by birth; they were John of S. Giles, and Alexander of Hales. The first was remarkable for proficiency in natural, as well as theological science, and
his early reputation had been gained by his lectures on
medicine. But laying aside these pursuits in order to
devote himself to the exclusive study of religion, he
received the degrees of doctor, and finally a professor's
chair from the University of Paris. A day came, however, when he was to present the world with one of those
great practical lessons, more eloquent than any words.
The chapter general of the Friars Preachers was then
assembled in the French capital under the goverment
of blessed Jordan; and on a certain day John of S. Giles
appeared in the pulpit of S. James's church to preach to

[*] Balmez, chap. 71.

a vast assembly of his admirers. His sermon was on the
vanity of the world, the worthlessness of its riches, its
honours, and of all it had to give. In the midst of his
impassioned oratory, as he was listened to in profound
silence by the breathless audience, he suddenly stopped,
descended the palpit steps, and, kneeling at the feet of
Josceline before all present, he asked and received the
habit of religion, and this being done, he finished his
discourse, having thus illustrated his subject by his
example as well as by his words. Nevertheless, in consequence of the urgent solicitation of the students, he
did not discontinue his lectures as professor; and this,
according to Nicholas Trivet, first gave rise to the erection of the Dominican chair of theology at the University.
He adds that there were many others illustrious at once
for their learning and virtue, who about the same time
renounced everything that the world had to give, to
embrace the voluntary poverty of Jesus Christ, retiring
into the orders of the Friars Preachers, or the Friars
Minors. Alexander Hales was one who joined the ranks
of the Franciscans; but among the illustrious Dominicans of this period none held a higher reputation than
Bacon and Fishacre, of whom we have before spoken.
Matthew Paris does not hesitate to say of them, that
England had none to compare with them for greatness
of learning or sanctity of life. They both took the habit
of the Preachers at Oxford about the same time that
John of S. Giles embraced the institute in Paris; and,
like him, they continued to fill their professional chairs,
adding to their studies the exercise of the apostolic
duties.

The jealousy of the secular clergy, however, headed by
the rector of the university of Paris, William de St. Amour,
soon directed a violent assault on the position assumed
by the two orders in the French capital. In the long
contest of forty years which ensued between the University and the mendicant friars, and which has been
rendered illustrious by the joint defence offered for the
latter by S. Thomas Aquinas, and S. Bonaventura, the
champions of their respective orders, the seculars dis

tinguished themselves by the violence of their invectives, and the grossness of their libels. According to them, the friars were hypocrites and false prophets, and everything spoken of in the Scriptures concerning the forerunners of Antichrist was to be interpreted of them. It was not until the year 1255 that this celebrated quarrel was finally settled by the decision of Pope Alexander IV., which put the two orders in possession of all their contested privileges; and, amongst others, of that so dearly prized, of being eligible for the university professorships. In fact, when the struggle was over, the Dominicans may be said to have taken possession of the universities of Europe. John of S. Giles, already mentioned, held the chair of theology in no fewer than four; and the two professorships already claimed by the order in Paris, were secured to it by the authority of S. Louis; whilst Oxford and Bologna, which had already given so many of their doctors to the new institute, now received back their most renowned professors from its ranks. From this period must date the development of the second great mission of the Friars Preachers,—their influence on theology and learning: their ranks were already rich with the names of apostles and martyrs; they were now to be equally prolific in those of doctors. Their schools everywhere started up side by side with the numerous universities which that age of scholastic enthusiasm produced at Orleans, Toulouse, Montpellier, and other places which it would be wearisome to enumerate. They may be said to have created the university of Dublin altogether; while their influence continued paramount in those of Oxford, Paris, and Bologna; "where," says a writer of our own day; "they did more than any other teachers to give the knowledge taught in them its distinctive form."

But the influence produced by the learning of the Dominicans was far from being confined to theology; their institute embraced no smaller idea than that of Christianizing the very well-spring of science; so that, as its thousand streams flowed forth to irrigate and fertilize the world, there should mingle with their floods

the ... and healing of the waters of life. Nicholas
Trevet, the English historian, and a member of the order,
is described, for instance, by Le Gendre as " a good
religious, a good poet, a good philosopher, a great mathematician, and a profound theologian." At an age, therefore, when England is commonly said to have had no
literature (Henry III. Edward I.), the order of Preachers
gave her this great writer, whom Touron declares to have
possessed all the sciences, and each one as perfectly as
if he had made it his exclusive study." And the list of
his varied acquirements is but a sample of those in which
his brethren have by turns excelled. Much of this learning, it must be remembered, was conveyed, not through
writings, but from the lips of skilled and eloquent preachers; and hence the very calling and office of a Dominican
gave him familiarity with the great medium of popular
instruction in those days. We can scarcely estimate the
effect of the sudden expansion of the office of preaching
which followed on the establishment of the mendicant
orders, as it was felt not only in religion, but in language
and general education. The intellects, as well as the wills of
men were enlightened by the sermons of such teachers as
Taulerus and Suso; for we must remember that preaching
was not now, as formerly, confined to the towns and
universities, and the resorts of the learned and opulent;
every country village and mountain district was in turn
visited by the wandering friar, who often taught his simple
audience the elements of thought and language with the
same accents with which he spoke to them of penance
and of faith. This, which is no fanciful supposition, may
be illustrated by the example of blessed Jordan of Pisa,
a man asserted by contemporary writers to have been at
once " a prodigy of nature, and a miracle of grace," but
whose reputation, like that of so many of his brethren,
has scarcely survived his own day, through the modesty
of his order, whose historians are never so tantalizing in
their brevity as when speaking of the illustrious members
of their own society. He lived at the latter part of the
thirteenth century, a time when the language of Italy
was still unformed, and presented a rude chaotic mixture

of the barbarous dialects left by the inundations of the northern nations. The "*lingua Toscana*" as yet had no vocabulary; and, we are told, the first to harmonize and combine its scattered elements was this preaching friar, whose eloquence, rich in classic erudition and the grace of native genius, was uttered in a style at once new and perfectly intelligible to his hearers ; so that the few fragments that remain of his sermons may even now be taken as examples of correct and musical Italian. He, too, was one of the varied geniuses of his order. Not only was he a great philosopher and theologian, "joining the eloquence of Tully to the memory of Mithridates," but, we are told, "he was a perfect master in the art of teaching men with equal facility on any subject that he chose."[*]

We may at the same time mention two others whose influence on what we might call the civilization of language was not less remarkable. The first is Bartholomew à Sancta Concordia, also a Pisan, who flourished about the middle of the fourteenth century. He wrote in his native tongue, and his little work entitled "Teaching of the Ancients," is praised by Leonardo Salviati, who speaks of the "force, brevity, clearness, beauty, grace, sweetness, purity, and simple ease which are there to be seen expressed in language worthy of the best era or literature." And again he says, "This work is written in the best and noblest style which the age had yet produced, and it would be fortunate for our language were the volume larger." The other writer to whom we referred is Father J. Passavanti; and his "Mirror of True Penance," originally written in Latin, but translated by his own hand into Italian, is thus praised by the editor of the Della-Cruscan Academy, who undertook a reprint of the work in 1861 :—"The 'Mirror of True Penance,' by Father P. ssavanti, a Florentine by birth, and a Dominican by religious profession, written in the style of his day, but adorned with the purest of gold of the most refined eloquence, has gained a more than ordinary applause, both for the sacred matter it contains and the charm and

---

* Marchese, quoted from Leander Albert.

beauty of its composition. And as many have thought that it might without disadvantage be compared with the writings of the most learned among the first fathers of the Church, so we may also consider it as inferior to none of the choicest and most renowned masters of the Tuscan tongue." These men, together with another Dominican preacher, Domenico Cavalca, are named by Pignotti among the fathers of Italian literature.

Poetry, too, the most popular of all branches of literature, was not without receiving some influence from the order whose mission was to popularize the faith by infusing it into science, and to teach men through all channels and by all ways. We have already alluded to the power of its theology over the muse of Dante. Without such a check, what might not have been the fate of that wild and daring genius? But in him, happier than so many to whom the laurel has been a poisoned wreath, imagination owned the mastery of faith, and his imperishable verses bear on to all ages the dogmas of the angelic doctor. And if the Dominicans may thus half claim the poet as their theologian, they may more than half claim for their great theologian the laurel of the poet. None can read those beautiful hymns of the Church, given to her by the inspired pen of S. Thomas,* without acknowledging their poetic as well as their devotional excellence. And this is yet more true of what we may fearlessly venture to call one of the finest lyrics in any language,—we mean the "*Dies Iræ*," a production which, though its authorship is contested, is most commonly attributed, and with the greatest appearance of probability, to the Dominican Cardinal Latino Malabranca, or Frangipani, who died in the year 1294.

The greater part of the preaching talent of the order has, of course, left no monument behind it which might enable us to measure the work done by it, or the intellect which produced it. We gather only a general, and certainly an astonishing, idea of the greatness of the

* The "Adoro Te," "Pange Lingua," "Verbum Supernum," "Lauda Sion," and "O Sacris Solemniis."

mediæval preachers by the position which their office
assumes in the history of the times. What wonderful
pictures, almost remantic in their colouring, may be
found, for instance, in the lives of saints such as S. An
thony of Padua among the Friars Minors, or Blessed
Matthew Carrerio among the Dominicans, or a hundred
others who might be named, and who really seemed to
have the world at their command by the force of their
eloquence. Half the influence produced by these orders
on society is beyond our power to estimate, for it was
exerted by their daily association with men, and the
power of their personal words or presence. Hitherto,
let it be remembered, the sanctity and learning of the
cloister, and that wondrous, indescribable power felt even
by those who most abhor it, which is possessed over the
world by the men who have renounced it for ever.—
all this had been for the most part withdrawn from
the popular view; and the deserts of Citeaux or the
Chartreuse, or the craggy summits of Monte Cassino,
shut out religion from the familiar eye of men. Now it
was in their streets; the poor could gaze at it and be
familiar with it, for it came under the garb of poverty;
the rich and the learned felt its sway, for under the
ragged tunic there lay those high gifts whose power they
were forced to own resistless. The influence of religion
and education thus popularized, and widely diffused in its
living representatives, must have been something equal
to, if not surpassing, the modern action on society of the
press. We can scarce open a book which treats of these
times, without meeting with some additional evidence of
this. The friars were the favourite confessors of kings,
and their coarse habits were familiar in the gayest courts;
yet they were also the brethren and companions of the
poor. Most of our popular devotions, those best adapted
to sink into the hearts of the common people, and by
their very simplicity to win for themselves universal
acceptation in the Church, have come to us through the
hands of the friars. Thus the devotion of the Stations
of the Cross, is said to have originated with the Blessed
Alvaro of Cordova, of the Order of Friars Preachers,

, whom we are told, in the breviary-office on his feast, that he constructed in his convent of Scala Cœli, representations of all the holy places of Palestine connected with the Passion, so disposed that each of the mysteries of our redemption was thus exhibited together, and that after his time this pious custom spread to other convents. In later times, we know, it has found its chief propagators in the sister Order of S. Francis. Again the Angelus, that most popular, and, as one might say, most Christianizing of all minor devotions, bringing as it does the thought of Christ incarnate to men's minds thrice a day, and forcing them by a sweet compulsion to kneel and worship in the field or the thoroughfare, whenever the bell for the Ave Maria falls on their ear, was first instituted by S. Bonaventura, and propagated among the people by his directions after the general chapter of the Friars Minors held at Pisa in 1262. The influence of the Rosary, the peculiar devotion of the Dominican order, it is impossible to over-estimate. It has been the defence of the faith itself against heresy and unbelief, and it would require a treatise to tell of all the wonders worked on society by this one devotion alone. Indeed, the institution of all kinds of lay confraternities for devotional purposes may be said to have arisen out of it ; and these associations beginning with the Dominicans, were afterwards taken up and propagated with equal ardour by the Franciscans ; so that in the annals of the Friars Minors the first establishment of these pious societies is attributed to S. Bonaventura.

The presence of the friars among them was eagerly courted by a grateful people, who knew that the white scapular of S. Dominic, or the cord of S. Francis, brought with them their own blessings. How often do we find mention of this hearty welcome of the mendicants among the people to whom they came to preach ; an enthusiasm which in some degree explains their rapid extension over Europe, for churches and monasteries sprang up for them wherever they appeared ; and we are told that after the sermons of S. Francis it was common for the people of the town or country where he preached to offer to build a convent. It was thus that the mountain of Alvernia was bestowed on him by Orlando, where, as we read in the exquisite chronicles of the order, on his sending two of his brethren to take possession of the chapel and monastery, they were welcomed to the solitude by the cries of the birds who came forth to greet them. And if we consider the works of active charity practised by the friars, so many of whom fell victims in their services to the plague-stricken, and the innumerable hospitals and institutes of mercy that owed their origin to them, as the orphanages founded by S. Vincent Ferrer in almost every city of Spain, this view of their beneficial influence on society, apart from their writings or actual apostolic labours, may be largely extended. Nay, were we to attempt anything like an examination into the subject, we might startle our readers by the variety of inventions and institutions of practical and social utility,* quite distinct from religion, which have originated with the friars of both orders, and which show at once their kindly sympathy with the people's wants, and their universal influence for the amelioration and civilization of society. In the words of Balmez, "if the illustrious Spaniard, Dominic of Guzman, and the wonderful man of Assisi, did not occupy a place on our altars, there to receive the veneration of the faithful for their eminent sanctity, they would deserve to have statues raised to them by the gratitude of society and humanity." Then, after rapidly sketching the change beginning to be felt in Europe at the time when the mendicants first arose, he proceeds to draw the portrait of these new orders in words which need no apology for their insertion. "They are not," he says, speaking of the friars, "anchorites living in remote deserts, nor monks sheltered in rich abbeys, nor clergy whose functions and duties are confined to any particular place; they are men without fixed abodes, and who are

* For instance, the institution of the "Monte di Pieta," so well known in Catholic countries, and so admirable a substitute for the pawnbroker's shop, is to be attributed to a friar minor, Barnabo di Terni, who made the first experiment of the kind at Perugia during the pontificate of Leo X.

found sometimes in populous cities, and sometimes in
miserable hamlets ; -to-day, in the midst of the old continent, to-morrow on a vessel which bears them on peril-
ous missions to the remotest countries of the globe ;
sometimes they are seen in the palaces of kings, enlight-
ening their councils and taking part in the highest
affairs of state ; sometimes in the dwellings of obscure
families, consoling them in misfortune, reconciling their
differences, and giving them advice on their domestic
affairs. These same men who are covered with glory in
the chairs of the universities, teach the catechism to
children in the humblest boroughs ; illustrious orators
who have preached in courts before kings, go to explain
the gospel in obscure villages. The people find them
everywhere, and meet them at every step—in joy and in
sorrow ; these men are constantly ready to take part in
the happy festivities of a baptism which fills the house
with joy, or to lament a misfortune which has just covered
it with mourning. We can imagine," he continues, " the
force and ascendency of such institutions. Their influence on the minds of nations must have been incalculable :
the new sects which had aimed at misleading the multitude with their pestilent doctrines, found themselves face
to face with an adversary who completely conquered
them. They had thought to deceive the simple by the
ostentation of austerity, and to strike the imagination by
the sight of exterior mortification and poor clothing ;
but the new institutions united these qualities in an
extraordinary degree ; and the true doctrine had the
same attributes which error had assumed. Violent
declaimers had sought to take possession of the minds of
the multitude by their fiery eloquence; but in all parts
of Europe, we meet now with burning orators, pleading
the cause of truth, who, well versed in the passions, ideas,
and tastes of the people, know how to interest them, and
use in *defence* of religion what others avail themselves of
to attack her. They are found wherever they are wanted
to combat the efforts of sects. Free from all worldly
ties, belonging to no particular Church, or province, or
kingdom, they have the means of passing rapidly from

one region to another, and are found at the proper time
wherever their presence is most urgently required.',*

But there is just one peculiarity in the mission of the
friars to society at large on which we must briefly touch ;
it is the part they took as the peacemakers of the world.
Whether we look to what they did as popular mendicant preachers scattered over the face of the world, or to
the influence exerted by their chiefs and great dignitaries,
we shall always find the same spirit evinced ; and these
persecutors of the people, and enemies of freedom, as
some have loved to represent them, are emphatically men
of peace.   Beautiful upon the earth were the feet of those
who brought the glad tidings which healed the feuds and
factions of those turbulent ages : of some, like the
English Lawrence, and S. Vincent Ferrer, we read, that
they never left a town or village without having chased
away all hatreds and discords from the place.   Others,
like Crescenti in Russia, were legates of peace to distant
countries.   The pontificates of two of the Dominican
Popes, Innocent V. and Benedict XI., short as they were,
were both distinguished by successful exertions in extinguishing the bloody and rival factions of the time.
Cardinal Latino Frangipani went about through Italy on
this heavenly mission, and received the title of the prince
of peace ; and the same might be said of a vast number
of others whose names would fill a volume.†   But that
our readers may form some idea of the lovely character
of these missions of peace, we will add a passage from
the life of the blessed Ventura of Bergamo.   He was one
of those gentle and loving men whose tenderness draws
to their feet the greatest criminals, whose hardened hearts
are melted by their charity and their tears.   It is
thus that Oderic Raynaldus describes his labours at
Bergamo in the cause of peace.   The fruits of his preaching were visible in a vast crowd of penitents, who abjuring
their ancient animosities, were formed into a united confraternity, and conducted by the blessed father on a
pilgrimage to Rome.   Thus, at the time when the lords

* " Protestantism and Catholicism Compared," ch. 43.
† See " Mores Catholici," book ix. ch. 12

and tyrants of Italy, busy with the thought of satisfy-
ing their ambition, their avarice, and their cruelty, were
deluging her cities with blood. Ventura, full of zeal for
the salvation of souls, determined to oppose to these devices
of the demon of discord a holy society of Christians, who,
led by a different spirit, should have no other standard than the cross, and no other device than the three
words, "Peace, Penance, and Mercy." These pious
pilgrims to the number of 10,000, and followed by an
almost infinite multitude of people, journeyed along, wearing white robes, with a little cloak of a blue colour. The
cross was seen on one side of their habit, and on the
other a dove with an olive branch in its mouth. In
their hands they bore instruments of penance, and still
as they went they chanted the praises of God, or those
oft-repeated words, "Peace, Penance and Mercy." The
order they preserved in their march filled all men with
admiration; they went two and two, and kept close
to the rules prescribed by their holy leader. And so
they travelled till they reached Rome, where they
solemnly sealed the reconciliation of all their feuds on
the tomb of the apostles. We are assured that the
spectacle of this singular procession, and the very sound
of the words they repeated as they marched, brought
peace and mercy " to the cities through which they passed,
and inspired with compunction the hearts of the greatest
sinners.

We read the same of almost all the early preachers
of the order; as of Angelo of Perugia, the angel of
peace to Florence, "where he caused all hatreds, quarrels and ancient feuds to cease, and reconciled the chief
families of the city." Of John of Vicenza we have elsewhere spoken; but we cannot refrain from inserting
in this place the description given us of his labours in the
words of an ancient historian: "Never," he says, "since
the time of our Lord Jesus Christ, were there seen such
multitudes gathered together in His name, as were assembled to hear this friar preach peace. He had such power
over all minds, that everywhere he was suffered to
arrange the terms of reconciliation; and through reve-

rence for him the greater part of the multitude used to
listen to him with bare feet. Many who had been mor
tal enemies, moved by his preaching, of their own accord
embraced and gave each other the kiss of peace."* And
of the great preaching in the meadows of Verona, we read
in a contemporary chronicle :—" Such a multitude assembled as had never been before seen in Lombardy, it being
by the river-side, about four miles from Verona, and there
he proposed the authority of Christ, ' Peace I give to
you, my peace I leave with you,' and preached peace to
Lombardy and all Italy, adding warnings and denunciations against any who should dare in future to interrupt
that blessed peace."

We must return from the digression, which seemed
necessary in referring to the influence of the friars on
society, so much of which was exerted, not through their
writings, but by the effect of their personal presence and
intercourse in the world ; and which, powerful as it was,
has of course left no monuments behind it, so that in
many cases those who have done the greatest works are
the least known to posterity. We have alluded to the
preaching of Taulerus and Henry Suso ; but with them
the case has been different, for they were also writers,
and their works† which remain among us have preserved
their fame, and conferred on them a high rank in the

---

* Life of Ricciardus, Count of S. Boniface.

† We are glad to take this oportunity of reminding our readers
that the admirable work of Suso, his " Little Book of Eternal
Wisdom," has been recently translated into English, and it is to be
hoped that his beautiful life will soon also be known among us.
Nor can we omit in this place quoting the words of one of the
greatest modern writers of Germany, Frederic Schlegel, as he contrasts the *language* of the Catholic ages, with that which has prevailed since the rise of Protestantism. " Besides à Kempis,"
he says, " there are several other religious writers of the fifteenth
century, and even of an earlier period, who, though less known.
were distinguished by a similar spirit, partly among those who used
the Latin language, then universally current. and partly among
those who, like Taulerus, made the German the vehicle of their
thoughts. Were we to compare the gentle simplicity, the charming
clearness of thought and expression which reign in the works of
these writers, with the productions of the following age of barbarous polemic strife, we should be furnished with the best criterion
for duly appreciating the earlier and the later period."

school of mystic theology. But, as we have before said,
it was not merely as theologians that the Dominicans
distinguished themselves in this first century of their
career. The part they took in the general revival of
learning was equally great, and we may particularly refer
to their cultivation of the Oriental languages, a study
which has been always in a particular manner cherished
by the order. It was John the Tewtonic, the fourth
general of the Friars Preachers, who, at the general
chapter at Metz in the year 1251, added the greater
part of those statutes to the constitutions which refer to
the regulation of the studies; and it was to him, in company with S. Raymund Pennafort, that we may attribute
their first direction to the cultivation of Oriental literature. Not that these great men can at all claim to be
the first who rendered this branch of learning popular in

It is a little singular that Schlegel should not have more particularly alluded to Henry Suso, whose works might be more fairly
compared, in point of style, with those of Thomas à Kempis, than
the writings of Taulerus. He might have added, that, along with
the charm of simplicity, these early German writers have a depth
of pathos, and a beauty of imagination unknown to the controversialists of modern times. Nothing, we suppose, can go beyond the
winning plaintiveness of Suso's style; and both he and Taulerus
are, as it were, personally made known to us in the singular and
exquisite biographies which are attached to their works. We may
add, that for those who find the Germanism of blessed Suso a little
rugged in his English dress, Monsieur E. Cartier has furnished a
modern French version which is everything they can desire.
We can but hope that the day is not far distant when the biography and writings of Taulerus may also find an English translator. It was the consideration of the advantages to be gathered
from the study of his works that obliged Cardinal Bellarmine to give
him the just and glorious title of "a preacher eminent for piety and
learning," and the celebrated Louis of Blois, who defended the
purity of his teaching against the indiscreet and uncharitable zeal
of those who sought to bring suspicion on it, boldly calls him "the
zealous defender of the Catholic faith, whose writings are not merely
orthodox, but even divine." A celebrated prelate of France, moreover (Sponde, bishop of Pamiers), who has continued the history of
Cardinal Baronius, hesitates not to assert that "he is a man worthy
of all admiration, and that his works are full of the unction and
grace of the Holy Spirit;" to which he adds a very remarkable
fact, namely, "that by a kind of prophetic spirit he has predicted
the heresies which only rose in later ages, and groaned in tenderness over those wounds of the Church which are not inflicted till
long after his death." (From the advertisment prefixed to the
French translation of the Institutions of Taulerus, 1684.

Europe. During the Moorish dominion in Spain the Arabic philosophy, grounded as it was on the writings of Aristotle, had become the rage in Europe; and we know that the ardour with which it was pursued in the 13th century appeared so dangerous and excessive to Innocent III. as to call forth from him a decided censure. But with the Dominicans Orientalism was cherished, not from the love of vain philosophy, but, as became their apostolic vocation, as an assistance and necessary instrument in the defence of the Christian faith. The Jews and Moors were in those days the formidable adversaries of religion; they possessed many sources of learning shut out from the Christians; and the fact that the "Summa" of S. Thomas was principally directed against their controversialists, may give us some idea of the position they then held as enemies of the faith. Spain was the great battle-field of Christianity against infidelity, and it was there that, among his other great labours, S. Raymund of Pennafort used his influence with the kings of Arragon and Castile for the establishment of colleges for the express study of the Oriental languages, as an indispensable weapon to be used in the disputes with the Jewish and Mahometan doctors. To him also the world probably owes the great work of S. Thomas to which we have just referred, for we are told that it was written at his request and suggestion. Nor were his efforts without success : Christianity seemed to make instant head against the infidels on the adoption of those studies in the colleges of the order; and Clement VIII. did not hesitate to say that by the introduction of Hebrew and Arabic learning S. Raymund had contributed to the glory both of Spain and of the Church, and been the cause of the conversion of thousands. In fact, we have his own testimony in a letter to Humbert, the successor of John the Teutonic in the government of the order, that no fewer than 10,000 Saracens had been received to the Christian faith, since the commencement of these studies, and, among them, many of their most learned men. The cultivation of the Greek and Hebrew languages is expressly provided for in the constitutions; and we shall

find on examination that a very large proportion of the
great writers of the order have been chiefly distinguished
for their proficiency in these studies, and in those so
closely connected with them, namely Biblical learning and
criticism.*

We cannot of course propose to ourselves to give even
the names of all who claim our notice as stars in the
Dominican heaven; but the mention of Biblical learning
suggests one, even in those early times, too distinguished
for his services in that branch of science to be passed
over in silence; this was Hugo à Sancto Charo, the first
cardinal of the order, and the author of the first Concord-
ance of the Bible ever attempted. Mariana tells us that
no fewer than 500 religious of the order laboured at this
great work under his direction, and that those afterwards compiled by the Jews and Greeks were in imitation of it; nor can we over-estimate the encouragement
which such a work must have given to the study of the
Sacred Text. His piety was equal to his learning, and
his exertions had no small share in the establishment of
the feast of Corpus Christi; the devotion to the Blessed
Sacrament being one of the objects to the propagation of
which he may be said to have dedicated his life.

But the learning of the Dominican order was the least
remarkable feature which it displayed during the first
century of its existence. We may venture to point to
its great men, *as men*, and to the singular force and heroism of their character as offering the best explanation of
the rapid extension of their institute over the world.
Let us take the first five generals of the order after the
death of S. Dominic. We can hardly picture to ourselves
a group of more remarkable and admirable characters.
There was the blessed Jordan with his divine simplicity,
his good humored *bonhomie* of disposition, and his fearless courage, which prompted him to utter the boldest
truths even to such men as Frederick II. There was
S. Raymund of Pennafort (for the Friars Preachers were

* Blessed James of Voragine, archbishop of Genoa, known as the
author of the Golden Legend, was the first translator of the Bible
into the Vulgar tongue. His Italian version of the Old and New
Testaments was made in 1254, or thereabouts.

happy in this also, that they were ruled in those early
ages by a dynasty of saints), but of him we shall presently
have to speak more particularly. Then comes John the
Teutonic, the fearless preacher of peace, whose bold re-
bukes, strangely enough, like those of blessed Jordan,
also won the friendship and confidence of Frederick. Notwithstanding the extraordinary difficulty of his position,
placed as he was between the contending interests of the
Pope and the emperor, he displayed a firmness and
prudence which would have proved equal to the government of a kingdom. Under him the order is thought to
have attained its highest glory, and his generalship may
be considered the most brilliant period of its history.
Paris, Bologna, Cologne, Montpellier, and London, witnessed those chapters of the Friars Preachers which were
recognized as the assemblies of saints. Our readers will
pardon us for inserting an extract from the letter addressed
to the Prior of Montpellier by Guy Fulcodi, afterwards
Pope Clement IV. He had come to town, in company
with his sister, to witness the deliberations of the fathers.
It was the festival of Pentecost, and it is thus he describes
the scene; "We entered your church, where, whilst she
[his sister] prayed, humbly prostrate on the ground, and
entreated the Lord to look favourably on so many of those
who laboured for His glory, she felt her confidence increase
with her importunity; and as the choir intoned the ' *Veni
Creator*,' she beheld descending from on high a great flame
which covered all the choir and remained above them till
the conclusion of the hymn."

What shall we say of the blessed Humbert, the successor of John, and the author of those Chronicles whose
charm and grace have surely never been surpassed? Who
can read his letters to his brethren, and not feel his own
heart kindled with some touch of that heroic zeal which
breathes in every line! What noble and elevating
thoughts, what a great and gallant spirit, must have dwelt
in the heart that thus pours forth its animating exhortations, ever reiterating the old battle-cry of the order,
"God's honour, and the salvation of souls!" And in all
these men, with all their splendid qualities, how vainly

should we look to find one spark of that ambition so
common with the simply great men, whose greatness is
not linked to the humility of the saint. S. Raya and
resigned his office, having held it only two years. Humbert did the same at the chapter of London, after a
government of no more than nine years. "He has been
considered," says Touron, "as the perfect model of a wise,
zealous, and vigilant superior; able to bear with the
infirmities of the weak, but incapable of admitting aught
that could enervate the vigour of regular discipline." He
was a great writer, and even in our own day the order feels
his influence, and may drink his spirit in the various commentaries and explanations on the Rules and Constitutions
which he has left behind him

Again, as confessors and spiritual guides to the people,
the influence of the friars was felt even more universally
than as preachers or men of learning. As the counsellors
of kings, they had a vast share in giving that Christian
tone to the government of the day which is so striking a
feature in the history of the thirteenth century. For
instance, where can we look for higher ideals of Christian
monarchy than in the examples of S. Louis of France,
James of Arragon, Alphonsus III. of Portugal, and S. Ferdinand of Castile? They are the noblest types of royalty
which the mind can picture, and have excited the enthusiasm even of Protestant eulogists. Yet it is impossible
to doubt that much of that sanctity which renders them
so admirable, is to be attributed to the character of their
spiritual advisers, and these were all Dominicans. S. Peter
Gonzales was the confessor of S. Ferdinand; Geoffrey de
Beaulieu held the same office to S. Louis of France;
S. Raymund of Pennafort enjoyed the unlimited confidence of James of Arragon; and, in short, we are told
that, during the government of John the Teutonic, the
kings of France, England, Castile, Arragon, Portugal, and
Hungary, invariably chose their confessors and chaplains
from the ranks of the Friars Preachers. The whole history of such men as S. Peter Gonzales and S. Raymund
exhibits them to us in what we might call a semi-political
character, labouring to sanctify a royal court and army;

and though S. Raymund's eminence as a canonist, and the
celebrity of his works on penance, as well as the fact of his
having had so large a share in the formation of the Constitutions of his order, entitle him to rank as one of its most
distinguished writers, yet it is not as an author that we
know him best: by those who are familiar with his life he
is rather remembered as a great man and a great saint.
And because authorship is at best but a human thing,
we will leave it for a moment to glance at one episode in
the life of S. Raymund which is connected with another
of the glories of his order; its influence, namely, in the
formation and reform of other religious bodies.   In the
same work, from which we have already made such frequent quotations, Balmez distinguishes, as among the
most remarkable institutions of the thirteenth century,
the rise of the orders for the redemption of captives.
Certainly, in days when the abolition of slavery has been
so popular a theme, and freedom so national a boast, there
should be peculiar sympathy for the work of heroic charity
to which the two Institutes of Mercy and the Trinity so
nobly devoted themselves.   The latter, indeed, we may
almost claim as an English order, so large a share had
our own nation in its first foundation* and government;
while its calendar of saints and martyrs is enriched with a
catalogue of English names which England has well-nigh
forgotten.

The deep sympathy felt by the Order of Preachers
for this work of the redemption of captives is evident
from many facts. We have in a previous page related
how S. Dominic himself was on one occasion so moved
by the sufferings of his captive brethren, as to offer to
be sold to the Moors in order to procure the redemption
of a poor woman's son.   Many writers of the order add,

* Among the fellow-students of S. John of Matha in the university of Paris, who first joined his order, were John of England,
William of Scotland, and Roger Dee, also an Englishman, and a
learned doctor of the day.   John and William were the chief co-
operators with the holy founder in the beginning of his enterprise,
and successively governed the order after his death; whilst among
its canonized saints is the English martyr S. Serapion, with others
of less note.

at he had resolved at one time to consecrate his life to
the undertaking, but that God made known to him by a
particular revelation that it was the work reserved for S.
John of Matha, and that his calling was rather to labour
in the conversion of heretics. We may consider it almost
certain, that these two great men were known to one
another, and that S. John did actually co-operate with
S. Dominic in his labours among the Albigenses; for it is
said that in the year 1202 he was charged by Pope Innocent III. with a mission to the Count of Toulouse and
the Albigenses, and that he preached in Languedoc on
his return from the court of Rome to Spain; which
seems the more probable from the fact of his order
having been at that time established in Provence. If
then, as seems likely, the two founders were personally
known to one another, we may imagine how deep must
have been the sympathy of minds whose objects and desires
were so alike.

It is not, however, of the Trinitarian Order that we
are about to speak in this place, but of the sister Order
of Mercy, in whose establishment S. Raymond Pennafort
had so large a share, and whose founder was also, as is
more than probable, a familiar friend of S. Dominic ;
for the first time we meet with the name of S. Peter
Nolasco, it is as a crusader in the army of Count Simon de
Montfort. At the victory of Muret, Peter, then twenty-
five years of age, played a distinguished part; and when,
on the death of King Peter of Arragon, the fortune of
war threw his infant son, Prince James, into the hands
of the conqueror, De Montfort, with the chivalrous
feeling for which he was so remarkable, having a tender
regard and compassion for his little prisoner, selected
the young soldier, as the bravest and noblest of his
knights, to be the guardian and tutor of the prince, and
sent them both back to Barcelona, then the chief residence of the court of Arragon. To this brave and truly
Christian soldier King James owed the blessings of his
religious education, and had reason to look back on the
defeat of Muret as one of the chief blessings of his life.
If the infancy of the prince was thus connected with

one of the great incidents in the life of S. Dominic, his manhood was passed under the guidance and influence of the order of preachers; for S. Raymund of Pennafort was, as we have said, his most intimate adviser, and held the office of confessor both to him and to S. Peter Nolasco. The circumstances which led to the foundation of the Order of Mercy are among those supernatural events, the evidence of which has been placed beyond the possibility of a doubt. On the same night, the Blessed Virgin appeared in three distinct visions to S. Peter, King James, and S. Raymund, and charged them to commence the establishment of an order for the redemption of captives among the Moors, promising them her patronage and assistance. It was at once begun, and on the feast of S. Lawrence, 1223, the king and S. Raymund led S. Peter to the Cathedral church of Barcelona, where the bishop Berengarius received his religious profession, adding to the three essential vows of religion one to devote his life, substance, and liberty to the randsoming of slaves. Then was presented one of those striking scenes so common in the ages of faith: S. Raymund ascended the pulpit, and announced to the assembled people the Divine revelation which had given rise to this foundation, and declared the manner with which the will of God and the favour of Mary had been made known at once to himself, the king, and the saint who stood before them; after which he gave the habit of the new order to S. Peter with his own hands, as we learn on the authority of Mariana.

The constitutions of the Order of Mercy, as it was thenceforward designated, were entirely drawn up by S. Raymund, whose peculiar skill in this branch of legislation was well known; and he is even reckoned as its second founder. But nothing in connection with this singular history has, as it seems to us, a deeper interest than the words of the saint himself, still preserved in the letter of S. Peter Nolasco; in which, when many years had passed over their heads, he reminds him of that eventful night, when both of them had gazed upon the face of Mary. For S. Peter, overburthened by the charge of superiority, at one time thought of imitating the example of S. Raymund and laying down the government of his order, to seek repose in a humbler and more obscure position. S. Raymund, however, well knew the necessity of his continuing at the head of the institute he had founded ; and the letter by which he succeeded in turning him from his design is still extant. He had himself resigned the mastership of the Order of Preachers, and was forced to use much ingenious humility to persuade his friend that in so doing he had not given him a precedent. Then he continues in the following terms : " But for you, dear brother, rejoice in the Lord ; or at any rate afflict not yourself because you see yourself at the head of your order ; for it is not your own choice, but the very oracle of the Mother of God that has placed you there. To what other pastor has that Queen of Virgins ever said, ' Feed my sheep ?' Would you then resist her will ? I cannot think this of you. I conjure you, by the holy love we must all bear that Blessed Virgin, never to abandon the flock she has entrusted to your care. Recall, dear father, the thought so sweet and consoling of that happy night, illumined, as it seemed, by a ray of Eternity, when your merits made me also to share in the blessedness of the heavenly citizens. I mean that night when we were both honoured by the visible appearance of Her whose divine beauty surpassed the beauty and brightness of the sun. Ah ! how can you ever yield to sadness—you who have been consoled by the choirs of angels, and by the favourable looks of Her who conceived the very Word of God ? Could it have been for the loss of any one ? or must it not have been for the salvation of those who were perishing that the Mother of mercy thus deigned to show herself to her servants ? If, therefore, it is any sentiment of humility which urges you to resign your rank, remember in what manner you were called to it, and be persuaded that what is contrary to that Divine vocation can never come from God." There is something of most thrilling interest in this allusion to the vision of Mary ; nor can we recall anything in the lives of the saints which more *realizes* a supernatural visitation than these words, in which the recollection is so tenderly and devoutly brought to mind.

In alluding to other orders in whose foundation or reformation the Dominicans have taken part, the order of *Servites*, or Servants of Mary, should not be forgotten. The singular origin of this order is probably familiar to many of our readers. Seven rich merchants of Florence, members of a devout confraternity dedicated to " our Lady of praise," were praying in the oratory of their confraternity on the festival of the Assumption, when each felt himself moved by a secret and powerful impulse to dedicate himself in some special way to God and our Lady. Communicating their impressions to one another, they resolved on distributing all their wealth to the poor, and abandoning the world to embrace an austere and cremitical life. They accordingly retired to some cells on Monte Senario, about six miles from the city, and on their first appearance in the streets of Florence in the rough penitential habit they had assumed, the people to whom their persons were familiar, gathered about them with surprise, and the children ran after them crying out " See! there go the servants of Mary!" This cry was, it is said, repeated by an infant of five years old who was carried by in his nurse's arms. The child was afterwards S. Philip Beniti, the great ornament of the order of Servites; and the name thus bestowed on the little company was ever afterwards retained by them. It was the time when the Church was suffering grievously from the disorders of the Manichean heretics, and when S. Peter Martyr so nobly upheld the standard of the faith in the northern provinces of Italy. He filled the office of Inquisitor of the faith under the Pontiffs Gregory IX. and Innocent IV., and on the accession of the latter to the Holy See, the task of examining the character of the new society, whose members had rapidly increased, was laid on S. Peter. His inquiries resulted in a warm approval of their spirit and manner of life; and his cordial recommendation of them was quickly followed by the formal confirmation of their order by the new Pontiff. No doubt the tender and special devotion ever borne by the great martyr of the Friars Preachers to the Mother of God, was one chief secret of the earnest support he gave to her servants, who from the first commencement of their association had made the dolours of Mary the peculiar object of their reverence; so that they may be considered the great propagators of that most touching devotion. Some writers even go as far as to assert that the first idea of erecting the pious association into an order originated with S. Peter, and though this wants confirmation, yet it is probably true that the plan of withdrawing them from their exclusively contemplative and solitary life, and employing them in active labour for the salvation of souls, was of his suggestion. Touron speaks only of his diligent and exact examination of their rule, and recommendation of it for confirmation to the Holy See, but in the original chronicles of the order of Servites the story is given with the addition of some of those circumstances of supernatural interest, which the French historian so universally rejects from his narrative, but which form the peculiar charm of the old writers.

According to F. Michael, the Servite chronicler, it would seem that the interest felt by S. Peter in the hermits of Monte Senario was the result of a divine revelation. Many a time did he, being in ecstacy, behold before the eyes of his soul a mountain surrounded by most clear light, adorned with every kind of flower, among which seven lilies of dazzling whiteness far surpassed the rest in beauty and delicious perfume; and his wonder and admiration increased when he beheld them gathered by the angels, and presented to the Mother of God; and accepted by her with a joyful and gracious countenance. He often pondered over this vision, but never understood its meaning till he came to the holy mountain of Senario; there the life of the solitaries, who had left the world to dedicate themselves to God and our Lady, and to cherish a loving commemoration of Her sorrows, seemed to explain the

mystery, and he was enlightened to discern the grace
which dwelt in these men, and specially of their seven
founders ; whose cause and order he thenceforward
generously protected and advanced.   Nor were the
Servites backward to express their gratitude.   S. Peter
Martyr has always been honoured amongst them as their
second founder, and after his glorious martyrdom and
subsequent canonization, he was enrolled among their
chief protectors and patron saints.   In the notice of his
martyrdom inserted in their chronicles, he is called by
the common appellation of "*familiar* of our order."*

We might mention other orders which felt the influence of the Friars Preachers, especially the Carmelites.
Their rule appearing to many excessive in its austerity,
the religious applied to Pope Innocent IV. for some explanation of its obscurities ; and Hugo a Sancto Charo, the
cardinal of Santa Sabina, was the person selected for the
task.   Three centuries later, when the Dominicans had again
so great a share in the reform of the same order, S. Theresa refers to this their first connection, in the following
words : "We observe," she says, "the rule of our Lady
of Mount Carmel, without any mitigation, as it was
ordained by Father Hugo, cardinal of Santa Sabina, and
confirmed by Pope Innocent IV."   This revision of the
Carmelite rule took place during the generalship of S.
Simon Stock.

To these orders we may add the Congregation of the
Barnabites of S. Paul, whose rule was committed to the
revision and examination of Leonard de Marini, Papal
Nuncio at the council of Trent, by Pius IV. before
granting it his confirmation ; the Order of Grandmont,
whose rule was revised by Bernard Geraldi, appointed
visitor to the order by Honorius IV. in 1282 ; and
several Benedictine reforms, in which the eminent men of
the Order of Preachers had a prominent share.   It is
time, however, for us to bring this chapter to a close, that
we may enter on the general history of the order during
the second century of its foundation.

* See Touron, Vie de S. Dominique, liv. 5. and Chron. Ord. Serv.
p. 11—15.

CHAPTER II.

WHILST glancing, in the last chapter, over some of the great men and distinguished writers of the Dominican order, we have for a time abandoned the course of its history. The contest with the universities was not the only one in which it had to bear a leading part ; and the second great struggle in which it was engaged brings us to consider what we may call its influence on the politics of the Church. If the thirteenth century was busy with the disputes of the schools, the fourteenth was torn by distractions of a far more grievous kind : it may be termed the century of schism. The two great factions of Guelf and Ghibelline, Italian in their origin, extended in their spirit and effect throughout the whole Church ; and in every country of Europe ecclesiastical privileges had to sustain a fierce attack from the encroachments of the civil power. The most important of these contests was, of course, that to which the names of the two factions is more particularly applied—namely, that between the emperors and the Popes. In the long and complicated history of that quarrel we find the Order of Friars Preachers offering to the chair of S. Peter a defence, the loyalty and devotion of which is not to be surpassed even by that of the illustrious society which has made allegiance to the Popes an obligation to which its members are bound by vow. The emperors and the antipopes seem to have had a sort of instinctive horror of the Friars Preachers, as of their natural enemies ; and we accordingly find Louis of Bavaria, and his nominee to the schismatic tiara, Nicholas V., driving the order

out of every convent in Germany, and such cities of the
north of Italy as acknowledged their obedience. For
three years the order suffered the most violent persecution
for its adherence to the rightful Pontiff. John XXII.,
which was only terminated by the death of the emperor
and the consequent fall of the antipope. In 1348, a new
calamity fell on the Church in the terrible plague which
ravaged Europe and desolated whole provinces. so that,
we are told, many districts remained wholly without
inhabitants. the domestic animals became fierce and wild,
and cultivated regions fell back again into vast untenanted
deserts. The great novelist who has given us a sketch of
some of the terrors of that dreadful time, has left us
likewise an idea of its frightful demoralization. Men
grew familiar with death till they ceased to fear it, and
there appeared among them that strange form of sensuality which would make the most of the brief hour which
separates it from the grave, and even links its licentiousness
with the idea of the pestilence which it defies—a sensuality
which has been exhibited in our own day, and in our own
day also has found a novelist worthy to be the chronicler
of its abominations.

The very year when this pestilence broke out was that
which gave to the world one of the brightest ornaments
of the Dominican order. We can scarcely picture to
ourselves the state of the world during those thirty-three
years that S. Catherine of Siena was its glorious apostle.
It was a period of universal decay; and the religious
orders felt the effects of the universal declension equally
with the rest of the Church. The Friars preachers. who
had nobly exposed themselves to the relief of the plague-
stricken, died by thousands; and those who were the
worthiest in their ranks were the surest to be taken,
falling victims to their noble charity to the sick and dying.
Nor was the reduction of their numbers the only or the
worst evil resulting from the scourge. A time of pestilence is never a time of strict observance. and when the
scanty remnant that survived the epidemic beheld their
order reduced to a tenth of its former numbers,—some
conven s left wholly without inhabitants,—others with

communities of twos and threes, where formerly they had
been reckoned by hundreds, they yielded to a fatal human
prudence ; and by the way of filling up the empty ranks
admitted all kinds of subjects under all kinds of dispensations, relaxing the rule, even allowing community life to be
relinquished in many places for the sake of securing to the
order the adherence of those who were in reality unfit
for its duties or its austerities.

A grievous and universal relaxation was the inevitable
consequence of this unhappy policy ; and when, in 1378,
the great schism of the West broke out, and Europe,
already suffering from the demoralizing influence of long-
continued pestilence and famine, was again distracted by
a divided spiritual allegiance, the miserable state of all
classes of society became such as it is difficult to believe,
and impossible to describe. This was the period during
which S. Catherine lived and wrote ; and it is just that
we should have some knowledge of the causes and extent
of that fearful corruption which she was raised up by
God to denounce and to reform, if we desire to have
any idea of her true historical character. It was doubtless one wholly extraordinary, but so were the times ;
and we need to be in some degree aware of their deep
degradation to understand those bold and severe denunciations of vice in every form, in every class, which
are to be found in her inspired writings. At once the
chief support of the Papacy and the apostle of the age,
S. Catherine has other claims which have perpetuated
her name to the veneration of the faithful, far beyond her
own day. As a mystic writer, she holds a rank in the
Church, which we cannot well place too high ; and the
term "inspired," which we have just ventured to apply
to her writings, will scarcely seem exaggerated to those
who are familiar with their profound and most heavenly
teaching. As a saint, she is perhaps the most perfect
type of the Dominican ideal ever given to the world.
Her mind, her life, and her writings, are all steeped in
the essential spirit of the order. Large and free, full of
enthusiasm, and full of good sense ; chivalrous in every
impulse and purpose, devoted with unswerving loyalty to

the Holy See, and full of divine and infused science, we see in Catherine an epitome of the Dominican character. Nor can we anywhere seek for a more perfect example of that which is the primary idea of the institute, namely, the union of the active and contemplative states, than is to be found in the life of one who soared to the very heights of divine contemplation, not in the solitude of conventual enclosure, but amid the jarring vexation of ordinary domestic duties, or the distractions of what we might almost call a public and political career. In her are combined the seemingly opposite characteristics of other saints;—the wisdom and theology of the doctors of the Church, with the simplicity of him whose title, as well as whose supernatural and mysterious privilege of suffering she shared, namely, the seraphic* saint of Assisi.

The great schism lasted 70 years; and we must not be surprised if during the perplexities of that unhappy period we find good men coming to a different decision on the claims of the rival candidates. It is easy for us in our day to go over the problem as it has been worked and solved by others, and to come to the ready conclusion that Urban was Pope, and Benedict and Clement were antipopes; just as it is easy for us to see the landmarks about us when we have emerged from a fog, and have made our way to a higher ground, whilst it is still thick darkness to those whose eyes are blinded with the mist. Doubtless its difficulties must have been very great; and sorrowful as is the fact, we must not be hasty in our judgment of it when we find the already enfeebled order in part sharing in the schism, and the provinces of France, Castile, Arragon and Scotland, with their general, Elias Raymund, under the obedience of the antipopes,

* The title of "Seraphic" given in common parlance to the whole Franciscan Order is not, so far as we are aware, bestowed on any individual saint except S. Bonaventure, the Seraphic doctor, S. Catherine, and S. Francis; the two latter having also this peculiar privilege, that the Church has recognised and honoured their reception of the stigma by appointing festivals for their commemoration; a distinction which, we believe, is exclusively their own.

whilst the rest of the order adhered firmly to the cause of
Urban and his successors. But in the history of orders,
as in that of the Church itself, the period of relaxation is
followed by that of reform. The relaxation must indeed
have been great, if we may trust the words of Michel
Pio, who, writing in the seventeenth century, acknow-
ledges that its effects were still felt even in his day. The
reform, however, which was chiefly worked out under
Raymund of Capua and Bartholomew Texier, grievous
as were the evils in which it originated, exhibited in a
remarkable manner the vitality of the Dominican rule,
which even in decay has ever possessed within itself
the power of regeneration. There were no new ordinances or rules drawn up; and when we use the word
" reform," our readers must understand the expression
in a totally different sense to that which it would have in
speaking, for instance, of the Capuchins or Cistercians,
who when they returned to their original rule, broke off
at the same time from the unity of the parent stem. But
this has never been the case with the Dominicans; their
unity of government has remained absolutely unbroken,
and their reforms have consisted only in a return to the
observance of that rule to the fulness of whose provisions
nothing could be added. This return to strict observance
was not indeed universal; and hence we sometimes find the
terms conventual and observant used, as among the Franciscans, to distinguish the stricter from the more relaxed communities; but nevertheless, the government of the order
has never once been divided, save in the case of the great
schism of which we have spoken above.

During this reform begun by Raymund of Capua, the
order produced a harvest of great and saintly men, worthy
of its best days and primitive fervour. Marcolino of
Forli, and John Dominic of Florence, both of whom the
Church has ranked among her beatified heroes, might
have been novices of Dominic or of Reginald; and they
shed a sweet odour of sanctity over a troubled time. To
the latter, indeed, who sat in the Council of Constance as
Cardinal Legate to Pope Gregory XII., the final extinction
of the schism must be in a great measure attributed. It

was he who advised, and at length succeeded in effecting,
the resignation of all the contending claimants ; a step
which was immediately followed by the election of Martin
V., and the restoration of peace to the Church.

It is impossible to pass over the period of the great
schism without noticing the extraordinary man whose
apostolic labours shed a light upon the troubled times,
while he took an active share in the great question which
then agitated the Church. We allude to S. Vincent
Ferrer, the Thaumaturgus of his order, and one of its
most distinguished ornaments, who previously to the
decision of the Council of Constance, took in common
with his countrymen, the side of Peter de Luna (Benedict XIII.) in the long controversy. But his support of
the Cardinal de Luna's claims had nothing in it of parti-
sanship : his constant endeavours were directed to persuade him to resign his pretensions as the only means of
restoring peace and unity to the Church ; he lived on
terms of the closest intimacy with John Dominic and the
other adherents of Pope Gregory, and his conduct on the
final decision of the question by the election of Martin
V. exhibits one of the most admirable examples of submission to the authority of the Church which stands
recorded. United by personal intimacy and ties of
private interest to Peter de Luna, he never hesitated as
to the course to be pursued when the doubt which had
distracted the Church so long was at length removed.
From the moment the decree of the Council was published, he withdrew all obedience to the authority of him
whom till then he had regarded as the rightful Pontiff ;
and the rest of his life was spent in unwearied exertions
to procure the entire extirpation of the schism, and to
bring the kingdom of France and Aragon to acknowledge the authority of Pope Martin.*   Of S. Vincent's

* Lest the fact of S. Vincent having at one time espoused the
cause of an antipope should perplex any of our readers, and induce
them to imagine him involved in the charge of schism, we will
quote the words of Gerson, who himself lived in those times, and
who writes as follows: "In the present schism which is of so
doubtful a character, it would be a most bold, injurious, and
scandalous assertion, to say that those who embraced either one

career as an apostle it is difficult to speak; not to mention his miracles, which are of a character and authority which justify us in ranking him amongst the most extraordinary of all the saints, his life was a miracle in itself. He was the apostle not of one province or country, but of the world; in almost every town and village of Spain, France, Italy, and we have a pride in adding, of England, Scotland, and Ireland, he preached with a success that has no parallel in history. In Spain alone he is known to have converted more than 8,000 Moors and above 35,000 Jews; whilst if we take the accounts of the Jewish rabbins instead of Christian authors, we may increase this last number to that of 200,000 of their nation whom they affirm to have been moved to receive baptism and embrace the Christian faith by the preaching of S. Vincent. Gerson did not hesitate to apply to him the prophecy in the Apocalypse of "one mounted on a white horse to whom was given a crown, and who went forth conquering, and to conquer." Others understood the prophecy given by the same Evangelist, of the winged angel who was to preach the everlasting gospel through the heavens, as referring to him; and hence in Christian art he is commonly represented with wings. In fact, the boundless influence he possessed over men's minds in his own day cannot be overrated; yet he is of the number of those who have left little behind him for posterity. His sermons, a few letters, and a golden treatise on the spiritual life, are all the authentic writings which remain of this wonderful man, whose greatness was essentially of that personal description to which we

side or the other, or who remain neutral, incur any censure or suspicion of the guilt of schism; for there never has been a schism in which there is more room for doubt than in this; the opinions of the greatest doctors and most holy men on both sides being so opposed. S. Vincent is not the only saint we find taking a part now universally judged to be erroneous. Blessed Peter of Luxemburg, beatified by Clement VII., was an adherent of another Clement, one of Peter de Luna's predecessors. We may add the fact that John de Poinox, general of that portion of the order which recognized Benedict XIII., afterward became confessor to Martin V., and, like S. Vincent, used all his influence with Benedict to induce him to resign.

alluded as the one most commonly to be found in a preaching and apostolic order.

We will not dwell further on the period of the schism, which, even in the midst of the most painful and humiliating circumstances attendant on a time of religious declension, furnishes us nevertheless with one remarkable feature in the character of the Dominican order—we mean its extraordinary vitality. It cannot be crushed, and it will not decay; even when seemingly most dead it raises itself to new life, not, like other orders, demanding new constitutions or new founders, but ever the same, with its rule, its government, nay, its very habit unchanged since the days of its first foundation. We have spoken of the influence of the order on the politics of the Church, and specially of its devotion to the Holy See in opposition to the attacks of the Ghibeline emperors; but this devotion was equally displayed through all the struggles which the Pontifical power had to maintain during the thirteenth and fourteenth centuries. Conrad of Brescia, the reformer of the convent of Bologna, was among those most remarkable for his noble and disinterested efforts in defence of the Papal authority, at the time when the Bolognese were in open rebellion against the government of the Holy See. He was at the mercy of the insurgents, shut up in their city, and wholly dependent on their favour and support; the city was laid under an interdict, but none dared to publish it, until Conrad, laying aside every thought save that of loyalty to the chair of Peter, boldly proclaimed it in the great piazza of the city, and was instantly seized and cast into prison, where he was left without food for many days. Released, and imprisoned a second time, he was at length condemned by the popular party to be starved to death; and the sentence would undoubtedly have been executed but for the open and manifest protection of heaven; for his enemies were forced to acknowledge, after a lengthened trial, that man "lives not by bread alone," and that the saints of God have meat that the world knows not of. "In fact," says Leander Albert, "the prison of Conrad was a Paradise, rather than a place of torment, by reason

of the heavenly consolations with which he was favoured."
So finding that starvation had no power over one who lived
on prayer, they again released him; but when the news
of his liberty was brought to him he only sighed: " I
had thought," he said, "that the wedding-feast was at
hand, and that you had come to call me to the nuptials;
but God's will be done; I am not worthy to die for
Christ." Martin V., who constantly looked on him as a
martyr in will, and who attributed the peace which was
soon afterwards concluded between the Holy See and
its Bolognese subjects, to the heroic sacrifices of this
admirable religious, offered him the purple; but he resolutely refused every dignity and begged as the only reward
of his services, to be suffered to spend his life in labour
for his order and the Church. He died, as became
him, in the service of the plague-stricken, at the age
of 31, and though never solemnly beatified, no writer
speaks of him in other terms than as " the blessed
Conrad."

This loyalty to the See of Rome we shall always find
exposing the Friars Preachers to persecution from the
enemies of the Church. That it was, as we have said,
their peculiar characteristic cannot be doubted, when we
find such bodies, for instance, as the schismatical Council
of Basle making an invasion of the privileges granted to
the Dominicans, one of its first measures, and at the very
same time when, as we shall see, it was directing its pre-
sumptuous attacks against Eugenius IV. If, too, we
examine the tendency and character of the writers who
have attacked or depreciated the order, as Matthew Paris
and others, we shall invariably find them to be Ghibeline in
their principles.

We have spoken of the periods of decay and of reform;
another must now be alluded to, and it is the period of
revival. The labours of Raymund and of Texier were
crowned with an abundant success; and if we desire
proof of the extent to which the new impulse was felt
throughout the order, we may find it in the fear which
was expressed by its superiors, lest it should suffer from
its very greatness, and from the dangers which seemed

to threaten it from the vast numbers now raised to ecclesiastical dignities from its ranks. Every province was then rich with men of learning and sanctity; the world had thought the order dying and degraded, and were astonished to see reappearing on all sides religious men zealous for primitive discipline and full of the heroism of their institute. The apostolic spirit revived, and fresh missions were sent out to labour among the northern regions of Russia, and the schismatical provinces of the East. Not that the missionary labours of the order had ever been wholly interrupted, even when the deplorable schism of the Church had checked and in great measure hindered their success. It was in the very midst of that disastrous time that blessed Alvarez of Cordova was pursuing his most painful and untiring labours in the Holy Land; and the preaching of the Dominicans in the eastern empire, now rapidly falling before the victorious arms of the Turks, was not without success even among the Mussulman conquerors themselves. The eastern missions, as well those of the Franciscans and Dominicans, as of other religious bodies, seemed to have received a fatal blow on the fall of Constantinople in 1453, and the consequent triumph of the Turkish arms in every part of the East. Great, however, as were the obstacles thenceforward opposed to the success of the Christian missionaries, they were far from abandoning the apostolic work; and Providence raised up a series of pontiffs with the continued support and encouragement of the Holy See.

Since the time of S. Hyacinth there had existed in the order a congregation for the extension of the faith, called "the Congregation of the Pilgrims of Jesus Christ." This ancient association was suppressed in 1462 by F. Martial Auribelli, master-general of the order, but was restored under the government of his successor, Conrad of Asti, and greatly encouraged by Pius II. We may judge of the amount of the missionary work at this time undertaken by the order, by the account given us of the countries and convents over which this congregation alone presided. Besides many convents belonging to it

in the East, we find others in Hungary, Poland, Lithu-
ania, Podolia, Russia, Moldavia, and Wallachia. The
superior of this congregation was F. Benedict Filicaja,
"a man," says Fontena, "who desired nothing better
than to die for Christ and the gospel." The fruits of its
re-establishment were very great. In Russia alone, then
a barbarous and in some degree an idolatrous country,
we read of one Dominican of Erfurth converting 5,000
persons to the Christian faith ; and the success of others
was much in the same proportion. We cannot, however,
undertake to give even the briefest sketch of the Dominican missions ; for it is a subject which would demand as
many volumes as we have pages to devote to it. It is
much to be hoped that some day the vast treasures of
information which lie hidden in the original and unpublished documents preserved in the order, may in some
shape or other be given to the public. The more than
indifference which the order of Friars Preachers has continually exhibited to make its prodigious labours manifest
to the world, is not one of its least remarkable characteristics ;* but much as we may admire the carelessness of

* We are surely justified in pointing to this singular modesty of
the Friars Preachers as a characteristic of them as a body. With
them it has ever seemed enough to do their work, and think no
more about it. Our readers will remember their extraordinary
indifference even to the canonization of its holy founder. "Every
one, they said, knew that he was a saint; to what purpose enter
on a long process to prove it?" Many of the biographies of their
great men are lost, or so imperfectly preserved as to give no
idea of what they actually performed. And not to speak further
of the singular reserve they have shown with regard to many of
their most wonderful missionary undertakings, of which the world
knows nothing, we observe the same peculiarity in the conduct of
individuals among them. Thomas Turco, for instance, general of
the order in 1649, never published any of his own writings, whilst
he spent the greater part of his leisure in superintending new
editions of those of others; and in Louis Sousa, the Portuguese
historian of the order, this simplicity and perfect absence of literary
vanity was very remarkable. He was chosen by Philip IV. to write
a history of the life and reign of John III. of Portugal; and having
completed the work, he committed the manuscript to the hands of
the person who was charged with its publication; but from some
accidental cause the history never was published, and Sousa lost
all his manuscript, for he had never taken the ordinary precaution
of preserving a second copy of his work when he gave up the ori-

popular applause, we must feel mankind to be losers by
the suppression of so valuable a portion of the history of
the Church.

Imperfectly as we possess the details of these apostolic
labours, they are of the deepest interest; and many
circumstances concurred just at this period to give an impulse to the Church's missionary zeal in spite of the
check which it had received from the victorious arms of
the Turks.

New discoveries were every day adding unknown countries to the geography of the world. In these discoveries
the Portugese took the lead under the enterprising and
zealous encouragements of Prince Henry of Portugal;
and wherever the Spanish and Portuguese navigators
appeared, laying open new islands and continents to
European commerce, they were quickly followed by the
indefatigable missionaries of S. Francis and S. Dominic.
It is, indeed, very gratifying to find the close union subsisting between the two orders in their apostolic labours, at
a time when they were often engaged on opposite sides in
controversial questions, and when differences in their theological systems sometimes placed them in apparent rivalry.
Whatever their disputes as theologians, as apostles they
ever worked side by side with most generous and united
devotion; nor can we discover a single trace of that
jealousy which might easily have arisen from the circumstances in which they were placed. In Livonio, for
instance, where the Friars Preachers were first in the
field, we find the Grand Master of the Teutonic Order,
to whom the sovereignty of the country belonged, coming
to their assistance when the work was beyond their
strength, and founding three convents of Franciscans to
assist the Dominicans in their laborious struggles against
the infidels on the boundaries of Christendom. So, in like
manner, we find Dominicans labouring in those holy places
in Palestine of which the Franciscans were the appointed
guardians, and not a vestige of any unwillingness on the

ginal, so little did he know of ambition or ostentation of a mere
author.

part of the Friars Minors to admit them to a share in the
glorious work.

Sometimes, indeed, as in the accounts of the first preaching of Christianity to Congo, we find the honours disputed
by the historians of the two orders: but the rivalry natural
to authors seems to have been unknown to the missionaries
themselves; and the controversy does but furnish us with
a proof that both Friars Preachers and Friars Minors
were engaged in the apostolic work at the same time, and
with equal energy and success. In fact, to study the
history of the missions founded by one order, is to become
acquainted with the achievements of the other; for during
the three first centuries of their foundations the Franciscans and Dominicans were, almost exclusively, the apostles
of the world.

Reserving a more particular notice of the missionary
character of the order for a later date, when we shall have
to speak of the apostolic labours of the Friars Preachers
in America and in China, we will return to the general
history of the Dominican institute at this period, which
may be considered that of its greatest glory and most
perfect development. An allusion has been made to the
number of bishops and dignitaries chosen from its ranks
during the two centuries that followed the close of the
great schism; and so great was their number and reputation, that we may venture to point to the character of
the great Dominican prelates as one among the most
beneficial influences which the order was destined to
shed upon the Church. At all times, indeed, the order
of Preachers has produced great prelates, for the papal
authority very soon overruled the objections made by the
founders of the two mendicant orders to the holding of
ecclesiastical dignities by their followers. Gregory IX.,
to whom, whilst yet cardinal, that joint disapprobation
had been expressed, was the first to act in opposition to
it by the appointment of John the Teutonic, afterwards
master general of the order of Preachers, to the bishopric
of Bosnia. Hugo di Sancto Charo, one of the earliest
of the Dominican theologians, was the first cardinal of
the order, having received the purple in the year 1244

T

from the hands of Innocent IV. It would be in vain
to attempt anything like an enumeration of the great
bishops afterwards given to the Church by the Friars
Preachers; we will select one only as an example of
pastoral excellence; and our choice naturally turns in
the first place to the great S. Antoninus of Florence,
who may be taken as the fairest model of the Dominican
episcopate.

And we may here remark the very striking similarity
of character which distinguishes all the great prelates
of the order. There is a kind of family likeness among
them: the four Dominican popes,—of whom one is a
canonized and another a beatified saint,*—S. Antoninus
of Florence, Bartholomew of the Martyrs, Jerome Lanuza, and others who crowd upon the memory, were all
alike in the general outline of their lives. In public,
they spoke and acted as great prelates, all being particularly distinguished by their zeal for the preservation
or restoration of ecclesiastical discipline; but in private
they were poor religious. They kept the rule and wore
the habit of their order: their revenues were lavished
on the poor, and their great work was invariably one of
reform, and a living protest against the corruptions of
the day. In S. Antoninus and Bartholomew of the
Martyrs this resemblance is rendered yet more striking
by the similarity to be found in various circumstances of
their lives. The zeal and charity of both were exhibited
during a time of pestilence and famine, their own hands
ministering to the sick and dying when others fled from
the sufferers in disgust. The lives of both were exposed
to the attacks of assassins, whom they converted by their
prayers; and in both the natural sweetness and gentleness of their dispositions did not prevent them from
severely enforcing the ecclesiastical canons on clergy as
well as laity, in pursuance of their vigorous reforms. In
the laborious visitations of their dioceses, which they
performed on foot like humble religious, amid the snows
and cataracts of mountainous districts, both were equally

S. Pius V and blessed Benedict XI.

indefatigable; and when we remember that Antoninus
was selected by Pius II. to attempt that very reform of
the Cardinalate which was afterwards so courageously
and successfully insisted on at the Council of Trent by
Bartholomew, the likeness between these two brothers
of the same illustrious family, separated as they are by a
century and a half in point of time, appears singularly
complete. In fact, the Dominican prelates were always
foremost in the work of ecclesiastical reform; and
perhaps their rigid advocacy of evangelical poverty may
have partly arisen from a remembrance of the fact, that
the first step of their great founder in his apostolic
career was a protest against the luxury of the legates and
bishops associated with him in his mission against the
Albigenses.

The name of S. Antoninus is distinguished not merely
for his merits as a pastor, but also as a doctor of the
Church. Theological greatness is, as it were, the heritage of the illustrious men of his order, and S. Antoninus
ranks with the very first of its theologians. But had his
Summa of Moral Theology never been written, we should
still cherish the memory of the great archbishop of
Florence as presenting us with a perfect model of sanctity
in the episcopate. " The hands of the poor," says Pope
Pius II., " were the depository of all he possessed."
In fact, the revenues of his diocese were entirely expended
on their relief; for himself he retained within his archie-
piscopal palace the same rule of life which he had observed
in the cloisters of Fiesole or S. Mark. There was, to
use the words of Touron, a "heroism" in his mode of
government which produced astonishing results. He
succeeded in bringing about a reformation of manners
in the city of Florence, the mere attempt to effect which
would seem in our day like the schemes of a visionary.
But Antoninus was armed with the strange irresistable
power of sanctity. " He rose with all difficulties,"
says his biographer, " and not only was his chapter
and clergy placed under the restored discipline of the
ecclesiastical canons, but the people themselves felt the
influence of his apostolic and paternal rule; so that

before long, gaming and blasphemy were unknown in
Florence, usury and other disorders of a social character
were abolished, private quarrels and dissentions were healed,
and, to use the words of Pope Pius, ' all enmities were
banished out of the city.' He was, in fact (if we may so
say), canonized whilst yet alive, in the heart and judgment of the world. Pope Nicholas V. ordered that no
appeals against any of his sentences should be received at
Rome ; and Pius II. concludes the eloquent eulogy of him
which he has inserted in his Commentaries with the
remarkable expression, that ' from the day of his death,
he was with reason regarded as an inhabitant of the
heavenly city.' "

The Dominicans, in their character as theologians,
have naturally played a great part in the councils of the
Church, and, at the period of wl ich we speak, distinguished themselves in a particular manner in the deliberations of the Council of Basle, by their zeal against the
heresy of the Hussites, and by their efforts for the reconciliation of the Greek schismatics at that of Florence.
The age was in fact rife with error; and in Bohemia the
fanaticism of the followers of Huss and Zisca had produced a bloody and disastrous insurrection.   Those who
are willing to believe that the Church has known no other
method of dealing with heretics than that of fire and
sword, would do well to study the manifesto of Father
John Nyder, one of the Papal Nuncios despatched by
the Fathers of Basle against the Bohemian insurgents.
It is given at length by Bzovius, and is remarkable for
its tone of sweetness and moderation, and its strain of
exalted piety

But our chief motive for referring in this place to the
Council of Basle, is for the sake of the illustration which
its history affords of that devotion on the part of the
Dominicans to the interests of the Holy See, of which we
have before spoken as one of their most striking characteristics.   The unfortunate conclusion of the council
is well known.   On the attempt of the Pontiff Eugenius IV. to remove the assembly to Ferrara, the prelates
not only opposed his resolution with their remonstrances

a step which was probably justified by the peculiar circumstances in which the negotiations with the Bohemian heretics had involved them), but, on his persisting in his design, they proceeded to open resistance of his authority, and even ventured to pronounce his deposition from the Papal chair. Not to enter on the great theological questions which engaged the pens of the controversialists assembled at Basle, we may be permitted to notice the course pursued by the Dominican theologians during this painful crisis, and their resolute defence of the Papal authority, with sentiments of just admiration. The services rendered by them to the Fathers of the Council in the whole course of the proceedings against the Hussites, and the labours of Nyder, Montenigro, and above all, of John Torquemada, the Master of the Sacred Palace, had been warmly acknowledged by the assembled prelates. It is evident that they shared the views of those who looked on the removal of the Council as a dangerous and ill advised step; nevertheless, the moment that an attack seemed threatened against the integrity of the Holy See, the instinctive loyalty of the order to the Chair of S. Peter was manifested. No doubt the crisis was one of no common importance; the proceedings of the Council of Constance were considered by some to offer a precedent to those of Basle, although in fact the cases were totally different. Nevertheless, recent events, and the grievous effects of a long schism, had contributed to lower the idea of the Papal supremacy, and to exalt the authority of councils. The danger of this feeling, at the very moment when heresy was raging without the fold, was quickly apprehended by the watchful eyes of the Dominican theologians, who accordingly withdrew from Basle, and hastened to join the new council assembled under the authority of the supreme Pontiff at Ferrara.

It was under these circumstances that Torquemada published his two treatises on the power of the Popes, and the authority of general councils; and at Fiorence, whither the prelates assembled at Ferrara adjourned soon

The Immaculate Conception; defined by the fathers of Basle, and at that time warmly disputed by opposite schools of theology.

afterwards, he distinguished himself in so remarkable a
manner by his defence of the Latin dogmas, and especially
of the Roman primacy (which was defined by the council
and acknowledged by the Greek bishops) that he received
from Eugenius the glorious title of "Defender of the
Faith," less fitly borne in the following century by the
English tyrant Henry VIII.

Torquemada was, in fact, one of the most illustrious men
of the time ; and it is not until we fully appreciate the dangers of the age in which he lived, that we can justly estimate the services rendered to the Church by him and
others of his order, in their firm resistance to the schismatical spirit then so general, and their devotion of every
energy to maintain inviolate that supremacy of the See of
S. Peter which each succeeding age has recognized with
greater distinctness to be the bulwark of the Christian
faith.   As Cardinal-legate and Papal ambassador to
half the courts of Europe, Torquemada occupied a distinguished position in the sight of the world ; and yet so
little of the worldly spirit clung to him in his greatness,
that we find him retiring to his convent at Florence for
two years " busying himself with his own sanctification
and the practices of a private religious." " His great
dignities," says Leander Albert, " in no way interrupted
his ordinary exercises of piety and penance, or diminished
ought of his religious modesty.   His habit and exterior remained unchanged ; what he was among his
brethren he was also among the princes of the Church ;
humble, recollected, penitent ; full of zeal for the salvation
of souls, of tenderness for the poor and of love for his order,
which he honoured yet more by his virtues than by
the purple." *

We will now pass to a subject closely connected with
the period of religious reform ; carrying us, however, to

---

* Our readers must not confound John Torquemada, the cardinal
of S. Sixtus of whom we have spoken above, with his nephew
Thomas Torquemada, the celebrated Spanish inquisitor, whose
severe measures in defence of the Christian religion, then furiously
attacked by the Jews and Saracens, have rendered his name so
terrible to English ears.

for different thoughts from those suggested by the disputes of councils; yet we can probably scarce find a better illustration of the largeness and diversity of the Dominican spirit, than by turning from the great questions of ecclesiastical and political interest which engages the theologians of Basle and Florence, and dwelling for a few moments on the gentler,—but who shall say less powerful? influence of that art which, like theology, was to find its "sublime dictator" among the ranks of the Friars Preachers.

At this period of active contest and controversy, it is pleasant to turn to the sunny hills and silent cloisters of Fiesole, where the glorious genius of one whom the voice of the world has consented to beatify, was laying a sweet and powerful grasp upon the imagination and the heart of Christendom. The order which had already produced an angelic doctor was now giving to the world that saintly artist, to whose name also the title of "Angelic" was to be perpetually associated.

—𝕯.—

CHAPTER III.

Santa Maria Novella. Passavanti. Connection of Art with religious reform. B. John Dominic. Foundation of the convent of Fiesole. Fra Angelico. Savonarola; his idea of Christian art and literature. His fall. Fra Bartolomeo. Bartholomew of the Martyrs at the court of Pius IV. Later artists of the order.

THE connection of the Dominican order with Christian art dates almost from its foundation. It was in 1278 that the first stone of the church of Santa Maria Novella at Florence was laid under singular and impressive circumstances. The feuds between Guelf and Ghibelline were then at their height, and Fra Latino Malabranca, nephew to Pope Nicholas V., after travelling through all the cities of Romagna, preaching peace and reconciliation to the opposing factions, at length arrived at Florence to commence the same work of mercy. He assisted at the blessing of the foundation-stone of the new church, and took occasion of the multitudes assembled to witness the ceremony, to address them in so powerful a strain of eloquence that the disputants agreed to forget their enmities, and, flinging their arms round one another's necks, embraced as brothers. The same scene was witnessed not long after within the walls of the newly-erected building on the solemn publication of peace, which was delivered by Latino from its pulpit; and thus the very foundation of this church, afterwards so celebrated in the order, may be said to have been laid in mercy. Its architects and designers were the two lay brothers Fra Sisto and Fra Ristoro; and the glorious temple raised under their direction was exclusively built by the hands of the religious brethren themselves, without the assistance of a single secular, " a thing," says Marchese, " very rare in the history of art."

It is unnecessary for us to speak in praise of a structure whose criticism from the lips of Michael Angelo must be familiar to all. He was wont to call it " his gentle and beautiful bride;" and his merits have even been celebrated in a treatise bearing the title " *De Pulchritudine Sanctæ Mariæ Novellæ*," which we find quoted in one of Savonarola's orations. It must ever possess a peculiar interest for the student of Christian art, who, retracing the six hundred years that have elapsed since its first erection, will recall the day when the walls were receiving their first frescoes from the hands of those Greek artists who had been invited to Florence by the Republic, and found their first and most generous patrons among the Friars Preachers. And as in fancy he watches them at their work, he may see stealing into the church a truant schoolboy, who has escaped from his books and lessons in the grammar-school opened by the Friars

immediately on their settlement in the convent, and has
found his way here to feast his eyes and imagination on
the paintings so far superior in design and coloring to
anything yet known in Florence. He is the scapegrace
of the school, and his name is Cimabue. The order of
Preachers cannot indeed claim him as a member, yet it
was within the walls of one of her most glorious temples
that the future founder of the Florentine school of
painting caught his first inspiration, and it was there, in
the Rucellai chapel, many years afterwards, that his
great *chef d'œuvre*, the Madonna, was carried in procession, and deposited by the hands of his enthusiastic
fellow-citizens.*

We should never end were we to attempt to chronicle
all the artistic glories of Santa Maria Novella, and our
design in speaking of them at all is that they furnish one
out of many illustrations which might be given, of the
manner in which art was used as a means of popular
teaching. The fourteenth century was an age (to use
the words of F. Marchese) "prolific in artists and glorious
for Christian art : every one desired to read on the walls
of the temple the most sublime stories of the Bible, the
popular legends of the saints, and the immortal strains
of Dante. Religion was then the fountain-source of the
artist's inspiration, and painting was employed as a grand
means of moral teaching, worthy of a Christian people."
Indeed, no one can fail to be struck with the contrast
exhibited between the whole system of composition at

The story told of the completion of this picture is illustrative
enough of the enthusiasm of the age in matters of art. Cimabue
was employed in putting his last finishing touches to the Madonna,
when Charles of Anjou passed through the city, and notified his
intention of visiting the artist's studio. Hitherto no one had been
admitted to see the painting; but the news of the prince's intended
visit getting wind, a vast multitude of the citizens followed in his
train, and insisted on the doors being thrown open to the public.
This was done; all Florence crowded to see the great masterpiece
of Cimabue, and so great was the joy and admiration it excited,
that the quarter of the town occupied by his house received the
name of the "Borgo Allegri;" and the painting itself was, as we
have said, borne in triumphant procession to the chapel, where it
still remains.

this period, and that adopted in the modern schools of painting. Mere picturesqueness of detail in form and colouring was not the great object of the painter's study; the aim of men like Memmi, Orgagna, or Taddeo Gaddi, was to employ religious, or, we might say, theological ideas; and thus the pencil of the artist was often guided by the theologian, and was devoted to the representation of a part of some complete system of doctrine or devotion. In fact, painting was unknown as an art of luxury, or apart from its great mission of popular instruction; and it is remarkable that cabinet pictures, that is, pictures merely intended to hang against the walls of private apartments as objects of taste, did not exist until a later period. Up to the time of which we now speak, paintings were to be found only on the walls of the church and cloister, on the doors of shrines and tabernacles, or other public places where they might best fulfil their avowed object as the books of the unlearned. It was in this way that the church of Santa Maria Novella became, under the direction of successive generations, a very museum of Christian art. Much was the work of the religious themselves; but they contributed to the formation of a high school of religious sculpture and painting not only by their own labours, but by their patronage and encouragement of others. None took a greater share in this undertaking than the celebrated Fra Jacobo Passavanti, of whom we have before spoken as the author of "The Mirror of True Penance," and one of the earliest fathers of the Italian idiom. His refined and admirable taste led him to form intimate ties with the distinguished artists of the day, such as Orgagna and others; and at his solicitation, under the superintendence of Fra Jacobi Talenti, they completed the edifice, and made it an almost unequalled gallery of sacred painting. Nowhere, perhaps, have the peculiar characteristics of the mediæval theology been so perfectly represented and preserved. Dante's mind and imagination seem to be embodied on the walls, and we have already indicated the source whence the great poet derived the religious coloring of his poems. To show how close the connection was in those days

between painting and theology, we may remark that
whilst Orgagna was employed in those wonderful frescoes
which represent the terrors of the "Inferno," Simon
Memmi was decorating the cloister with a series illustrative of the mysteries of the Church triumphant and
militant, where we find the Sacrament of Penance placed,
in a number of elaborate designs, as the entrance to the
Church triumphant, every image being taken from Passavanti's work. Indeed, we are expressly told that it
was he who superintended the whole undertaking, and
that the ideas and mode of treatment were all suggested
by him; a circumstance which explains the remarkable
unity of design and teaching which we find in the entire
series.

But it was not only as patrons of the arts that the
Friars Preachers evinced an appreciation of their power
as instruments of popular instruction. They were
artists themselves: and there is one remarkable feature
in the history of their cultivation of Christian art which
we particularly desire to notice in this place. Not only
was it essentially a Christian school of painting which
flourished in the Dominican order, but one which was
invariably associated with the spirit of religious discipline
and reform. Whilst the arts have elsewhere but too
often gained themselves an ill name by their connection
with an age of luxury and relaxation of morals, we find
that in the cloisters of the Friars Preachers they were
not only made compatible with the rigour of primitive
discipline, but were even used as a means of its restoration, where it was found to have decayed. The chief
patrons of art in the Dominican order have every one
been among her greatest and most austere reformers; so
that, in attempting a sketch of her painters and sculptors,
the names of her saints and ascetic men would necessarily
find their way into our pages. Blessed John Dominic,
S. Antoninus, and Jerome Savonarola, are among the most
conspicuous of those who fostered artistic genius in those
very cloisters into which they introduced so primitive and
austere a reform; and this fact will readily explain the
very spiritual and sublime character which attaches to

productions which were undertaken in close association with a revival of religious observance,—nay, often as the very instruments of effecting it.

No man probably stands more distinguished as an ecclesiastical reformer, whether in the Church at large or in his own order in particular, than he whose name we have already so often referred to,—the blessed John Dominic, Cardinal of S. Sixtus. In history he must always be remembered as one who bore the greatest part in extinguishing the fatal schism of the west. He also took the lead in the reform of his own order, and was the founder of several convents which he established on the principles of strict regular observance, to serve as nurseries of sanctity, and models of the institute at large. He was himself an artist of no mean capacity, and during the early years of his religious life in the convent of Santa Maria Novella attained to singular excellence as a miniaturist; many of the choral books illuminated by his hand at this period being still preserved. It was, therefore, experience rather than theory which taught him the use which might be made of religious art as an instrument of community reform; and in his after career we are told that in every convent of the order, whether of men or women, whose regular discipline he reformed, nay, in every convent that he built from the foundations, " he invariably laboured to introduce the most noble art of painting, whose tendency is to raise the soul and the heart to chaste and holy thoughts." Many of his letters on this subject, written to the nuns of the convent of Corpus Domini at Venice, remain to attest the truth of this assertion. In them he directs the religious to perfect themselves in miniaturing (by which is here meant the devout miniatures in choral books) and offers to complete some, the final tintings of which were too difficult for them to undertake.*

We shall select the history of one these convents of strict observance, both for the sake of its connection with Dominican art, and because we are persuaded that our readers will gather a better idea of the spirit of the order

* Marchese.

at this period of its revival and reform from such a narrative, than by a separate notice of the illustrious men whose names are associated with its foundation.

It was then, in the year 1406, that after reestablishing regular discipline in every convent of the Roman province, John Dominic determined, as we have said, on the foundation of several new houses, where the strict letter of the rule should be observed, and the spirit of the order carried out in its highest perfection. The sunny hill of Fiesole was chosen as the site of one of these; and if, as would seem, exterior beauty dwelt on in a religious spirit was judged in the mind of its founder to be a help to the devout contemplation of God, he could scarce have chosen a fitter spot than the one which he destined for his new convent of S. Dominic. The ground was given by Altovito, Bishop of Fiesole, himself a Dominican; and scarcely had the work been begun, when rumours spread far and near that the building then in course of erection was intended as a retreat of peculiar sanctity, or as one may say as an ideal of monastic perfection. S. Antoninus was among the first of those who presented themselves for admission, being attracted by the rumoured holiness of the new foundation; and he was followed two years afterwards by the two brothers Mugello, better known as Fra Benedetto, and Fra Giovanni Angelico da Fiesole. No noviciate being as yet attached to the convent, they were sent to Cortona, where the blessed Lawrence of Ripafracta became their novice-master; having held the same office to S. Antoninus, who has left a eulogium on his venerable guide and teacher in the spiritual life, which has been confirmed in our own day by his solemn beatification. "By reason of his purity of heart," says Bzovius, "he doubted not to call him blessed." And besides these joined with them in the ties of holy friendship, there was the blessed Constantius Fabriano, afterwards the reformer of Ascoli, a man illustrious for miracles and the gift of prayer; and Pietro Capucci, to whom is also sometimes given the title of blessed. In fact, Cortona and Fiesole were the nurseries of saints, and it was in such a home, and in such fellowship, that the genius of Angelico received its stamp of sanctity. Of all the painters of the mystic school (by which we intend to designate the followers or imitators of Giotto in opposition to the naturalists who received so powerful an encouragement from the patronage of the Medici), Angelico stands undoubtedly highest; and his merits as a painter, nay more, the singular and irresistible spiritual influence of his works, have been acknowledged by critics like Vasari, whose mind was certainly cast in a wholly different mould. Yet his sketch of the Dominican painter is itself so beautiful and truthful a delineation that we will give it as it stands, feeling sure that our readers will gain their best idea of the character of his paintings by knowing something of the character of the man. His words are as follows : " Fra Giovanni was a man of holy and simple habits ; he lived a pure and sanctified life, and was ever the friend of the poor on earth, as I believe also that his soul is now in heaven. He was always painting; and never wished to produce anything save for the saints. He was wont to say that true riches consist in being content with little. He might easily have attained to high dignities, but he did not esteem them, saying that the only dignity he desired was to escape hell, and to win paradise. He was very gentle and sober, and used to say that artists needed quiet, and should be free from interruptions ; and that he whose works related to Christ should be ever communing with Christ. Never was he known to exhibit anger, and when he had occasion to admonish any, he did it with a gentle smile. When others sought works from his pencil he was wont to tell them with extraordinary amiability that so long as the prior was satisfied he would not refuse them. In short, both in actions and words, he was most humble and modest, and in his painting simple and devout ; the saints he painted have more the air and resemblance of saints than those of any other artist. He never retouched or heightened the effect of any of his works, but left them just as they came from his pencil, believing that such was the will of God. Some say he never took up his brush without first having recourse to prayer. Whenever he painted a crucifixion the tears streamed down his cheeks, and it is easy, in the very countenances and attitudes of his figures, to see the purity of his heart, and his devotion to the Christian faith." In fact, to use the words of a more modern critic, "painting was his ordinary prayer," the very means he used to raise his heart to God. What wonder that the works of such a man should bear in their silent eloquence something of that strange power over the soul which attaches to the speech or the writings of the saints? A power which genius alone, even the genius of Rafaele or Michael Angelo can never attain to when the supernatural element is wanting.

The influence exercised by the poetry of Dante over all the painters of the mystic school was of a very singular character. Giotto, we know, was the friend and close associate of the great Florentine, and may be said to have illustrated the Divine Commedio by his pencil. Nor was Angelico insensible to the influence of that master mind. "Dante," says Marchese, in his work on the Dominican painters, "mated the doctrine of S. Thomas to the harmony of his verse; and I would venture to affirm that Angelico incarnated and coloured the conception of these two great men. If we compare his pictures with the writings of the philosopher and the poet, we shall have little difficulty in detecting the identity of thought that characterized the Italians in their theories of the supernatural, and the imagery in which they clothed them." To which we will add, that a study of the works of these three minds will probably convey the most perfect idea that could be formed of the Christianity of the middle ages, and would enable us to form a high conception of the extent to which the theolgy of S. Thomas, illustrated and popularized as it was to men's hearts by the genius of the poet and the painter, diffused its influence over all classes, and found new ways of exercising its dictatorship of Christian philosophy.

How vast a distance separates this school of supernaturalism from that of the succeeding centuries! Two words rise to our lips as we stand before any of the great

works of the Angelico: they are simplicity and faith; and
these two qualities, whilst they express the whole character
of his mind and of his paintings, seem also to express the
religious spirit of his age.   What their influence may have
been in keeping alive spirituality and asceticism we can but
estimate by contrasts.   Let us turn to the productions of
a later school, to the churches restored, as it was called, by
the enthusiasts for pagan art, whose walls are defaced by
those gross imitators of nature who seem to value the art
of delineation only so far as it reproduces the idea of flesh
and blood; and when we feel the evil power possessed by
such representations, of obliterating spiritual impressions,
and substituting in their room the merest images of sense,
we feel also how different and wholly unearthly must have
been the thoughts and tone of mind of those trained to
prayer and contemplation in the midst of that supernatural
system which in the ages of faith was preached from the
very walls of church and cloister.

The reforms begun by John Dominic were carried out
in the same spirit by his disciple S. Antoninus, who, previous to his elevation to the see of Florence, governed
successively the convents of Rome, Naples, Gaeta, Cortona,
Siena, Fiesole, and Florence.   At the latter place Cosmo
de Medici made over to the Friars Preachers the convent
of S. Mark, which he endowed with his usual munificence,
and S. Antoninus became prior of the new house, to which
Angelico and his brother were soon summoned, and where
they have left the most glorious monuments of their genius.
S. Mark's soon became another Fiesole, a home and nursery of sanctity, and at the same time a gallery of the
most glorious productions of Christian art.   Indeed, we
know that S. Antoninus, like his predecessor, John Dominic,
was not only a patron and encourager of art, but was
himself possessed of considerable skill in painting, and
many of the choral books of S. Mark's still claim to be
those which received their illuminations from his venerable
hands.   And widely different as their part in life was destined to become, the name of Antoninus, the mirror of
prelates, the reformer of his order, the doctor of the
Church, is always sweetly and closely associated with that

of Fra Angelico whose life was so essentially hidden and contemplative, and whose only learning was that of his pencil. Every one knows the story of his visit to Rome, and how Eugenius IV. is said to have been so struck with his peculiar sanctity, that he would have elevated him to the vacant archbishopric of Florence, had not the painter declined the dignity, and suggested Fra Antonio as the fitter person for so exalted an office; so that, if the tale be authentic, and there seems no reasonable ground for doubting it, we may consider the glorious episcopate of S. Antoninus as in no small degree to be attributed to the recommendation of his friend. Those who are familiar with his story will remember also that instance of his *naïve* simplicity, so like what we realize of his character, when we are told how, on being invited to dine with the holy father, he declined, saying he could not eat meat, without his prior's permission, quite forgetting the dispensing power of the supreme Pontiff. He lies in the church of the Minerva, and it is said the Pope himself wrote the inscription we read over his tomb; remarkable for the circumstances that even there, and so immediately after his death, the expression occurs which has been sanctioned, if not by the formal declaration of the Church, at least by the common consent of her people. The words ran thus:

Here lies the *Venerable* Painter,
Brother John of Florence, of the Order of Preachers.

Fra Angelico had no disciples among the ranks of his own brethren, nevertheless, though he can scarcely be said to have formed a school, or to have trained others in his peculiar style, there were many of the order who trod in his footsteps, though there were none who came near to him in artistic skill. Thus we read of a certain Fra Girolamo Monsignori, whose character, sketched also by Vasari, is precisely of the same stamp as that of the great painter: "He was chiefly distinguished," he says, "for his love of prayer and seclusion, and his indifference to the world. The money which he earned by his works, and expended on the purchase of colours, was hung up in an old box without a lid, so that any one who wanted it

might come and use it. To avoid all trouble about daily
food, he cooked every Monday a pot of beans, and this
supplied him during the week. When Mantua was visited
by the plague and every one fled in alarm, he, moved by
charity, refused to abandon the sick fathers, but tended
them with his own hands. So, sacrificing his life to God,
he caught the contagion and died, being of the age of
sixty." How full, too, of the religious spirit of Angelico
is the inscription which we read on the painted window
in the church of S. Dominic at Perugia, which tells us
that the window is consecrated " to the honour of God
and of the most Holy Virgin, of S. James, and the blessed
Dominic, and of the celestial choir, by Brother Bartolomeo,
the least of the order of Preachers, who, with the Divine
aid, furnished it in the year 1411." Glass-painting,
indeed, was an art particularly cultivated in the order, and
produced the only *really* beatified saint who was distinguished as a painter; this was the blessed James of Ulm,*
a lay brother in the convent of Bologna, and the master
of a school of artists who rivalled him both in genius and
in sanctity.

But we must pass on to another period when the connection between religious art, as cultivated by the Dominican
order, and a spirit of ecclesiastical reform, was destined
to be more fully and strikingly illustrated than even in
the example of the Cardinal John Dominic. In speaking
of it we must necessarily carry our narrative to a later
date than that with which we concluded our last chapter;
but as it is not our intention to return to this subject, we
shall refer to the one or two facts which seem to claim
our notice, without attending to the chronological order
of our sketch; and there seems no fitter place than this
in which to speak of one whose enthusiasm for Christian
art is certainly not the least remarkable feature in
his character: we refer, of course, to the unfortunate
Savonarola.

We have already mentioned Cosmo de Medici as
having endowed the order of Friars Preachers with the
convent of S. Mark's at Florence. He was the first of

* See No. XIX. of "Tales and Legends from History."

his family who attained to the chief and supreme rule in
the Florentine republic, and under him and his successors
it may, indeed, be said that the state was a republic no
longer. The very name of his race carries with it the
idea of all that is splendid and refined; the restoration of
learning, and encouragement of science and commerce,
and, above all, a special patronage of the arts. And yet,
for all this, we can scarcely be wrong in saying that
Christian art and feeling had no more fatal enemies in
the fifteenth century than the illustrious members of the
Medici family; and that it was they who chiefly gave
that impulse to pagan literature and pagan philosophy
and art, from whose deadly effects the world is only in
our own day beginning to revive. The fall of Constantinople drove multitudes of Greek scholars and artists into
Europe, and nowhere did they receive a more princely
welcome than at the court of Cosmo the Magnificent.
A fashion, if we may so say, set in for classic studies;
Plato took the place of S. Thomas, and we begin to hear
in the popular writers of the day more of the " virtues of
philosophy," and "the sublime mysteries of Platonism,"
than of either the virtues or the mysteries of the gospel.
" In fact," says a modern historian of this period,
" Florence was heathenized by the Medici, and pagan
philosophy was made the rule of life for the scholars and
sages of this new Athens of intellectual refinement."
Yet the evil had its commencement only in the lifetime
of Cosmo.

The dazzling brilliancy of the age of the Medici has
too often blinded the eyes of its historians, as it did
those of contemporaries, and concealed from their view
the fatal character of that revolution which was effected
in society during the fifteenth century. If we consider some of the elements then at work, we may easily
perceive that in no way could the world have escaped
a period of powerful agitation and intellectual excitement. At one and the same time, the stores of ancient
classic learning were being poured into the capitals of
the west, brought thither after the fall of the eastern
empire, by the crowd of refugee scholars and philosophers

who found their chief asylums at Rome and in the northern
cities of Italy ; whilst the newly-discovered art of
printing lent its aid to diffuse these new studies, and,
in the words of Marchese, " sowed broadcast the seeds" of
pagan erudition.

Old principles of thought were breaking up: Aristotle
and his school of Christian interpreters were abandoned ;
and Plato, who took his place, was thought to need no
Christian interpreter at all. No century could, probably,
be selected so brilliant in names of literary greatness ;
but when we glance at the character of their genius, we
tremble at the combination of so much mental power with
so enormous a depravity. The world was no longer to
be ruled by the brute force of barbarous ages, and the
people showed a disposition to free themselves from the
yoke of their feudal rulers, whose power was everywhere
giving way before the refinement and civilization of the
age. But, in exchange, they fell under a different and
more subtle tyranny. It was the age of Machiavelism, and
the principles of state policy, and we may add, of state
iniquity, were in the vigour of their first developement.
" In wickedness of policy," says Marchese, " no age ever
surpassed the fifteenth century, for it fought, not with
arms and valour, but with fraud and poisons, and few
ever equalled it in the corruption of its morality." In
Tuscany the Medici, in their attempt to secure the
supreme power, not only pursued this object with a total
indifference to the protection of morals, but made the
indulgence of the people in a certain licence of manners
one of the most approved methods of acquiring the
dominion at which they aimed. It has ever been the
line of all who have grasped at a usurped dictatorship, to amuse and intoxicate the multitudes by
pageant and festivals, by which their senses are dazzled,
and their minds distracted from an apprehension of their
real danger. This was the peculiar policy of the Medici,
and they cared little for the licentiousness which quickly
infused its poison into every vein of society, so long as
the world applauded, and the state submitted ; and
Florence was content to sacrifice its liberty in exchange

for the enjoyment of that unbridled freedom which disfigured the very arts of which they claimed to be the special and most magnificent patrons. Alas! these great patrons of art were, in too many ways, its great corrupters. What could be anticipated from an intellectual movement so thoroughly and essentially pagan in its tendencies, that we find examples like that of a certain Florentine canon, who, in his idolatry of Plato, went so far as to burn a lamp in his chamber before an image of his favourite philosopher!

Whatever may be the merit of the Medici as the revivers of classical learning, and the great encouragers of genius in every shape, the *prestige* of their magnificence is something tarnished when we view it closer. The imaginative arts had hitherto been the weapons of Christianity against the world; they now became arms in the hands of the world, warring against Christianity. Let us hear a modern author speaking of the period when Lorenzo de Medici ruled the republic of Florence as its absolute sovereign:—" Among the means adopted by this great and astute man to secure his power, always increasing, over the Florentine people, he imagined a new style of poetry which he called "*Cesti Carnascialeschi,*" or carnival-songs, in order to give more effect to certain masquerades in which some triumph or subject of art was represented. He spared no expense to render these orgies attractive and brilliant. The chariots and carousers went about the city from after dinner to two, and even three, hours of the night, men wearing masks following them on horseback, richly apparelled, with flames and torches. In this order they paraded the city with singers and musicians, singing ballads and madrigals suitable to the character of each masquerade." He then gives us the names of subjects of some of these representations, some being heathen fables, as "The triumph of Bacchus and Ariadne;" others of a satirical character, adding that these festivals, and the poetry which was sung in them, "were for the most part indecent and immoral."* In fact, one cannot

* De Rians.

acquit the Mecaenas, or the Augustus of Florence, as his flatterers loved to call him, of a deliberate plan for securing his power over the populace by means of the corruption of the public taste and manners. Nay, what was the very art that he encouraged and revived? We may quote a French writer of our own day, one of those many generous champions of Catholic faith and purity who, thanks be to God, are fast obliterating from the literature of their country the associations of a past age of infidelity. "Antiquity," says Carlier, "was patronized by the Medici only on the side of sensuality. Their love for pagan art was not a classic taste, but a voluptuous passion. In literature, Ovid, Catullus, and Tibullus, were in greater favour with them than Homer, Cicero, and Cæsar. Their celebrated garden at Florence became the sanctuary of a nude naturalism in art. Developments of form—the mere manifestations of physical perfection—statues of divinities who presided of old over the orgies of unbridled vice,—these attracted the public admiration, and found a species of worship in obsequious criticism, in poetry, and even in philosophic contemplation."[*]

Such was the state of things in Florence, when a chance meeting at the chapter-general of the order, held at Reggio in 1445, introduced Jerome Savonarola to the notice of one of the most remarkable men of that remarkable age. This was John Picus Mirandola, "the phœnix of intellects," as he was styled: a prodigy of learning, whose wonderful mind had happily early drunk deep at those sacred sources of Christian theology which made all things pure to him. The intellectual wonder of his age, he was able to say with the profound conviction of one who utters the experience of a life, "Philosophy seeks for truth, theology finds it, religion possesses it."[†] Among all the great intelligences whom the Medici had attracted to their court, there was none so distinguished for his vast attainments, his undisputed taste, and his lofty and irreproachable character, as the young prince of Mirandola;

* Carlier, Æsthétiques de Savonarola
† Epist. Joh. Pic. Mir.

and at his first meeting with Savonarola, "spirit sprang to spirit," and a friendship was formed between them which remained unbroken during the whole of their lives. On his return to Florence, Mirandola exerted all his influence with Lorenzo de' Medici to invite the gifted friar to his capital, and five years afterwards Savonarola was established in the convent of S. Mark, and was almost immediately elected prior of that community.

Of all the illustrious men of the Dominican order there is none whose name has such a world-wide interest as that of Savonarola. Something of the spell which attracted men to him during his life almost against their will, still attaches to his memory; and sparks of that enthusiasm which he kindled by his strange eloquence even now survive among us. His career, from the time of his entrance into Florence to the day of his ignominious death, occupied the short space of eight years; during that time he combated single-handed against the corruptions of the world around him: against licentiousness of morals, corruptions in public government, and paganism in literature and the arts. As a religious, he was the strictest, yet the gentlest of reformers; we see him, in our mind's eye, walking through those glorious cloisters of S. Mark's, rich with the fairest creations of Angelico's imagination, with the ivory death's-head that he was wont to carry in his hand, and with that look of sweetness and repose about him which, we are told, was one of the secrets of his influence over others, and which kindled an indescribable feeling of interior consolation in all who approached him. His first work as a reformer, and that which was the most successful and abundant in its fruits, was in his own order. Everywhere he endeavoured to introduce the old spirit of poverty and religious simplicity: a spirit little in accordance with the manners of the time, but which he found ways and means of fostering out of the richness and fertility of his own inventive genius. What cannot one master mind effect when, in addition to its greatness and its power, it knows how to charm by a sweet familiar intercourse with all ranks and all ages; when it can be grave with sadder and elder

hearts, and can unbend to children; can discourse of
divine things, and expound the sacred Scriptures with
theologians, or gather the novices and little ones of
Christ, and exert all its skill and all its gracious
pleasantry to amuse! And so it was with the prior of
S. Mark's. We can watch him in the convent garden,
singing canticles with his novices, or sitting under the
shadow of the fig-tree, amusing them by cutting out the
pith of trees into images of little doves, or teaching them
simple games, wherein some saint of pure and holy life
was commemorated, and praises and divine songs were
sung in honour of the Child Jesus, or of the blessed
Virgin. This was one of his methods of guidance;
another was the introduction of habits of industry among
all the members of the community. He contrived to
infuse his own spirit among them, and one of the great
weapons used by him for the preservation of this spirit
of primitive and spiritual religion was the introduction
and cultivation of Christian art. In every convent over
which his influence extended, and in all which he founded,
whether of men or of women, the arts of painting and
modelling were introduced, and carried on in strict accordance with those maxims which our own day is fast
recognizing as the truest definitions of beauty ever given
to the world.

We should be exceeding the limits of our subject were
we to give the extracts from Savonarola's sermons and
writings, wherein he lays down the rules of spiritual
beauty, and attacks with a bold and fearless eloquence
the profane and abominable representations from the
school of naturalism which had found their way into the
holy places. Art was in his eyes one of the great
elements by which men were to be humanized and
christianized: he considered it as a want of the people,
and, unlike others who had entered on the task of
reform, far from proscribing it, he encouraged it with
all the force of his enthusiastic eloquence; his denunciations fell only on the sensualism which had usurped
its name. We refer the reader to the beautiful work of
Rio, "La Poësie en l'Art," to Marchese's "Lives of the

Dominican Painters and Sculptors," and to Carlier's
articles on the ".Esthetics of Savonarola," if they would
form any idea of the corruptions which he attacked, or
of the principles which he brought into opposition. No
one can rise from the perusal of these authors, or of
those passages of Savonarola's own writings which touch
on the subject without feeling that he in the most
intimate and delicate manner apprehended that supernatural and spiritual idea of art which had found its
incarnation in the works of Angelico ; while, on the
other hand, he will receive an impression of the character of that classic revival so lauded by the admirers of
the Medici, which makes us glad to leave the task of
exposure to other hands and other pages. Let him turn
to the Lenten Sermons in which the great orator attacks
the profligacy of the church-decoraters in such indignant
strains of eloquence, and in the same breath defines the
idea of beauty, apart from form, as something whose
essential principle must be light and purity. Powerful,
indeed, must have been that oratory, whose effects are
said by Burlamacchi to have been like an irresistible
magic, even on hardened and debased minds like those of
the Florentine artists. As in the days of the Apostles,
they came and laid at their feet the materials of their
unholy trade. Baccio della Porta, afterwards known in
religion as the celebrated Fra Bartolomeo, with several
others, brought all their designs and works of a reprehensible character, and offered to destroy them before his
eyes. Others left his presence with vows on the lips,
never again to degrade the art of sculpture or painting
by prostituting them to the encouragement of vice. The
change effected by his fervid oratory was felt, not among
the artists alone, but in all ranks and professions. The
quick and ardent sensibilities of the Florentines were
captivated by that eloquence which undoubtedly, in its
bewitching charm, surpassed everything which the world
of antiquity had known.

"The people," says Burlamacchi, " rose from their
beds at midnight to go to the sermon, and waited uncovered

at the doors of the cathedral till they were opened, never complaining of the inconvenience, or exposure to the cold air, of standing in the winter time on the bare marble; and amongst them were young and old, women and children, of every class, all filled with great joy, and going to the sermon as to a wedding. In the church was profound silence; not a whisper heard in the great multitude till the children came, who sang some hymns with such sweetness that Paradise seemed opened. And so they would wait three or four hours till the father ascended the pulpit. Profane songs were now no longer heard, but spiritual canticles, often the composition of Savonarola himself; these they sometimes chanted in chorus on the highways, as friars do in the choir. Mothers were seen in the street reciting the office with their children. The women, now dressed with modesty, and even the children, sent a deputation to the governors of the city praying them to enact laws for the protection of good morals." All classes crowded round the wonderful friar, and gave in their enthusiastic adhesion to his plan of social reform. "The grand intellects," says Marchese, "whom the Medici had attracted to their court, all bowed before the majesty of his surpassing eloquence." There was the Count de Mirandola, who after renouncing his government, desired to enter the order of S. Dominic; but, death preventing the accomplishment of this design, he directed that at least his body should be buried in the holy habit, which was accordingly done. There was Zanobi Acciajuoli, the classic scholar of his day, and Politian, the most refined and elegant of Lorenzo's courtiers. Such a crowd of Florentine nobles solicited the habit that S. Mark's had to be enlarged; and, on the death of Savonarola, the convent counted upwards of two hundred friars, and eighty novices, *all of whom,* we are assured, persevered. As to the artists to whom Savonarola unfolded his glorious idea of beauty, Vasari compares their enthusiasm to a delirium. They threw themselves into the ranks of the order like volunteers flocking to a patriot band; and, indeed, at that time the purification of art and of literature was regarded as a kind of patriotism. On the one hand were those who usurped a despotism over Florence, and sought to govern her by her degradation; on the other side was the cause of the republic; and, as Savonarola would fain have had it thought, that cause was indissolubly tied up with social reform, and the restoration of Christian purity in morals, letters and education. It was a tremendous struggle, and we well know how it ended. Yet, ere the bloood of the great victim flowed, he had achieved a triumph, the memory of which was not to be effaced even by the fury of the Arrabbiati.

Not to dwell too long on the details of a period whose interest insensibly carries us beyond our limits, we must just give the account left us by Burlamacchi, of one of the reformed carnival festivities. A year or two before, these hoildays had been ovations to vice : they were now made the solemn inauguration of restored Christianity.

" At the beginning of the carnival, 1497, the father ordered that there should be a very solemn procession, full of mysteries; and he caused to be erected in the Piazza dei Signori, a large cabin, within which were collected all vain and abominable objects which the children had gathered from all parts of the city. The joiners had constructed a pyramid, and in its hollow placed a great quantity of brushwood and gunpowder. On its steps were laid and arranged all the various offensive objects. On the first step, most precious tapestries, whereon indecent figures had been worked ; above them figures and portraits of the fairest damsels of Florence ; on another step, cards, dice, and such like diabolical inventions ; on another, musical instruments of all kinds. Then came the adornments of women : false hair, mirrors, perfumes, cyprus-powder, and similar varieties. Then masks, beards, and other carnival trumpery. Then the works of the Latin and modern poets, Boccaccio, Petrarch, and the like. Then many most beautiful works of the chisel and the pencil, with some ivory and alabaster chessmen for which a certain Venetian merchant had offered 20,000 crowns; but, instead of letting him have them, they painted him to the life, enthroned him at the

top as the king of all these vanities. Then the whole
was set on fire, the flames mounted up to heaven, and all
these vanities were consumed."

Some of our readers may think this indiscriminate
destruction of the *chefs d'œuvres* of the Florentine artists
a strange instance to cite in illustration of the services
rendered by Savonarola to the cause of art ; and coupling
such a fact with the circumstance of his oppposition having
been directed against works of the pagan or classical
school, they may receive an impression that the question
was a mere rivalry of styles, and that the zeal shown by
the Dominican friar was but a development of that
bigoted mediævalism which would limit Christian art to
one form of expression, and would resist the *renaissance*
of the 15th century simply as being a departure from the
antique ecclesiastical type. To hold up such a principle
as worthy of veneration and imitation would not only be
a mistake, but even a dangerous one, calculated to foster
that insidious error so inseparable from an heretical
spirit, the inclination, namely, to petrify truth into some
particular form arbitrarily chosen, denying to the Church
her power of adopting every variety of style and system,
and bending them to her purpose ; and above all it would
be to encourage that disposition to exalt antiquity over the
Church's living authority, which, even when it does not
extend to an actaul revolt against her teaching, argues
but a cold sympathy with her in matters of feeling, and has
been the Jansenism of every age.

For it cannot be forgotten that, whatever be each one's
taste in such matters, there could plainly be no question
of orthodoxy involved in the struggle between mediæval
art and the *cinque cento*. Even if there were a secret
danger lurking in the revival of a style closely associated
with paganism, the Church had power to annul the evil by
consecrating those classic forms to Christian purposes;
and that she has done so, and in the centre of Christendom has permitted the modern taste to prevail
over the Mediæval style, ought not to be without its
significance to those amongst ourselves who would pin
down Catholicism in art and architecture to the taste of

any particular century chosen by themselves. We are aware that the advocates of the modern classical renaissance go even farther, and not only marvel how the grotesque forms of the middle ages can be preferred to the truer delineation of nature, and bolder design of the school of artists who sprang up during the age of the Medici, but assert that the genius of the great men of the fifteenth century has created a new era in Christian æsthetics, and that the result has been not merely the adaptation of the classical forms to the warmer and more joyous spirit which characterizes the modern Church, but the creation of a style by which that spirit must be almost exclusively expressed. Nor is it wonderful that they who have drunk in Catholic devotional feeling under the wonderful dome of Michael Angelo, or before the unscreened altars of modern Rome, and who find in the Madonnas of Rafaele and his contemporaries their highest ideals of human beauty, should come to associate Grecian architecture and the productions of a school of painting which avowedly drew its inspiration from life and nature, with their own tenderest impressions of Catholic worship; and that, overlooking with an indulgent partiality the sensualism which too often mingles with the beauty, they should claim the pre-eminence in Christian art for that style which is identified in their minds with modern Rome.

We have no wish to impose the severer rules of ancient taste on those with whose devotion it has ceased to harmonize; doubtless, what spiritual writers affirm of the individual soul is true of the world at large, and to adopt the expression of S. Catherine, "the heart cannot always abide in *one* mode of receiving the Divine visitation, as though God were not able to act through other means and in other ways."* Nor would we overlook the fact that one secret of the Church's strength lies in her power of absorbing into herself all popular emotions, and pressing them into the service of the faith. As she seized on the military enthusiasm of a semi-barbarous age, raising out of it the beautiful

* Dialogo, cap. 71.

fabric of Christian chivalry, and at a later period overpowered the relationship of the schools by adapting their
system into her own scheme of Christian philosophy,
—and as in each succeeding age she has kept her mastery
over the world less by crushing than by directing those
varying forms of popular enthusiasm which in bodies
separated from her guidance have resulted in wild and
fanatic excess,—so there cannot be a doubt that she did
well and wisely in receiving the classical *renaissance* into
her bosom, and robbing its beauties of their paganism
by identifying them with the associations of Christian
worship.

Against this principle Savonarola's zeal was in no
way directed : his crusade was against sensualism in
art, wherever it might be found existing; but we can
nowhere find any condemnation pronounced by him of
one style rather than of another. So far from wishing
to stifle the study and imitation of nature under due
restrictions, or from attempting to stiffen Christian art
into any given shape no longer in harmony with the
popular taste and feeling, we know that the disciples
whom he formed on his own principles did not any of
them follow the mediæval models, and that the greatest
of them all, and he who certainly was most profoundly
imbued with his master's teaching, Fra Bartolomeo, is
thought in his boldness of conception and design to
follow closely on the steps of Michael Angelo, whom he
is often said to resemble. No doubt the eagle eye of the
Dominican friar saw the weak point of the rising school,
and was forewarned of the inevitable consequence of taking
any standard of human beauty for the ideals of divine
forms. If, when he denounced in such tremendous terms
the "gross materialism" which was taking the place of the
purely spiritual creations of elder days, and so often set
before his hearers, in discourses whose sublimity has never
been surpassed, the idea of Jesus as the type of regener-
ated humanity, he showed little mercy on genius when
defaced by what he deemed the evil stamp of a licentious
character, this was no mediæval bigotry ; although we
may fancy his half-prophetic soul looking on through the

centuries that followed, beholding the *naturalizing* of art resulting in little else than its degradation. Surely, without risk of being thought to advocate the imposition of any peculiar views as a rule of taste, we may ask ourselves whether Christian art may not have suffered something when it consented to take its inspiration from no higher source than that which moved the genius of pagan artists in the delineation of pagan divinities, when nature was made the standard of ideals that were *above* nature; when human beauty was thought enough to constitute a model for the Immaculate Mother, whatever were its character, and the artist's studio not only lost its almost religious character, but came to be looked on as a dangerous school for morals. Nor can we be otherwise than struck with one singular and significant fact in connection with this subject. Whatever may be said of the undoubted superiority of the modern school of painters, considered simply as artists, the *religious* heart of Christendom has refused them its homage. Their exquisite works are to be oftener found in our galleries and dining-halls than in our churches; of all the incarnations of grace and beauty which Rafaele has given us in his Madonnas we know not of *one* which has ever become the object of popular religious veneration;* and the multitude, so true in the

---

* We do not mean to assert that no modern picture has become an object of popular veneration, or even been honoured by miraculous graces. More instances than one occur to our minds which would be sufficient to establish the contrary. But we must needs admit that where this has been the case the pictures in question are neither in the artistic merits, nor in the religious demerits of the great masters. One in particular suggests itself to the writer's mind, painted but a few years since by a very neophyte in the art of fresco, innocent of the mysteries of chiaro 'scuro, and as stiff and unskilful in its design as though copied from an early mosaic; yet it has a character of inexpressible purity and sweetness, or, it may be, the air of the little chapel of the "Mater Admirabilis" is so redolent with devotion that we involuntarily ascribe something of sanctity to the character of the painting. It is in the convent of the Trinità dei Monti at Rome; and the numberless graces granted at the little sanctuary are known to all who have ever visited the Holy City, and not long since procured from the Sovereign Pontiff

long run to religious instincts, keep faithful to those
more ancient representations which, with less of material
beauty, possess the higher qualifications of *devotion*, and
have been honoured by those miraculous graces which
seem withheld from the highest productions of human
genius. The Madonnas of Rafaele will, no doubt, command the homage of our admiration as long as their canvas
holds together; but they will never draw away the love and
worship of the people from the old sanctuaries where the
images of Mary borrow nothing of their power from the
skill of the painter, and where the supernatural beauty
which is so often discernible in spite of the rudeness of
their design, is as far as possible removed from the stamp
of sensualism.

Our readers must pardon us if we have in some degree
wandered from our subject, but it seemed necessary, to
avoid misconception on a matter where it is so easy a
thing to write or read as a partisan. Savonarola's name
is so closely associated with the advocacy of Christian
design, and the condemnation of paganism in art and
literature, that it would not be unnatural for a eulogy
of his principles in this matter to be taken as bearing
on some particular questions warmly contested in our
own day, and he might come to be looked on as having
desired to *crush* rather than to spiritualize art. But we
may remind any who might be inclined thus to interpret
the scene which we have described on the Piazza dei
Signori, that the man who thus encouraged his fellow-
citizens to sacrifice without mercy " all vain and lascivious
things" was the same who, in reviving primitive observance
at S. Mark's, resolved (in the words of Marchese) " to
promote the study of the arts of design which he considered *essential* to his grand reform. He determined
that the lay brothers should devote themselves to some
of the arts not likely to distract them, such as sculpture,
painting, mason's work, writing, &c." And no fewer
than nine of the first artists of Florence received the
religious habit from his hand, and were encouraged by

the grant of a golden crown to the picture, together with many
indulgences to those who offer their devotions before the altar.

him not to abandon their art, but to consecrate their
genius within those cloisters rendered already glorious
by the pencil of Angelico. Even in the Dominican convents of women his influence introduced a cultivation of
the arts of design, specially in that of S. Catherine at
Florence, founded by Camilla Ruccellai, where painting
and modelling were studied by the religious at his suggestion, and where a succession of excellent artists continued
to flourish down to the period of the suppression of the
religious orders in the last century. The two sisters
Plautilla and Petronilla Nelli were both members of
this community, the former of whom was a paintress
of no mean celebrity, while the latter devoted herself
to literature, and has left, among other works, a life of
Savonarola still preserved in manuscript. Plautilla Nelli
is compared by Vasari to the celebrated and unfortunate
Properzia de' Rossi, whose skill, he says, was rivalled by
that of the Dominican nun. But if equal in genius,
by how vast a distance are they separated in the story of
their lives! Properzia died a victim to the world's most
cruel sorrow: Plautilla consecrated her glorious gifts
to God's service, and was yet more admirable for the
prudence and piety with which she governed her monastery, than for those endowments which she valued
only as a means for promoting the honour of her Divine
Spouse.[*]

Savonarola's whole design seems to have been the
substitution of Christian ideas, as objects of literature
and art, for those which were in themselves essentially
pagan. He was never foremost in that popularization of
devotion by means of songs and pictures, which has done
such admirable service to religion in the struggle she has
waged with modern heresy. His "Laude," or Divine
Songs, were written to take the place of those very
Carnival verses of a licentious character which he had
so summarily destroyed; and we can confidently affirm
that none who read those exquisite verses, ode as to the

* See the interesting chapter in Marchese's work on the "Dominican Artists," which is devoted to the female painters and authors
of the order.

X

soul," and others of equal merit recently translated and
given to the public in his biography by Dr. Madden, can
refuse to acknowledge his claims to true poetic feeling,
even though he placed the works of Petrarch among the
"vanities" of his bonfire. The fact that S. Philip Neri,
closely identified as he was in after years with what we
may call the modern popular school, passed his youth
and formed his first religious impressions in the cloisters
of S. Mark, where the spirit and principles of Savonarola
were still warmly cherished and preserved, would be
enough to show that those principles must have been
wholly distinct from the mere purism of antiquarian
bigotry.

The political career of Savonarola, and his subsequent
condemnation by the Holy See, are foreign to the purpose with which we have introduced his name into our
present sketch, which has been solely as an illustration
of the part always taken by the Dominican order in the
cause of Christian art. His story has continued to furnish
matter of warm and often of bitter controversy even
down to our own day, and it is not the least singular
fact in connection with the great republican friar, that,
after the lapse of four centuries, his name is still able to
rouse the enthusiasm both of friends and enemies, so that
it is hard for either to reason save as partisans. Doubtless,
the purity of the cause to which he first devoted his noble
energies, and the heroic constancy with which he struggled
single-handed to stem the corruption of the age, must
command the sympathy of every generous heart; and
if, during his closing years, the excitement of political
agitation absorbed those powers which should have
been spent on worthier things, and, gradually warping
his judgment, and (it may be) marring the perfect
equilibrium of his mind, led him into the fatal error of
assuming a position of hostility to the supreme authority
of the Church, it is scarcely surprising that the sufferings
by which he expiated his fault, and the character of his
persecutors, should have induced many to forget and
almost to palliate the fault itself. It is, however, one
of those cases in which an indulgence of our sympathies

would lead us astray; the fact remains uncontroverted, that not only did Savonarola resist that supreme authority, submission to which is the primary law of Christian obedience, but justified his resistance in words[*] which bear unmistakeable evidence of an appeal to interior inspiration against the claims of obedience. Such a pretence has been the groundwork of all heresy and unbelief; and, feeling this, we shrink from the popular canonization of the great Florentine, as we should from all attempts to substitute sentiment in the room of principle. His career and his misfortunes, if they are a problem in history, afford at least a profound lesson in morals, and one suited to no age better than to our own. For in him we see a soul far on the track of sanctity, endowed with the highest gifts of genius, and the most keen and exquisite perceptions of truth, ever soaring to the highest standard, and content with nothing short of the beauty or the truth of God, thrown out of its course, and wrecked at last, when it came to identify a political creed with the cause of Christianity, and when the love of truth became insidiously and imperceptibly blended with the fatal love of self.

We hold it for something more than a probability, that the highly wrought and excitable temperament of Savonarola had before his death contracted the first seeds of mental disease. And this appears in a certain vein of fanaticism, and extravagance, and an assumed tone of authority, only comprehensible in one of his greatness of understanding under the supposition that his mind was overstrained. We know that such aberrations of genius and imagination are not rare; yet it would not be too bold to say that, although such a supposition must

---

[*] "I act in coming here in obedience to authority. To whom? To the Signoria? You wish not to believe me, because, as you say, I am not bound to obey them. It is, then, you will say, to obey your prelates, your superiors. But nothing of the kind has been directed me by my superiors. Know, then, that I have ascended the pulpit this day *to obey him who is the Ruler of us all*, the Supreme Pontiff of all popes, and who makes known to me what is contrary to His will, and in nature opposed to it, &c."

extenuate much in his conduct which otherwise appears
indefensible, it of itself presupposes a defective humility,
for without the admission into the soul of some such
error in principle, or the yielding to some interior temptation, enthusiasm can never gain such mastery over a
mind as to throw it off its balance. Yet, be the case how
it may, the name of Jerome Savonarola will always be
held as one of the greatest in his order, and the memory
of his errors is well-nigh consumed in the flames of his
expiatory sacrifice. When the mob of the Arrabbiati
stormed the convent of S. Mark on the 9th of April,
1498, and the partisans of Savonarola prepared for
defence, and the short struggle was terminated by the
voluntary surrender of the great victim into the hands of
his enemies,—there were none on whom the catastrophe,
which closed the drama of his life, fell with so overwhelming a power as on those artists of Florence who had
adopted the principles of his reform. Many paid for their
devotion to his cause with their life. "Others," says
Marchese, "when the terrible tragedy was ended, abandoned the cultivation of those arts which had formed
their delight during the lifetime of Fra Girolamo."
Among these was Baccio della Porta, who during the
attack on S. Mark's had made a vow that should God
spare his life, he would take the habit of S. Dominic, and
end his days in the cloister. He kept his word, and
when the dreadful scene of the 23rd of May was over,
and Florence (so true in her likeness to Athens) had
scattered the ashes of her greatest citizen on the waters
of the Arno, he surrendered all his patrimony to his
brother, and, renouncing the world, and as he thought,
the arts also, for ever, he took the religious vows in the
convent of Prato. But the genius of Baccio della Porta
was to revive in a more splendid form in Fra Bartolomeo,
a name destined in the chronicles of Dominican art to be
second only in celebrity to that of the great Angelico.
At first, indeed, the bitterness of his grief rendered the
very thought of resuming his pencil odious to him. But
on his return to Florence he was thrown in company
with Sanctes Pagninus, then a member of the community

of S. Mark's, and himself a disciple and admirer of
Savonarola. This celebrated man, of whose extraordinary
learning we shall have occasion to speak in another place,
being elected prior of the convent, was the means of
inducing Fra Bartolomeo to resume the study of his art,
and eventually Pagninus became to Porta what S.
Antoninus had been to Angelico. He soon attained a
reputation which justifies Rosini in calling him " the star
of the Florentine school." And when, in 1506, the
young Rafaele d'Urbino arrived at Florence to study the
works of Michael Angelo and Leonardo da Vinci, he
placed himself under the tuition of the Dominican painter,
as the nearest to them in his knowledge of colouring,
while Fra Bartolomeo at the same time learnt from his
illustrious pupil a more perfect theory of perspective. The
friendship between these two great masters forms one of
the most refreshing incidents in the history of art ; it was
free from the least shadow of a professional jealousy,
and more than one picture exists on which their pencils
have worked together, and in which Rafaele, even when at
the summit of his glory, did not disdain to finish subjects
commenced by Della Porta.

His after career found him competing for renown by
the side of Buonarotti, whom perhaps he most resembled in the grand and majestic character of his
designs ; and living as he did, at the period when art
had reached its highest glory, and the rival schools of
Venice, Florence, and Rome, were producing the greatest
artists the world has ever known, his name ranks among
the most illustrious of them all. Nevertheless, we should
err did we seek to convey the idea that he revived the
supernatural school of painting which had found its
matchless representative in Angelico. He never, indeed,
departed from those principles which he had learned
from his first master Savonarola, and art was never
debased or degraded in his hands ; but we miss the
mystic spirituality of his predecessor, although there is
ample evidence that Bartolomeo ever placed before his
eyes the life of the saintly artist as his guide and model.
He was himself a true and excellent religious. Vasari

tells us that "he arrived at length at the wished-for
power of accompanying the labour of his hands with the
uninterrupted contemplation of death." He was also,
like so many other of the pupils of Savonarola, a poet
and a musician, and some of his pious verses have
been found traced on the back of his pictures in his
own hand. He died when only forty-eight, having in the
brief period of seventeen years produced a marvellous
number of works, the list of which is given by Marchese.
The close friendship existing between him and Rafaele
may possibly have had some share in bringing about,
what Marchese calls "the most splendid religious re-
habilitation of Savonarola—the most luminous proof of
his innocence, and the most convincing proof of the
perfidy of his persecutors." We allude to the introduction of the great reformer in the grandest work of
Rafaele's genius—the "Disputation on the B. Sacrament," where he is painted among the doctors of the
Church, the face being, as it is thought, an exact copy
of the likeness of Fra Girolamo, painted by Della Porta
many years before. This magnificent work was executed
only ten years after the death of the friar ; it was undertaken by the command of Julius II., and adorned the
very halls of the Pontifical palace, and may be considered
as offering almost as complete a vindication of his name
from the aspersions of his enemies as that given by Paul
III., who hesitated not to declare "that he should regard
that man as heretical who dared to accuse Savonarola
of heresy."

But we have already gone far beyond our limits in
treating of the connection of the order with religious
art, and must hasten to bring this chapter to a close.
There is a crowd of illustrious names which might be
given in illustration of the fact that the Dominican order
has never relinquished its principle of cultivating and
sanctifying the imaginative arts, as means of influencing
the popular heart, and guiding men's minds to God by
possessing itself of every avenue by which to reach them.
Some of these were simple lay-brothers ; others, like
Ignatius Dante (of the family of the poet) attained the

highest ecclesiastical dignities. And let it be remembered, that the art encouraged by the Dominican painters and sculptors has always been essentially *Christian*; and that Savonarola's denunciations against the corruptions of heathenism in art and literature have been faithfully re-echoed by other champions of Christian purity. In the succeeding age the classic imitators had it their own way; the world, as we know, was flooded with pagan literature, and the beautiful monuments of the ages of faith were, in too many cases, swept away to make room for clumsy imitations of heathenism. Popes and cardinals vied with one another in their enthusiastic patronage of brick and mortar, and in the bad taste with which they used them; but even at the court of Pius IV., a Dominican was found to lift his voice against the prevailing corruptions. The Pontiff was himself a great encourager of the classical *renaissance* then in fashion. He was a great builder, and a patron of architects and men of taste. In the summer of 1561, however, he was entertaining one who seemed insensible to all which he beheld; it could not be stupidity, for Bartholomew of the Martyrs, the primate of Portugal, was not a stupid man; nevertheless, when the new buildings at the Belvidere were submitted to his view, he only shrugged his shoulders. "What do you think of the Belvidere, my lord of Braga?" inquired the Pope. " It is for me to admire and not to judge," was the reply. " Your excellency, however, intends adding to the episcopal palace of Braga; I am told it is in the old style, quite unsuitable to our modern taste." " Your holiness is probably aware that I have no money for building." " Come, I am determined to know your opinion of my architect; I will know what you think of the Belvidere and its statues: they at least are full of merit." " Since your Holiness commands me to say *what I think*," at length replied the imperturbable archbishop. " *I think* the Son of God will one day come to burn up palaces such as these: *I think* they are quite worthy of their architect, but not of your holiness, whom God has placed in the Church to rear up lively temples for

Himself. As to the paintings, I care for those only which trace the image of God on the souls of the faithful: this, Holy Father, is what I think." It was certainly a fair specimen of Dominican freedom of speech, but the words of Bartholomew are every way remarkable. So too was the Pope's reply. " I see how it is,—you and Charles Borromeo have been together; you are just a pair; he cares no more for my statues than you do, and I will answer for it when he gets to Milan, his palace will be the counterpart of yours."

The strictures of two such men as Bartholomew and S. Charles were doubtless levelled, not merely at the expense but also at the character of these decorations. Bartholomew could scarcely have been insensible to the claims of that religious art, the appreciation of which was hereditary in his order; his censures were not directed against the frescoes of Angelico, at that moment rotting on the walls of their neglected chapel, but rather against that school of restored paganism which has not hesitated to place in the basilica of S. Peter's, and on the very tombs of the Pontiffs, statues which modern refinement has been compelled to veil. Nevertheless, the spirit of the age was then too strong to be resisted. For three centuries art was well-nigh lost to the cause of religion, and, like all creatures of his imagination when emancipated from the control of the faith, it became only the minister of sensuality. Yet there are indications that even during this period, the tie between the Dominican order and the Christian use of art was never wholly severed. Besides those architects and sculptors of the seventeenth and eighteenth centuries, an account of whom will be found in the work of Padre Marchese, we find incidental mention of the cultivation of painting among some of the South American missionaries, and that for a purpose purely religious. Gonzalo Lucero, provincial of Mexico in 1550, a man possessed of much of the peculiar genius of his order, is spoken of as painting a series of all the chief mysteries of the faith, and preaching from them to the people, thus carrying out the old principle of Passavanti, that " pictures were the books of the unlettered." And the same is told us of other and later missionaries in the same field.

It cannot, indeed, be pretended that all the Dominican artists followed in the steps of Angelico, or that the genius of such men as Marcillat could be claimed as doing much credit to their order. But these were exceptions : in general the character of the painters, equally with that of their paintings, was devout and spiritual. Out of many names we may select that of Fra Paolino Signoraccio, who, when a young novice in the convent of Prato, evinced so much artistic talent as to induce his superiors to place him as a pupil under Fra Bartolomeo. Almost his first essay in modelling was made on the clay figures for the Christmas crib of S. Magdalene's hospital, in whose books there occurs an entry of the said figures "made by little Paul of Pistoja," with the memorandum that they are already hard, "for he made three years before and painted them, to the honour of God, S. Dominic, and S. Magdalen." Little Paul, as he is here called, was but thirteen when he commenced his career as an artist. He followed the style of his master, Fra Bartolomeo, and if he was inferior to him in boldness and originality of design, he is acknowleged to have excelled him in the devotion and "celestial beauty" of his representations of the Madonna. In fact, Paolino was an excellent and worthy religious, "simple, upright, devout, modest, and obedient."* He was the friend of S. Catherine de Ricci, and of Plautilla Nelli, and he ever aimed at rendering his talents subservient to the cause of religion.

Yet more celebrated in his own peculiar art was Damian of Bergamo, the renowned worker in wood mosaic, or, as it is technically called, *tarsia*. His extraordinary works far surpassed anything of the kind which had been hitherto seen, and are still the wonder of all who beheld them. They excited the incredulous admiration of Charles V., who, on his visit to the friars' church at Bologna, could not be led to believe that what he saw was really worked in wood, till he had convinced himself by unsheathing his dagger and chipping off a

* Razzi.

portion of the work. He gave his imperial testimony to the singular merits of the artist, by visiting him in his humble cell. It was on that occasion that Damian gave the greatest monarch in Christendom a memorable lesson of independence. The emperor was followed by Alfonso of Este, the Duke of Ferrara, but Damian refused him entrance: the duke's officers had been guilty of some unjust and tyrannical impositions, and the sturdy lay brother had determined he should never see his works till he had done him justice. His independence of character, however, had nothing in it that was morose; he was the favourite of his convent, and not only a man of genius, but a holy and excellent religious.

We have mentioned the name of Ignatius Dante, whose celebrity was perhaps rather as a mathematician and an engineer, than as an artist. The singular and beautiful maps still to be seen in the galleries of the Vatican, however, evince no inconsiderable degree of taste, as well as of science. He was appointed to superintend the works at the Vatican under the pontificate of Gregory XIII., and his influence was of the happiest kind, "for to his knowledge of art," we are told, "he added the most unblemished morality." The same may be said of Fra Portigiani, the architect, and the celebrated worker in bronze, whose piety and devotion have found honorable records in the annals of his convent of S. Mark.

Paganelli, another engineering genius of the order, and architect to Paul V., was held in equally great repute for his skill in the sacred sciences; and, as became a member of the order, ever zealous for the purity of ecclesiastical discipline, was one of the congregation appointed by the authority of the council of Trent, for the reformation of the clergy.

The art of military defence perhaps scarcely merits to be included in our present subject; and that it should have found any to cultivate it among the ranks of the Dominicans may possibly excite our reader's surprise. But the friars were the men of their age: they were ever ready to turn their talent in whatever direction it was needed; and so, when the republic of Genoa was straining every nerve to defend its liberties against the tyranny of Charles Emmanuel of Savoy, the enthusiastic citizens, who toiled day and night at the walls, did not appeal in vain to the patriotism of Fra Vincenzo Maculano, the most experienced engineer of the day, who filled the office of Inquisitor in the Genoese capital. After exhausting every resource of his genius on the military defence of Genoa, Maculano was called to Rome, where he rose to high repute as a theologian, and became master of the Sacred Palace. His skill as a military engineer, however, was destined to be once more exerted, and in a cause that was not unworthy his sacred profession. He presided over the works raised at Malta in 1640, when the island was threatened by the Turks, and on his return to Rome was created cardinal and archbishop of Benevento by Urban VIII. Marchese assures us that on two occasions he was within a single vote of being raised to the pontificate, of which dignity his virtues and talents rendered him not unworthy.

We may add, that even in our own day the arts still find those who cherish them in a truly Christian spirit, in the ranks of the Friars Preachers. The great church of Bologna, which contains the shrine of the holy founder of the order, has not long since been restored in excellent taste under the direction of one of the lay brothers, Fra Girolamo Bianchedi of Faenza, who also presided over the restoration of the Minerva in Rome. This church, the head-quarters of the order, originally raised by two Florentine Dominicans, presents one of the very few remains of the earlier ecclesiastical style still existing in that city. Its restoration is but partial; and Girolamo died a victim, it is said, to the terrors of the late revolution, before seeing the completion of his design. He did not live to witness what was a proud day for his order; when, on the feast of S. Dominic 1855, the church was reopened by the pope in person, and the relics of S. Catherine, which had lain since her death in the Rosary chapel, were solemnly removed to the high altar, under which they now repose. A proud day, we have

said, for the order; for on the evening of that day those
streets, which four centuries since had been trodden by
the feet of the seraphic saint of Siena, were filled with
the lines of an immense and splendid procession, in the
midst of which her relics, borne in a silver urn and
canopied with flowers, were shown for the veneration of
the enthusiastic multitudes.   The skill of Fra Girolamo,
who has thus enjoyed the happiness of restoring the two
churches of his order which contain the shrines of its
two greatest saints, and the principles on which he
conducted **his** restoration, which are essentially based on
the rules of Christian art, have received the sanction of
his present Holiness, who, when bishop of Imola, employed
the Dominican artist in the restoration of his own cathedral in that city.   We might mention other indications
that the artistic spirit of the order still survives among us,
but we have already exceeded our limits.   Yet we cannot
resist concluding this chapter in the words of the writer
so often quoted:—" The mission of our order," says Marchese, " is to infuse new life into hearts that have been
weakened by the corrupt influences of the times; to
consecrate our energies to the amelioration of the people ;
and to prove that religion, however inflexibly opposed to
a false and spurious progress, is, nevertheless, the truest
protectress of sound knowledge, and the most zealous
patroness of national prosperity.   Nor should we forget
the arts, for it lies on us to inspire them with noble and
sublime sentiments, and associate them with all that
is sanctified by religion.   Let him, therefore, who cannot
speak from the pulpit, or the professor's chair, speak
with the chisel, or the pencil, but let us all speak a
noble and a holy language.   Never let us forget that we
saved the arts in the days of barbaric devastation: and
that we sheltered and cherished them in the times of the
renaissance.   Never let us forget that we warmed them
with the breath of our hearts, and that we educated them
for the honour and glory of Christianity.   Thus shall we
convince men that we comprehend the full sublimity of
our vocation ; and for every benefit we bestow on the people, we shall receive the benedictions of grateful hearts."

CHAPTER IV.

Close of the 15th century. Discovery of America. First Dominican missions in the New World. Bartholomew de Las Casas. Jerome Loaysa. S. Louis Bertrand. The Philippine Islands.

As we draw on to the close of the fifteenth and the opening of the sixteenth century we are conscious of the approach of a great change; the infancy of the world is over, and its education complete; will, understanding, and imagination, have all come to maturity; the child has become a man, and is about to assert its independence, and to enter on a career which may display its energies to the full. Two great discoveries mark the commencement of this singular era, and in no small degree help on the designs of Providence: Columbus gives a new world to European enterprise by the discovery of America, and the invention of printing accomplishes the greatest social revolution the world has ever known; henceforth two thirds of mankind will be governed by the press. The Dominicans had hitherto claimed their share in each new influence to which the world had been subjected since the foundation of their order, and it was not to be supposed that they could remain insensible to the new field thrown open to their apostolic labours by the discovery of America, or to the demand made on them in their character of a teaching order by the revival of literature. The little flotilla which sailed from Europe on the 3rd of August, 1492, and was destined to gain a new world to Christendom, bore on the decks of its admiral's vessel three friars, the representatives of their respective orders—a Franciscan, a Dominican, and F. Solorzano of the order of Mercy, who acted as confessor to Columbus, and almoner to his fleet. The lands which the Genoese adventurer added to the empire of Spain, these three mendicant friars may be said to have

318   THE DOMINICAN ORDER.

taken possession of in the name of Christ; and the part
which succeeding brethren of those three orders were to
play on the soil of the newly discovered continent, made
the circumstance of their presence at that first landing a
peculiarly appropriate accident. In fact, Columbus owed
not a little of his success in gaining the consent and
protection of Ferdinand, to the orders of S. Francis and
S. Dominic. His two great advocates at the court of
Spain were the Franciscan, John Perez de Marchena,
and Diego Deza, Dominican professor of theology at the
university of Salamanca; and Remesal does not hesitate
to say, that Spain in a great measure owed the discovery
of her new empire to F. Diego. Marchena led a company of missionaries of his order to Haiti in the
following year, and the little hut which he erected at
Isabella, and where he celebrated Mass directly on his
landing, was the first Christian church erected by the
Spaniards in America. Diego did not himself enter on
the apostolate of the new world, but his nephew, Peter
Deza, was the first archbishop of Xaragua, and primate
of the American churches.

It is melancholy to read the solemn terms in which
that Alexandrian bull is couched which delivers the provinces of the new world to the keeping of the kings of
Spain, and charges them with the care of the souls of
their inhabitants, and their instruction in the Christian
faith "by the memory of their baptism, and by the bowels
of mercy of our Lord Jesus Christ," and then to remember that only ten years after the publication of that bull
the atrocities committed by the Spanish conquerors had
attained their height, and cruelty had already been formed
into a system which the indignant and courageous remonstrances of the Christian missionaries were unable to
suppress. Queen Isabella died in 1504; her death was,
in the words of Las Casas, the signal for the destruction
of the aborigines, and her last testament which gives such
evidence of the deep impression made on her soul by the
Papal charge of Alexander VI. was scarcely written ere
it was violated. Six years afterwards we find the first
regular mission opened in America by the Friars

Preachers, and in the same year Bartholomew de Las
Casas sang at Vega the first high mass which had been
heard in the new world. It was also his own first mass,
and he was then a simple secular priest; already full of
enthusiastic kindness for the natives, whose language he
had learnt with a view of devoting his life to their service and conversion. The celebration of that high mass
of Bartholomew would form no bad subject as an historic
picture. By command of Diego Columbus it was accompanied with the greatest pomp. "Every one then at La
Vega," says Herrera, "assisted at it, and a vast number
of the inhabitants from other parts of the island were also
present, it being then the season of gold-finding. They
came from all quarters with quantities of the precious
metal as offerings to the new celebrant, who gave them
all to his godfather in the sacred ceremony, keeping only
a few pieces better cast than others." Well, indeed,
might the simple and trustful people of America crowd
instinctively around their future protector and offer him
their gratuitous homage. It was not long before Bartholomew, already disposed to compassionate the sufferings of the Indians, was induced, on a closer knowledge
of the cruelties practised on them, to embrace their cause
as his own; and, giving up the employments he had at
first accepted under the viceroy of Hispaniola, he resolved
to do and suffer anything in order to deliver the victims
of his countrymen's cruelty from the tyranny under which
they languished.

In this general resolve he was warmly encouraged by
the Dominican missionaries, under Peter of Cordova, who
had scarcely arrived at Haiti before they began their
bold and uncompromising protests against the injustice
and rapacity of the Spaniards. Their determined and
dogged assertion of evangelic truth soon raised a storm;
before many months Antonio de Montesino, the chief
orator in the defence of the Indians, was sent back to
Spain to plead their cause before King Ferdinand; and
though little real fruit came of the affair, the successful
advocacy of the natives before the Court at Burgos, was
a triumph of which their generous protectors might well

be proud. It was soon evident that if the missionaries would have free room for their labours, they must act independently of the Spanish authorities, and preach the cross in provinces where the Spaniards had as yet made no settlements, and created no prejudice against the name of Christian; and accordingly, in the year 1512, those missions were commenced on the continent of America, which gained so many a martyr to the order of Preachers, and so many a soul to the faith of Christ. And here again we have occasion to admire the admirable spirit of unity which marked the missionary labours of the orders of S. Francis and S. Dominic. When in 1516 Las Casas had so far interested the Spanish regency in the cause to which he had devoted himself, that they had nominated him Protector General of the Indians, and had induced Ximenes, then at the head of affairs, to enter warmly into his views, a great impulse was given to the zeal of the various religious orders; and F. Remi, a Franciscan of great interprise and courage, who had lately returned to Europe after many years spent among the infidels, set himself to organize a fresh body of labourers whom he collected from all countries, and with them prepared to set out a second time for the scene of his former missions. They were fourteen in all: among them it is interesting to read the name of F. Remigius Stuart, a member of our own royal and unfortunate house. He was the brother of King James IV. of Scotland, and not less distinguished for his religious zeal than for his illustrious birth. When the little company of Franciscans were ready to sail, Ximenes added several Dominicans, who joined the body, and acknowledged Remi as their leader and superior.

In 1518, the conquest of Mexico was undertaken by Fernando Cortez, and the first missionaries who entered on this new field were of the order of mercy. They were, soon followed by the Franciscans, under the celebrated Martin de Valencia, the blessed Martin, as he is deservedly called, who, as Wadding tells us, began to preach the same year that Luther commenced spreading his doctrines in Germany; "so that it would seem as if

the providence of God had disposed that one Martin
should repair, by the conversion of new kingdoms, the
loss caused to the Church by the corruptions of another
Martin." But very soon after the country had fallen
under the Spanish dominion the Dominicans were sent
thither by the command of Charles V., and we again read
that " they were received by the Franciscans with no less
charity than joy, and abode with them for the space of
three months, until their own habitations had been prepared."* They were twelve in number, and were destined
eventually to become the founders of those provinces of
Oaxaca and Guatemala, whose chronicles rival in romantic and pathetic interest anything which one can find in
the fabulous pages of Cretta.

The names of Dominic de Betanços, the founder of
more than a hundred convents, and of his deacon and
disciple, Gonsalvo Lucero, suggest tales of such surpassing beauty that, did we once enter on their narration we
should be beguiled into a prolixity which our limits
forbid. It was a hard struggle at first: at one time
Dominic was left the only priest of his order in Mexico,
the others had died, or been forced to return to Spain;
and one of the charming tales which occur in the life of
Lucero shows him to us the only inhabitant of his convent, having on his shoulders the apostolic care of a vast
district, and the maintenance of religious rule and discipline, which spite of every difficulty he never abandoned.
But this did not last long: other missionaries soon
poured into America in great numbers, owing to the
edict of the emperor that no vessel was to leave Spain
without carrying a certain number of religious on board,
and such was the zeal and sanctity of Betanços, that
crowds of young Castilians who had left their native land
in search of riches or adventures, laid aside their dreams
of worldly advancement, and received the habit of religion
at his hands. Meanwhile Las Casas was toiling at a
fruitless cost. Again and again did he return to Europe
to plead his cause, and to lay new schemes for the protection of the natives before the royal council. His first

* Fontana, Monumenta Domenicana.

Y

plan, whose consequences, little forseen by its author, have brought great and undeserved obloquy on his name, was to increase the importation of the African negroes to supply the place of the native Americans, whose delicate an l feeble constitution unfitted them for severe lab our. This plan did not originate with Las Casas; it had been adopted from the commencement of the century. To use the words of a well-known Protestant historian,* " It was a suggestion of humanity, however mistaken; and considering the circumstances under which it occurred, and the age, it may well be forgiven in Las Casas, especially, inasmuch as, when more enlightened, he, with deep humiliation, confesses his regret at having countenanced the measure, since, to use his own words, ' the same law applies equally to the negro as to the Indian.' "

The next scheme was bolder, and most characteristic of Bartholomew's ardent and imaginative mind. It was to obtain the grant of a vast district and commence a Christian colony, independent of the military authorities, whose atrocities had made the very name of European hateful to the natives. He had the idea that by adopting a different dress, which was to be white with the cross of Calatrava, he might persuade the Indians to believe that the new colonists were of a different nation from their persecutors. Fifty Dominicans were to accompany the colony, and a military order was to be established for its defence. His eloquence, as he advocated his plan in the presence of the emperor, prevailed, and he was suffered to make the attempt. It failed, through the malconduct of the Spaniards of a neighbouring settlement; and, compelled to abandon his project, he retired to the Dominican convent of Hispaniola, to hide his chagrin and his disgrace. " It is impossible," says Prescott, " not to recognize in the whole scheme the hand of one more familiar with books than with men, who meditated his benevolent plans without estimating the obstacles in their way, and counted too confidently on meeting the same generous enthusiasm which glowed in his own bosom." He found his consolation, however,

* Prescott.

for in that period of disgrace and disappointment, when the sympathy of the friars formed his only resource, he received the call to religion; and, becoming a member of the order he had ever so dearly loved, he passed some years in retirement, and in the discharge of the duties befitting his new character; at which time it was that his great work on " The History of the Indies," was commenced, though it was finished only a few years before his death.

When we next find him at the Spanish Court, many years had passed over his head, but they had not changed his purpose or his constancy. A great change had, however, come over the royal councils. The presidency of the Indian Council was filled by no less a man than Garcias de Loaysa, the confessor to the emperor, and General of the Order of Preachers. The renewed appeal of Las Casas produced most important regulations on behalf of the American subjects of the Spanish Crown, and a code of laws was passed, "having for its express object the enfranchisement of the oppressed race; and in the wisdom and humanity of its provisions it is easy to recognize the hand of the Protector of the Indians."* In fact we are bound to admit that little or no blame attaches to the Spanish government in their dealings with their colonies: to use the words of the writer just quoted, " the history of Spanish colonial legislation is the history of the impotent struggles of the government against the avarice and cruelty of its subjects;" and certainly neither Ferdinand nor Charles ever showed themselves insensible to the charge laid on them by the sovereign Pontiff to regard the dominions given them by Providence as a cure of souls. In 1544, Bartholomew de Las Casas, then seventy years of age, was consecrated Bishop of Chiapa. He was well-nigh worn out with toil and disappointment; he had already crossed the Atlantic on four several missions to the court of Castile, and now he did not shrink from returning to his adopted country with the fresh burden of the episcopate on his venerable shoulders. He had need of all his heroic courage to face the storm that

* Prescott.
Y 2

greeted him on his landing. The colonists saw in him the
author of the new code which laid so powerful a restraint
upon their cruelty and rapacity. He was everywhere
received with an outcry of hatred and contempt, "which,"
says Touron, "he accepted as the appanage of the apostolate." Violence was even offered to his person; yet
never did the tide of opposition prevail with him so far as
to induce him to yield one point of what he deemed the
cause of God. Up to the last he refused to admit to
the sacraments any who still held an Indian in bondage
contrary to the regulations of the new code.

But he was powerless to check the flood of iniquity
which desolated the unhappy country: his own eyes were
witnesses of those enormities which his pen has so vividly
portrayed;—he saw infants torn from their mothers'
breasts, and dashed against the wall, or thrown into the
river. He beheld the unhappy natives, with noses and
limbs cut off, thrown, in the sport of cruelty, to be
devoured by dogs. He witnessed the brutal wagers of
the Spanish conquerors, where a trifling bauble was the
prize of his dexterity who should strike off an Indian's
head at a single sabre-stroke. He tells us of massacres in
which 500 of the chief caciques were slaughtered in a
day; and of one occasion when 4,000 Indians were slain,
700 of whom were thrown alive from the summit of a
precipice, so that you might have seen the air darkened
by the cloud of their bodies as they fell, and were dashed
to pieces on the rocks. Eighteen millions of Indians are
reckoned to have perished in these wholesale slaughters;
and the number every day delivered to the flames or the
wild beasts was so great, that, he assures us, a certain
vessel made the voyage to S. Domingo from some distant
island without the aid of a compass, being guided thither
only by the dead bodies which floated over the water by
thousands.[*]

At length even the hope and courage of Las Casas was
unequal to continue the struggle, and he determined to
withdraw from the scene of abominations which he had no

[*] Touron, quoted from the "Relation of the extinction of the
Indians."

longer any power to restrain. He resigned his bishopric,
and again returned to Europe, to die among his brethren;
he appeared once more as the champion of the Indians in
the famous dispute with Sepulveda, who had undertaken to
justify the proceedings of the Spanish conquerors in a
work entitled, "The Justice of the War of the King of
Spain against the Indians." In this book the learned
author endeavoured to make the most of the dominion
over the new world granted to Spain by the Alexandrine
bull, and to deduce as a consequence that the Spaniards
might do what they liked with their own. The book
was suppressed owing to the instances of Las Casas, but
Sepulveda at length obtained permission for a solemn
disputation on the question to be held between him and
his opponent before the royal council. Dominic Soto
was appointed arbiter, and the aged champion of justice
to the Indians had thus an opportunity of striking a
last blow in the cause he had so faithfully and devotedly
served. His triumph was undisputed, especially in the
propositions, wherein he clearly demonstrates that the
grant made by the Holy See rested on the condition
of the conversion of the natives to Christianity; and
though this argument seemed to attack the very integrity
of the Spanish colonial empire, Las Casas was regarded
with too much respect for the court to take offence.
He died at length in his 92nd year at the convent
of Atocha, near Madrid. His character is one concerning which the judgments of men have never differed:
Protestants and Catholics have rivalled one another in
doing justice to his heroic memory. "He was one
of those," says Prescott, "to whose gifted minds are
revealed those glorious moral truths which, like the
lights of heaven, are fixed and the same for ever; but
which, though now familiar, were hidden from all but
a few penetrating intellects by the general darkness of
the times in which they lived. He was inspired by
one great and glorious idea. This was the key to all
his thoughts, and to every act of his long life. It
was this which urged him to lift the voice of rebuke
in the presence of princes, to brave the menaces of an

infuriated populace, to cross seas, to traverse mountains and deserts, to incur the alienation of friends, the hostility of enemies, and to endure obloquy, insult, and persecution." " His only fault," says the Père Charlevoix, the Jesuit historian of S. Domingo, " was an over-ardent imagination, by which he at times allowed himself to be too much governed." In short, his faults were those of a generous enthusiasm, his virtues those of the purest Christian heroism.

We have devoted so large a space in speaking of this most illustrious of all the early Dominican missionaries of America, that we must necessarily pass very briefly over the names of others who claim our notice. The greater proportion of the first American bishops were chosen from the order of Preachers :* among them Jerome de Loaysa, first bishop of Carthagena, and afterwards first archbishop of Lima, presents us with the perfect model of an apostle. He may be said to have been the founder of all the future glory of the Peruvian Church ; and Lima, so rich in saints and saintly men, owes a debt of gratitude to her first primate, the extent of which can never be rightly measured. He laboured equally at the conversion of the Indians, and at the far harder task of Christianizing the Spanish colonists ; and such was his success, that he is reckoned, in all the soberness of historic truth, as having made up by the souls he gained to Christ in the new world, for the losses the Church was then suffering in Europe at the hands of the Lutheran heretics. We have said that Lima is indebted for no small part of her religious glory to the labours of Loaysa. Her university owes its foundation to him, as well as that celebrated convent of the Rosary, whence the university drew its chief professors. We will not attempt the task of reckoning all the congregations and orders, the religious and charitable foundations, he introduced into the city ; we will content ourselves with remarking that the establishment of the Tertiaries of S. Dominic at Lima was

* See the list of the bishops who sat in the two first provincial councils of Lima, given in Touran's " History of America.'

his work, and from that stem blossomed the first and
sweetest saint of the new world, S. Rose of Lima, whose
sanctity would be glory enough to the country which gave
her birth, even if it did not claim the right of reckoning
her as only the first of a long calendar of saints.* Val-
verde, the first bishop of Casco, died a martyr's death,
being seized by the cannibals of La Puna, and torn
to pieces, whilst in the act of celebrating the sacred
mysteries. Bernard Albuquerque, bishop of Guaxaca, is
another whose life has the charm of a romance, and whose
character is essentially of the heroic stamp; and one
scarce knows which most to admire, his untiring and
prodigious labours, his life of secret prayer, or that sweet
and strange humility, which made his more worldly colleagues affirm that " he knew better how to be a saint than
how to be a bishop."

We must hasten, however, to bring this subject to
a close, and conclude our scanty sketch of the South
American missions with the notice of one name greater
than any yet mentioned, S. Louis Bertrand, the Xavier
of the Western world. In doing so we must necessarily
pass on to a later period; and before entering on the
labours of this, the most illustrious apostle whom the
Dominican order had produced since the days of S.
Hyacinth, we must beg our readers to understand, that,
in speaking of the services rendered to the faith in
America by that order, nothing is further from our
intention than to claim for them the exclusive honours
of the American apostolate. The Franciscans in a par-

* Among the saints of the Liman Church we may specially notice
the Indian half-caste, Martin Porres, a lay brother in the Dominican convent of the Rosary. The beatification of this holy man
seems the crowning example of that spirit which has been the
special glory of the Dominicans of America; who, in the elevation
to their altar of an Indian slave, have in the noblest manner pronounced their condemnation of those prejudices which have disgraced the Christian world for three centuries. And whilst we see
the most Protestant of republics still vindicating the rights of
slavery and the wrongs of slaves, the veneration shown by the
Catholic Church to more than one saintly member of this despised
class, presents a contrast which we need not press upon the attention of our readers.

ticular manner divide the glory of that work, and we
might say that there is scarcely a religious order which
was not represented in the early South American missions,
and which did not distinguish itself by a noble advocacy
of the rights of humanity and justice.   But in our
narrow limits we are obliged to confine ourselves to one
branch of the subject, and certainly the consent of all
writers, even those who are alien from the faith, justifies us
in giving the Dominicans something of pre-eminence,
when speaking of the defence of the suffering Indians.
Their zeal was of so peculiar a kind as to have extracted
a tribute of admiration even from such a writer as
Robertson ; and the American author whom we have
already so often quoted, gives his testimony in their favour
in terms which evince how little he is inclined to speak
favourably of the Order of Preachers.   " The brethren
of S. Dominic," he says, " stood forth as the avowed
champions of the Indians on all occasions, and showed
themselves as devoted to the cause of freedom in the
new world, as they had been hostile to it in the
old ;"* an assertion of inconsistency in the conduct of the
friars which he has not thought it necessary to justify
or explain

It was in the year 1562 that S. Louis Bertrand,
whose fame for sanctity had already been established in
his own country, arrived at Carthagena, and found the
Christian faith rapidly spreading under the united efforts
of the Franciscans, the Dominicans, and the Order of
Mercy.   The admirable harmony with which these three
orders worked together deserves a tribute of respect at
the hands of the historian, and amid the many jealousies
and rivalries that force themselves on our notice when
we enter on the literary or political history of any
body of men, the evangelical love which was retained
unbroken between the missionaries of these different
societies is a subject of perpetually recurring consolation.   At the period of which we speak, we find John
de los Barrios, a religious of the Order of Mercy, bishop
of S. Martha, his first act being the establishment in

* Prescott.

his cathedral city of two communities, one of S. Francis, and another of S. Dominic. The Austin Friars were likewise there, and religious women of each order scattered over the diocese. The charge of education was given over to the Dominicans, who were laying the foundation of a future university at Lima. As to the work of preaching, it was common to all. The neighbouring diocese of Carthagena was governed by a Dominican, Gregory de Beteta; and by both these holy prelates the arrival of S. Louis was hailed with extraordinary joy. He almost at once entered on his apostolic labours in all the northern provinces of the Continent, and with such success that we are assured no less than 10,000 souls were gained by him to Christ in the short space of three years. The signs and graces promised to the apostles did not fail to follow on the preaching of this extraordinary man. His first prayer had been, to be understood by the people whom he should address; and the miraculous gift of tongues, which we know was so frequently granted to S. Francis Xavier, was granted to him also. Whilst he spoke no language but Castilian, he was understood by all the various tribes and nations among whom he preached.

But miracles are after all the least marvellous and least admirable part of the story of a saint; and when we read of the sick cured by the touch or prayer of the servant of God; of storms quelled, and ferocious animals tamed and domesticated by the sign of the Cross, these things seem little by the side of the constancy and sweetness and devotedness which gave a greater power to the preaching of S. Louis than all the marvels that he worked. The savage people crowded about him in wonder; their hearts opened to him as, drawn by an irresistible charm, they came and dashed their idols to pieces before his eyes, and with their own hands raised altars to the true God, and vowed to receive the doctrine of purity and of the Cross. So he passed from Carthagena to Tabara, and thence, when there were no more infidels to convert, to the territories of Cipacoa and Paluato. His fame went before him; the Indians knew him but by

one title, " the religious of God," and came down from
their mountains, and from the recesses of their forests,
to meet him on his way. Sometimes, indeed, he was
not so well received. We read of one tribe of Paluto
of whom two only were converted at the time ; but the
harvest of souls in this case was only delayed, and at
a later period the whole people embraced the faith.
Once, as he preached under a tree to a vast multitude,
a band of savages were seen approaching armed with bows
and lances, and with the avowed purpose of putting the
despiser of their idols to a bloody death. Louis was
warned to fly. " Fear nothing," he replied : " they will
not be able to do what they propose." The savages,
indeed, reached his presence, but instead of offering him
violence, they stood as though overpowered by a new and
strange sentiment of admiration. He continued to
speak, and when his discourse was ended, 200 of his
intended murderers cast themselves at his feet and
demanded baptism. He even penetrated alone among
the Carribees, where, after escaping innumerable attempts
against his life, he made many converts, and is said to
have sometimes won these fierce and savage people by
the charm of his music. At length, after eight years of
these labours, he returned to Spain, wearied out by the
hardness of heart, not of the heathens, but of the Spanish
Christians. On his death, he was fitly claimed by the
people of New Grenada as their patron saint, and was
solemnly declared protector of that country by Alexander VIII.

Of the long line of prelates which the order gave
to the South American provinces, our space will not
allow us to speak, though the name of Bartholomew
Ledesma, John Ramirez, Peter de Feria, and many others,
might fitly find a place among those which have most
worthily graced the episcopate. Let it be remembered that
those apostolic men, who evangelized the vast territories
of the American continent, were not content with simply
preaching and converting souls ; but they planted the
Church on solid and lasting foundations ; and wherever the
Dominican missions appeared, there sooner or later were

established hospitals, religious houses, and colleges for education of all kinds. At Lima they founded the great university, which was entirely conducted and taught by their professors. At Puebla, in Mexico, and in many other cities, as afterwards at Manilla, in the Philippines, their colleges received the university privileges. The hospital of S. Alexis, at Guatemala, where the sick natives were served and nursed by the hands of the religious, owed its erection to the devoted and heroic zeal of F. Matthew of Peace; and scarce a town of Peru and Mexico but bears even to this day marks of the pious labours of these admirable men, whose names are unknown and forgotten save in the chronicles of their order, and in the book of life

Whilst these things were going on in the Western world, the discoveries of Magellan in the Eastern Archipelago were hardly less important in their results. It was in the year 1521 that the Portuguese navigator discovered that group of islands, which being afterwards in 1555 formally taken posession of by Philip II., received from him the name of the Philippine Islands. The Augustinian and Franciscan friars were the first to take advantage of the ground thus opened; but it was not long before F. John de Castro, one of the most illustrious of the Dominican missionaries of South America, was

---

The story of this foundation is a beautiful illustration of the character of these early missioners. Matthew, whilst still very young, entirely devoted himself to the service of the natives: he begged alms in the street for their necessaries, and shared all their hardships and sufferings. He had built a little sanctuary at Guatemala in honour of our Lady, where he collected his Indians every day, and prepared them for the sacraments. The sick he received in a little hut adjoining the chapel, which he had built with his own hands, of straw and the branches of trees. Here he nursed and tended them; and not a day passed but this humble servant of the despised Indian slaves might be seen seeking new objects of charity in the streets, and carrying them on his back to his little hospital. It was there he lived; and neither the infection of the place, nor the difficulties he encountered among the Indians themselves, ever wearied out his patience. This was the beginning of the hospital of S. Alexis, afterwards constructed on a larger scale, and served by the Dominicans of Guatemala.

appointed vicar-general of a new mission destined for the
East, and became the founder of the celebrated Philippine
province of the Holy Rosary. 1579, Dominic Salazar, a
Dominican by profession, had been appointed first bishop
of Manilla; and it was probably about five years after
his elevation that the new missionaries arrived in his
diocese. Among them we find the name of Michael
Benavides, who afterwards succeeded Salazar in the
government of Manilla, when the church was erected
in to an archbishopric. Previous to this elevation, he
devoted himself with enthusiasm to the scheme, always
so dear to Catholic missionaries, of penetrating into
China. The settlement of the Philippines offered singular
advantages for facilitating this enterprise; and, indeed,
the great value of these islands as a *religious* possession,
was their position half-way between the South American
provinces and China. Benavides succeeded in entering
the Celestial empire, but was obliged after a while to
return to Manilla without effecting any permanent
results. From this period the influence of the Dominicans became paramount in the Philippine Islands, and
has continued to be so even to our own day. A long
line of illustrious bishops of their order have governed
the Church of Manilla; and at a time when almost every
other religious house was suppressed by the revolutionized
government of Spain, it was found necessary to preserve
one convent of the Friars Preachers (that of Ocagna) for
the purpose of supplying the missions of the Philippine
province.

We have already exceeded our limits in speaking of
this subject; we can, therefore, only add that the apostles
of the Order of Preachers were to be found during this
and the succeeding century in almost every country of
the east. In Hindostan, they preceded the Jesuits; in
Ceylon, the Moluccas, Siam, Corea, and China, we might
reckon the names of their missionaries and martyrs by
hundreds. Nor were the old fields of Armenia and
Persia neglected for these newer regions of enterprise;
whilst from the island of Scio, a home and nursery of
the order, went forth a crowd of zealous missionaries to

all the coasts of the Archipelago and Levant. And we may again remark the solid character of the work undertaken by the order; it always had its eye on the firm establishment of the Church in the countries it evangelized, by means of educational institutions; and it is entirely in accordance with the spirit and example of his predecessors that we find Seraphino Siccus, the master-general of the order in 1622, establishing the college of Nakchivan in Armenia; whilst not content with this, the order founded within a few years another Armenian college at Rome, the rules of which were drawn up in the general chapter of 1644.

Indeed, we may safely affirm that the generals of the sixteenth and seventeenth centuries were men worthy of succeeding to the office which had been made so illustrious by the first masters of the order. Such men as Seraphino Siccus, Nicholas Rodolph, Thomas Tarcus, and their successors, present us with splendid examples of religious superiors; and the study of their biographies furnishes us with some idea of the vast spiritual dominion then included within the government of the Friars Preachers; reaching, as we might say, over the whole known world, and illustrated during those centuries with a continual succession of martyrs and apostolic men. And it will be seen that even at a period when the order had lost something of its influence in Europe, and was evincing symptoms of languor and decadence, it never lost anything of its fresh and primitive vigour in the fields of the apostolate. The first blessing has rested on that work, wherein the first fervour of its missionaries has never cooled; and the annals of China in the eighteenth and nineteenth centuries present us with the same pictures of constancy and devotion as we may find in the Tartar or American missionaries of earlier ages.

CHAPTER V.

The 16th century. Revival of biblical learning. Zenobius Accia-
joli. Giustiniani. Sanctes Pagninus. Sixtus of Siena. Cajetan.
Scenes of the Reformation. Persecutions in Ireland. Irish
Martyrs. Dominican popes. The Council of Trent.

WHILST the discoveries of navigators were daily
throwing open new fields to the labours of the Dominican
missionaries, the order was not idle at home. The sixteenth century is, indeed, an eventful one in history, and
the unhappy religious revolution which distinguished it
could scarcely fail to call forth all the energies and
talents of that institution which has deserved the title of
the "hammer of the heretics." But even without this
stimulus to activity it could not but be roused to extraordinary exertions in an age which was *par excellence* the age
of the restoration of letters, and we naturally look in its
ranks, at this period, for a more than ordinary display of
learning, and of literary greatness.

And here we may remark how much the influence of
Savonarola's teaching was felt in the generation which
succeeded him. All the men of eminence formed in his
school had received a particular bias in the direction of
their studies, the utility of which in the questions which
afterwards rose to agitate the world was, certainly, in no
degree foreseen by Savonarola at the time it was first
suggested by him. We allude to the substitution of
scriptural criticism and the study of the oriental languages, in place of scholastic or classical learning, which
we find general among his disciples, and which gave the
same impulse to the renewed cultivation of what one
might call the biblical sciences, as we have before noticed
as taking place in the thirteenth century. The restoration of biblical learning just at a period when the heretics
of Germany were about to claim the Scriptures as their

rule of faith, and when spurious translations of the sacred text were to be placed in the hands of the unlettered multitudes, may be deemed a Providential circumstance, and one most important in its results.

One of the most distinguished literary disciples of Savonarola was Zenobius Acciajoli, to whom we have before alluded as the friend and associate of Mirandola Politian, Martiales Ficinius, and other men of learning and genius who adorned the court of the Medici, and among whom the study of orientalism was a favourite pursuit. After his entrance into the Order of Preachers, he consecrated all his literary powers to the service of religion, and in the preface to his translation of a treatise of Eusebius against Hierocles, we find him dedicating to Lorenzo de Medici, " this the first fruits of his studies since his entrance into the Dominican order, whose special profession it is to neglect nothing which can contribute to the defence of the Catholic faith."

His chief labours were spent on the translation of the works of Justin Martyr and Theodoret ; the latter work having, as he says, been suggested to him by John Francis Mirandola as an antidote to the dangerous idolatry of Plato then so universal. He was promoted to a congenial and most suitable office by Leo X., being made Prefect of the Vatican Library, where every opportunity was afforded him of pursuing his favourite researches among the treasures of Greek and Hebrew literature. We shall find almost all the learned men of the order at this period turning their attention to similar pursuits ; among them we may mention Augustine Giustiniani, a member of that illustrious house which has supplied so many a great name to the ranks of the Friars Preachers. He, too, entered the order just at the time when Savonarola's system was becoming generally adopted, and the works he subsequently published prove, says Touron, " that Greek, Hebrew, Arabic, and Chaldaic, were as familiar to him as Latin." He adds, naïvely enough, that the application of Giustiniani to these studies was at first purely " the effect of his spirit of penance," but that they afterwards became his delight. Being invited to Paris by Francis I., he awakened the attention of the French prelates and literati to the importance of these pursuits, and introduced the cultivation of oriental learning into the university of Paris. His Psalter in five languages was but a sample of what he purposed to have done; his plan being to give similar versions of each of the sacred books; but he lacked a patron to assist him in the completion of this gigantic undertaking.

Not to accumulate the mere names of learned men, we shall content ourselves, in this reference to the revival of biblical literature, with mentioning that of Sanctes Pagninus, the wonder of his age, and one who, like the others we have named, was led to scriptural criticism, and the study of the oriental languages. His Latin translation of the Bible from the original tongues was a work which received the approval of Leo X. That great pope, whom Protestant critics have not hesitated to term exclusively heathen in his tastes, was one of the most magnificent encouragers of sacred letters whom the Church ever produced, and death alone prevented him from undertaking the publication of Pagninus's work at his own expense. It is said to have occupied its author for more than thirty years; during which time he produced a variety of other learned works, chiefly intended to facilitate the study of the Hebrew and Chaldaic languages. Nor can we omit recalling to mind the fact that this man of letters was also the apostle of the south of France, and a hero of charity. Of the seventeen years of his residence at Lyons, fourteen were spent amid the horrors of pestilence; and Lyons has to thank him for that magnificent hospital which was built for the sufferers at his suggestion by Thomas Guadagni.

The name of Sixtus of Siena claims our notice not only for his own merit as an author, but on account of his connection with the early career of S. Pius V. It is well that our readers should see something of a Dominican Inquisitor, and we know no better example with which to present them than that of Michael Ghislieri. Sixtus was by birth a Jew: we know nothing of the story of his conversion, but there is sufficient evidence that his bold

genius very early showed a disposition to original and
dangerous speculation. It was in the year 1500 that F.
Michael Ghislieri, in the discharge of his duties as Com-
missary-General of the Holy Office, entered one day the
prisons of the Inquisition, not for the purpose of superintending the torture, as some of our readers might
believe, but in order to see and speak with the prisoners,
and inform himself personally of their state. There he
found Sixtus, then just thirty years of age: he had been
adjudged guilty, not of heresy only, but of relapse into
heresy, and lay under sentence of death. Ghislieri was
touched with compassion, and by his means the unhappy
man was convinced of his errors, and induced to lay aside
the haughty resolution he had formed to die rather than
to submit, and so appear again in the world humiliated
and disgraced. The commissary of the Inquisition left
the prison to throw himself at the feet of the Pope and
obtain the pardon of the prisoner; but this was not all;
he determined to charge himself and his order henceforth
with the care of this erratic and untamed genius, and his
charitable and urgent solicitations won from the Pope a
permission rarely if ever granted: which was, to receive
the condemned but repentant heretic into the ranks of the
order.

Fifteen years afterwards, in his dedication of his great
work, the Biblioteca Sancta, to S. Pius, Sixtus thus
addresses his generous deliverer:—"I could not seek a
more friendly or more powerful protector than you, who
once, in old times, delivered me from the very gates of
hell, and restored me to the light of truth, and to a yet
more perfect state. When you deigned to receive me
into your order, you were pleased to clothe me with your
own hand, and even with *your own habit*, and at the same
time adopted me as your spiritual child."

He had, indeed, in Sixtus, saved a glorious soul. The
powerful grasp of religious discipline completed the conversion of heart which was begun by those first loving
and charitable words in the dungeons of Rome. Sixtus
never relapsed, and his vast learning and intellectual
powers were thenceforth directed to the service of the

faith. He was specially employed in combating Judaism, at that time active and powerful in its attacks on Christianity. His reading, like his writing, was all on a prodigious scale; we have the list of his numerous works, mostly criticisms on the Scriptures and biblical languages; but with the characteristic impetuosity of his nature, he threw them all into the flames with his own hand, with the exception of the Biblioteca Sancta, which was the only one which had reached completion at the period of his death. This work, besides containing criticisms and commentaries on the sacred books, and a vast amount of curious biblical erudition of all kinds, gives an exact account of all the writers who have treated on similar subjects down to the middle of the 16th century; in the course of which he has become the historian of many distinguished authors of his own order.

We have perhaps said enough to suggest to our readers an idea of the direction which had been given to the studies of the Dominicans just at the period when this kind of learning was most called for by the special needs of the Church. We might add many names to those given above; but we shall do no more than allude to that of Thomas de Vio Cajetan, known to every reader of the history of the Protestant Reformation as that Cardinal Cajetan to whom, as Legate of the Pope, Martin Luther made solemn profession of his willingness to submit to the judgment of the Roman Church, and to whom he gave his written declaration that "he repented of his failure of respect to the Pope, and demanded nothing better than in all things to follow the decision of the Holy Father." Previous to his elevation to the purple, Cajetan had been general of the order, and had done good service to the Holy See by a defence of its prerogatives, in a treatise on the comparative authority of a council and the Sovereign Pontiff—the old traditionary battle-ground of the Dominican champions of the Papacy. He, too, was a biblical commentator, and an expounder of the doctrines of the Church on those points attacked by the Lutheran heretics. But it was perhaps more even in his public than in his literary character, that his name is illustrious,

remembered and often maligned as it is in our own country
on account of the firm opposition he offered to the divorce
of Henry VIII. When he fell into the hands of the
Imperialists at the sack of Rome, it is said that Clement
VII. mourned over his loss more than over that of his
capital, and declared the cardinal of S. Sixtus to be " the
light of the Church."

His name brings before us the great feature of that
strange century, which dates, like the commencement
of modern history, as a new era in the destinies of Europe,
and the history of the Church. Far be it from us to
say of that century, what may be said of no period without gravely impugning the fidelity, or the providence of
God, that its fruits were unmixed evil. On the contrary, we know and are assured that the Catholic Church,
whilst it had to deplore whole kingdoms lost to the
unity of the faith, has gained by having to battle face to
face with a form of unbelief avowedly *without* her pale ;
and that the age of reform, falsely so called, was one of
true reform to her, in which the limits of her faith
received their last and exactest definitions, and her discipline put on something of that primitive beauty which
had been lost during the turbulent centuries which had
preceded it. But still the history of the Reformation is
a book written within and without with lamentation, and
mourning, and woe. And the order which follows the
fortunes of the Church, as a guard of honour clings to
some crowned master in the hour of triumph or defeat,
that order on which we have seen a sovereign Pontiff
bestowing the title of the " Order of Truth," shared in
all the sufferings of this unhappy period. In those terrible
struggles, when so much blood was shed amid the violent
disorders which everywhere followed on the preaching
of the new doctrines, the Dominicans gave a crowd of
martyrs to the Church. In France alone it is calculated
3,000 ecclesiastics and 9,000 religious perished by the
swords of the Huguenots; whilst the profanations and
crimes that accompanied these murders were too shocking
to describe. We hear much of the massacre of S. Bartholomew, but France could tell other tales, less familiar

to our ears, of thirty-five convents of this one order alone
fired by these same Huguenots, and their inhabitants driven
out, tortured,* or put to the sword. In Germany they
suffered yet more. Whole provinces had to be abandoned,
with their convents, in Poland, Moravia and Bohemia.
In the Low Countries frightful cruelties were practised :
at Ghent, for instance, the brethren were seized to the
number of a hundred, tied two and two, and placed in
their own refectory to be starved to death ; but at the
end of three days their captors determined on shooting them
to shorten their trouble, and were about to execute their
design, when the senate interfered and desired that the
friars should only be driven from the country. And this
was instantly done ; the half-dead and famishing religious
being compelled, though scarce able to stand, to begin the
journey, in the course of which many perished on the road-
side of hunger and exhaustion.

But it may perhaps be thought unfair for Catholics to
complain of persecution, as though their adversaries enjoyed
a monopoly of cruelty in a persecuting age. The Huguenots of France, it may be said, had to bear as much as
they inflicted. We will, therefore, turn to a country where
there has been no rivalry in the matter ; in whose history,
at least, Catholics can only appear as sufferers, the voice
of whose wailing has gone forth to the ends of the earth,
and whose emerald soil has been dyed red in the blood of
martyrs. We will pass over the suppression of the order
in England, where forty-two convents were swept away by
Henry VIII. with the usual scenes of sacrilege and
violence which accompanied the proceedings of that illus-

---

* Among other methods of slaughter, it was the practice of the
Huguenots to tie the priests to a crucifix, and in this way make them
marks for their arquebus-shots. "Who can relate all the martyrdoms and persecutions suffered by the Fathers," says Michel Pio,
"and that not in one place, but in every part of France? Some
were cut to pieces, others thrown into wells, others dragged about,
poisoned and pierced with swords and arrows;" whilst, venting
their rage even on the dead carcases, they would stuff them full of
corn and hay, and so make them eating-troughs for their horses. "In
the midst of these inhumanities," he adds, "the Huguenots would
raise the cry, ' Vive l'Evangile !' "—(Travagli dell' Ordine, p. 353)

trious reformer, and where the nation showed .s reviving appreciation of letters by publicly burning the works of the angelic doctor. The English province was entirely destroyed, and though partly restored by Queen Mary, the renewed persecution under Elizabeth completed its extinction. An interesting letter is given by Michel Pio, from the English provincial of the period, F. Richard Hargrave, to the master-general, describing the exile of a community of Dominican nuns of Dartford, and the state of destitution in which they were then living in the island of Zealand. One of the religious of this little community, the last remains of the English province, was a sister of the martyred Fisher, bishop of Rochester, "and a martyr of no less will and constancy," says F. Hargrave, "than was her brother."

In Ireland, however, many circumstances rendered it difficult for the English sovereigns to carry out their measures for the destruction of religion with the same success as had attended their efforts in their own island. They were there wholly without popular support, and though the laws against Catholics were framed for both countries, yet they were never able to root up the Church or her religious orders, as they had done in England. Nevertheless, the Catholic religion endured great sufferings. We will give one specimen of the system pursued by Elizabeth on her accession to the crown, taken from the "Epilogus Chronologicus," of Father John O'Heyne. It was in the year 1602, that a number of religious, Benedictines, Cistercians, and others, together with seven Dominicans, were assembled in the island of Scattery, under orders to leave the kingdom. A royal ship of war took them on board, with the purpose, as was pretended, of conveying them to the coasts of France or Spain. But though this was the *professed* design, the captain had his private orders conveyed by a royal mandate; and so soon as they were out of sight of land, every one of the prisoners, to the number of forty-two, was thrown overboard. Elizabeth, however, had a character to keep up, and therefore, on the return of her officers, after despatching her royal orders, they and all on board were cast into prison. But let not the reader suppose that this was intended as any mark of displeasure on the part of their sovereign;—on the contrary, having by this act sufficiently vindicated her reputation for justice and toleration, the prisoners were after a few days released, and by another mandate rewarded for their good service by being put in possession of the very abbey-lands which formed the property of their victims.

Protestant writers of course pass over facts like these; and their Protestant readers will therefore go on to the end extolling the glories of that " bright occidental star," whose rising put an end to the inhuman cruelties of the Papists. That can be scarcely called ignorance which refuses to know the truth ; and the martyrdoms of Irish Catholics under Elizabeth were not few in number, neither are they left without full historical records. They put the inquisition to the blush ; hanging was thought too mild a death to inflict on the victims of " religious tolerance." The ingenuity of the Indian savages was imitated in the devising of new and strange tortures. They were roasted, and pressed to death ; their nails were slowly torn from their feet and hands ; they were exposed to die of cold and starvation ; and the imagination of their tormentors was racked to invent originalities in the way of cruelty. What, for instance, are we to think of the punishment inflicted on Dermot Hurle, archbishop of Cashel, a Dominican ? He was sentenced to be hanged ; but previously to his execution, was subjected to an extraordinary barbarity. His entire legs and feet were covered with a corrosive plaster made of pitch, sulphur, brandy, salt, and other combustible materials, which slowly consumed the flesh ; the plaster was renewed hour after hour, till the arteries and muscles were destroyed, and the very bones appeared ; and his enemies, having thus satisfied their savage malice, then conducted him to the scaffold, though we are told they did so *before break of day*, lest the circumstances of his previous tortures should become public.

A great number of the religious of the order suffered during the reigns of James I. and Charles I., yet still it

survived in spite of all that the rack and the gibbet could
do to extinguish it. But during the conquest of the
island by Cromwell, Ireland was made to drain to the very
dregs the chalice of her misery. We have neither space
nor inclination to dwell at length on the barbarities inflicted by that champion of religious liberty, yet we
cannot omit an allusion to one or two among the many
illustrious martyrs whose deaths shed an additional lustre
over the Irish province of the Friars Preachers. There
is something that reminds us of the acts of the early
Christian martyrs in the account, for instance, given us
of the death of F. Richard Barry, prior of Cashel, who
was seized in the church with a number of other
Catholics, both secular and ecclesiastic, after having
insisted on his brethren seeking safety by flight. He
was a man of noble and stately bearing, and when the
leader of the hostile troop came into his presence, he was
so struck by his appearance that he offered him his life
if he would only consent to quit the religious habit.
But Father Barry rejected the offer with heroic disdain.
"These garments," he said, "are the livery of Christ,
and represent to me His Passion; they are the banner
of my military service to Him; I have worn them from
my youth upwards, and never will I put them off."
Enraged at his obstinacy, they determined to make an
example of him, and collecting a fire of sticks on the rock
of Cashel, they burnt him slowly from his feet upwards,
and at length ended his sufferings with a thrust of a sword.
Or again, how beautiful is the story of Father Lawrence
O'Ferall of Longford, who, being remanded for three
days, secretly prayed to God that the palm of martyrdom
should not be denied him. When led to the scaffold, he
threw his rosary round his neck, and meekly folding his
hands under his scapular after the manner of his order,
he submitted to the hangman with a sweet and cheerful
countenance. As he hung suspended in the air, by a
marvellous prodigy, he withdrew one of his hands from
his scapular, and with it held his cross high above his head,
in token of victory and triumph, until all was over.

But we must remember that we are not writing a

martyrology. In spite of torrents of blood and continual banishments, the Irish province lived on, and its succession of provincials has remained unbroken even to our own time. We have already spoken of the grant made by Clement VIII. to the Irish branch of the order, of the convents of S. Clement and S. Sixtus at Rome. It likewise possesses other foreign establishments, such as the college at Louvain, erected by permission of Philip IV. in 1655; and that at Lisbon founded in 1615, whose first prior, F. Dominic O'Daly, has left several interesting works on the history and sufferings of his order.

We must pass from this part of our subject to glance for a moment at some of those great theologians whose services were called forth by the peculiar exigencies of the times. In the history of the Protestant Reformation, the names of some of these Dominican defenders of the faith have attained an immortal celebrity. None, perhaps, offered a more formidable opposition to the new sectaries than John Faber, one of the chief Catholic theologians at the celebrated Conference of Baden (in which the doctrines of Luther and Zuinglius were definitively condemned), and at the subsequent Diet of Spires. The two Soto's, Dominic and Peter, with Melchior Cano, upheld the theological renown of the order in Spain. Peter Soto was the friend of Cardinal Pole, the last Dominican whose voice was heard in the schools of Oxford. During the temporary restoration of the faith in England under Philip and Mary, he was established professor at the university, and revived for a brief space the ancient scholastic and theological studies that had formerly flourished there. Associated with him in this work were several others of his order, amongst them Bartholomew Carranza and John of Villagracia; and we are assured the conversions effected by them were very numerous. Dominic Soto was one of that great body of Dominican theologians who took so large a share in the deliberations of the Council of Trent; and during the first six sessions of the council he was appointed to represent the general of the order. He was placed, moreover, at the head of all the theologians sent by the emperor; and among the fifty fathers of his order who were present in that august assembly, he was considered the one of highest repute. This certainly is no light praise, when we consider who these Dominicans were who filled the ranks of the Tridentine Fathers. There was, at a later period of the sessions, Leonard Marinis, the archbishop of Lanciano, who sat there as Papal legate, to whom, in company with two others of his order, Giles Foscarari and Francis Forerio, was committed the drawing up of the Catechism of the Council of Trent. There was Bartholomew of the Martyrs, the saintly archbishop of Braga, and the unflinching promoter of ecclesiastical reform, the friend and adviser of S. Charles Borromeo, and, we might say, the model on which he formed his idea of sanctity. There also was the companion and chosen associate of Bartholomew, Henry of Tavora, afterwards archbishop of Goa, a man of singular and primitive simplicity: these, and others equally illustrious, represented the order of Preachers in that great council, where one and all distinguished themselves with extraordinary unity of sentiment as the champions of Church reform. No one will mistake the sense in which we use these words, and certainly the Dominican order is not the body which lies open to the suspicion of favouring novelties and innovations. The reform aimed at by the Tridentine Fathers was the universal restoration of that primitive discipline which we see carried out in the episcopates of such men as Bartholomew of the Martyrs, S. Charles Borromeo, Lanuza, and other saintly bishops who illustrated an age rendered yet more distinguished as the age of ecclesiastical reform by the pontificate of S. Pius V.

In fact, it is well known that some of the most stringent measures of ecclesiastical reform originated with the Dominican members of the council. One of the prelates in attendance resolutely opposed some of these; and, in particular, ventured to press the propriety of exempting the cardinals from the effect of the reforming decrees. "The most illustrious and reverend cardinals," he said, in the pompous style of a court eulogist, "can stand in need of no reform." Bartholomew of the Martyrs imme-

diately rose to reply. "The most illustrious and reverend
cardinals shall have a most illustrious and most reverend
reform;" and his opponent was soon obliged to give up the
point before the determination of the Portuguese primate.
We have already alluded to his strictures on the building
tastes of Pius IV. His name is to be had in benediction
as one of the most glorious examples of pastoral excellence
the order ever produced, and as the guide and teacher
of one who surpasses him in the glory of actual canonization, yet was but the disciple and imitator of his episcopal
career. It was probably after some such scene as that we
have described in the Belvidere gardens, that the young
Cardinal Borromeo followed him to his room, and opened
his whole heart to the first man who had ever seemed
worthy of his confidence. "There is none here but God
and ourselves," he said, closing the door behind him,
" and you must hear me, for I loved you from the first
moment that we met; and I well know that it was for
my sake God sent you hither. You see what it is to be
nephew to a Pope; I am young and care for none of
these things. I shall resign all my preferments and
retire to some monastery of strict observance, for I desire
only to save my soul." If S. Charles was preserved in
his exalted position, and exhibited to all future ages as
the model of the episcopate, it was owing to the advice
and guidance of Bartholomew at that critical moment.
His work, entitled the "*Stimulus Pastorum*," being
instructions for those entering on the pastoral office, is
said to have been the constant companion of the saint; he
carried it in his bosom, and the living example of its
incomparable author was the rule by which he guided his
subsequent career.

We have alluded to the pontificate of S. Pius. Two
other members of the Order of Preachers had already
ascended the chair of S. Peter. Peter de Tarentasia,
under the title of Innocent V., in a short reign of five
months, had accomplished the reconciliation of the Guelph
and Ghibeline factions of Tuscany, and left a name so
dear and venerable, that though no office has been
granted in his honour, his name is often distinguished

with the popular title of Blessed. Nicholas Bocassini, the ninth general of the Dominicans who, true to the loyal instincts of his order, stood by the unfortunate pontiff Boniface VIII., when all else deserted him, on the fatal day of Anagni, became his successor, and is known in history as the blessed Benedict XI. His pontificate lasted but a single year; but, like that of Pope Innocent it was long enough to be deemed illustrious, and to fill the distracted Church of the 14th century with the sweet and gracious odour of peace. "Wars and dissensions fled from Rome," says an ancient author, quoted by Oderic Raynaldus, "when Benedict appeared." Peace too was restored by his fatherly hand between France and the Holy See; and the grievances which had arisen in the reign of Boniface were healed and reconciled. In every country the legates of the blessed Benedict were to be found preaching the same gospel of peace and reconciliation; and if, as is thought, his early death was caused by poison administered by his enemies, we may pronounce his eulogium in the words of Touron, and say that, "the victim and the martyr of peace, he lived but to preach its doctrines, and reigned only to make it reign."

Benedict XI. has received the solemn beatification of the Church. It remained for her to bestow a yet higher honour on the third Dominican who succeeded to the sacred tiara. This was Michael Ghislieri, of whose character as grand inquisitor we have already spoken. The whole idea of the pontificate of S. Pius was one of ecclesiastical reform; and if something of severity appears to attach to his government, let it be remembered that this severity was directed in most cases, not against seculars and heretics, but against the Catholic clergy themselves. Rome under his rule became once more worthy of the title of the Holy City:—nor was there a country in the wide range of Christendom that did not feel the effects of his parental solicitude. We can find in the annals of no single pontificate, if we except that of Innocent III., such examples of vigilance over all people, and all churches that owned the rule of Peter, as we find in the history of S. Pius. And when we remember the

period during which he held the reins of government,——
a period when Europe was on one side revolutionized by
the madness of sectaries, whilst on the other the power of
the Ottomans was every day advancing nearer and nearer,
and destroying one by one her bulwarks of defence,—
we shall be better able to do justice to the qualities of
one to whose greatness the world and the Church alike
bear witness in his threefold character of pontiff, prince,
and saint. His election to the chair of S. Peter was the
work of S. Charles Borromeo, whose influence was paramount in the conclave that assembled on the death of
Pius IV. He may be considered the last, and in some
respects the greatest, of that long line of popes whose
temporal and political power almost equalled that of
their spiritual supremacy. After his time, the political
influence of the Roman pontiffs gradually declined; it
had rested on the religious unity of the European states,
and when that unity was broken, the Roman see, which
had formed its centre, naturally lost much of the power
it had hitherto possessed. But though the causes which
effected the change were already in operation during the
reign of Pius V., they had only begun to work, and the
crisis of extraordinary danger which, in the middle of
the 16th century, well nigh laid Europe at the mercy
of the Turks, was the last occasion when a Roman
pontiff was seen acting as the father of the Christian
world, animating the distracted sovereigns to courage
and unity with his single voice, and directing all that
was left in Europe of faith and chivalry against the
hosts of the Mussulman invaders. The Christian league,
whose victory at Lepanto broke the naval power of the
Turks, and saved Europe from unimaginable sufferings,
was the creation of S. Pius; nothing short of his unwearied constancy, and the influence of his venerable
authority, could have cemented such a league in that
hour of discord; the glorious result of the great struggle
belongs to him and to his order; and its results, as well
as the sagacity and pious zeal of him who was the
presiding spirit of the Christian confederacy, extorted
from Bacon the memorable words, "I marvel that the

Roman Church has not yet canonized this great man."
In the following century, however, those honours were
formally granted to S. Pius which had long before been
his by popular acclamation. He had earned them, not
merely as the victorious defender of Christendom, but
by the merits of a pontificate which aimed at, and in no
small degree succeeded in, restoring to the Church its
primitive purity and beauty. The part he had taken in
drawing up the reforming decrees of the Council of
Trent was very considerable, but still greater was his
share in enforcing them. And lest, in representing him as
the uncompromising advocate of ancient discipline, any
should think of him as acting on that narrow-minded
bigotry which refuses to mould itself to the views and
necessities of the age, let them remember that he was
the warm advocate of popular education, the founder of
the Confraternity of Christian Doctrine, and the liberal
patron of parish schools, and factories, on the foundation
of which latter establishments he expended 100,000
crowns, in order to supply some means for correcting
the idleness, as well as the ignorance, of his people. Nor
is the Church without her obligations to him in matters
which might be deemed of lighter import. True to the
traditions of his order, he supported the principles of
Christian art, against the abuses of the renaissance.[*]
The same sensuality which had debased the arts of
painting and sculpture had, towards the middle of the
16th century, infused its poison with no less subtlety
into music; so that the Council of Trent, which had
passed a severe condemnation on the character of the
pictures and images then being introduced into the
churches, felt called on in like manner to censure the
worldly and effeminate music which had taken the place
of church harmony. S. Pius, when cardinal, formed one
of the commission before whom the question was finally
brought, which was to decide whether, in consequence of
these abuses, the use of all ornamental or figured music

[*] By order of S. Pius all statuary of a reprehensible character in
the gallery of the Vatican was removed, and the pieces of any
artistic merit placed in the collection at the Capitol.

should not be abandoned. It was the genius of Palestrina which alone prevented such a result. The Mass, commonly known as that of Marcellus II., on which the trembling hands of the composer, who knew how much depended on the judgment to be formed of his work, had traced the words, " Deus adjuva me," convinced all who listened, that music, like painting, in religious hands, could minister to a religious end. The question remained undecided, however, until the accession of S. Pius, who immediately appointed Palestrina master of the papal chapel, where the spirit and traditions of the great master of sacred harmony still survive.

We may finally remind our readers, that by English Catholics the name of S. Pius should ever be held in peculiar veneration : he never failed to show a warm, paternal sympathy in their sufferings; and his correspondence with Mary Stuart, the unhappy victim of Elizabeth's tyranny, is not among the least interesting pages of his life.

The order of Friars Preachers still continued fruitful in men of letters; and among them we find three who attained to eminence as historians,—Leander Albert, Malvenda, the annalist of his order, and Bzovius, to whom was committed the task of completing the Annals of Baronius. In Spain we seem to behold that group of illustrious Dominicans whose names are associated with the reform of S. Theresa, among whom are to be reckoned S. Louis Bertrand himself, her friend and supporter in many difficulties, and Dominic Bannez, her confessor through the most stormy period of her life. Indeed the close connection of the order with the life of this great saint is not among the least interesting chapters of its history; and if, in God's Providence, many of its saintly men were suffered to co-operate with her in her work, it received its reward in the precious testimonies of esteem which it has received from her pen.

The mention of the Spanish Dominicans of the 16th century recalls one name, probably more familiar to our readers' ears than any we have yet given,—that of Louis of Granada, whose works have found a home in every

language, and are esteemed even by those who widely
differ from his faith. Among the mystic writers of the
order, he has had a more world wide influence and
reputation than any who preceded him. Doubtless in
his writings we miss the sweet antique pathos of Suso,
or the terrific majesty of Thaulerus; he comes to us in a
more modern guise and spirit; nevertheless, the author
of the "Guide of Sinners" is certainly one of those to
whom the Christian world stands most indebted. In his
own day his works were read and esteemed in every
European country, and yet it is even more his sancity
than his genius that we love to commemorate. A peculiar
beauty ever attaches to the friendship of the saints, and
there are few more delightful passages in the history of
Louis of Grenada than those which exhibit him to us
in his familiar intercourse with S. Louis Bertrand, and
the great archbishop of Braga. No office or dignity in
the Church could have been too high for him to aspire to,
and hardly one exists which was not pressed on his
acceptance; but he refused them all, and when his
acceptance of the purple was urged on him by Gregory
XIII. he replied to the pontiff's solicitations in the words
of Job, "In nidulo meo moriar;"—"I will die in my
little nest."*

Once more we repeat, it is not as writers and men of
letters that we most desire our readers to admire the
posterity of S. Dominic. Even during this century,
when the heretics declaimed so loudly against the corruption
of the Church and her religious, it is remarkable that the
order, and we might add the Church at large, was richer in
saints, and saintly men and women, than at almost any
other period.† The religious spirit had not departed from
the cloisters of the Friars Preachers, and those whom the

* Job xxix. 18.
† The century of the Protestant Reformation was illustrated in
the Catholic Church by the lives of some of her very greatest saints.
We find all living at the same time, S. Pius V., S. Philip Neri,
S. Ignatius Loyola, S. Louis Bertrand, S. Francis Borgia, S. Theresa, S. Catherine of Ricci, S. Peter Alcantara, S. Charles Borromeo,
S. Andrew Avellino, S. Francis Xavier, S. Pascal Baylen, S. Stanis-
laus Kotska, S. Aloysius Gonzaga, and many others of almost equal
note.

world celebrated for their learning and literary distinction
were rather valued among their own brethren for their
sanctity and prayer. And lest our readers should carry
away the idea that lectures and disputations, and the dangers of learned celebrity must necessarily have effaced
the monastic simplicity of the former ages, let them consider the example of F. Bartholomew of Valenza, a disciple
of S. Louis Bertrand, and a great theological lecturer in his
day. When he addressed his scholars, we are told, do
what he would, his lectures fell into the language of prayer.
He always spoke in abstraction, to God, and not to them
—" Jesus, my love," he would say, " Thy servant S.
Thomas in this question considers the difference between
time and eternity : do Thou deliver me from time, and
conduct me to a blessed eternity, even to Thyself, O God.
Amen. But in the reasoning of Thy servant Thomas,
there arises difficulties which I know not how to answer ;
O Master of my soul, give me Thy Holy Spirit to understand that which I shall one day see. Thy servant Cajetan
on the same subject says so and so. May he ever enjoy
Thy blessed vision who, by Thy inspiration, has spoken of
Thee so wisely and so well. But to me it seems that there
is such or such a distinction : pardon my arrogance, O
Lord of angels, those beings drawn out of time, and now
tasting of eternity, and give to me, a sinner, grace to
enjoy it one day with them, through the merits of Thine
own blood. Amen." In this way he would go on,
mingling his speculations with devotions, oft rapt in
ecstasy, whilst his auditors heard him with tears, and
a feeling of solemn awe, as though listening to some
superhuman colloquy. We do not give his style as a
model for the imitation of theological professors, but
merely to illustrate the fact that at this peiod of sharp
and bitter controversy, when so much of the religious
feeling of the past was crumbling away, instances were
not wanting to prove that the Dominican professor was
still something more than a mere man of letters, and was
worthy of reckoning his descent from that noble ancestry
of the 13th century which filled the lecture-rooms of the
universities with beatified saints.

CHAPTER VI.

Declension of Religion in the 17th century. Distinguished reformers of the Order. Sebastian Michaelis. Anthony le
Quien. John B. Carre. Cardinal Howard. Massoulie. Natalis Alexander. Distinguished religious women. Juliana
Morelle. Vittoria Dolara.

ALTHOUGH it can scarcely be doubted that the effect
of the revolution of the 16th century was eventually
beneficial to the Church, and brought about a real
reformation within her pale, of a different character
from the unhappy schism which assumed the name, yet
neither can we deny that its immediate results were
disastrous and ruinous in the extreme. "It would be
impossible to paint in too lively colours," says Touron,
"the injury which the Church received in the 16th
century, from the spirit of error and licentiousness
which was supported by all the powers of hell." Not
to speak of the fatal contagion of such a spirit, the
religious orders of this period suffered in some measure,
as they had done during the great plague of the 14th
century, and with something of a similar result. Thousands of religious fell under the swords of the Huguenots
and German sectaries, and the gaps left by their removal
were not easily filled up; for those readiest to give their
lives for the faith were sure to be the worthiest members
of their body. All men are not purified by persecutions,
and when Vincent Giustiniani, one of the last who filled
the office of Provincial of England, was elected to the
mastership of his order, he found, in the course of the
general visitation, together with much of noble zeal and
fidelity among his subjects, many tokens of relaxation
and decay. We have sufficient evidence that the evil
was only partial; nevertheless, we know that even S.
Theresa, in the description she gives of the great order,
traditionally interpreted to signify that of S. Dominic,

2 A

which was to revive in the latter times for the confusion
of heresy, represents it as being in her day in the commencement of her decline. It can be no great matter of
wonder that it should be so, for it is with the religious
orders as with the dynasties and kingdoms; they rise and
fall, and their history is full of variations. The order of
Friars Preachers was certainly neither superanuated nor
effete; but its greatest era was past, and the new society
of Jesus, fresh in the vigour of a young foundation, and in
the full fervour of its first generation of saints and heroic
men, in some degree took its place, and became, if not the
most popular, at least the all-powerful order of the two
succeeding centuries.

Nevertheless, this period of partial declension was
illustrated by the zeal of many bold and fervent advocates of religious reform. Whilst Hippolitus Beccaria
ruled the order and toiled with unwearied zeal for the
universal restoration of regular discipline, the province
of Provence was governed by one who was well fitted to
carry out the general's designs. This was F. Sebastian
Michaelis, who proposed to himself nothing short of an
exact return to the spirit and discipline of the first ages.
His visitations as provincial were made in the very
spirit and method of those of S. Dominic. Perhaps the
historical associations of his province, the very birth
place of the order, and the scene of S. Dominic's first
and most heroic labours, contributed to cherish these
feelings; for it sounds like a passage out of the life of
the great patriarch, when we read of the chapter held by
Michaelis at Fangeaux, the scene of that celebrated
miracle which attested the triumph of S. Dominic over
the Albigenses. Michaelis' labours were not without fruit,
and the communities reformed by him, especially that
of Toulouse, became, as in old time, the nurseries of
saints. Indeed, we have evidence that not in France
only, but in Spain, and Italy, especially at Naples and
Salamanca, the reformed convents restored the regular
observance of the rule with a severity and zeal which is
truly extraordinary. We have F. Marchese's description
of the convent of Salamanca, of which he was himself

a member; and our readers will allow that the religious spirit was not yet extinct among the Friars Preachers, whatever may have been the partial relaxation. "In that convent," he says, "the happy state of primitive religion seemed never to have grown old. It was a perpetual alternation of prayer and study, so that the religious were always employed either in the praises of God, or in attending to the salvation of souls. No indulgence was admitted in the rigours of fasting, the exactness of inclosure, or the observation of silence, which last was indeed but little felt; for the work was so continual that even had any desired to speak they would have found no time to do so." Some of the most interesting sketches left us by this writer are of the Neapolitan religious whom he had himself known, and whose lives are a sufficient evidence that the cloisters of the Friars Preachers were still nurturing chosen souls to the heroic degrees of sanctity.

The reformation of their own order and the defence of the Church against the progress of heresy were the two objects to which the efforts of the Dominicans were now directed; and none was more distinguished for his zeal and devotion in both these objects than the celebrated Anthony Le Quieu, who embraced the religious life in the convent of the Annunciation, founded by the Père Michaelis as the model house of his reform. In this house he became the master of novices to many of those destined eventually to revive the spirit of religion throughout the order; but even the strict observance of this foundation did not satisfy him, and his ardent temperament was ever devising schemes of new establishments, wherein the exact observance of the constitutions should be united to an apostolate for the extinction of heresy in every province where the new convents should be erected. We can scarcely study the history of any order without being forcibly struck by the singular family likeness that exists among its great men: we see not only their virtues, but their infirmities continually reproduced, and it is evident that the same rule and spirit attracted to itself men of congenial natures. If one may systema-

tize in such things, we should be inclined to say, that
a certain romance and enthusiasm, sometimes carrying
its possessors beyond the bounds of discretion, but
always noble and full of chivalry, was the hereditary
infirmity of the Friars Preachers ; it sometimes gave to
their plans of perfection, as in the case of Bartholomew
de Las Casas, a character rather ideal than practical, and
in that of Le Quieu eventually led him to go beyond the
very constitutions whose exact observance he desired to
revive.   Nicholas Rodolph, the general of the order,
entered warmly into his views, and after receiving the
benediction of the Sovereign Pontiff, he proceeded to
enter on his work, and became the founder of six convents
in various provinces of France, which were united together
under the title of "the Congregation of the Blessed
Sacrament."   In these we must particularly admire the
way in which he succeeded in bringing out the great idea
of the Dominican institute in its integrity ; namely, its
union of the contemplative and the apostolic life ; his
religious were men of prayer and men of preaching, and
in the description left us of these convents, as in those
founded by Michaelis, we seem to see a reproduction
of the early foundations of S. Dominic.   The indiscretion
of Le Quieu to which we have alluded consisted in his
desire to introduce the custom of going barefooted ; a
practice which had never existed in the order, or formed
any part of its rule, and which would inevitably have led
to some separation from the main body of the order, and
thus have deprived it of what has been one of its greatest
glories and privileges, its unbroken unity.   The scheme
was, however, overruled by the authority of the general,
and Le Quieu was in future obliged to content himself
with the degree of poverty and austerity prescribed by
his rule.

Ten years before his death he commenced his apostolic
missions in the territory of Geneva.   The heretics of the
south of France had already learnt to fear him, as once
their forefathers had feared the preaching of S. Dominic,
and now the whole diocese of Annecy (whither the
bishops of Geneva had removed their episcopal see) felt

the influence of this extraordinary man. "Wherever he preached," says his biographer, the Père Archange, "he introduced the devotion of the Forty Hours. He preached twice and sometimes three times every day, and would spend ten or twelve hours in the confessional, passing the nights on the altar-step. His repast was only a handful of bread, and he might often have been found on the wayside taking it by the margin of some running stream which supplied his drink, and this when he was seventy-five years of age." His singular devotion to the Blessed Sacrament led to his forming a foundation for the express purpose of promoting its honour. This was a convent of nuns of the Perpetual Adoration established at Marseilles in 1659, and one of the first establishments of the kind of which we find any notice in history.* They followed the rule of S. Austin, with constitutions of their own given them by Le Quieu, which were approved by the Holy See. This convent still existed at the period when Touron wrote his history.

The only other of these modern reformers whom we will mention is F. John Baptist Carré, the founder of the Noviciate-General of Paris, who, like Le Quieu, was a disciple of the reform of Michaelis, and had received his religious education in his convent at Toulouse. He also filled the same office of novice-master at the Annunciation, and in 1632 the admirable scheme for the establishment of one noviciate for the whole of the French provinces was carried out, and placed under his management by Nicholas Rodolph the general of the order. Indeed at this

---

We say one of the first, for the first convent of this description was undoubtedly that founded in Paris in the year 1653 by Catherine de Barr, under the patronage of Anne of Austria. This community followed the Benedictine rule. Marchese mentions a convent of Dominican friars in Spain about the same time, where the Perpetual Adoration was kept up. In fact, devotion to the Most Holy Sacrament has always been a distinguished feature of the order of Preachers; we find the arch-confraternity of the Blessed Sacrament established at the Minerva by Paul III. in 153-, from which other branch-confraternities took their rise, though that of S. Martin at Liege was probably of yet earlier origin.

period France may be considered as the rallying ground
of the Dominican Institute. In spite of the spread
of Jansenism, and the attacks on the liberties of the
Church which mark the ecclesiastical history of France
in the seventeenth century, there was probably no age
when the ranks of her clergy were filled with more illustrious members. Among these the most distinguished
of all may be claimed by the order of S. Dominic, of
which he was a professed tertiary. We allude to M.
Olier, the founder of the seminary of S. Sulpice, and one
whose influence over the society of his day was of the
most extraordinary kind. It is well known that the
sanctification of this great man, and his devotion to the
work which afterwards produced such vast results on the
whole body of the French clergy, has been formally
acknowledged by many of the Sulpician ecclesiastics as
principally owing to the influence of the Venerable Agnes
of Jesus. Perhaps it was his close connection with this
celebrated religious of the Dominican order that moved
him with the desire to attach himself to the same institute.
As he knelt to receive the scapular in the chapel of S.
Sulpice, we are told that "he confessed with lively emotion
that he owed every grace he had up to that time received
to the order of S. Dominic." " I am rejoiced," he added,
" to see myself a child of S. Dominic, and more than ever
a brother of the revered Mother Agnes of Jesus, to
whom I owe so much." Following his example, many
other priests of the seminary entered the third order about
the same time.

Whilst speaking of those who *reformed* the order, the
English Dominicans ought never to forget one to whom
they owe in no small degree the restoration of its existence
among themselves. This was Philip Thomas Howard,
one of the noble house of Norfolk who entered the order
in the year 1645, and during the Protectorate of Cromwell founded a monastery of English friars at Bornheim
in Flanders, and a convent of nuns of the second order at
Vilvorde, which was afterwards removed to Brussels,* his

* We have called Sister Antoinette Howard, *sister* to the cardinal,
on the authority of Touron, but by the unpublished manuscript

own sister Antoinete Howard being the first of the English nation who offered herself to join the proposed foundation. At the French revolution in the following century, when so many religious communities took refuge in England, these two houses were broken up, and their inmates settled in our own land, which thus saw the

memoirs of the community of Vilvorde (now settled at Atherstone in Warwichshire), it would not appear that she was so nearly related to him.

She was but sixteen years of age when she took the habit, having removed from the convent of Tempes with two of the religious of that community, for the purpose of commencing the new foundation. " She was the first Englishwoman," says the MS., "that had taken the habit of the holy father since the unhappy fall of religion in England. A short time of her noviceship passed when it pleased God to try her with a grievous sickness; and He rewarded her virtuous intentions and fervent desires to be consecrated to Him in holy religion, with a clear sight of His Sacred Mother, the ever-blessed Virgin, about an hour before her happy death, which took place on the 8th day of October, 1661, four months after she took the holy habit." After some particulars of her illness, the account continues as follows: " A little while after, she fell into a trance, in which for about a quarter of an hour she appeared quite dead ; then smiling, she opened her eyes with great signs of joy, and presently after fell into another trance, which lasted not so long, but by the signs of joy and satisfaction far exceeded that that she had showed before; this moved the father confessor to ask her the cause of her joy, to which she made no reply, but looked upon him and us that were by her very cheerfully and made some signs with her hand which we could not understand. Then her confessor, much surprised to see this strange satisfaction, so very unusual at such a time, said thus to her, " Child, I command you in virtue of holy obedience, to declare the cause of your joy at this dreadful time, when you are going to give a strict account of every thought, word, and deed, which God exacts with such severity that the greatest saints have trembled to think of it." She without any change of countenance, answered, " I see it.' " Child," said the father, " what do you see? tell what you see.' She said, " I see our Blessed Lady with a crown in one hand and a rosary in the other—a fine crown." " Child," said the father, "have a care what you say ; do you see our Blessed Lady ?" She very cheerfully replied, " Yes, I do see our Blessed Lady with a fine crown and rosary, O! fine crown! O! fine rosary! I desire to see no more of this world." Then the Confessor (F. William Collings) said to her, " Child, would you have the absolution of the rosary ?" She answered, " I made signs for it many times when I could not speak." Then devoutly preparing herself to receive it, he gave it to her, and presently after, with a pleasant smiling countenance, she left this wretched life to pass to eternal felicity —She was professed on her death-bed.

restoration of the order just two hundred years after the nuns of Dartford had been driven from her shores in the manner we have described. F. Howard was raised to the purple in 1675, and at the instance of James II. was afterwards declared Cardinal Protector of England. He was also the founder of a new college at Louvain in favour of religious of his own order and nation. Towards the end of the seventeenth century the opinions of the Quietists began to trouble the Church; their errors had long before been minutely described and confuted by Taulerus; and in their modern form they found a vigorous opponent in Père Anthony Massoulié, the enthusiastic defender of S. Thomas, whose principles of theology are the weapons he uses, in his celebrated treatises on prayer, and the love of God, to condemn the erroneous doctrines of his adversaries. Other writers of the greatest eminence flourished about this time : among whom we may notice Goar, the illustrious convert from the Greek schism, but, in particular, the theologian and ecclesiastical historian, Natalis Alexander, whose works were declared by Cardinal Orsini to be a library in themselves.

We find among the literary notices of this century the name of one writer, whose celebrity is of so curious a kind that we shall not hesitate to give her story at length. It is well known that not a few of the religious women of the Dominican order have in all ages maintained the character of their institute for learning and the cultivation of the arts, and have found means to unite these pursuits to the virtues of their vocation in a truly admirable manner. We have alluded to the two sisters, Plautilla and Petronilla Nelli, the painter and authoress, of the Ruccellai convent at Florence. During the same century a singular amount of talent was to be found in convents of the female Dominicans. The nuns of Florence were among the earliest and most zealous encouragers of the art of printing. Their spiritual director, Fra Domenico of Pistoja, established a printing-press in their convent, which they worked with their own hands. Marchese mentions Sister Aurelia Fiorentini, of the convent of Lucca, one of whose paintings may yet be seen over the high altars of S. Dominic's Church in that city, where it was placed after the removal of the Madonna della Misericordia, the *chef d'œuvre* of Fra Bartolomeo. Besides a great many of other female painters whose names have been recorded by Marchese, the convent of Prato, celebrated as that of S. Catherine of Ricci, was the residence of the well-known elegiac poetess, Lorenza Strozzi, of whom Echard has given a long and interesting account. After her entrace into religion she applied herself to the study of languages, and became a perfect mistress both of Greek and Latin. Her Latin hymns and sapphics, for the feasts of the Church, have been translated into French verse, and were much esteemed. But the learning of Sister Lorenza fades into nothing by the side of that of Juliana Morelle, to whom we made allusion above. She was a native of Barcelona; and previous to her entrance into religion, her father, Anthony Morelle, applied himself to the task of cultivating her natural talents by devoting her to a course of study very unusual in those of her sex. We are told that when only twelve years old she spoke Castilian, French, Italian, Greek, and Hebrew, with perfect facility. She employed nine hours every day in study, and attained such eminence in the sciences of logic, and of physical and moral philosophy, that in 1607 (she being then but thirteen years of age), she sustained public theses of philosophy at Lyons, and which were afterwards published, and dedicated to Margaret of Austria. Besides these acquirements, she studied metaphysics, jurisprudence, and music. Her father wished her to take her degree as *Doctress* in Law, and for this purpose conducted her to Avignon. The whole city was stirred at the news of her arrival, and the most distinguished persons of either sex were eager to see and speak with her. By her wisdom and erudition, but far more by her singular modesty and humility, she excited general admiration; and the vice-legate of Avignon, wishing to have some proof of her learning, appointed a day for a public disputation to be held at his palace, in the presence of the Duchess of Condé, and a crowd of illustrious ecclesiastics and religious, with other persons of rank and eminence. Juliana for the second time was obliged to defend the public theses, answering every argument and objection of her opponents with so much depth and readiness as to astonish all who listened. Nevertheless, in the midst of all the flattery which was heaped upon her, her humility never once gave way; and the simplicity and sanctity which were observable in her conduct rendered her far more worthy of applause than did the learning on which her father and the public set so high a value. She very early took the resolution of retiring from the eyes of the world, and entering religion; and took the veil in the convent of S. Praxedes, at Avignon, when only fifteen years of age; so brief had been the career that created so extraordinary a renown.

Probably some of our readers may have formed no favourable idea of the young doctress and public disputant, but they must surely admire the purity and true spirituality of a soul that could unite such gifts, and a reputation so uncommon, to the virtues of a religious vocation. They must forgive Juliana her learning, should that be an offence in their eyes, when they hear how she bore herself in her religious probation. In the midst of the most humbling trials to which her superiors considered it right to subject her, in order to prove her vocation, and to prevent her from being puffed up by her extraordinary knowledge, she always showed herself equally humble, patient, submissive, and grateful to all. She never exercised her talents save with permission of her superiors, or for the service of the sisters. When, in order to test her, they would show contempt for the explanations she gave of anything, Juliana lost nothing of her customary sweetness and humility. She was a most exact observer of her rule, and was several times elected novice-mistress and prioress of her community, always discharging these offices with a union of zeal, sweetness, and spiritual wisdom. She had a great love to the poor, and distributed to them everything in her power to give. At length, after twenty-five years of constant sickness, she died in 1653, and several miraculous cures were attributed to her after her death. "This great religious," continues the author of the *Vie Spirituelle Universelle*, "whom several learned authors have not hesitated to call the honour of her sex, the wonder of her age, the glory of her monastery, and one of the brightest ornaments of her order, has left several devout works. Among these are a 'Retreat of ten days on Eternity,' a beautiful commentary on the 'Treatise on the Spiritual Life' of S. Vincent Ferrer, together with a commentary on the rule of S. Austin, some Latin prayers, and a history of the reform of her monastery of S. Praxedes. Besides these, she wrote a brief exposition of the dispositions proper for religious profession." She is spoken of in terms of eulogy by Lopez de Vega, and several other authors. Later in the same century, Sister Maria Villani, of the convent at Naples, attained a yet higher reputation as mystic writer. Few biographies can rival hers in beauty and interest, for she was of most saintly life. She has "eleven large volumes full of the profoundest doctrine," says Echard, who gives a list of her works in his "History of the Dominican writers," where we shall find an interesting notice of all the illustrious women of the order.

Their reputation has been supported nearer our own time by Sister Anna Vittoria Dolara, prioress of the monastery of S. Mary Magdalen on Monte Cavallo, founded by Magdalen Orsini, and now inhabited by the nuns of the Perpetual Adoration. She was alike remarkable for her piety, her poetical genius, and her excellence as a painter. When Pius VI. was carried into exile by the soldiers of the French republic, they spared the convent of the sisters, but at the same time stripped it of all means of support. Vittoria Dolara contrived in this emergency to raise a sufficient subsistence for herself and her sisters by incessant application to her pencil, and it was during this period of suffering that she wrote the "Complaint of the Roman Virgins," a little poem of singular beauty and pathos. "This accomplished nun," says Marchese, "possessed a considerable knowledge of

Latin; she was also well skilled in vocal and instrumental music, and was wont to cheer her afflicted sisters with her melodious strains. Pius VII., who held Sister Dolara in the highest esteem, often visited her, and more than once sat to her for his portrait. These likenesses were admirably painted, and Leo XII. conferred a similar honor on this ornament of the cloister. Thus were all the accomplishments of Plautilla Nelli the paintress, and Lorenza Strozzi the poetess, revived in the person of the gifted Dolara." She died in 1827, aged 63 years.

—cℴ—

CHAPTER VII.

Pontificate of Benedict XIII. Missions and Martyrs of China. Dominican Saints. Conclusion.

On the death of Innocent XIII. in 1724, the fourth and last pontiff of the Dominican order ascended the chair of S. Peter, in the person of Cardinal Orsini, archbishop of Benevento, who assumed the title of Benedict XIII. His pontificate, which lasted six years, was chiefly remarkable, like those of his predecessors, for its measures of peace and conciliation; and, we may add, for the singular zeal displayed by the venerable Father in the discharge, not only of pontifical, but of pastoral functions. The times were not heroic; and there was little opportunity for a display of great or brilliant qualities; nevertheless, there is a character of touching simplicity in the narrative of Benedict's career, which supplies for the want of more striking interest. But if the Church history of Europe in the eighteenth century was in some degree wanting in sublimity, the same could not be said of her missionary annals. We have necessarily been compelled to pass over in silence much that exhibits the order of Friars Preachers to us in its grandest character, as one of the chief apostolic bodies existing in the Church. Nevertheless, the missions and martyrdoms of China which took place during the pontificate of Benedict XIII. form so very remarkable a portion of her history, that we cannot omit some notice of them in this place.

The number of Christians in China had been greatly increased during the course of the seventeenth century by the labours of the missionaries of various religious orders, especially of the Jesuits and Dominicans. Among the latter, John Baptist Morales, Dominic Navaretto, and Gregory Lopez, a native Chinese, who entered the order of Preachers, and became the first of his nation elevated to the Christian episcopacy, had evangelized a vast tract of country, which retained its hold of the faith in spite of the cruel persecutions to which the new converts were subjected. It was in 1715 that Peter Martyr Sanz set foot on the soil of China; and after the course of a few years he was consecrated bishop of Mauricastro, just at the time when a new persecution of the Christians was in contemplation by the government. The number of converts made by Sanz and his companions was altogether extraordinary, and the rage of the Chinese magistrates was the more excited from the circumstance of many of the highest rank being among their disciples. But what gave a singular and striking character to the apostolic labours of the bishop of Mauricastro, was his success in winning the Chinese not merely to embrace the Christian faith, but to aim at the highest grades of perfection. The number of Christian virgins desirous of consecrating themselves by vow to God was so great, as to recall the days of the primitive Church, and Sanz knew no better way of meeting their wishes, and giving a lasting character to the religious feeling which had been excited among them, than by the establishment of the third branch of his own order, whose habit was accordingly received by a very considerable number of the new converts.

A very extraordinary revival of fervour followed on

this step, but the Christians were not long left in
tranquillity. In the month of June, 1746, the bishop
and his four companions were seized and carried before
the tribunals, whilst at the same time eleven holy women
of the third order, suspected of having assisted and concealed the missionaries, were likewise arrested. The
Chinese seem on this occasion to have lost the timidity
which so generally distinguishes them. They evinced
their fidelity to their pastors by signs of the most
extraordinary attachment. They followed them on the
road to Fochcu, the capital of the province, kissing their
chains and habits, and refusing to be driven away.
"These Christians," said one of the governors, "honour
the Europeans as though they were gods, or their own
fathers." At Fochcu they were examined under the
torture. The courageous answers of the Christian
virgins were worthy of the saints of the primitive ages;
five of them, after enduring cruel torments, were sent
back to their own homes; the rest were condemned to
the cangue, and other punishments, but their lives were
spared. As to the bishop, he was adjudged worthy of
death, " for perverting the souls of men;" and after
being tormented in the most barbarous manner, beaten,
and torn on the face with iron-pointed gauntlets, the
sentence was carried into execution on the 26th of May,
1747. This glorious martyrdom received additional lustre
from the manner in which it was commemorated by the
supreme pontiff, Benedict XIV., who, in a secret consistory held in the September of the following year,
pronounced a magnificent allocution on the death of
Peter Sanz. By many he was regarded as the proto-
martyr of China, but the Pope corrects this error,
adjudging that honour to belong to another of his
order who had suffered in the previous century, F. Francis
de Capillas.

The names of the four companions of the bishop
deserve our remembrance; they were Francis Serrano,
Joachim Royo, John Alcober, and Francis Diaz. When
the holy prelate was condemned to death, the same
sentence was pronounced on the other missionaries,

and cut in *Chinese characters*, on their f... They were, nevertheless, detained for twenty-eight months in prison, at the end of which time they were ... strangled. During this time the persecution wa... directed against the Chinese Tertiaries, whose num... was very great. We read of one noble confessor of the faith, himself enrolled in the order, by name Liu Matthias, whose three daughters were all consecrated to God under the habit of S. Dominic. In vain did the mandarins call on him to abandon his profession, and give his daughters in marriage. "I will never renounce the holy law of God," was his reply, " nor give my daughters in marriage, who are devoted to serve God in holy virginity." It is with a singular interest that we follow the story of these brethren and sisters of the order among the native Chinese, whose devotion and heroic charity are the reproduction of the virtues of those whose names they bore. One admirable woman expired under repeated torture, and the sisters of the third order at Lienba, where she died, braved every danger to gather round her bed and tend her in her last moments. Many of them were driven into exile; others were cast into prison and cruelly insulted. Some seem to have been living together in a kind of community, for we find a letter from the mandarin charged with the conduct of the persecution, describing his entrance into a house inhabited by four devout women, named Ursula, Lucy, Petronilla, and Isabella, where he had seized books, images and rosaries, belonging to their " perverse law;" and it is evident that whole families of the Christian converts of the martyred missionaries were united in the fellowship of the order. The particular fate of each of these has not been preserved; but though few probably actually suffered death, they must in some sort find a place in our commemoration of the Dominican martyrs of China.

Even in our own day the order has given its blood to the same ungrateful soil. The whole province of eastern Tong-King may be considered as a Dominican mission; and it was there that in 1838, Ignatius Delgado, who had laboured as vicar-apostolic of the province for forty years, expired in prison from the effect of his sufferings ; while his companion and coadjutor, Dominic Henarez, with several religious of the order, was beheaded a few days later. Seven members of the third order likewise gave their blood for Christ at the same time. One of these, Joseph Cank, an old man of seventy, insisted on going to the place of execution clothed in the white habit of his order. Five others were only novices, and not being able to receive the missionary of the district in their prison, they sent him their profession in a letter ; this was in the August of 1839. Our readers will peruse the simple expression of their fervour and faith with no common interest. " We are, all five, novices of the third order," they write, "and we can observe the fasts prescribed by our rule on most days, but not always. We, therefore, beg the father to extend some indulgence to us, and to pardon his children. Moreover, we entreat to be allowed to make our profession according to the said rule of the third order ; and we conjure the father to admit and receive our professions, here written, as if we made it in his hands. Therefore, to the honour of Almighty God, Father, Son, and Holy Ghost, we, Francis Xavier, Dominic, Thomas, Agustin, and Stephen, in your presence, Reverend Father Juan, in the place of the Most Reverend Master-General of the order of Friars Preachers, and of the third order of Penance of S. Dominic, make profession, and promise to live acccording to the rule and constitutions of the third order of S. Dominic, even until death."

" Is it not a touching spectacle," says Père Jandel, the present general of the order, in his preface to the rule of the Tertiaries, " to see five young men, subjected for more than a year to all the horrors of a cruel captivity, accusing themselves and begging pardon for not always observing the fasts and abstinences of their rule with sufficient exactitude." A great number of infidels imprisoned with these generous confessors of the faith were instructed and baptized by them, and afterwards shared their martyrdom, which took place at length eighteen months after their first arrest. They were all strangled, invoking the name of Jesus, on the 19th of December, 1839. These seven Tertiaries were declared venerable by Gregory XVI., who, imitating the example of Benedict XIV., pronounced the eulogy of all the martyrs of the persecution, in a secret consistory held in February, 1840. He gave his approval to the introduction of their process of beatification and canonization in the June following, confirmed by a later decree in 1843; so that it is probable that at some future day the order will be enabled to venerate those heroic martyrs with the highest honours of the Church

Our task is well-nigh ended. Not, indeed, that we pretend to have offered in these hurried and imperfect notices anything like a complete sketch of the Dominican order—hardly even so much as to have indicated the direction in which its most illustrious men are apt to be found. Least of all have we in the foregoing pages given any idea of that which constitutes the true greatness of an order, namely, the calendar of its saints. Yet even this is scarcely to be taken as the fair measure of its sanctity. "Count the stars if thou art able," was the reply given by one of the Roman pontiffs to a person who asked him the number of the Dominican saints. They include a vast variety: men and women of all ranks and all countries, and all phases and developments of holiness, high and low, active and contemplative; yet all with the generic Dominican character of heroic zeal for souls

Twelve, besides the great patriarch himself, have received canonization; namely, S. Hyacinth, S. Raymond Pennafort, S. Peter Martyr, S. Thomas Aquinas, S. Vincent Ferrer, S. Antoninus, S. Louis Bertrand, S. Pius V., S. Catherine of Siena, S. Agnes of Monte Pulciano S. Catherine Ricci, and S. Rose of Lima. Sixty-six have received the inferior order of beatification, twenty of whom are women. Three of the canonized female saints are claimed by the third order, with seventeen of those beatified; whilst among the men, B. Martin Porres, and B. Albert of Bergamo, were also Tertiaries. The rest belong to the two first branches of the order. But it would be an error to suppose that this includes all those whose sanctity is acknowledged by the popular prefix of " Blessed." In fact, scarcely a year now passes without adding to the list; and the newly beatified saints are mostly those of the earlier centuries, who have long been known and revered as such in the chronicles of their order.

And the order is not yet obsolete; involved as it was in the general decay which affected all religious institutions during the last century, we have even in our own day seen it revive with redoubled vigour. France, once the nursery of infidelity, but, as it would seem, destined also in God's Providence to be the nursery of Catholic regeneration, gives her best blood to the ranks of the Friars Preachers,* whose restoration in all the purity of their primitive discipline is going on side by side with the advance of the Catholic Church. Everywhere the white scapular of S. Dominic is reappearing; Italy, France, Belgium, America, and England, are all witnessing the second spring of this obstinate family which follows the fortunes of the Church, and, like her, will not die. Those who watch the times predict for the Church a coming era of unusual greatness; nor can we doubt that if it be so, the order of Friars Preachers will once more have a prominent part to play. We would not, however, be misunderstood; nor in using the words *revival* and *restoration,* would we point to any fanciful bringing back of manners and modes of feeling impossible perhaps in our day. But if we have shown anything by the glance over the history of the Friars Preachers which has occupied these pages, it is that they are emphatically the men of their age, and are ever ready to minister to its

* Not to speak of the influx of French subjects into the religious houses of the order, and of the illustrious living members of the Institute which is carrying on its reform under the government of a Frenchman, the popularity of the Dominicans in France is evinced by the fact that the third order, revived by P. Lacordaire, reckoned already upwards of 2,000 members within five years from its re-establishment.

needs, not by an idealism of the past, but by a vigorous adaptation of their vast resources to the necessities of the present day.

In what way the eternal counsels of God may direct the freshly waking energies of the Church in the next generation, time alone can show ; but if the glories of the Friars Preachers are indeed to have that great revival in the latter times long since prophesied by S. Teresa, we know that they will be developed, as of old, in a loyal adhesion to her living principles ; and that wheresoever and howsoever the Church may pursue her heavenly calling, there will the order of S. Dominic be found labouring in her foremost ranks.

THE END.

A LARGE DISCOUNT *on the annexed prices allowed to the Trade, and to all who buy for sale or distribution.*

CATALOGUE

OF

BOOKS, RELIGIOUS ARTICLES, &C.

PUBLISHED, IMPORTED,

AND FOR SALE,

WHOLESALE AND RETAIL,

BY

P. O'SHEA,

27 BARCLAY STREET, NEW YORK.

COMPRISING

NEW YORK:

P. O'SHEA, 27 BARCLAY STREET.

1867.

P. O'SHEA'S NEW PUBLICATIONS.

THE MOST SPLENDID AND USEFUL WORK EVER ISSUED FROM
THE CATHOLIC PRESS IN AMERICA.

The General History of the Catholic Church,

From the commencement of the Christian era until the present time. By M. L'Abbé J. E. DARRAS, with introduction and notes by the Most Rev. M. J. SPALDING, D. D., Archbishop of Baltimore.

4 vols. 8vo, cloth, beautifully illustrated.........$12 00
    "   "   " beveled edges...................14 00
    "   "   " sheep, marbled edges..........16 00
    "   "   " half Morocco extra............20 00
    "   "   " half Morocco antique..........24 00
    "   "   "   " calf, gilt backs, extra.......24 00
    "   "   " Turkey Morocco, extra gilt edges.32 00

This great work, warmly commended by His Holiness Pope PIUS IX., by the most celebrated Archbishops and Bishops of France and Italy, by the Most Rev. Archbishop SPALDING, of Baltimore, the Most Rev. Archbishop McCLOSKEY, of New York, the Most Rev. Archbishop PURCELL, of Cincinnati, the Most Rev. Archbishop ALEMANY, of San Francisco, and by nearly all the Bishops of the United States, has been published in a style of unsurpassed elegance.

It has been introduced as a TEXT BOOK in the most distinguished Catholic seminaries and colleges in Europe.

It is recommended by the Most Rev. Archbishop SPALDING to every Catholic family in the United States. "AND TO OUR NUMEROUS SEMINARIES, COLLEGES, AND ACADEMIES."

RECOMMENDATIONS

OF

THE GENERAL HISTORY OF THE CHURCH.

Letter from His Holiness Pope Pius IX. to the author of
"The General History of the Church."

DILECTO filio presbytero J. E. DARRAS, Lutetiam Parisiorum

To our beloved Son, J. E. DARRAS, Priest at Paris

PIUS P. P. IX.

PIUS P. P. IX.

Dilecte Fili, Salutem et Apostolicam Benedictionem:

Litteræ Tuæ XIII. Kalendas Aprilis proximi ad nos datæ, quibus exemplar offerre nobis voluisti operis de historiâ Ecclesiæ generali, fuerunt nobis ipsis quam gratissimæ. Significas enim id Tibi fuisse consilii, quod virum certe decet germanæ doctrinæ studio ac singularis erga Nos ipsos sedemque Apostolicam devotionis et observantiæ laude præstantem. Si, ut confidimus, consilio ipsi opus quod adhuc legere Nos non potuimus, exacte respondeat, magno illud usui erit istic futurum addetque omnibus stimulos ad gravissimam eam ecclesiasticorum studiorum partem pœnitius internoscendam. Meritas pro oblato ipso operis munere cum Tibi, Dilecte Fili, persolvimus gratias, omnipotentem Dominum suppliciter

Beloved Son, health and the Apostolic Benediction:

Your letter of the twentieth of March, accompanied by a copy of your General History of the Church, was most grateful to us. The plan of your work testifies your zeal for sound doctrine and your singular and praiseworthy devotion toward us and the Apostolic See. If, as we trust, the work (which we ourselves have not as yet been able to read) fulfills the design proposed, it will be of the greatest use, and will tend to stimulate a more profound study of this most important branch of Ecclesiastical Science. We give you, therefore, beloved son, merited thanks for your offering to us, and we earnestly pray Almighty God that He will multiply and preserve His gifts in you. And as a pledge of this great favor, we

e ..., ut sua in te mu-
n multiplicet ac tueatur.
E' tanti hujus boni auspicium
adjungimus Apostolicam Benedictionem, quam intimo pa-
terni cordis affectu, ipsi Tibi,
Dilecte fili, amanter imperti-
mur.

add the Apostolic Benediction,
which, with the sincere affection of our paternal heart, we
lovingly impart to you.

Datum Romæ apud S. Petrum,
die 8 augusti, anni 1855,
Pontificatus Nostri anno X.

PIUS P. P. IX.

Given at St. Peter's, Rome,
the 8th of August, in the
year of our Lord 1855, and
the tenth of our Pontificate.

PIUS P. P. IX.

From the Most Rev. JOHN McCLOSKEY, D. D., Archbishop of
New York.

DEAR SIR:—I am very glad to learn that you are about
publishing an English version of the excellent Ecclesiastical
History of the Abbé Darras. The auspices under which the
translation is made, will, I am confident, secure for it both
elegance and fidelity. I trust that your laudable enterprise
will meet all due encouragement from the Catholic public.

Very truly, your friend and servant in Christ,

+ JOHN, *Archbishop of New York.*

P. O'SHEA, Esq.
New York, Dec. 12, 1864.

From the Most Rev. M. J. SPALDING, D. D., Archbishop of
Baltimore.

MR. P. O'SHEA:

The conviction grows upon me, that the History of Darras,
so warmly commended by many learned men in France, will
meet a want which has been so long felt in this country—that
of a good Church History, neither too lengthy nor too compen-
dious, and at the same time replete with interesting and
edifying details.

The four volumes which you are publishing contain a rich
array of facts, well stated and well put together, which will be
most agreeable and instructive to our Catholic people, all of
whom will of course seek to obtain the work for family use.
This Church History will also be found very opportune and
useful in our numerous *Seminaries, Colleges,* and *Academies.*
I wish you every success in your praiseworthy undertaking,

and hope you will receive sufficient patronage to defray all
expenses.

†   M. J. SPALDING, *Archbishop of Baltimore.*
Baltimore, *Dec.* 7, 1864.

From the Most Rev. J. B. PURCELL, D. D., Archbishop of
Cincinnati.

CINCINNATI, *Nov.* 15, 1864.
Mr. P. O'SHEA :
DEAR SIR:—Permit me to take this occasion, in answering
your Circular, to signify my concurrence in the judgment pro-
nounced on the Ecclesiastical History of the Abbé Darras.
Please send me five copies in volumes, cloth binding.
Respectfully yours,
†   J. B. PURCELL, *Archbishop of Cincinnati.*

EXTRACTS FROM THE LETTERS

OF

EMINENT FRENCH AND ITALIAN PRELATES,

TO THE

AUTHOR OF THE "GENERAL HISTORY OF THE CHURCH."

From MONSEIGNEUR PARISIS, Bishop of Arras.

I have read nearly the whole of the first volume of your
General History of the Church, and I have only congratulations
to address to you upon the work. Its spirit is excellent, its
doctrine sound, and its style clear and unaffected. To have
ranged the facts of ecclesiastical history according to the succession of pontiffs, just as the events of a kingdom are frequently related in the order of reigns, is a very happy innovation.
Your work is in every respect truly admirable. We see in it,
distinctly portrayed, the Fathers of the Church and their
writings, the martyrs and their sufferings, the heretics and
their numerous errors. The Holy Scriptures, the canon law,
and the whole discipline of the Church, are alike admirably
expounded.
I do not hesitate to say to you, if the other three volumes
are equal to the first, that your General History of the Church
will become a class-book of the highest usefulness in our
seminaries.
†   P. L., *Bishop of Arras.*

From MONSEIGNEUR DEBELAY, Archbishop of Avignon.

We have caused the work to be examined by a competent judge, * * * and knowing well the excellent spirit by which M. L'Abbé is animated and his filial love for the Church, we approve and recommend his work.

† J. M. M., Archbishop of Avignon.

From MONSEIGNEUR CASANELLI D'ISTRIA, Bishop of Ajaccio.

I received your first two volumes in Rome, and after having examined them in my own way, I submitted them to the examination of two eminent men of learning here, Monseigneur Tizzani, Professor in the Roman University, and the celebrated Jesuit Father, Rev. P. Ballerini, Professor in the Roman College, no less renowned in the Holy City for his profound erudition.

I have the satisfaction of making known to you the fact that these rigid censors agree with me in the high estimate I have formed of your work. If the last two volumes are equal to the first (and of this I have no doubt), I shall not hesitate to request the superiors of my seminaries to adopt it in their institutions as the text-book of Ecclesiastical History; and I shall congratulate myself on having been one of the first to profit by the fruit of your labors. Meanwhile, may your enterprise prove a complete success, and may God bless a pen so usefully employed in the service of our Holy Mother the Church.

† X. T. RAPHAEL, Bishop of Ajaccio.

From MONSEIGNEUR DE SEGUR, Auditor of the Tribunal of the Rota, at Rome.

For a long time past the friends of the Holy See and of the Church were anxious to see a good Ecclesiastical History, short yet complete, interesting in style, truly Catholic, yet moderate and impartial, and fit to be used both by the clergy and the laity. Allow me to congratulate you on your having been chosen by the Almighty to execute so important a work, and to have fulfilled so successfully all the conditions of your arduous task.

In this age of logic and common sense, the evil and the good tend more and more to separate, and soon there will be, without doubt, only two adverse camps in the world: - Christianity and the Catholic Church on the one side, socialistic revolution and infidel philosophy on the other. Let us all work, each according to his measure, to increase the ranks of God's army; and let us humbly thank our Lord when He permits us to serve in His holy cause. * * *

L. G. De Segur.

From Very Rev. FATHER ETIENNE, Superior-General of the Lazarists.

I have charged with the examination of your work two Fathers who have been Professors of History for many years in the schools of our society. They unite in praising it in the highest terms. I therefore cheerfully add my approbation of your History to the many indorsements which you have received, and which no doubt you will still receive from other sources.

ETIENNE, Superior-General.

Lingard's History of England.

From the latest revised London edition, in 13 vols., 12mo, beautifully illustrated with fourteen fine line engravings on steel, by GOODALL, including a beautiful and correct portrait of the author from an original painting by LOVER.

TERMS:

Thirteen vols., large 12mo, cloth....................$16 00
"   "   "   "   sheep, library style.........20 00
"   "   "   "   half-calf extra, marble edges..28 00

This is undeniably the standard History of England. No library should be without it. No other writer, it is universally acknowledged, has made use of the vast mass of materials bearing on the History of England, with so much impartiality, skill, industry and ability as LINGARD. MACAULAY and HALLAM, rivals in the same field, have both acknowledged his superior merits. DANIEL WEBSTER asserted that there was no other work worthy the name of History of England, except Lingard's. To the lawyer who would make himself thoroughly acquainted with the growth of the common law and the Constitution of England, Lingard's History is indispensable. To the general reader, perhaps there is no work so interesting and instructive. It abounds in events and incidents related in a style unsurpassed for beauty and elegance. The arrangement is clear and simple, and on the margin of each page are to be found the dates of the occurrences related therein.

The American Republic.

Its Constitution, Tendencies and Destiny. By O. A. Brownson, Esq., LL. D. 1 vol., 8vo, 456 pp.

Cloth plain.............................$3 00
Half calf extra...........................5 00

EXTRACTS FROM NOTICES OF THE PRESS.

After a general introduction, Dr. Brownson proceeds to discuss, in seven chapters, Government, its Origin, and its Constitution; and having thus settled the leading principles of his political belief, applies them to the consideration of the United States, the Constitution of the United States, Secession, Reconstruction, the Political Tendencies, and Political and Religious Destiny of the Republic. The topics are such as come home to every intelligent citizen, and they are treated in a manner which will interest large classes of readers who are commonly repelled by works on political science. As the ablest and most matured of the author's publications, it will doubtless receive what it unquestionably deserves—the thoughtful attention of thinking minds.

We have neither time nor space to indicate our points of agreement with, or dissent from, Dr. Brownson's logic, and indeed the interest of the book does not depend on the reader's sympathy with the writer's views. He is a born reasoner, as some other men are born poets; he must have toyed with the syllogism in his cradle; and among all American writers, he is perhaps the only one who has succeeded in giving to consecutive argumentation the interest and charm of narrative. His reasoning fastens the attention like other men's stories; he delights in the process himself, and his readers and hearers catch it by infection; and from the time he first unfolded to the working-men of Boston the metaphysics of Cousin, to the present day, he has never lost the power of presenting the most abstruse and intricate problems in clear, forcible, logically-connected and captivating statements. In the present volume this power is exhibited in its most attractive form; and as the subject is of the utmost importance, while its treatment is as vigorous as it is perspicuous, it would seem that the book must obtain a multitude of readers.—*Boston Transcript.*

This is no ordinary book. It gives us the mature conclusions of a mind long schooled in religious and political philosophies, and conscientiously devoted to the pursuit of Truth. It is undeniably of that class of intellectual achievements which build up the highest reputations, and resist alike,

1*

with a recoil fatal to all assaults, the artillery of denunciation and the slow corrosion of intentional neglect.—*New York Tablet.*

There can be no doubt that this work will give rise to conflicting opinions, and notices of the most antagonistic character. But the work will outlive it all, and remain a lasting monument of a great mind and a patriotic heart. We venture to say that this work will not only remain as one of reference, but actually a TEXT-BOOK in our Catholic schools. —*Boston Pilot.*

The Gentle Skeptic,

Or Easy Conversations of a Country Justice on the Authenticity and Truthfulness of the Old Testament Records. By Rev. C. WALWORTH. New and Revised Edition. 1 vol., 368 pp., 8vo.

Cloth......................................$1 50
" gilt edges, beveled......................2 50
Half-calf, extra...........................3 75

From the Catholic World of January, 1867.

"The Gentle Skeptic, by Rev. C. A. WALWORTH, now pastor of St. Mary's Church, Albany, treats of several topics here noticed in a cursory manner. This work is the result of several years' close and accurate study in theology and science. It has, therefore, the solidity and elaborate finish of a work executed with care and diligence by one who is both a strong thinker and a sound scholar. In style it is a model of classic elegance and purity, and in every respect it deserves a place among the best works of English Catholic literature. The author has broke ground in a field of investigation which it is imperative on Catholic scientific men to work up thoroughly. The entire change which has taken place in the attitude of science toward revealed religion within a few years, and in the doctrines of science themselves, makes the old works written on the connection between religion and science to a great degree useless. The subject needs to be taken up afresh, and handled in manner adequate to the present intellectual wants of the age."

Henry Clay's Works,

The Life, Correspondence, and Speeches of Henry Clay. Six volumes, 8vo. By CALVIN COLTON, LL. D.

Cloth, beveled, uncut edges..... .... $18 00

Sheep, library style............................ 20 00
Half calf, extra.............................. 25 00

FROM THE NEW YORK TIMES.

A new edition of the *Life, Correspondence, and Speeches of Henry Clay,* handsomely printed on tinted paper, in six portly octavo volumes, has just been published by Mr. P. O'SHEA. This important work, originally issued in separate volumes, at long intervals, under the editorial care of the late CALVIN COLTON, has undergone a thorough revision, both in the arrangement of the subject-matter and the correction of typographical and other accidental errors. It now appears in a form and dress worthy of the memory of one of the most illustrious statesmen of the Republic.

FROM THE NEW YORK TRIBUNE.

This edition of Clay's Works is gotten up in the very best manner.

FROM THE BOSTON PILOT.

We congratulate Mr. O'Shea on his being able in these hard times to bring forth another edition of such a *costly and splendid work* as the one before us. * * * * From no other work can our young men derive better materials or more reliable data to understand the working and nature of our Government, or draw purer inspirations to serve it faithfully, than from Mr. Colton's Life of HENRY CLAY.

The Complete Works of Dean Swift,

including a Life of the Dean, by ROSCOE. Six volumes, large 12mo. Illustrated with a Portrait.

Cloth, extra........................... ....$12 00
Sheep, library style........................ 16 00
Half calf, extra........................... 24 00

This is the only elegant, complete, and readable edition of Swift's Works extant.

EXTRACTS FROM NOTICES OF THE PRESS.

We commend strongly to our readers this magnificent edition of the greatest writer of his age. –*The Irish American.*

This edition of Swift's Works is above all praise. It has been carefully edited and beautifully gotten up.—*Philadelphia Press.*

Life of the Blessed Virgin Mary.

1 vol., 12mo. Printed on superfine paper, and beautifully Illustrated. By Rev. TITUS JOSLIN, author of "Life of St. Francis of Assisium," "Scenes from Life of the B. V. M.," "Star of Bethlehem," &c., &c.

Cloth, plain, illustrated with fine steel engrav-
ing of the Immaculate Conception..........$1 00
Cloth, gilt edges, 3 steel engravings............1 50
Turkey Morocco, extra.....................3 00

This beautiful tribute to the Immaculate Mother of God, from the glowing pen of its pious author, must prove a welcome acquisition to the Catholic literature of America. Its superb mechanical execution, embracing the finest paper, most beautiful typography, excellent illustrations, and richest binding, must render it as desirable an ornament in a Catholic household as its contents are interesting and edifying.

The Life of St. Joseph.

Translated from the French of the Abbé P—, Vicar-General of Evreux. To which are added Prayers and Devotions for the Month of March, consecrated to his honor. 1 vol., 12mo.

Cloth, plain............................. $1 50
"   gilt edges 2 00

The Life of St. Dominic,

and a Historical Sketch of the Dominican Order, with an Introduction by the Most Rev. J. S. ALEMANY, D.D., Archbishop of San Francisco. 1 vol., 12mo.

Cloth, extra $1 50
"   "   gilt edges.......................2 00

There is no department of Catholic literature so interesting and instructive as the Lives of Saints, and there is not, in the whole range of sacred biography, a more interesting and important work than the Life of St. Dominic and the sketch of his renowned Order now presented to American readers under the auspices of the learned and distinguished Archbishop of San Francisco.

The Life of St. Anthony of Padua.

By FATHER SERVAIS DIRKS, Friar Minor, Recollect of

the Belgian Province. Translated from the French.
1 vol., 12mo.

Cloth, plain.............................$1 50
"   gilt edges..........................2 00

The incidents of St. Anthony's life are here related in a
charming manner. Even without the fascination of style,
this book could not fail to be popular, so remarkable are the
various incidents and miraculous occurrences of the Saint's
life.

The Life of St. Zita,

A servant-girl of Lucca, in the thirteenth century. Translated from the French of the Baron DE MONTREUIL. To
which is added, the Life of Catherine Teaghokuita, the
Iroquois Virgin, by Father DE CHARLEVOIX, of the Society of Jesus.

1 vol., 18mo., cloth ....60 cents.
"   "   " gilt edges.............90   "

Here is a book which should be read not only by every
servant-girl, but also by every Catholic in America. It shows
how the Church, like her Divine Master, honors the poor as
well as the rich, according to their deserts. The Servant-girl
of Lucca is a model, which not only servant-girls, but all
others, will find worthy of imitation.

History of the Pontificate and Captivity of Pope Pius VI.;

Together with a glance at the Catholic Church. Translated from the French by Miss H***rit, a graduate of
St. Joseph's, near Emmitsburg, Maryland. 1 vol., 18mo,
cloth, 240 pp., 60 cents.

A more intensely interesting narrative has rarely, if ever,
been written. The heroic devotion and constancy of the
Pope, the insanely rabid conduct of his persecutors, his meekness under every contumely, *their* vexation at the calm resignation with which he bore every affront, together with the
many important events which then agitated the Christian
world, invest this volume with an interest which rarely attaches to any book.

The Star of the North.

Life of the Right Rev. Bishop MAGINN. By THOMAS D'ARCY McGEE, Esq. 1 vol., 12mo, cloth, $1.00.

NOTICES OF THE PRESS.

The life of this great champion of the Irish church, so full of apostolic zeal, moral courage, and iron fortitude, cannot fail to attract the Catholic reader.—*Baltimore Catholic Mirror.*

The history of the Right Rev. Bishop MAGINN is the history of one of the most deeply interesting epochs of Irish history—the close of a religious struggle for the freedom of religious worship, and the beginning of a yet unfinished struggle for national independence. * * * We commend this book as a valuable addition to Irish literature in America, which Mr. McGEE has done so much to foster and to establish.—*Philadelphia Catholic Herald and Visitor.*

We have not often read so interesting a work as this memoir is.—*N. Y. Truth Teller.*

Life of St. Francis of Assisium.

By Rev. TITUS JOSLIN. 1 vol., 18mo, cloth, gilt back, 45 cents.

NOTICES OF THE PRESS.

Thank you, Father JOSLIN, for writing this interesting and earnest little volume.—*N. Y. Freeman's Journal.*

It is a charming history of the life of one of the humblest and most devoted servants of the Lord.—*N. Y. Truth Teller.*

FATHER HEWIT'S

HIGHLY INTERESTING AND EDIFYING WORKS

I.

Life of Guendaline, Princess Borghese,

Translated from the German, with an introduction by Rev. A. F. HEWIT. 1 vol., 18mo, cloth, 45 cents.

We are delighted to see this admirable little life of so exemplary a Catholic of our own times. The subject is one of interest, and the style of the translator is particularly agreeable. *N. Y. Freeman's Journal.*

We have often to commend books with words of praise, since no other would be exactly suitable, although they scarcely merit what the words convey. The present volume is an exception. It is in reality equally interesting and edifying, and forms a most promising commencement of the New Catholic Library commenced by Mr. O'SHEA. The Life of Guendaline Talbot reads like a story of romance, yet it is all true. *St. Louis Leader.*

II.

Life of the Egyptian Aloysius;

Or, The Little Angel of the Copts, by Rev. Father BRESCIANI. Translated from the Italian by Rev. A. F. HEWIT.

```
1 vol., cloth, plain........................ ..................$0 75
    "       "      gilt edges........................1 00
```

NOTICES OF THE PRESS.

This is one of the most delightful little biographies we have ever laid eyes on, and we hope it will find its way into every separate school, and every other Catholic institution in the Province. A life of a saint of the ancient Coptic Church is a rarity, especially such an extended one as the present. *Toronto (Canada) Mirror.*

This English version is beautiful and fascinating. It is put forth as a literal one; but while we doubt not that it is an

exact reproduction of the original, we can recognize in it
none of the dryness or stiffness of style characteristic of proclaimed literal translations. Indeed, we cannot see any noble
feature in the English dress of the memoir, that is not to be
discerned in the translator's edifying introduction. The artistic and glowing touches of the same evenly guided pen are
visible throughout the whole work, and one must be hyper-
critical to an extreme who fails to observe and appreciate the
many charming merits either of the original prefatory remarks
of the translator or the translation of the biography itself.

Had we room, we would gladly quote some portions of the
work, which seems to us singularly beautiful and entertaining.
However, we are obliged to content ourselves with what we
have said in favor of the publication, and again recommending it to the notice of every thoughtful Catholic reader.—
N. Y. Truth Teller.

III.

Life of a Modern Martyr, Bishop Borie.

By Rev. A. F. HEWIT.

1 vol., 18mo, cloth, gilt back..................$0 50

NOTICES OF THE PRESS.

This is another of Father Hewit's edifying little books. His
name is a sufficient recommendation, yet we cannot avoid
calling especial attention to this life of a faithful servant of
God, not alone on account of the Christian heroism it illustrates, and the attractive style in which it is presented, but
also because the subject of Catholic missions is one which deserves the greatest attention.—*N. Y. Freeman's Journal.*

This beautiful book presents to us a memoir of one of the
most truly heroic men of modern times. His burning zeal
led him to the remote regions of Tonquin to spread the conquests of Christianity, where he labored, in despite of the
most cruel persecution, until his blood was shed under the
glorious banner of the Cross.— *Catholic Herald.*

The Life of Blessed Paul of the Cross.

Founder of the Congregation of Discalced Clerks, of the
Most Holy Cross and Passion of Jesus Christ. Written
by Father Pius of the name of Mary, consultor-general of
the same congregation. Translated by Father Ignatius
of St. Paul, consultor for the Anglo-Hibernian Province.
First American edition, with the approbation of the

Very Rev. Dominic Tarletini, Provincial of the Passionists
in the United States.

1 vol. 12mo, cloth $0 75
" " " gilt edge. 1 12

The Life of St. Bridget.

"The Mary of Erin." By an Irish Priest.

1 vol., 18mo, cloth plain. ... ...60 cents.
" " " gilt edges.............90 "

A more extended account of the life of this great Saint, so
much revered, and so dear to the Catholics of Ireland, had long
been looked for.

The publisher is happy to be able to announce at last the
publication of such a work.

The Life of Mary Magdalen;

Or, the Path of Penitents. By the Rev. THOMAS S.
PRESTON, author of the "Ark of the Covenant."

1 vol., 18mo, cloth.....................60 cents.

Such a book has long been needed. It now appears from
a masterly pen, and is well calculated to do all the good which
a work of this kind could be instrumental in effecting.

The Life and Miracles of St. Philomena, Virgin and Martyr.

Whose sacred body was lately discovered in the cata-
combs at Rome, and from thence transferred to Mugnano,
in the Kingdom of Naples. Translated from the French.

1 vol., 18mo, cloth ....60 cents.
" " " gilt edges............. 90 "

EXTRACT FROM THE PREFACE BY THE SISTERS OF CHARITY
MT. ST. VINCENT, N. Y.

We trust this little volume will serve to enkindle a tender
devotion to the Saint in many a young heart. At the early
age of thirteen years, this true heroine trampled all the vanities
of the world under her feet, and chose to endure multiplied
torments rather than renounce her vow to her crucified Saviour.
What a model of constancy and of every virtue does she
present to us. Let the youthful heart go to her when tried
and with unbounded confidence implore her intercession.

The Life of Bishop Brute.

First Bishop of Vincennes, with sketches describing his recollections of scenes connected with the French Revolution, and extracts from his Journal. By the Rt. Rev. JAMES R. BAYLEY, D. D., Bishop of Newark. New edition.

1 vol., 12mo, illustrated.................... $1 50

BOOKS OF

Instruction, Devotion and Meditation.

Most of these Books are highly approved for distribution at Missions.

THE

WORKS OF SAINT FRANCIS OF SALES.

I.

A Treatise on the Love of God.

By ST. FRANCIS DE SALES. A new translation.
1 vol., large 12mo, over 600 pp., cloth $1 75

NOTICES OF THE PRESS.

We have before us a new translation of that sublime and beautiful treatise on the Love of God by St. Francis de Sales. We have taken some pains to examine into the excellences which should characterize a new translation of such a work, and the ease and beauty of diction, together with the idiomatic correctness of expression throughout, are such as to enable us to give a *most favorable* notice of the rendering of this beautiful treatise.—*Philadelphia Catholic Herald.*

To those who have read the "Devout Life," it will be only necessary to say of the style of this treatise, that its beauties are those with which they are already familiar; but there is a depth of thought and of feeling here beyond what we find in any other writings of St. Francis. The translation is very creditable. We hope this work will meet with the circulation which it well merits, and of which the present excellent edition seems to promise assurance. —*Baltimore Catholic Mirror.*

This handsome volume is a valuable addition to the ascetic literature of the English language. It is a mine of rich thought concerning that virtue which was the distinguishing characteristic of its author. It appears to have been carefully translated, and to give the name of its publisher is equivalent to saying that it is a creditable specimen of book-making. *Boston Pilot.*

Of the work itself it would be superfluous to speak—a work which is remarkable alike for its deep philosophy and theology, and its sweet, unaffected piety. We are glad to see the work placed within the reach of the English reader, and we hope it will take the place of the light superficial, sentimental devotional works which have become so fashionable in late years. Its constant study and meditation will render our piety solid and robust as well as tender. St. Francis was in some sort the apostle of Calvinists, and his are the best works extant for Catholics who live in a Calvinistic country like ours.— *Brownson's Review.*

II.

The Introduction to a Devout Life.

By St. Francis of Sales. To which is added a Sketch of his Life.

    1 vol., 24mo, cloth, plain . . . . .60 cents.
      "   18mo,   "   " 75   "

This book is beyond all praise. Its reputation is world-wide. Perhaps there is no other work so universal a favorite or so generally useful as this.

III.

The Spirit of St. Francis of Sales.

By the Bishop of Belley. Translated from the French by a Priest of the Diocese of Boston.

    1 vol., 12mo, cloth, beveled $2 00

The *Philadelphia Catholic Standard* says:

"This work of Bishop Camus is so well known to the admirers of the sainted Bishop of Geneva, that the mere announcement of its appearance in an English dress will secure

for it a wide circulation. The author enjoyed for years the
familiar and intimate friendship of St. Francis de Sales, and
during this time treasured up many of his sayings and doings
which he has given to the world in this volume. Though St.
Francis is well known for his works, it is his "spirit" that
makes his name immortal. In this book, written by his friend,
he teaches by example, and instills into the mind and heart
some of his own gentle earnestness. It is peculiarly adapted
to ecclesiastics, who will find in it a mine of sound, practical
instruction."

THE BEST MEDITATION BOOK.

JUST PUBLISHED,

Crasset's Meditations for every Day in the Year.

Translated from the French by Mrs. ANNA H. DORSEY.
With an Introduction by Rev. C. WALWORTH.

1 vol., large 12mo, cloth $1 80

The Rev. Father Walworth, in his Introduction, says:

" Of meditation books we know of none which seem to
fulfill their purpose, except this work of Father Crasset. * * *
We repeat once more, for those who aspire, not simply to read
meditations, but to practice mental prayer, this work of Father
Crasset is the BOOK OF BOOKS.

NOTICES OF THE PRESS ON CRASSET'S MEDITATIONS.

These Meditations, perhaps the most popular and celebrated of any in Europe, rich in matter and well-arranged in
form, should be hailed with pleasure by English-speaking
Catholics. It is no common book of meditations, and should
receive no common welcome. Mrs. Dorsey is esteemed as a
translator, and has no doubt done her duty well. Mr. O'Shea
has had the book well printed and on good paper.—*New York
Freeman's Journal.*

The best of meditation books.—*New York Tablet.*

Many of the meditation books that are to be found in the
book-shops are mere books of spiritual reading, all the points
in them being elaborated to such an extent as to leave nothing
to the mind of the meditator to work out. Others err in the
opposite direction, and are mere bald collections of heads of
topics for meditation. Father Crasset's work is free from
both of these objections. It is eminently suggestive and practical. *For people living in the world, it is the best manual of
meditation that we know of.—Boston Pilot.*

('s Meditations, translated by Mrs. Anna H. Dorsey, is a most necessary book, for no one book of Meditations can supply the varied demand of those who cultivate mental prayer. We have now two solid, excellent works—Challoner's and Crasset's. In spite of our familiarity with the former, and our reverence for its sterling worth, we are almost forced to admit that for ordinary meditation *Crasset is the book of books*. It will bear comparison with the highest standards of piety. We wish it the widest circulation, for it will prove a spiritual treasure wherever its use obtains. *Catholic Mirror.*

The Sufferings of our Lord Jesus Christ.

By FATHER THOMAS OF JESUS. 1 vol., 12mo, cloth, beveled, $2. This is the great standard book of Meditation and Instruction on the Life and Sufferings of our Lord.

The *Catholic World* says of it:

"This is a work composed by a great saint, and justly deserving of the great reputation it has always enjoyed as one of the best of spiritual books. It contains an inexhaustible mine of meditation, sufficient to last a person during his whole life, and just as new and fresh after the hundredth perusal as during the first. It is as a book for meditation that it should be used, and for this purpose it cannot be too highly recommended to religious communities or to devout persons in the world who desire and need a guide and model for the practice of meditation."

The Sufferings of Jesus.

By CATHERINE EMMERICH. Translated by a SISTER OF MERCY. 1 vol., 18mo.

Cloth, with a fine steel Engraving of the
 "Agony in the Garden"................60 cents.

This is a very attractive little volume, relating to the passion and death of our Saviour. The authoress is represented as having been favored with visions during the holy season of Lent, in which she spiritually witnessed the progress of the "Sufferings of Jesus." What was thus revealed to her she describes in a graceful style, which this condensed translation presents unimpaired to edify the reader."—*N. Y. Truth Teller.*

Persons of contemplative minds can have no better guide to the thrilling scenes of Calvary than the Sufferings.—*N. Y. Tablet.*

Here is an excellent book, and is a valuable addition to our books of devotion. It is got out in good style, and is embellished with a beautiful engraving of our Blessed Lord in his agony.—*Boston Pilot.*

Spiritual Progress.

By Rev. J. W. Cummings, D. D., late Pastor of St. Stephen's Church, New York.

1 vol., 12mo, cloth, red edges................$1 50

The *Cincinnati Catholic Telegraph* says of it:

" After a careful perusal of the work, we beg to advise our readers to purchase, preserve, and attentively read it. It is a work of merit."

Selections from the Writings of Fenelon.

With an introduction by Rev. Thomas S. Preston, and a sketch of the life of Fenelon, by J. G. R. Hassard.

1 vol., 12mo, cloth, plain...................$1 25
"   "   " gilt edges 1 75

This book is a gem.—*Catholic Telegraph.*

We have nowhere else seen so much of beautiful sentiment, solid instruction, and sound philosophy combined.—*Nat. Quarterly Review.*

The Following of Christ.

In four books, by Thomas à Kempis. Translated from the Latin by Rt. Rev. Richard Challoner, D. D.

1 vol., 48mo, beautiful type, cloth, plain...... $0 40
"   "   "   "   " gilt edges... 60
Roan, gilt edges........ 75
Turkey Morocco, extra.....................1 50

The Spiritual Combat;

Or, the Christian Defended against the Enemy of his

Salvation. 1 vol., 48mo, uniform with "The Following of Christ."

Cloth, plain..............................40 cents.
   "   gilt edges........................60   "
Roan, "   " 75   "

The Spiritual Combat was the favorite book of ST. FRANCIS DE SALES. He always carried it in his pocket.

Instructions on the Commandments and Sacraments.

Translated from the Italian of ST. ALPHONSUS M. LIGUORI. 1 vol., 48mo, uniform with "The Following of Christ' Cloth, plain, 40 cents.

A Treatise on Prayer.

By ST. ALPHONSUS LIGUORI. 1 vol., 48mo, cloth, uniform with the above, 40 cents.

THE BEST BOOK FOR THE MONTH OF MAY.

The Ark of the Covenant :

Or, a series of short Discourses upon the Joys, Sorrows, Glories, and Virtues of the Ever Blessed Mother of God. By Rev. THOMAS S. PRESTON. 1 vol., 18mo, cloth, plain, 60 cents.

A Month of May:

Or, Scenes from the Life of the Blessed Virgin Mary. Arranged for the devotions of the month of May, with practices, prayers, and examples. 1 vol., 32mo, cloth, 38 cents

SOME OF THE NOTICES OF THE PRESS.

This is a precious little jewel case, containing a number of the most precious pearls of the crown of the Immaculate Virgin Mother. They are really brilliant, quite free from common place, and wrought in sparkling style, so that they are beyond all praise. We warmly commend this beautiful book to every household. It cannot be read without having our love for our Blessed Lady increased.—*Philadelphia Catholic Herald.*

This little book is a gem. * * * It is beautifully gotten up. —*N. Y. Freeman's Journal.*

The Little Month of the Holy Infancy;

Or, the First Mysteries of the Life of Our Lord Jesus Christ, PROPOSED TO THE IMITATION OF YOUTH. Translated from the French of the Abbé LETOURNEUR, V. G. of Soissons, and dedicated to the members of the Society of THE HOLY CHILDHOOD. 1 vol., 18mo, cloth, 63 cents.

This is the most instructive, interesting, and edifying book, especially for *youth*, that has ever fallen under our notice. It presents in the most charming manner an account of the first years of the life of our Divine Lord, with suitable reflections. Each chapter contains a happily conceived colloquy between the Infant Saviour and the youthful Christian reader, and closes with a beautiful HISTORICAL EXAMPLE well calculated to impress upon the mind principles of true Christian heroism, always inseparable from the performance of simple daily duties.

Give this book to your children and neglect not to read it yourselves.

Think Well On't;

Or, REFLECTIONS ON THE GREAT TRUTHS OF THE CHRISTIAN RELIGION for every day of the month. By Rt. Rev. R. CHALLONER, D. D. 1 vol., 32mo, cloth, 30 cents.

This is decidedly the most beautiful edition extant of this famous book of Bishop CHALLONER.

Via Crucis;

Or, the Stations of the Holy Way of the Cross. Paper covers, 6 cents. $4 per 100 copies.

New Testament.

24mo. A beautiful pocket edition. Printed from pearl

type. With the approbation of the Most Rev. JOHN
McCLOSKEY, D. D., Archbishop of New York.

No. 1. Cloth $0 40
      2. Roan, embossed, plain edges............ 60
      3.   "   "   gilt   " 75
      4. Turkey Morocco, extra................2 25

Douay Bible.

24mo. A beautiful pocket edition.   In press.

The Manual of the Confraternities.

Containing the Stations of the Cross, and the form of
erecting and blessing them; the Scapular of the Blessed
Trinity; the Scapular of the Passion; the Scapular of
the Immaculate Conception; the Scapular of the Seven
Dolors; the Scapular of Mount Carmel, Via Matris, Living Rosary, &c., &c.   1 vol., 32mo, cloth, 45 cents.

POEMS, TALES, LEGENDS, &c., &c.

The Rosa Mystica:

or, Mary of Nazareth. The Lily of the House of David.
By MARIE JOSEPHINE.

     1 vol., 12mo, extra, cloth, red edges $2 00
      "   "   "   "   gilt edges 3 00

The gifted author of this, while yet a Protestant, and with
no intention of becoming a Catholic, conceived the idea of
giving in poetry the life of the Blessed Virgin; and after she
had completed it, the present work, "Rosa Mystica," she
formally renounced Protestantism and professed Catholicism
a striking example of the fact that our holy religion requires
only investigation in order to be adopted. The work is an
unique gem. It possesses much fervent piety, poetical excellency
and originality. Its tender devotional sentiments toward our
Blessed Mother and its literary merits will instruct and please
any one who appreciates the good and the beautiful. *Cincinnati Catholic Telegraph.*

Rosa Immaculata.

or, Tower of Ivory in the House of Anna and Joachim.

A Poem by MARIE JOSEPHINE, author of "Rosa Mystica."
1 vol., 12mo, uniform with Rosa Mystica, $2; gilt
sides and edges, $3.

The Siege of Spoleto.

A Poem by MICHAEL J. A. McCAFFERY, M. A.

1 vol., 12mo, cloth...................... $0 75
"   "   superfineed................... 1 00

This is a poem of very rare merit. The story of the Siege
of Spoleto will always possess historic interest. It is recited in
this charming poem in a manner which happily combines
historic fidelity with poetical grace and vivacity.

Agnes Hilton ;

or, Practical Views of Catholicity, a tale of trials and
triumphs, by Miss MARY J. HOFFMAN. 1 vol., 12mo,
cloth, $1 50.

This is unquestionably the most charming, and at the same
time the most useful Catholic tale that we have yet had from
the pen of an American writer. It has received high praise
from the secular as well as the Catholic press. Perhaps
no better book could be placed in the hands of a non Catholic
reader in order to give in an attractive manner a broad and
clear view of the teaching and practices of the Church.

Bickerton ;

or, The Immigrant's Daughter. A tale of the times. By
the author of "Harry Layden," &c. 1 vol., 12mo, cloth,
60 cts.

NOTICES OF THE PRESS.

This is an excellent story, and well suited to the times.—
Brownson's Review.

Any work like the Immigrant's Daughter, whose tendency
is to wither or uproot bigotry and intolerance, ought to be
welcomed by every man who loves the country and its institutions, and is animated by the holy principle of Patrick Henry
—"Give me liberty or give me death."—*N. Y. Citizen.*

This is an excellent little work of fiction, grounded on the
present aspect of political affairs in this country. It is a true

narrative of the sufferings of many a poor immigrant, and will be read with interest. *N. Y. Irish American.*

This is an interesting story, and will be read with great interest at the present time, as it dips into the Know Nothings in grand style. The book is well gotten up by the publisher.- *Boston Pilot.*

Edma and Marguerite.

A tale by the author of the "Orphan of Moscow." 18mo, cloth, gilt back, 60 cents.

NOTICES OF THE PRESS.

It is a highly pleasing story for young persons, illustrative of the duty, pleasure, and reward of filial devotion, charity, and friendship. *Philadelphia C. Herald.*

A truly edifying and interesting story.—*N. Y. Truth Teller.*

The Young Communicants.

By the author of "Geraldine." 1 vol., 18mo, cloth, 38 cents.

It is unnecessary to point out the merits of a book written by the author of "Geraldine." It may not, however, be out of place to say that Father Joslin especially recommends it as a most instructive and interesting book, in a note in that excellent prayer book, the Star of Bethlehem.

Legends of the Blessed Virgin.

Translated from the French of Colin de Plancy, and published with the approbations of the Archbishop of Paris and his Eminence Cardinal Wiseman.

1 vol., 12mo, cloth $0 90
" " " gilt edges 1 50
These legends have a world wide celebrity.

Filial and Fraternal Piety

By Brother PHILIPPE, Superior-General of the Brothers of the Christian Schools. Translated from the French by CHRISTINE FARVILLE.

1 vol., 18mo, cloth......... .... 60 cents.
" " gilt edges..... .....90 "

This book contains over one hundred remarkable and well authenticated EXAMPLES of the blessings that attend filial duty, and of the awful retribution which has followed contempt or neglect of this sacred duty. Each of these examples is an interesting, sometimes a DELIGHTFUL OR A THRILLING NARRATIVE.

These remarkable narratives are presented under the following heads:

I. Love for Parents.
II. Respect for Parents.
III. Bearing with the Faults of our Parents.
IV. Respect due to Old Age.
V. Obedience to Parents.
VI. Bodily Assistance due to Parents.
VII. Spiritual Assistance due to Parents.
VIII. Concord between Brothers and Sisters.

The Children of the Patriarchs;

or, The Six Hundred Thousand Combatants Conquering the Promised Land. By Brother PHILIPPE, Superior-General of the Christian Brothers, author of "Examples of Filial and Fraternal Piety," &c.

1 vol., 18mo, cloth.........................$0 75
"   "   "   gilt edges................. 1 00

In this beautiful volume, all the more striking incidents of the Old Testament are presented in a manner admirably suited for young persons. It fills a void that has been long felt in our religious literature for the young.

The Sheaf.

By M. ALFRED DES ESSARTS. Translated from the French by CHRISTINE FARVILLE.

1 vol., 18mo, cloth $0 90
"   "   "   gilt edges............... 1 20

PREFACE.

As we deliver up to the public the simple narratives that form this volume, we think it well to explain both its title and its aim. There are all kinds of sheaves: sheaves of flowers in spring, sheaves of corn in summer. As provident people, let us make for the long evenings of the latter end of autumn, for those long nights that claim moral amusement, our sheaf of narratives.

Morality has also its flowers, it nourishes like the corn, and the nutrition it gives to the soul should be well chosen. On this head we hope to have attained the aim, and we trust that there will not be found in our sheaf one single sterile shoot that cautious censure would wish to cut off.

May Templeton.

A Tale of Faith and Love. By the author of "Tyborne, and Who Went Thither," &c., &c.

1 vol., 12mo, cloth, plain.. .... $1 50
"   "   gilt edges....................... 2 00

This is perhaps the most elegantly written work in the whole range of Catholic fiction. It exhibits, on the part of its distinguished author, a rare union of genius and common sense, with a very remarkable knowledge of the motives which prompt and influence human action.

Mignon.

A Tale. Translated from the French.

1 vol., 12mo, cloth......................... $1 25
"   "   "   gilt edges................... 1 75

This is a tale of great pathos and brilliancy. It excited a remarkable degree of interest in France, and no doubt will be no less welcome to American readers.

Charming Stories for the Young.

In beautiful bindings, suitable for premiums, and at *very low prices.*

SEBASTIAN'S ONE THOUSAND FRANCS.—Beautifully bound in enameled paper, with bronze lettering.
18mo................. .... $0 12

HENRIETTA. A true story, beautifully bound in enameled paper, with bronze lettering.
18mo 12

GRETCHEN; or, The Chapel of Winkelried. Enameled paper cover, with bronze lettering............... 12

THE FAIRY'S WELL.—Enameled paper cover, with bronze lettering 12

The Secret of Riches.—A Tale of the last Century. Enameled paper cover, with bronze lettering..... $0 12

The Sauremonde.—Tradition of the Black Mountain. Enameled paper cover, with bronze lettering...... 12

Cornelio ; or, the False Vocation.—Enameled paper cover, with bronze lettering.................. 12

Valentine, the Successful Student.—Enameled paper cover, with bronze lettering.............. 12

Adventures and Misfortunes of a Saxon Schoolmaster........................ 15

An Episode of the Russian Campaign........... 15

The same, beautifully bound, in six vols., cloth, viz:—

Sebastian and Fairy's Well.—1 vol., 18mo, cloth.. 30

Henrietta and Gretchen.—1 vol., 18mo, cloth...... 30

Secret of Riches and Sauremonde.—1 vol., 18mo, cloth........................ 30

Cornelio and Valentine.—1 vol., 18mo, cloth...... 30

The Saxon Schoolmaster.   "   "   " 30

The Campaign in Russia.   "   "   " 30

PRAYER BOOKS.

A SPLENDID NEW PRAYER BOOK,

The Manual of the Immaculate Conception.

A collection of prayers for general use, including the most approved devotions to the Blessed Mother of God, selected from authentic sources, with the approbation of the Most Rev. J. McCloskey, D. D., Archbishop of New York. Copiously illustrated with fine steel engravings.

It contains 1220 pages, 18mo, printed on fine white paper, and is the most COMPLETE, COMPREHENSIVE, USEFUL, and ELEGANT PRAYER BOOK now in use.

PRICE.

No. 1. Roan, embossed, 1 plate...................	$1 50
2. " " gilt center and edges, 1 plate....	2 00
3. " " " " " clasp, 1 plate....	2 50
4. " foil gilt sides and edges, 2 plates......	2 50
5. " " " " " clasp, 2 plates.........	3 00
6. Turkey morocco, extra, 7 plates.............	3 50
7. " " " " " and clasp.......	4 00
8. " " " " " beveled........	4 00
9. " " " " " and clasp.......	4 50
10. " " " " " paneled........	5 00
11. " " " " " and clasp......	6 00
12. " " block paneled and tooled edges....	7 00
13. " " " " and clasp........	8 00

In various styles of velvet bindings, from $8 to $20 each.

It had been for a long time the design of the publisher to publish a Prayer Book dedicated to the Patroness of America, and placed under her benign protection, under the title of her IMMACULATE CONCEPTION. It is now his privilege to have fulfilled this design. He devoutly trusts that the MANUAL OF THE IMMACULATE CONCEPTION will not be found unworthy of the high auspices under which it is offered to the Catholics of America. As a general Prayer Book, it will recommend itself to popular use by its COMPLETENESS, ACCURACY, and BEAUTY. But besides containing those devotions generally sought for in a Prayer Book, it contains, also, in a well-arranged manner, nearly all those beautiful prayers to the Holy Mother of God, upon which the Church has put the sacred stamp of her approbation.

NOTICES OF THE PRESS.

The Freeman's Journal says of it : "It is a general Manual of Devotions, and comprises many and well-selected meditations and instructions. Those pious enough to use large prayer books and many devotions will be well satisfied with it. It really strikes us as a meritorious and excellent prayer book."

The Cincinnati *Catholic Telegraph* says: "The 'Manual of the Immaculate Conception,' published by P. O'Shea, New York, and approved by the Most Rev. J. McCloskey, D. D. This is one of the most complete manuals of devotion that we have seen. Besides a large collection of the most beautiful prayers for general use, the Epistles and Gospels for every Sunday and holiday in the year, it contains all the most ap-

proved devotions to our Blessed Mother, under the auspice
the Immaculate Conception of whom it has been publi-l
The amount of matter it contains, all approved by the M.
Rev. Archbishop of New York, may be judged from the fact
that there are 1,114 pages in it. It is well printed, and taste-
fully illustrated, on good paper, and most beautifully bound in
fine morocco."

The St. Louis *Guardian* says: "Mr. O'Shea, the publisher
of New York, has rendered a lasting service to the Catholic
community, by issuing the above excellent book of Devotion.
It combines, with the ordinary prayer book, a manual of special devotions to the Blessed Virgin, with suitable prayers for
Novenas, offices of the Scapular, Epistles, Gospels, &c., for the
year.

The *Metropolitan Record* says: "The fullest and most beautiful manual of prayer ever issued by a New York publisher.
In its pages will be found the devotional exercises to which
the mind instinctively turns in joy or sorrow, in sickness or
suffering, as well as the public offices of the Church for penitential seasons, high festival times, or ordinary occasions;
novenas and litanies; and every approved form of private or
associated prayer. In addition, the 'Manual of the Immaculate Conception' is profusely illustrated, clearly printed, and
handsomely bound."

THE MANUAL OF THE IMMACULATE CONCEPTION contains,
besides the usual devotions to be found in large prayer books—
Novenas for the principal Feasts of the Blessed Virgin.
Novena to Saint Joseph.
Vespers for the Festivals of the Blessed Virgin.
Chaplet of Twelve Stars.
Chaplet of Seven Dolors.
Forty Ave Marie.
Little Office of the Blessed Virgin, in Latin and English.
Office of the Immaculate Conception.
A great number of Indulgenced Devotions to the Blessed
Virgin.
Mass of the Sacred Heart.
Devotions to the Sacred Heart.
Mass for the Dead.
Epistles and Gospels for the Sundays and Festivals through-
out the year, &c., &c., &c.

The Star of Bethlehem

A new and complete Prayer Book, containing—besides the
ordinary devotions to be found in other Prayer Books—

the Epistles and Gospels for all the Sundays and Holidays of the year; the songs to Vespers for Sundays and Festivals, with the original text *Music for each Psalm*. Compiled by the Rev. Titus Joslin. With the approbation of the Most Rev. J. Hughes, D. D., Archbishop of New York. Printed on fine white paper, and beautifully illustrated with fine steel engravings. 18mo, 810 pp.

PRICE.

No. 1. Roan, embossed, plain edges. 1 steel engraving. $1 25
2.   "   "   gilt edges.   2 " engravings.   1 75
3.   "   "   "   " and clasp. 2 steel eng's   2 00
4.   "   Imitation mor., gilt sides, and edges...... 2 00
5.   "   "   "   and clasps............ 2 25
6. Turkey morocco, extra, 6 steel engravings....... 3 50
7.   "   "   "   and clasps, 6 steel eng's   4 00
8.   "   "   beveled edges.   "   " .. 4 00
9.   "   "   " and clasps.   "   " .. 4 50
10.   "   "   paneled..................... 5 00
11.   "   "   " and clasps............. 5 50
12.   "   "   velvet, and clasps.............. 7 00
13.   "   "   " rims and clasps 9 00
14.   "   "   " full ornaments.......... 10 00
15.   "   "   " extra ornaments........

The Star of Bethlehem.

24mo. edition.

No. 16. Roan, embossed, plain edges.   1 plate........ $0 75
17.   "   plain edges, gilt sides.   " 1 00
18.   "   gilt edges and center.   2 plates 1 25
19.   "   "   "   and clasps.   " 1 50
20.   " imitation mor., gilt edges.   " 1 50
21.   "   "   "   and clasps.   " 1 75
22. Turkey morocco.   6 steel engravings.......... 3 00
23.   "   "   and clasps. 2 plates 3 50
24.   "   "   beveled 3 50
25.   "   "   " and clasps........ 4 00
26.   "   "   " paneled.   4 00
27.   "   "   and clasps 4 50
28.   "   "   velvet corners, and clasps 6 00
29.   "   "   " rims................... 6 75
30.   "   "   full ornaments 8 00
31.   "   "   **extra ornaments, from**.... $10 to 20 00

2*

WHAT THE CATHOLIC PRESS SAYS OF IT.

It compares favorably with any Prayer Book published in America.—*N. Y. Freeman's Journal.*

This manual reflects great credit on both the compiler and publisher. It contains over 800 pages of the best selected matter ever put into a Prayer Book, while the paper, printing, and binding are in character with the contents.—*N. Y. Tablet.*

This is a Prayer Book of the largest class, but the cheapest in price, just issued. We observe that those litanies which have been noticed by the most learned of our theologians have been entirely omitted. This feature will certainly commend it, and we speak for it a liberal share of patronage.—*Baltimore Catholic Mirror.*

From our own experience, we can say there is hardly any work so hard to find as a PRAYER BOOK, containing the various devotional aids which a Christian requires in daily life. THE STAR OF BETHLEHEM is most satisfactory in this respect. All the principal services of the Church, all the ordinary necessities of the Christian, are copiously provided for. The prayers at Mass, as well as the preparation for confession and communion, are especially full. *The Vespers also form a noteworthy feature of this volume. It includes the proper psalms for every feast in the year, accompanied by its appropriate bar of music, placed neatly and conspicuously over the psalms.* In short, THE STAR OF BETHLEHEM is a prayer book that can be relied upon. It is printed beautifully, carefully, and attractively, is illustrated with well-executed and appropriate steel engravings, and is substantially bound in a variety of styles, to suit the means of every Catholic.—*N. Y. Truth Teller.*

This very excellent compilation includes the gospels and epistles for the year, and various offices, special devotions, and masses, in addition to the usual contents. The book is well printed in large clean type, and will be found a useful companion and guide to the holy temple.—*Philadelphia Catholic Herald.*

We observe throughout this manual many useful notes and remarks, proofs of the Rev. FATHER JOSLIN's zeal for the interest and welfare of the people intrusted to his care.—*Baltimore Metropolitan Magazine.*

The Paradise of the Christian Soul.

Delightful for its choicest pleasures of piety of every kind. By JAMES MERLO HORSTIUS, of the Church of the Blessed Virgin Mary, in pasculo pastoris, at Cologne. A new and complete translation, by lawf'd authority. 18mo, 1083 pages.

THE PARADISE OF THE CHRISTIAN SOUL, to which access was only had in the Latin language, is the most complete manual of Catholic devotion, meditation, and instruction, ever published. It contains nearly eleven hundred pages of closely but beautifully printed matter, remarkable for its sweet and fervid piety, and its choice and useful instruction. It is, beyond all other books, a FAMILY PRAYER BOOK, and a copy of it should be in every Catholic family.

No. 1. Cloth, plain $1 25
    2. Roan, embossed, plain edges. 1 steel engraving. 1 50
    3.   "   "   gilt edges. 2 " engravings. 2 00
    4. American morocco, gilt sides and edges 4 steel
        engravings............................... 2 25
    5. American morocco, gilt sides and edges, and
        clasp. 4 steel engravings................ 2 50
    6. Turkey morocco, extra. 6 steel engravings.... 3 50
    7.   "   "   " and clasp. 6 steel eng's. 4 00
    8.   "   "   " beveled boards. 6 steel
        engravings. 4 00
    9. Turkey morocco, extra, beveled and clasp. 6
        steel engravings......................... 4 50
   10. Turkey morocco, paneled...... .... 5 00

WHAT THE CATHOLIC PRESS SAYS OF IT.

It contains the most soul-elevating prayers we have ever read.—*Catholic Herald.*

The Mission Book.

A new and improved edition. A Manual of Instructions and Prayers, adapted to preserve the FRUITS OF THE MISSION. Published under the direction of the Missionary Priests of St. Paul. 18mo, 500 pages.

No. 1. Roan, embossed, plain edges.................$1 00
    2.   "   full gilt sides, plain edges.............1 25
    3.   "   embossed, gilt edges...................1 25
    4.   "   "   "   " and clasp...........1 50
    5. Imitation morocco, full gilt sides and edges.......1 50
    6.   "   "   "   "   " clasp...1 75
    7. Turkey morocco, extra.......................3 00

```
 8. Turkey morocco, extra, clasps.... ...............$3 50
 9.     "          "       "   beveled............ ... ...3 50
10.     "          "       "     "    clasps...........4 00
11.     "          "       "   paneled ..............4 50
12.     "          "       "     "    and clasps.......5 00
13.     "          "       "   velvet corners and clasps..6 50
14.     "          "       "     "    rims and clasps.....7 50
15.     "          "       "     "    full ornaments... .9 00
```

The Mission Book.

24mo.

```
No. 16. Roan, plain.................................$0 75
   17.   "   gilt sides.............................. 90
   18.   "   embossed, gilt edges....................1 00
   19.   "       "       "     "   clasps..............1 20
   20.   "   full gilt sides and edges.................1 25
   21.   "       "    "     "        "   clasps...........1 50
   22. Turkey morocco.............................2 00
   23.     "          "     clasp.........................2 50
   24.     "          "     extra....... ............2 50
   25.     "          "     "   clasp....................3 00
   26.     "          "     "   beveled..................3 00
   27.     "          "     "     "   clasp............3 50
   28.     "          "     "   bands and ornaments......5 00
```

The Key of Heaven.

24mo. New and enlarged edition. Containing the Collects, Gospels, the Stations of the Cross, and the Scapulars.

```
No. 1. Cloth, plain.  1 plate.......................$0 50
    2. Roan, embossed................................ 63
    3.   "       "    gilt edges.....................1 00
    4.   "       "       "   and clasp..............1 20
    5.   "   full gilt sides.......................... 90
    6.   "       "    "   edges.  3 plates.............1 25
    7.   "       "    "     "   clasps................1 50
    8. Turkey morocco, extra.......................2 50
    9.     "          "      "   clasp ..............3 00
   10.     "          "      "   beveled. ...........3 00
   11.     "          "      "     "   clasp..........3 50
   12.     "          "   paneled, &c................3 25
   13.     "          "      "   and clasp............3 75
   14.     "          "      "   bands and clasps......5 00
```

15. Turkey morocco, velvet corners and clasps......$5 50
16. "   "   "   bands and clasps..........6 25
17. "   "   "   full ornaments............7 50
18. "   "   "   extra....................

The Key of Heaven.

18mo.   Large type, fine paper.   A superb edition.

No. 19. Roan, plain, with a fine steel engraving........$1 00
20.   "   embossed, gilt edges....................1 25
21.   "   "   "   "   and clasps...........1 50
22.   "   gilt sides............................1 25
23.   "   "   "   and edges....................1 50
24.   "   "   "   "   and clasps..... ....1 75
25. Turkey morocco, extra........................2 75
26.   "   "   "   and clasps........... 3 25
27.   "   "   beveled....................3 25
28.   "   "   "   and clasps...........3 75
29.   "   "   "   paneled......... ....4 00
30.   "   "   "   and clasps............4 50
31.   "   "   "   bands and ornaments ..6 00

The Christian's Daily Guide.

A Manual of Prayers, selected from the most approved sources; containing a great many Indulgenced Prayers. Printed in large type, on fine white paper; beautifully illustrated, with fine steel engravings, besides illustrations of the Rosary of the Blessed Virgin Mary. 32mo.   Approved by the Most Rev. J. McCloskey, D. D., Archbishop of New York.

No. 1. Cloth, plain.................................$0 40
2. Roan,   "   50
3.   "   gilt edges............................. 75
4.   "   "   "   and clasps..................... 90
5.   "   gilt sides 60
6.   "   "   "   and edges.................... 88
7.   "   "   "   "   "   and clasps.......... 1 00
8. Turkey morocco, extra....................2 00
9.   "   "   "   and clasps............2 50
10.   "   "   beveled....................2 50
11.   "   "   "   and clasps............3 00
12.   "   "   paneled..................3 75
13.   "   "   "   and clasps............4 25
14.   "   "   "   ornaments and clasps...5 00

The Christian's Treasury.

A most beautiful, complete, and useful prayer book; containing all the most approved prayers, with the Epistles and Gospels, and the appropriate Vespers for every Sunday and holiday in the year. Printed on fine paper, in large type; with a variety of fine illustrations. Approved by the Most Rev. J. McCloskey, D. D., Archbishop of New York.

No. 1. Cloth, plain, 24mo $0 60
    2. Roan,   "   75
    3.   " gilt edges..................................1 00
    4.   "   "   " and clasps.....................1 25
    5.   " gilt sides............................... 90
    6.   "   "   " and edges...................1 25
    7.   "   "   " and clasps...................1 50
    8. Turkey morocco, extra........................2 50
    9.   "   "   " and clasps..............3 00
   10.   "   "   beveled...................3 00
   11.   "   "   " and clasps...........3 50
   12.   "   "   paneled...................4 00
   13.   "   "   " and clasps...........4 50
   14.   "   "   " bands and clasps......5 00

The Little Path to Paradise.

48mo. A very complete, portable, and elegant Prayer Book.

No. 1. Cloth, plain....................................$0 30
    2. Embossed..................................... 38
    3.   "   gilt edges............................ 50
    4.   "   "   " and clasp.................. 63
    5.   "   gilt sides............................ 45
    6.   "   "   " and edges.................. 63
    7.   "   "   "   "   " and clasp.......... 75
    8. Turkey morocco, extra........................1 25
    9.   "   "   " and clasps..............1 62
   10.   "   "   bands and clasps.............2 50

The Flowers of Paradise.

24mo, 512 pages. Containing the Collects and Gospels, the Confraternities, and Indulgenced Devotions.

No. 1. Cloth, plain. 1 plate........................$0 50
    2. Roan, embossed. 1 plate..................... 63

3. Roan, embossed, gilt edges..................$1 00
4.   "   "   "   "   and clasp..........1 20
5.   "   full gilt sides, 2 plates................. 90
6.   "   "   "   "   and edges...........1 25
7.   "   "   "   "   "   " clasps............1 50
8. Turkey morocco, extra, case.............2 25
9.   "   "   "   flexible..........2 50
10. "   "   "   clasp 3 00
11. "   "   "   beveled.............3 00
12. "   "   "   "   clasps..........3 50
13. "   "   bands and ornaments..........5 00

Velvet, from $3.75 to $15.

The Flowers of Paradise.

32mo.

No. 14. Cloth, plain..................................$0 45
15. Roan,   "   50
16.   "   gilt sides.... 60
17.   "   embossed, gilt edges.................... 75
18.   "   "   and clasp.................... 90
19.   "   gilt sides and edges..................... 90
20.   "   "   "   "   "   clasps.............1 12
21. Turkey morocco, extra.....................2 00
22.   "   "   "   clasp....... ....2 50
23.   "   "   "   beveled.................2 50
24.   "   "   "   "   clasp...........3 00
25.   "   "   bands and ornaments........4 00

Velvet, richly ornamented, from $4 to $12.

The Diamond Manual.

A beautiful pocket Prayer Book, containing all the necessary prayers.

No. 1. Cloth, gilt......................................$0 25
2. Embossed roan, gilt edges..................... 45
3. Tucks (pocket-book form), gilt edges........... 63
4. Turkey morocco..............................1 00
6.   "   "   clasps...... ....1 25

Velvet and ornaments, from $1.50 to $6.

The Child's Catholic Manual.

Containing short abridgment of the Christian Doctrine, Prayers for morning and evening, Instructions and Pray ers for Mass, with handsome ILLUSTRATIONS OF THE MASS, Instructions and Devotion for Confession, Holy Communion and Confirmation, and a selection of beautiful and suitable Devotions, Hymns, &c., &c.   32mo.

PRICE.

No. 1. Cloth..................................... $0 30
    2. Roan, plain.............................   38
    3. Cloth, gilt center and edges...............   50
    4. Roan,   "   "   "   "   75
    5.   "   "   "   "   " and clasp........   90
    6.   "   gilt sides, plain edges...............   60
    7.   "   "   "   and edges...............   88
    8.   "   "   "   " and clasps........ 1 00
    9. Morocco, extra... .... 2 00
   10.   "   " and clasp.................. 2 50

The Purgatorian Manual;

or, A Selection of Prayers and Devotions, with appropriate reflections, for the use of the members of the Purgatorian Society, and adapted for general use. By Rev. THOMAS S. PRESTON.   Approved by the Most Rev. JOHN McCLOSKEY, D. D., Archbishop of New York. 18mo beautifully illustrated with steel engravings.

PRICE.

Cloth, plain.......... .... $1 00
Roan,   " 1 25
   "   gilt edges.............................. 1 50
   "   "   " and sides...................... 2 00
Turkey morocco, extra...................... .... 3 50

CONTENTS.

    I. The Purgatorian Society in the Diocese of New York; its history and the conditions of membership.
   II. The Doctrine of Purgatory stated and demonstrated.
  III. A Devout Method of hearing Mass for the benefit of the Suffering Souls.
   IV. The Office for the Dead.
    V. A Collection of Prayers Indulgenced by the Church.
   VI. Novena of St. Alphonsus, for the nine days preceding All-Souls' Day.

VII. Octave of Father Faber for the Souls in Purgatory.
VIII. The Way of the Cross by St. Alphonsus M. Liguori.
IX. Reflections for such as seek purification in this life.

CATHOLIC CATECHISMS.

Challoner's Catholic Christian Instructed.

16mo.   Flexible cloth...........................   45

Challoner's Catholic Christian Instructed.

16mo.   Paper...............................   30

Butler's Catechism.

With the Scriptural Catechism. Per hundred. $4 50   0 08

Butler's Catechism.

Detroit edition........................... 4 50   0 08

A Catechism for General Use.

By Rev. J. McCaffrey, D. D., President of Mt. St.
Mary's College.   Approved by the Most Rev. J. Mc-
Closkey, D. D.; Most Rev. M. J. Spalding, D. D.; Rt.
Rev. J. F. Wood, D. D., and several other Bishops, for
use in their Dioceses.

18mo. large type, good paper, per 100.......... $5 00
24mo.   "   "   "   " 2 75
"   abridged........................... 1 75

On the favorable report of our Examiners of Books, we take
pleasure in approving the Catechisms recently composed by
Rev. Dr. McCaffrey, President of Mount St. Mary's College,
the revised edition of which is to appear. . . . And I we permit and every recommend their use in our Archdiocese.

Baltimore, April 12, 1866.

M. J. Spalding,
Archbishop of Baltimore.

We approve the Catechisms prepared by the Very Rev. Dr McCAFFREY, both the larger one and the Abridgment, and recommend their adoption in the various schools of our diocese.

JOHN, Archbishop of New York.
New York, July 16, 1866.

CATHEDRAL, LOGAN SQUARE.
Philadelphia, Jan. 11, 1867.

We cheerfully concur in the recommendation of Catechisms lately published by Very Rev. Dr. McCAFFREY, knowing and appreciating the care and labor bestowed on their preparation by the Very Rev. author.

JAMES F. WOOD,
Bishop of Philadelphia.

FROM THE BALTIMORE CATHOLIC MIRROR.

The great desideratum in a Catechism is brevity, simplicity, and a plainness of style which enables the young mind to take in without effort all that it propounds and teaches. Dr. McCAFFREY's Catechism, while it fully states the elements of Christian doctrine, comes nearer, in our opinion, to what is needed in these particulars, than any thing of the kind that has yet been published. It is not to be expected that any human effort will ever reach perfection in a work of this kind, yet we much doubt if any future attempt that may be made will ever surpass, if it equal, this one of Dr. McCAFFREY. It is a pleasure to know that in our opinion of this little catechism we differ in nothing from many of our Archbishops, Bishops, and the body of our venerated clergy.

A Short Abridgment of the Christian Doctrine.

Revised for the use of the Catholic Church in the United States. Per hundred..............$2 50 $0 05

Catechism for the Use of the Sick Poor.

By a Sister of Mercy......................... 03

General Catechism of the Christian Doctrine.

Prepared by order of the National Council....... 05

Short Catechism.

Price...................................... 03

School Books.

The following School Books have been adopted for use by the Sisters of Charity, Ladies of the Sacred Heart, Sisters of Mercy, Brothers of the Christian Schools, &c., &c. They are used, also, in most of the best conducted private schools in the vicinity of New York.

I. The Primary Spelling-Book.

An easy introduction to the "Columbian Spelling-Book," in which the spelling, pronunciation, meaning, and application of almost all the irregular words in the English language are taught in a manner adapted to the comprehension of young learners, by means of spelling and dictation exercises. 1 vol., 12mo, half bound $0 25

II. The Columbian Spelling-Book.

A complete Manual of Orthography, Orthoepy, and Etymology. A new and easy method of teaching the spelling, pronunciation, meaning, and application of almost all the difficult and irregular words in the language, by means of Spelling and Dictation Exercises. 1 vol., large 12mo, 310 pp............. **45**

The Primary Reader.

By J. B. TULLY. Illustrated with several beautiful wood-cuts. Half bound........ .... 12½

The Second Reader.

By J. B. TULLY. 18mo, 188 pages. Half bound.. **25**

The Third Reader.

By J. B. TULLY. 12mo, half bound, roan, back lettered............................... **63**

The Fourth Reader.

By J. B. TULLY. 12mo, 432 pages............. 1 00

The Columbian Orator ;

Or, The Fifth Book of the Columbian Series of
Readers and Spellers, with illustrations and explanations of the various attitudes suitable to the
orator.

This book contains, besides an admirable selection from the best authors, several dialogues, prepared especially for it, which will be found to supply a want much felt hitherto by our schools. 1
vol., 12mo.. 1 50

TESTIMONIALS.

**FROM BROTHER HABACUC, DIRECTOR OF THE CHRISTIAN BRO-
THERS' ACADEMY OF THE ASSUMPTION, UTICA.**

"I have just received a copy of the 'Primary Spelling-
Book,' by Mr. Tully, and I am delighted with it. It is at once
the most simple, practical, and scientific English Spelling-Book
I have ever seen.

"BROTHER HABACUC."

FROM THE CONVENT OF MERCY, HOUSTON STREET, NEW YORK.

"We like your series of Readers very much, and shall use
them hereafter in our school."

FROM M. J. O'DONNELL, ESQ.

"After a careful examination of 'Tully's Columbian Spelling Book,' I adopted it in the higher classes of this school.
The success which has attended its use has verified my expectations of it, and convinced me that it is not only a book of
exceeding merit, but that it is decidedly the *best of its kind* of
any that has ever come under my observation. I cordially
recommend it to general patronage, in the conviction that,
wherever it may be adopted, its use will confirm the opinion
I have expressed in regard to its superior excellence.

"M. J. O'DONNELL, Ward School No. 5."

FROM THE NEW YORK EVENING POST.

"We are pleased to see that the text-book ('Columbian
Spelling Book'), to which we invite our readers' attention,
ascribes great importance to the practice of dictation. Besides adequate provisions for oral recitation, it furnishes
abundant exercises especially arranged for writing. The work
is thoroughly prepared and issued in a convenient and durable
form."

THE CHRISTIAN BROTHERS' SERIES OF READERS.

First Book of Reading Lessons.

By the Christian Brothers 0 12

Second Book of Reading Lessons.

18mo, half bound   25

Third Book of Reading Lessons.

24mo, roan, back lettered   36

Carpenter's Scholars' Spelling Assistant.

A new stereotype edition. 1 vol., 18mo   20

School Diaries.

Per dozen   20

Copy Books.

Per dozen, from 60 cts. to 1 20

Exercise Books.

Per dozen, from $1.50 to 3 00

The Practical Dictation Spelling Book.

In which the spelling, pronunciation, meaning and
application of almost all the irregular words in the
English language are taught in a manner adapted
to the comprehension of young learners, by means
of SPELLING and DICTATION EXERCISES. By ED.
MULVANY. 12mo, half bound   30
      This book is admirable in plan and execution, and
ought to be introduced into all our schools.

Price's Practical Arithmetic.

12mo, half bound   65

General Alphabetical List of Books,

Published and for Sale by

P. O'SHEA, 27 BARCLAY STREET,

NEW YORK.

A.

A General History of the Catholic Church, from the commencement of the Christian Era, until the present time. By the Abbé DARRAS. 4 vols., 8vo, cloth..$12 00

     Sheep, marble edges........................... 16 00
     Half morocco, extra........................... 20 00
     Half morocco, antique......................... 24 00

American Republic. By O. A. BROWNSON, LL.D. 1 vol., 8vo, cloth.............................. 3 00

Agnes Hilton, a Tale of Trials and Triumphs. By Miss HOFFMAN. 1 vol., 12mo, cloth.............. 1 50

Adventures and Misfortunes of a Saxon Schoolmaster. 18mo....................................... 30

An Episode of the Campaign in Russia. 18mo, cloth.. 30

American Revolution. By MICHAEL DOHENY. 18mo, cloth....................................... 75

Appleton's Sermons. 1 vol., 8vo..................... 3 00

Adelmar, the Templar. Cloth..................... 30

All for Jesus; or, The Easy Ways of Divine Love. By FABER....................................... 1 50

Alice Riordan; or, The Blind Man's Daughter......... 50

Alton Park....................................... 1 25

Ailey Moore....................................... 1 00

Alice Sherwin; or, The Days of Sir Thomas More..... 1 13

Art Maguire; or, The Broken Pledge. By CARLETON. 75

Anima Devota; or, Devout Soul..................... 60

Archconfraternity of the Heart of Mary............. 30

Ark of the Covenant. By Rev. T. S. PRESTON....... 60

Angelical Virtue................................. 38

Apologia pro Vita Sua. By Dr. NEWMAN............ 2 00

Aspirations of Nature. By Rev. I. T. HECKER...... 1 00

A Method of Prayer. 12mo. Cloth.......... . $1 75
Adventures of an Irish Giant.................. 49
A Treatise on the Love of God. By St. Francis De
    Sales. 1 75
Alphonso; or, The Triumph of Religion............ 80

B.

Brownson's American Republic.................. 3 00
Black Baronet. By Carleton................. 1 00
Brooksiana............................. 50
Balmes on European Civilization. 8vo.......... 3 00
Balmes's Essay on Divine Faith............... 1 25
Balls and Dancing. By Abbé Hulot............. 50
Bertha; or, The Pope and the Emperor. By McCabe. 1 00
Bible against Protestantism. By Dr. Sheil.......... 75
Bible Question Fairly Tested.................. 50
Beauties of Sir Thomas More.................. 1 00
Beauties of the Sanctuary................... 75
Bickerton; or, Immigrant's Daughter............. 60
Blakes and Flannigans...................... 1 13
Blind Agnes.............................. 50
Blanche. A Tale........................... 30
Bossuet's History of the Variations of the Protestant
    Churches. 2 vols. Cloth................... 2 50
Boschool of Great Painters. 2 vols. Cloth........ 1 20
Bartoli's Life of St. Ignatius. 2 vols............ 3 00
Blessed Sacrament. By Faber................ 1 50
Brownson's Essays and Reviews of Theology, Politics,
    and Socialism. Cloth.................... 1 75
Butler's Lives of the Saints. New and beautiful edition.
    12 vols., half morocco, extra.................. 30 00
       (This is the best edition extant.)
Butler's Lives of the Saints. 4 vols. Cloth......... 8 00
Butler's Catechism......................... 8
Butler's Catechism for the Diocese of Detroit........ 8
Bryant on the Immaculate Conception............. 75
Ballad Poetry of Ireland. By Charles Gavan Duffy.
    1 vol. 18mo. Cloth...................... 75
Boyne Water. By Banim..................... 1 00
Bishop England's Works (scarce)...............
Bishop Maginn, Life and Letters of. By Thomas
    D'Arcy McGee. 1 vol., 12mo................ 1 00
Bishop Brute, Memoir and Journal of. By Bishop
    Bayley. 1 vol., 12mo.................... 1 50
Brother James's Library. 12 vols., cloth. Each. 30
Burke's Speeches. 1 vol., 12mo 2 00

C.